Shojo Beat

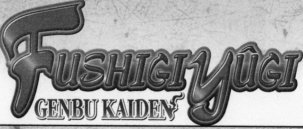

FUSHIGI YÛGI
GENBU KAIDEN

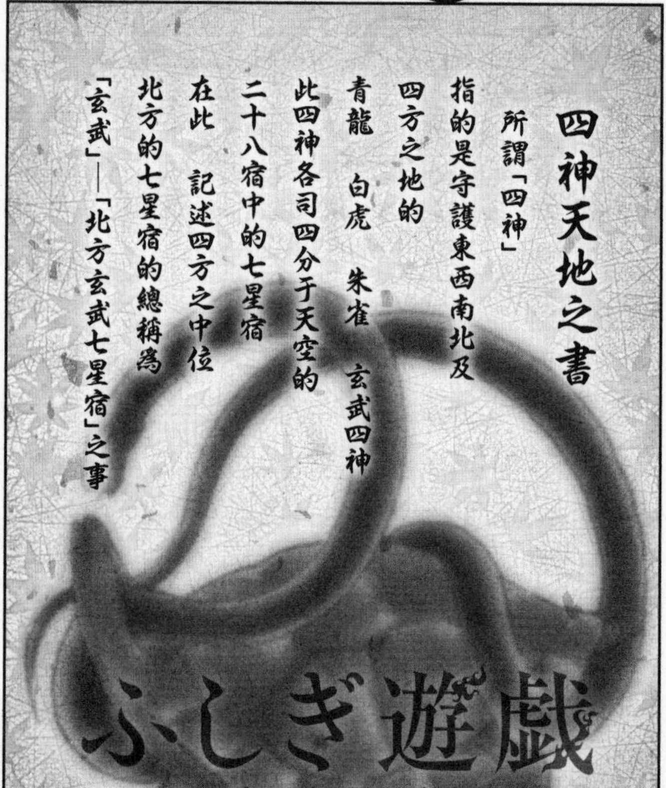
四神天地之書
所謂「四神」
指的是守護東西南北及
四方之地的
青龍　白虎　朱雀　玄武四神
此四神各司四分于天空的
二十八宿中的七星宿
在此　記述四方之中位
北方的七星宿的總稱為
「玄武」——「北方玄武七星宿」之事
ふしぎ遊戯
玄武開伝
渡瀬悠宇

story and art by **YUU WATASE**

Vol. 1

CONTENTS

TRANSLATION OF "THE UNIVERSE OF THE FOUR GODS"

In Chinese tradition, Seiryu, Byakko, Suzaku, and Genbu are the four gods who guard over the four cardinal points: East, West, South, and North, respectively. They divide the twenty-eight heavenly constellations into four houses, with each god ruling over seven constellations. This is the legend of Genbu and the Northern Seven Constellations.

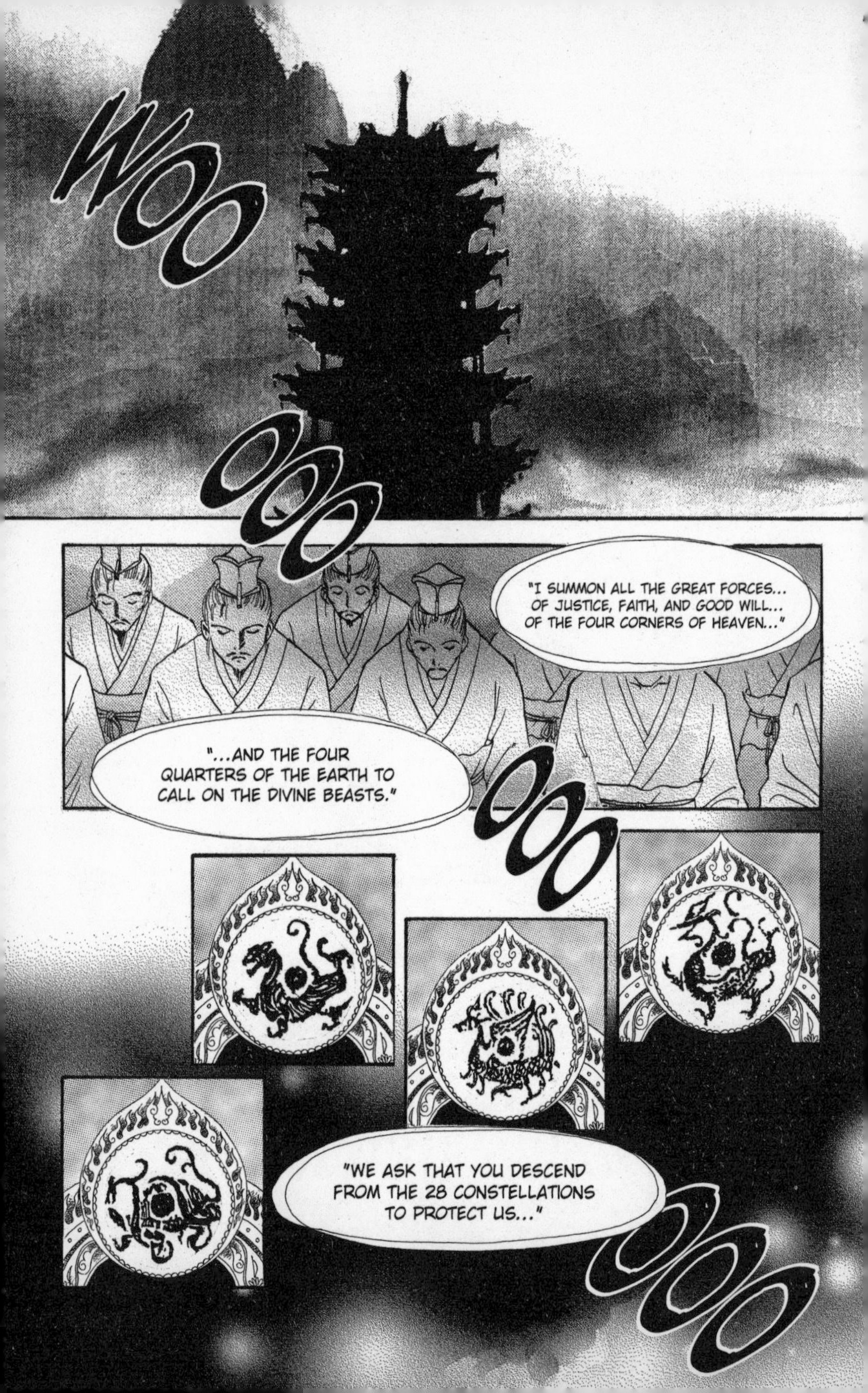
WOOOOOOOOOOOOO
"I SUMMON ALL THE GREAT FORCES... OF JUSTICE, FAITH, AND GOOD WILL... OF THE FOUR CORNERS OF HEAVEN..."
"...AND THE FOUR QUARTERS OF THE EARTH TO CALL ON THE DIVINE BEASTS."
"WE ASK THAT YOU DESCEND FROM THE 28 CONSTELLATIONS TO PROTECT US..."

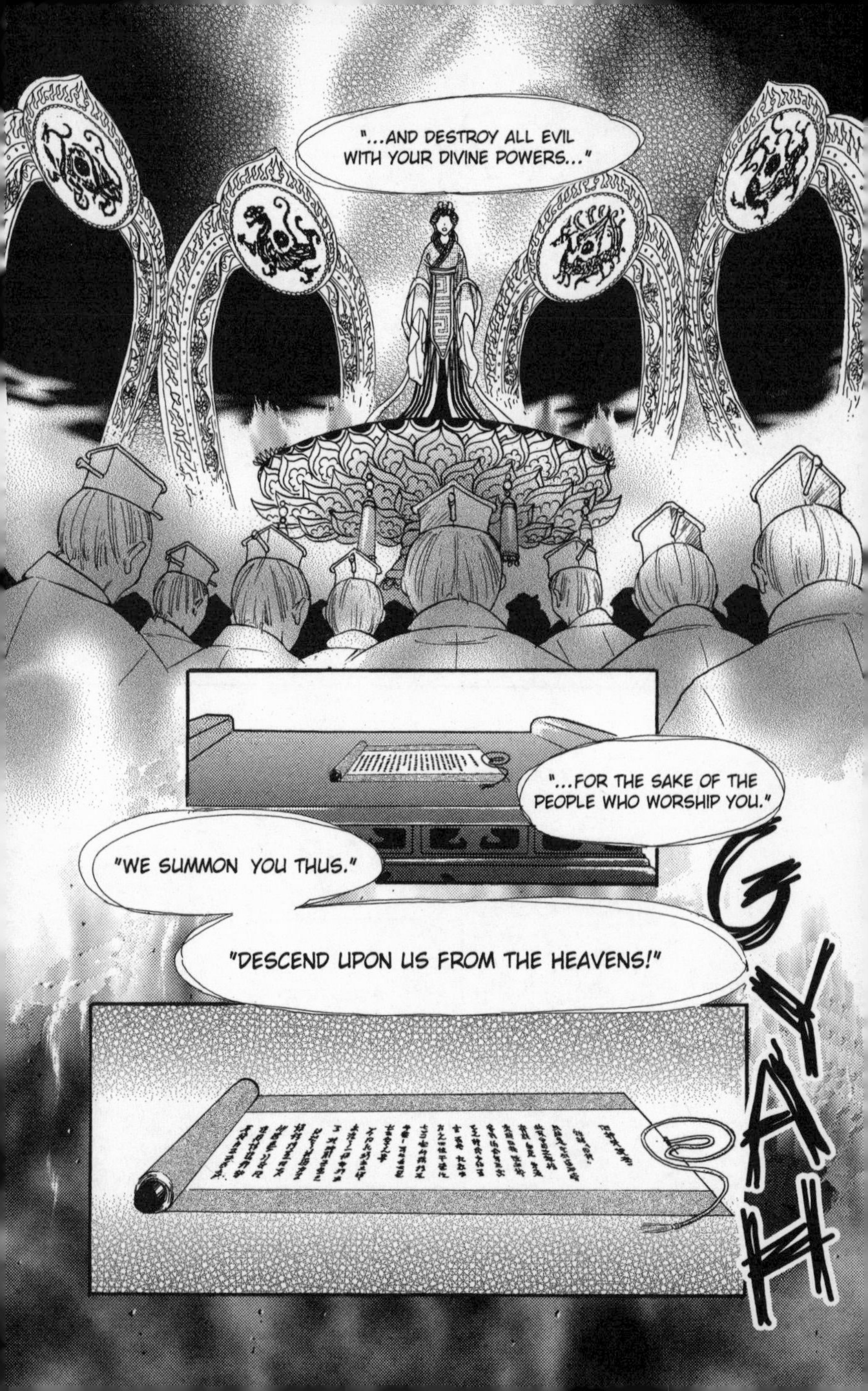
"...AND DESTROY ALL EVIL WITH YOUR DIVINE POWERS..."
"...FOR THE SAKE OF THE PEOPLE WHO WORSHIP YOU."
"WE SUMMON YOU THUS."
"DESCEND UPON US FROM THE HEAVENS!"
GYAH

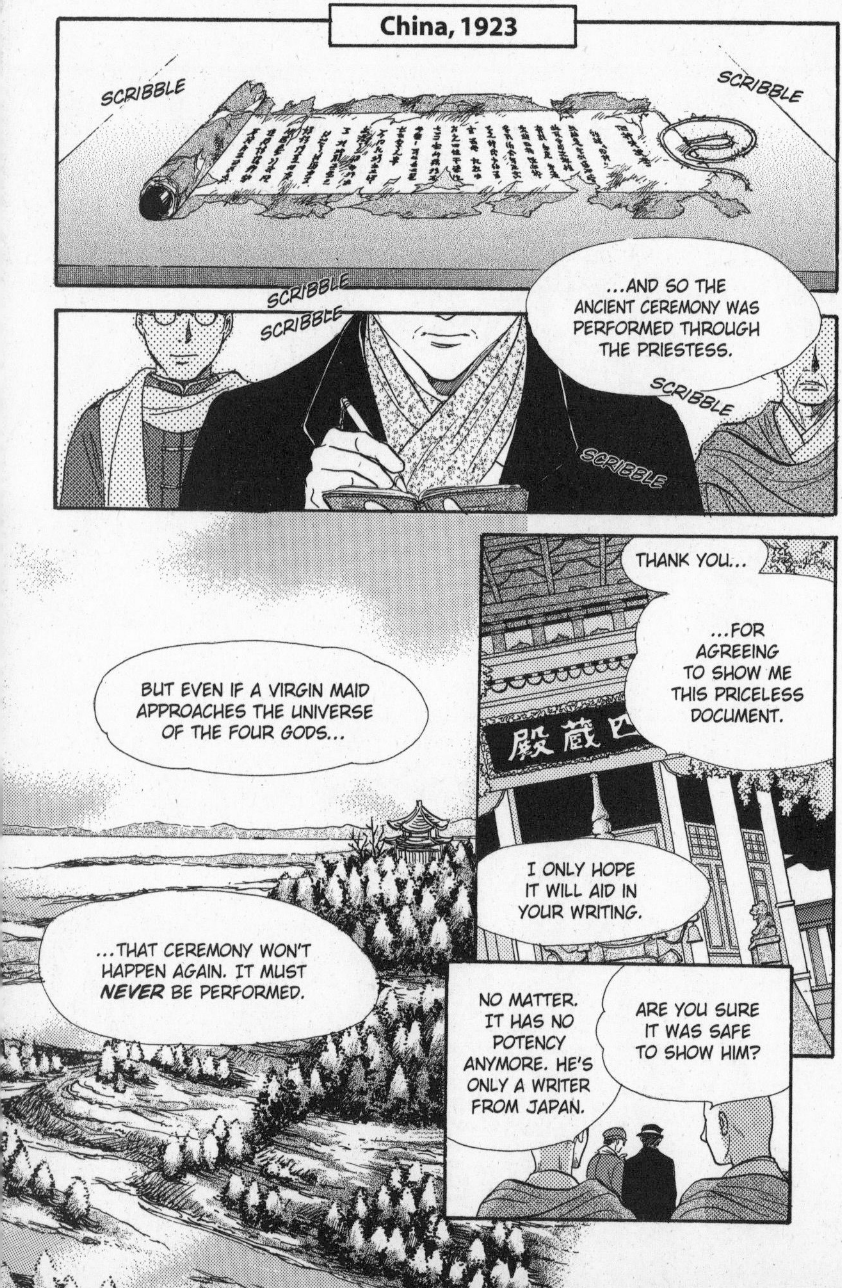
China, 1923
SCRIBBLE
SCRIBBLE
...AND SO THE ANCIENT CEREMONY WAS PERFORMED THROUGH THE PRIESTESS.
SCRIBBLE
SCRIBBLE
SCRIBBLE
SCRIBBLE
THANK YOU...
...FOR AGREEING TO SHOW ME THIS PRICELESS DOCUMENT.
I ONLY HOPE IT WILL AID IN YOUR WRITING.
ARE YOU SURE IT WAS SAFE TO SHOW HIM?
NO MATTER. IT HAS NO POTENCY ANYMORE. HE'S ONLY A WRITER FROM JAPAN.
BUT EVEN IF A VIRGIN MAID APPROACHES THE UNIVERSE OF THE FOUR GODS...
...THAT CEREMONY WON'T HAPPEN AGAIN. IT MUST ***NEVER*** BE PERFORMED.

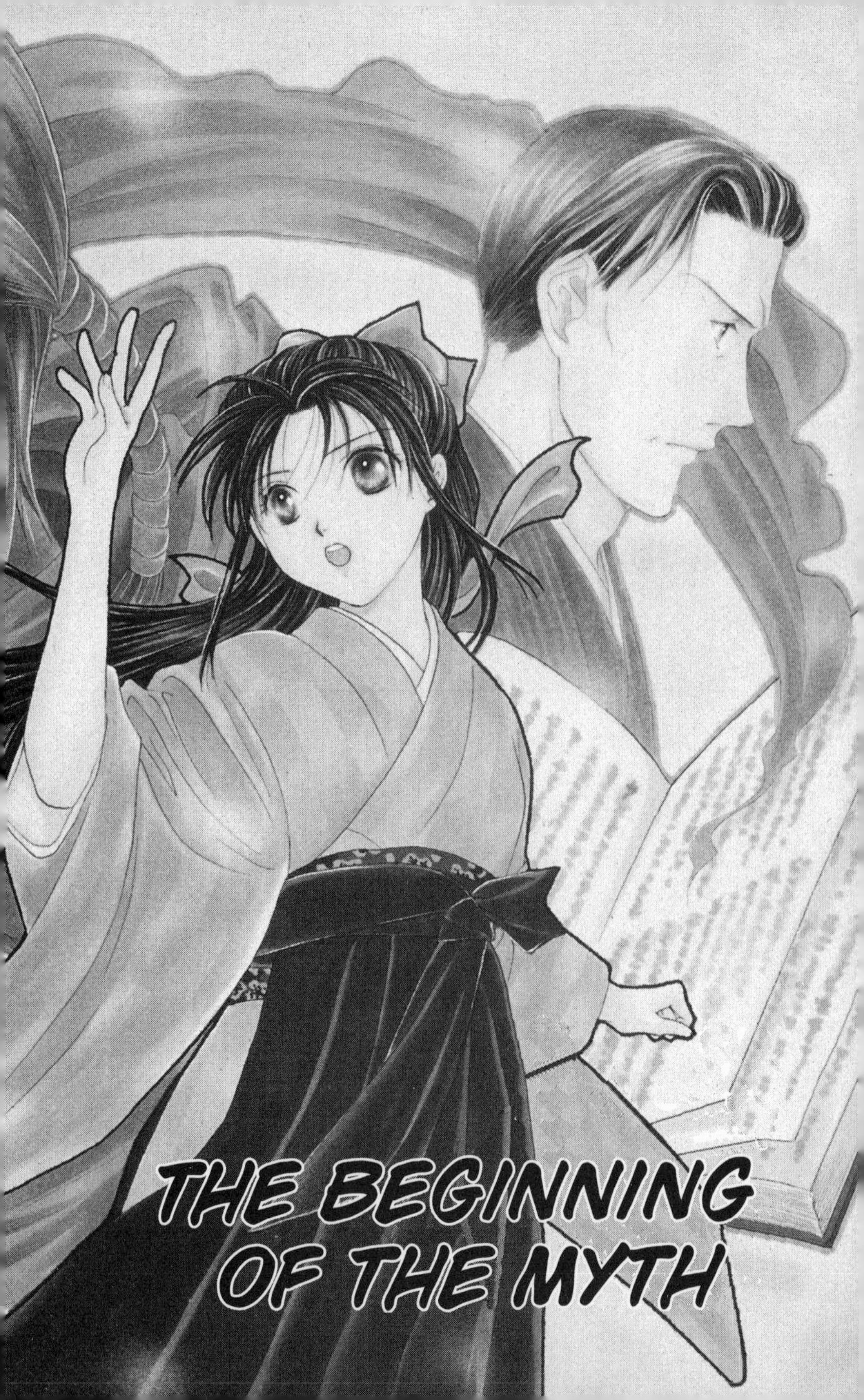
THE BEGINNING
OF THE MYTH

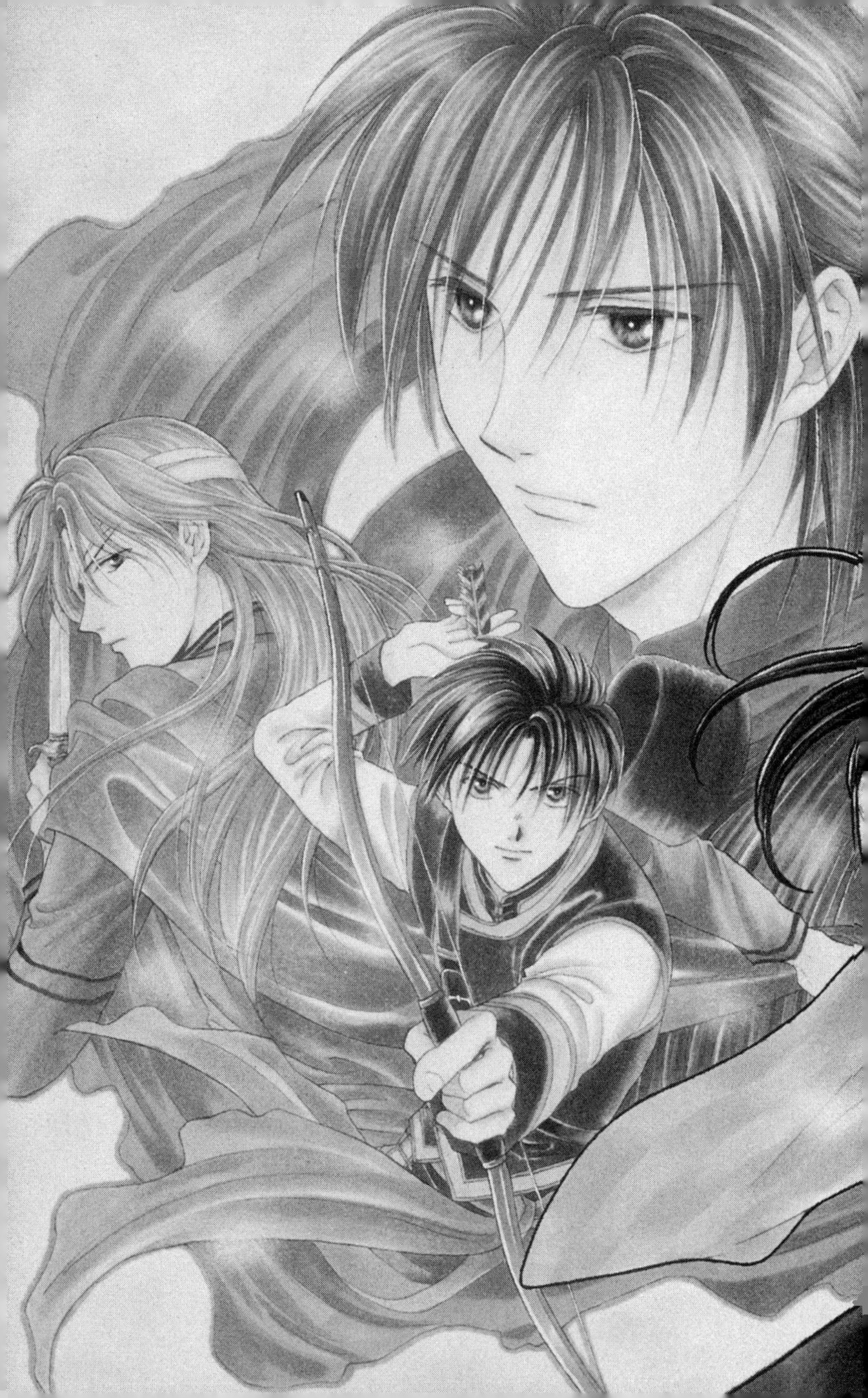

FUSHIGI YÛGI:
GENBU KAIDEN

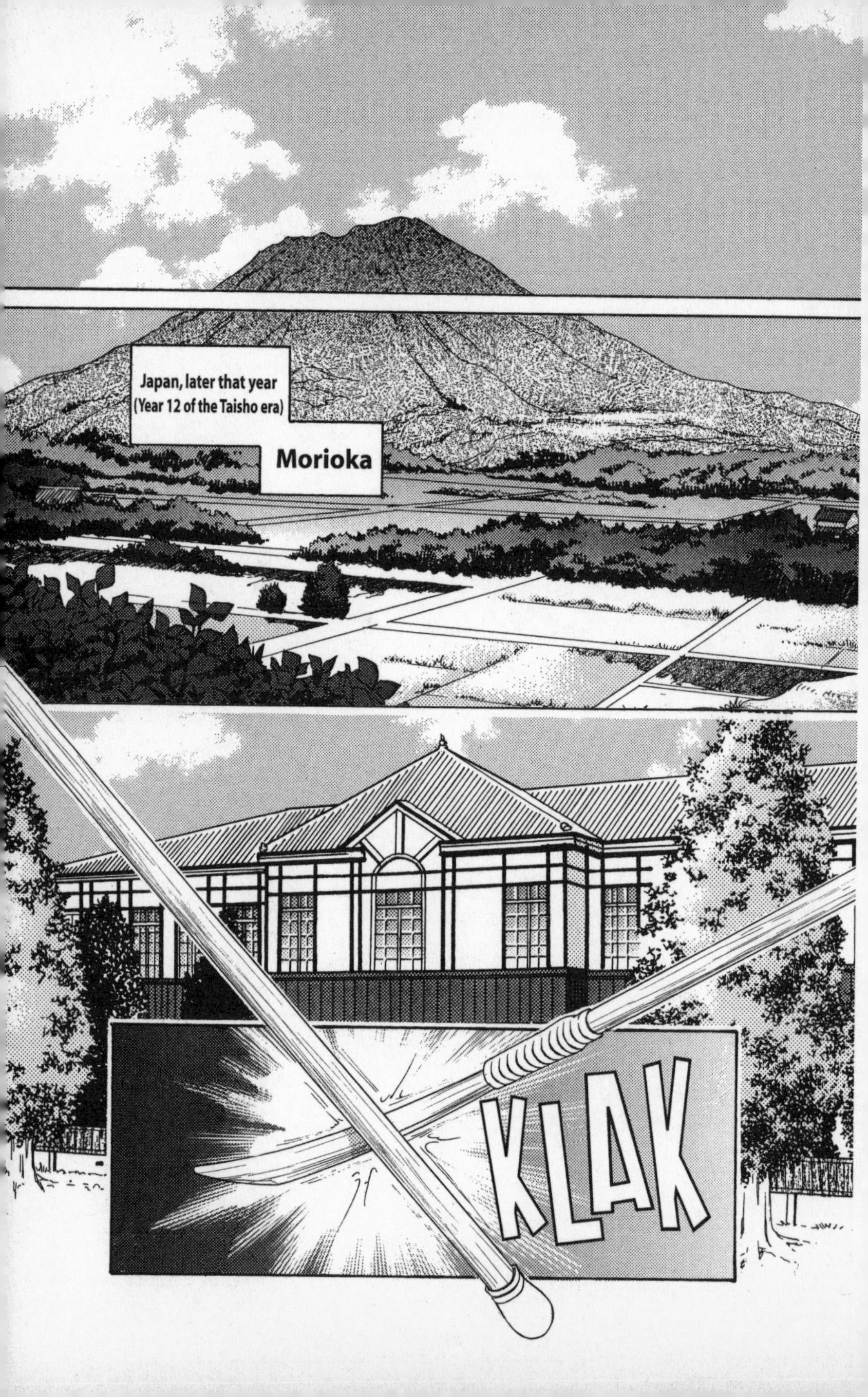
Japan, later that year
(Year 12 of the Taisho era)
Morioka
KLAK

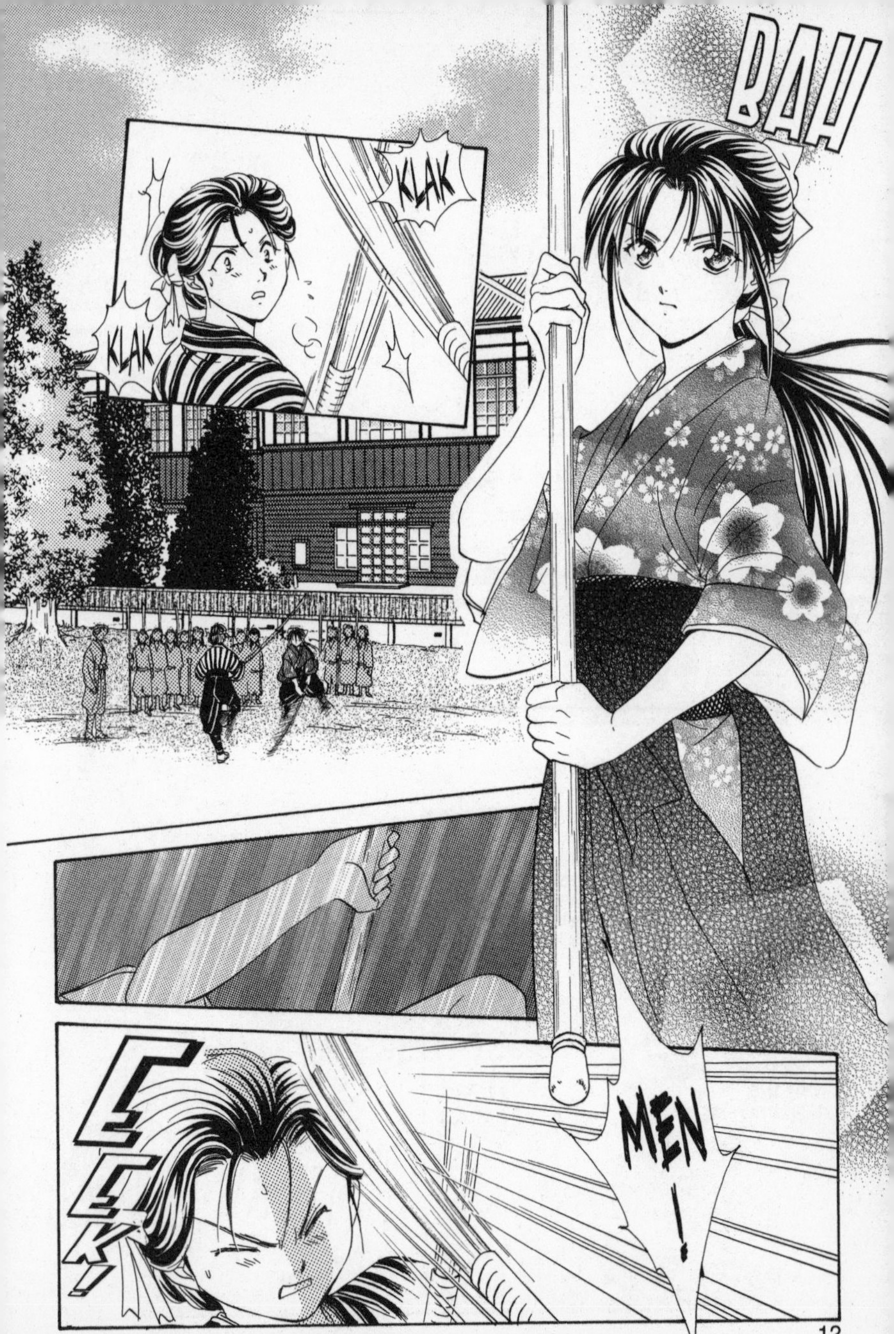
BAH
KLAK
KLAK
MEN !
EEEK!

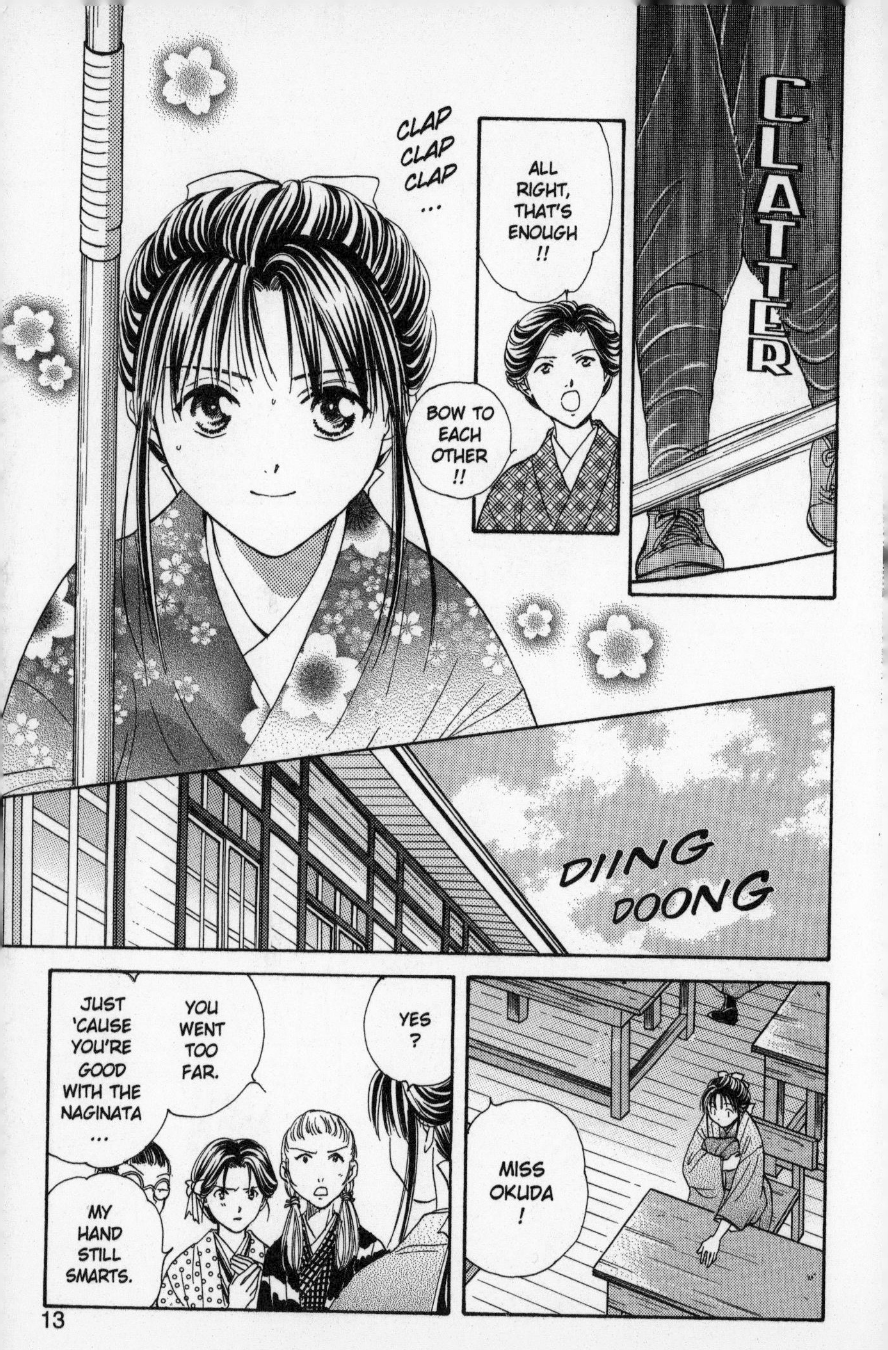
CLATTER
ALL RIGHT, THAT'S ENOUGH !!
BOW TO EACH OTHER !!
CLAP CLAP CLAP ...
DIING DOONG
MISS OKUDA !
YES ?
YOU WENT TOO FAR.
JUST 'CAUSE YOU'RE GOOD WITH THE NAGINATA ...
MY HAND STILL SMARTS.

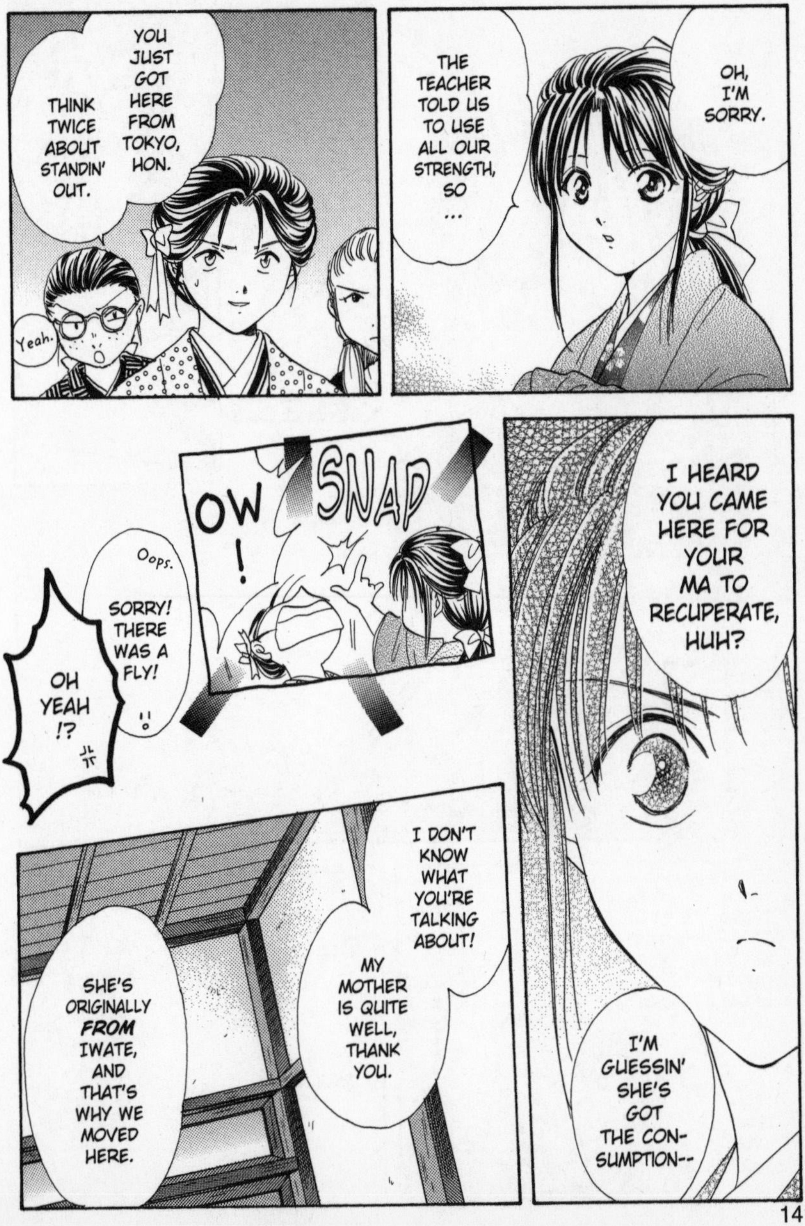
OH, I'M SORRY.
THE TEACHER TOLD US TO USE ALL OUR STRENGTH, SO ...
YOU JUST GOT HERE FROM TOKYO, HON.
THINK TWICE ABOUT STANDIN' OUT.
Yeah.
I HEARD YOU CAME HERE FOR YOUR MA TO RECUPERATE, HUH?
I'M GUESSIN' SHE'S GOT THE CON-SUMPTION--
SNAP
OW!
Oops.
SORRY! THERE WAS A FLY!
OH YEAH!?
I DON'T KNOW WHAT YOU'RE TALKING ABOUT!
MY MOTHER IS QUITE WELL, THANK YOU.
SHE'S ORIGINALLY ***FROM*** IWATE, AND THAT'S WHY WE MOVED HERE.

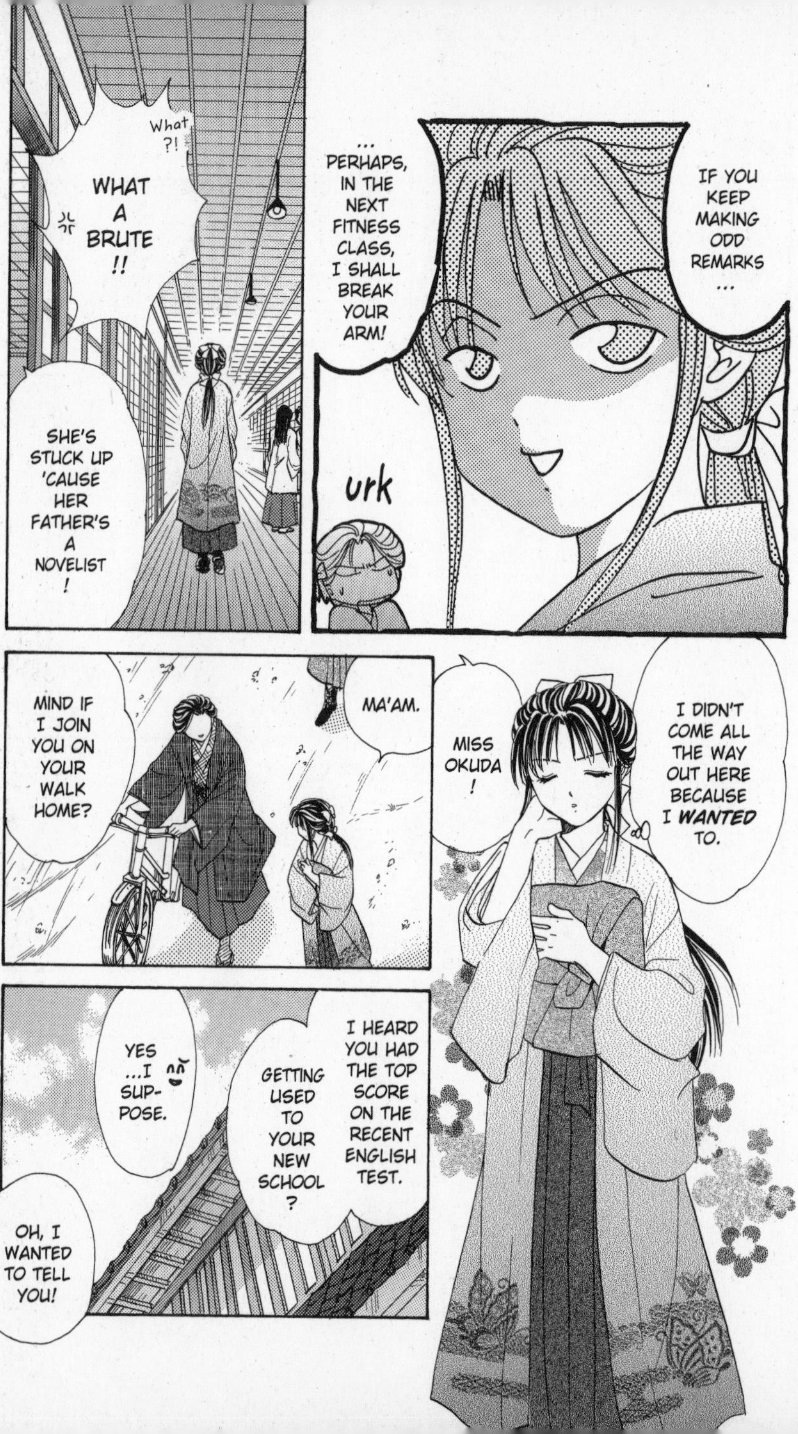
IF YOU KEEP MAKING ODD REMARKS ...
... PERHAPS, IN THE NEXT FITNESS CLASS, I SHALL BREAK YOUR ARM!
urk
What ?!
WHAT A BRUTE !!
SHE'S STUCK UP 'CAUSE HER FATHER'S A NOVELIST !
I DIDN'T COME ALL THE WAY OUT HERE BECAUSE I *WANTED* TO.
MISS OKUDA !
MA'AM.
MIND IF I JOIN YOU ON YOUR WALK HOME?
I HEARD YOU HAD THE TOP SCORE ON THE RECENT ENGLISH TEST.
GETTING USED TO YOUR NEW SCHOOL ?
YES ...I SUP-POSE.
OH, I WANTED TO TELL YOU!

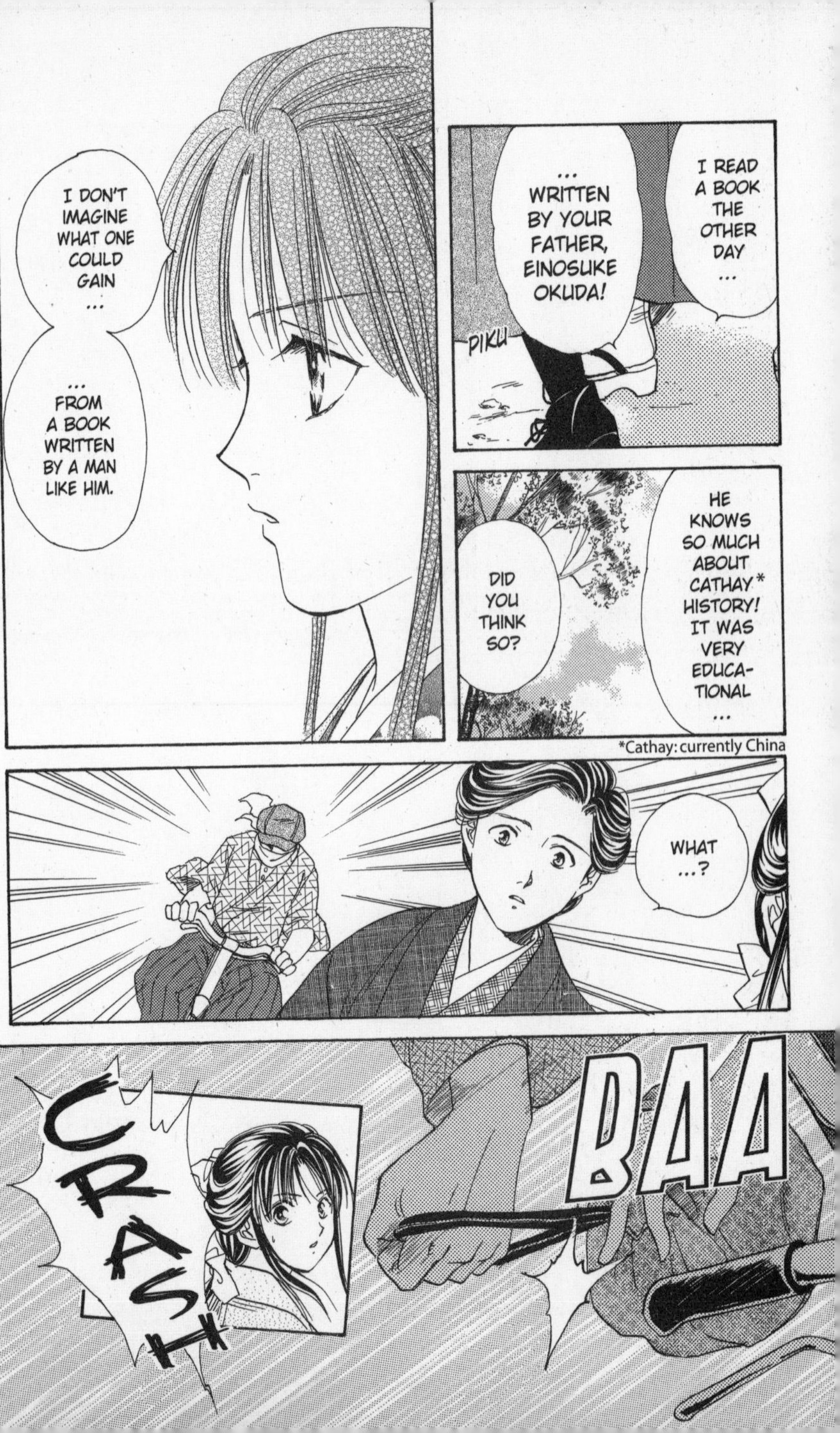
I READ A BOOK THE OTHER DAY ...
... WRITTEN BY YOUR FATHER, EINOSUKE OKUDA!
PIKU
HE KNOWS SO MUCH ABOUT CATHAY* HISTORY! IT WAS VERY EDUCATIONAL ...
DID YOU THINK SO?
I DON'T IMAGINE WHAT ONE COULD GAIN ...
... FROM A BOOK WRITTEN BY A MAN LIKE HIM.
WHAT ...?
BAA
CRASH

*Cathay: currently China

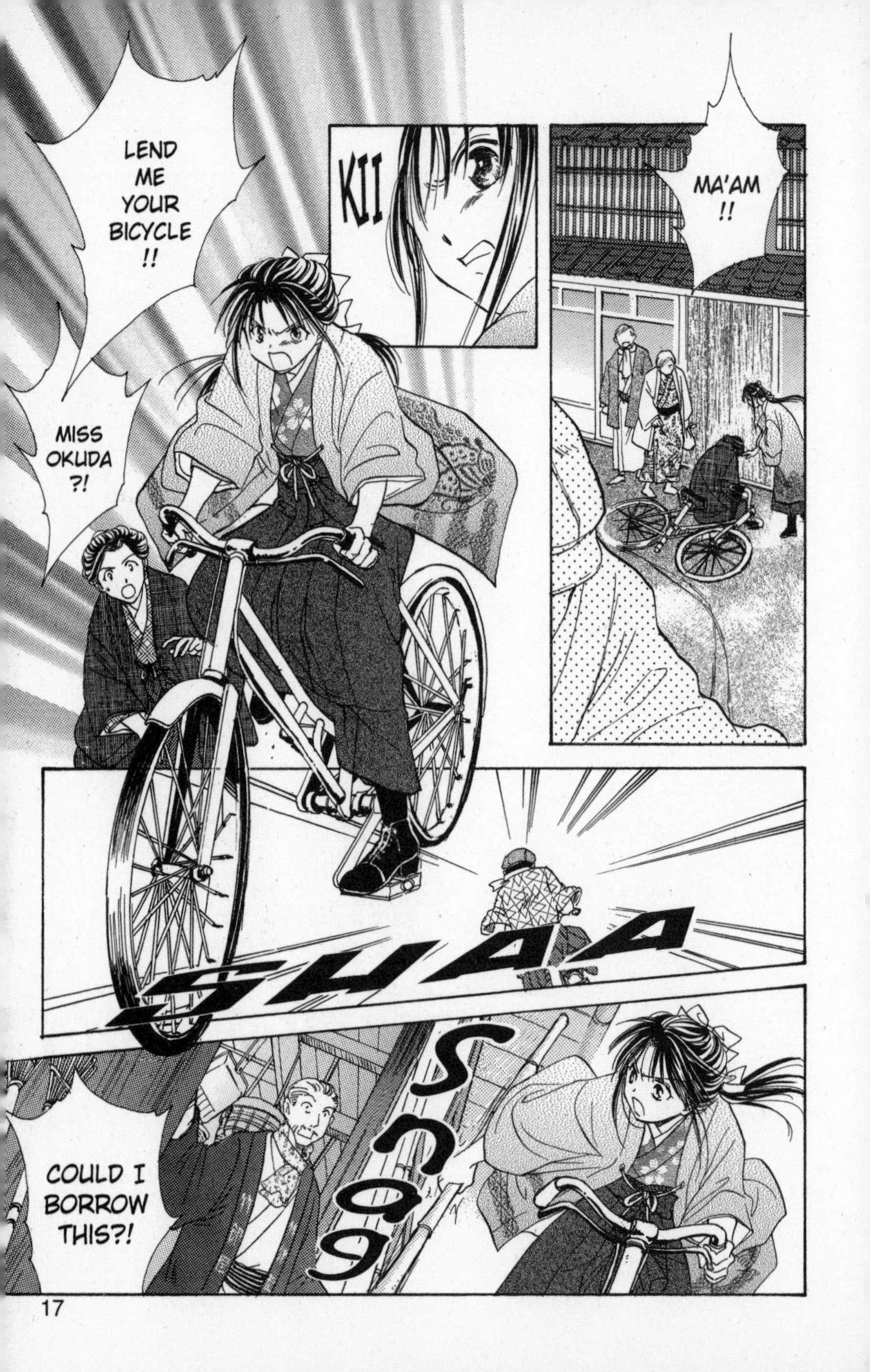
MA'AM !!
KII
LEND ME YOUR BICYCLE !!
MISS OKUDA ?!
SHAA
SNAG
COULD I BORROW THIS?!

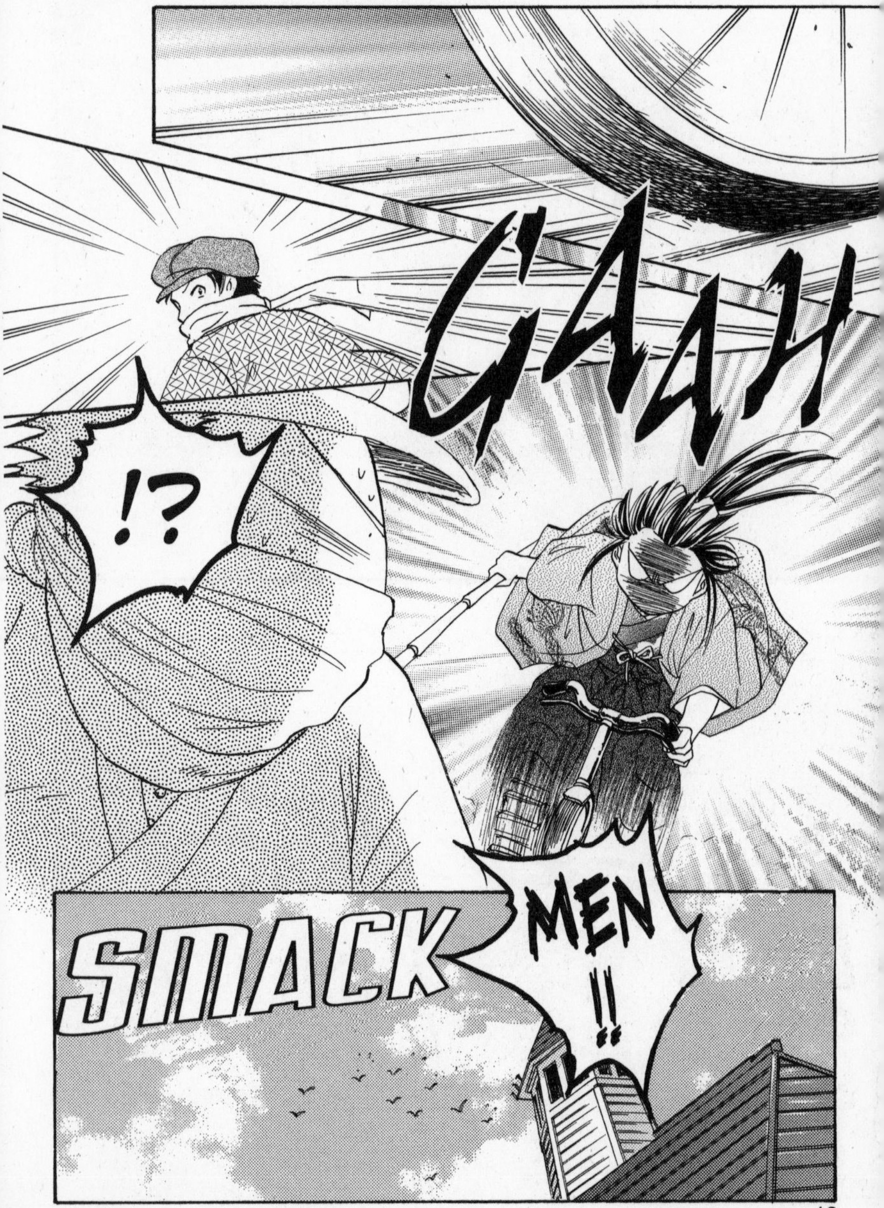
GAAH
!?
MEN !!
SMACK

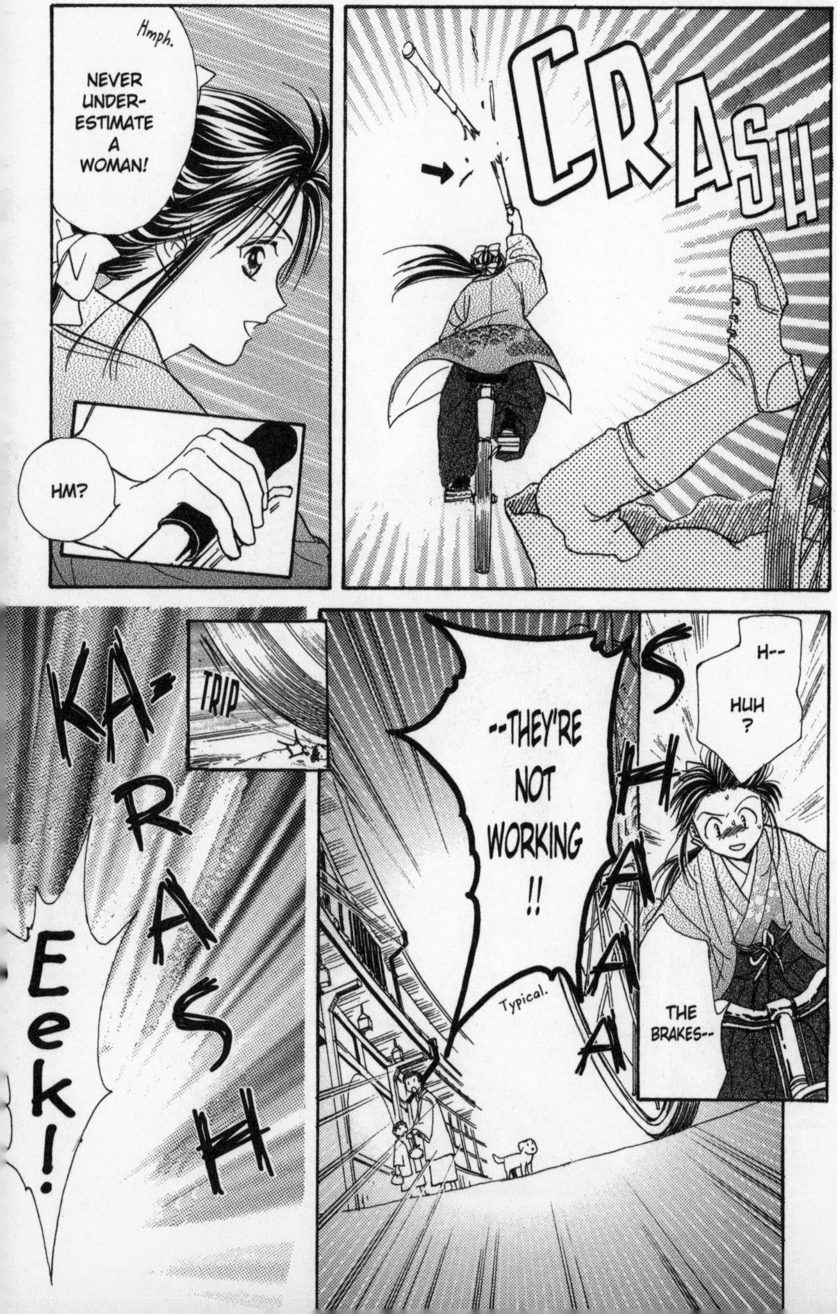
CRASH
Hmph.
NEVER UNDER-ESTIMATE A WOMAN!
HM?
H--
HUH?
THE BRAKES--
--THEY'RE NOT WORKING!!
SHAAAA
Typical.
TRIP
KA-RASH
Eek!

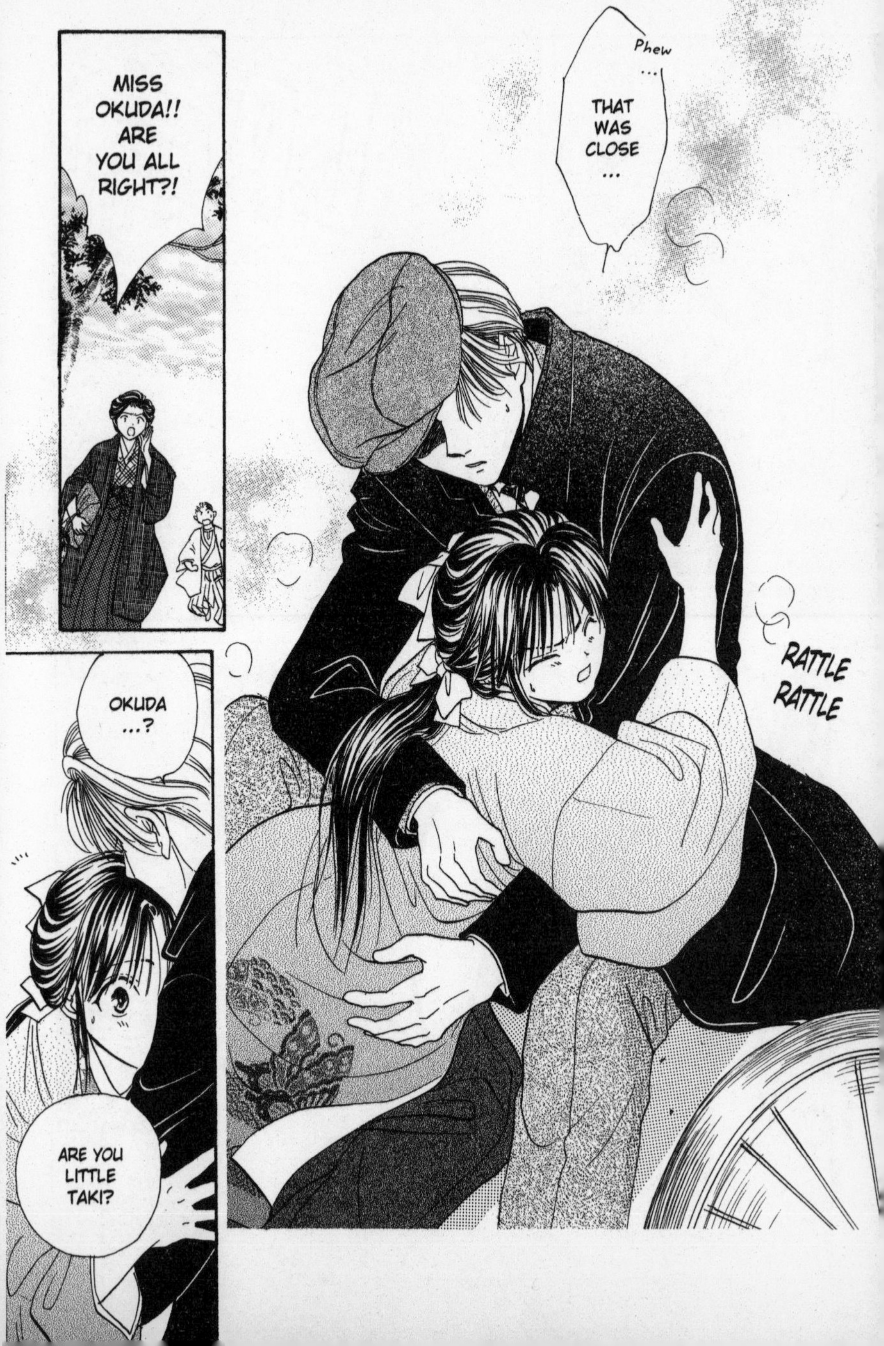
Phew ... THAT WAS CLOSE ...
RATTLE RATTLE
MISS OKUDA!! ARE YOU ALL RIGHT?!
OKUDA ...?
...
ARE YOU LITTLE TAKI?

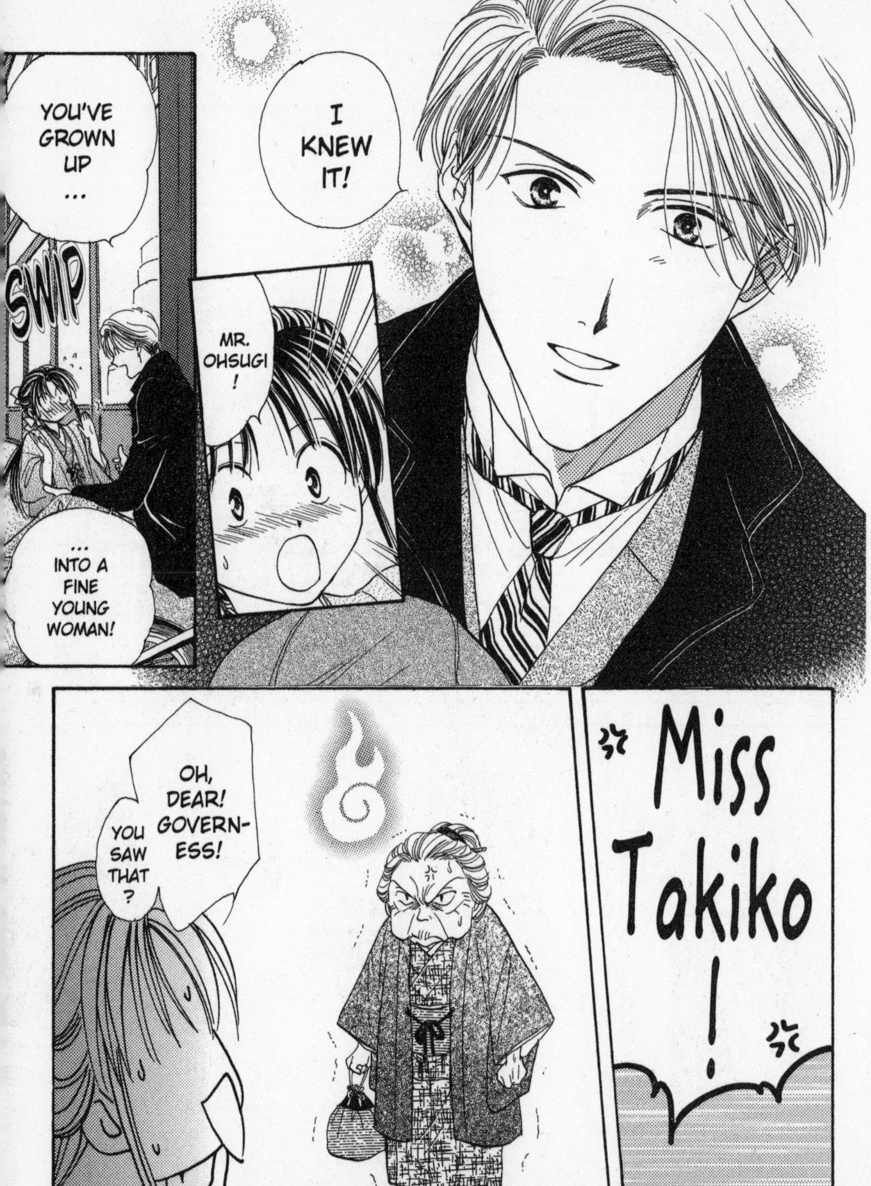
I KNEW IT!
MR. OHSUGI!
YOU'VE GROWN UP ...
SWIP
... INTO A FINE YOUNG WOMAN!
Miss Takiko!
OH, DEAR! GOVERNESS!
YOU SAW THAT?

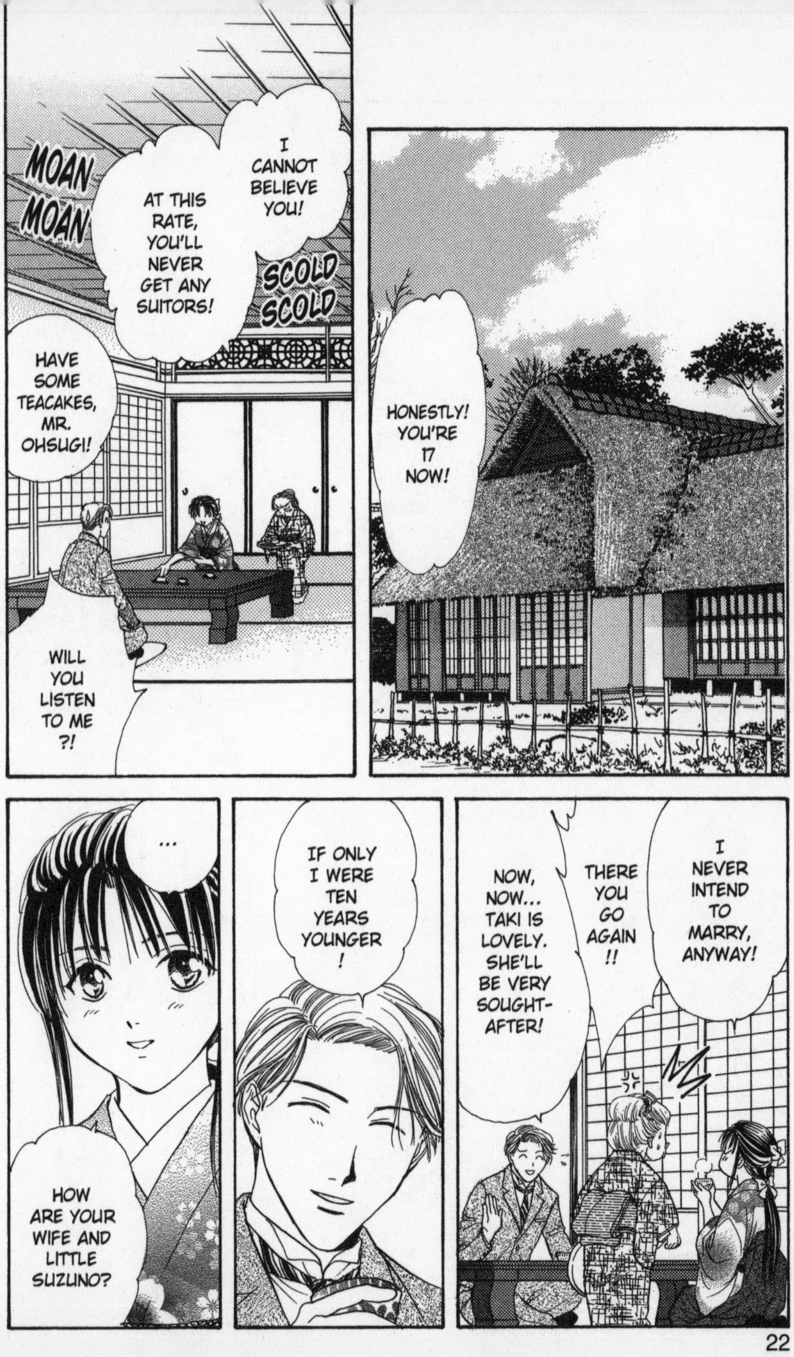
HONESTLY! YOU'RE 17 NOW!
I CANNOT BELIEVE YOU!
SCOLD SCOLD
AT THIS RATE, YOU'LL NEVER GET ANY SUITORS!
MOAN MOAN
HAVE SOME TEACAKES, MR. OHSUGI!
WILL YOU LISTEN TO ME?!
I NEVER INTEND TO MARRY, ANYWAY!
THERE YOU GO AGAIN!!
NOW, NOW... TAKI IS LOVELY. SHE'LL BE VERY SOUGHT-AFTER!
IF ONLY I WERE TEN YEARS YOUNGER!
...
HOW ARE YOUR WIFE AND LITTLE SUZUNO?

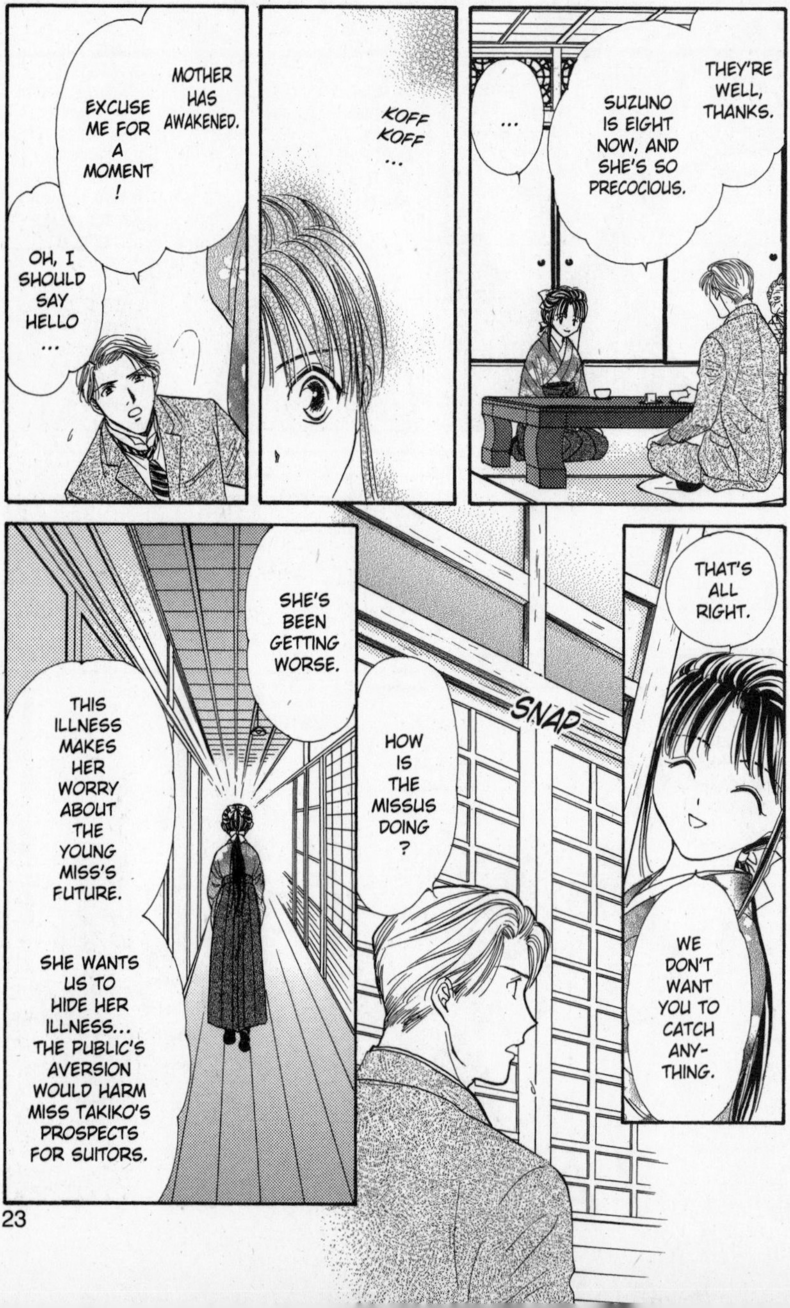
THEY'RE WELL, THANKS.
SUZUNO IS EIGHT NOW, AND SHE'S SO PRECOCIOUS.
...
KOFF KOFF ...
MOTHER HAS AWAKENED.
EXCUSE ME FOR A MOMENT!
OH, I SHOULD SAY HELLO ...
THAT'S ALL RIGHT.
WE DON'T WANT YOU TO CATCH ANY-THING.
SNAP
HOW IS THE MISSUS DOING?
SHE'S BEEN GETTING WORSE.
THIS ILLNESS MAKES HER WORRY ABOUT THE YOUNG MISS'S FUTURE.
SHE WANTS US TO HIDE HER ILLNESS... THE PUBLIC'S AVERSION WOULD HARM MISS TAKIKO'S PROSPECTS FOR SUITORS.

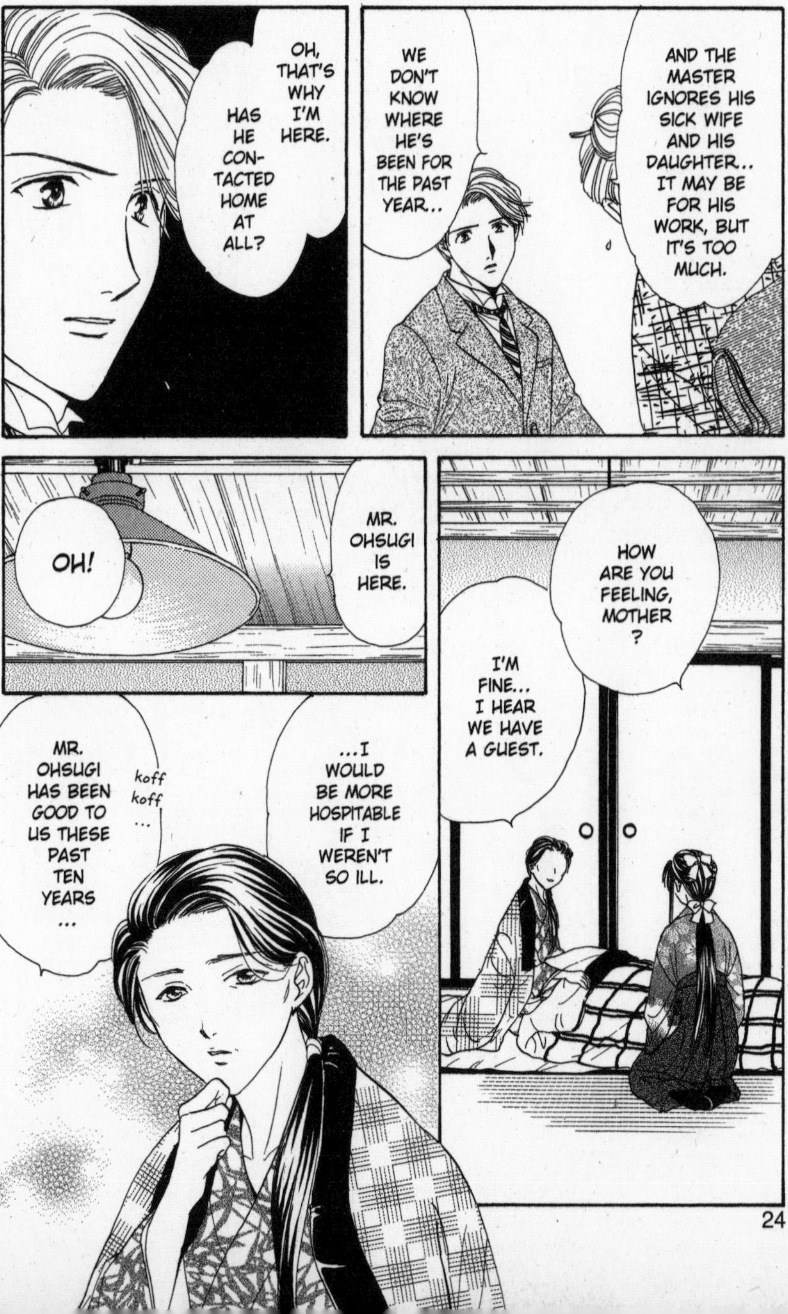
OH, THAT'S WHY I'M HERE.
HAS HE CONTACTED HOME AT ALL?
WE DON'T KNOW WHERE HE'S BEEN FOR THE PAST YEAR...
AND THE MASTER IGNORES HIS SICK WIFE AND HIS DAUGHTER... IT MAY BE FOR HIS WORK, BUT IT'S TOO MUCH.
OH!
MR. OHSUGI IS HERE.
HOW ARE YOU FEELING, MOTHER?
I'M FINE... I HEAR WE HAVE A GUEST.
MR. OHSUGI HAS BEEN GOOD TO US THESE PAST TEN YEARS...
koff koff ...
...I WOULD BE MORE HOSPITABLE IF I WEREN'T SO ILL.

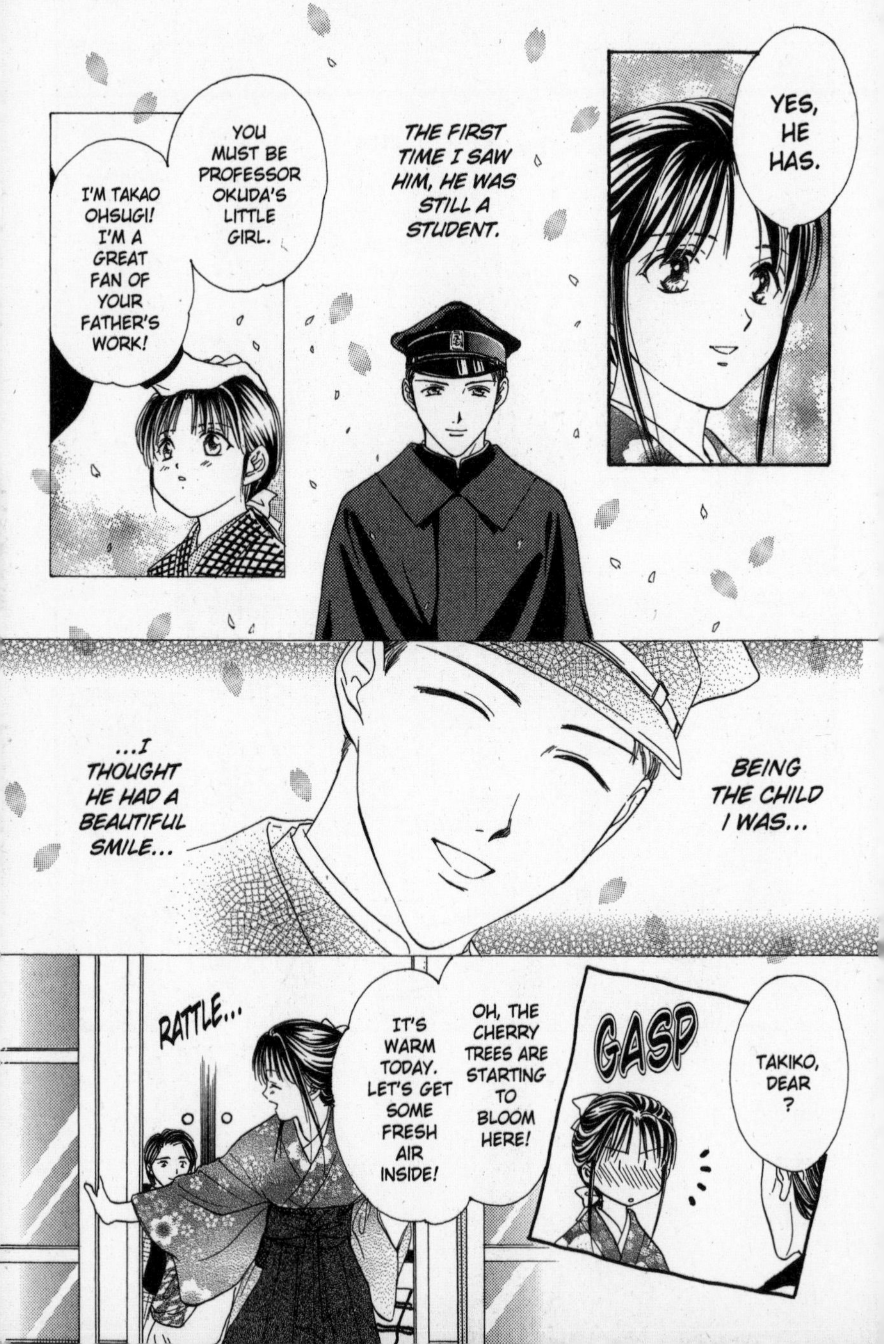
YES, HE HAS.
THE FIRST TIME I SAW HIM, HE WAS STILL A STUDENT.
YOU MUST BE PROFESSOR OKUDA'S LITTLE GIRL.
I'M TAKAO OHSUGI! I'M A GREAT FAN OF YOUR FATHER'S WORK!
BEING THE CHILD I WAS...
...I THOUGHT HE HAD A BEAUTIFUL SMILE...
TAKIKO, DEAR?
GASP
...
OH, THE CHERRY TREES ARE STARTING TO BLOOM HERE!
IT'S WARM TODAY. LET'S GET SOME FRESH AIR INSIDE!
RATTLE...

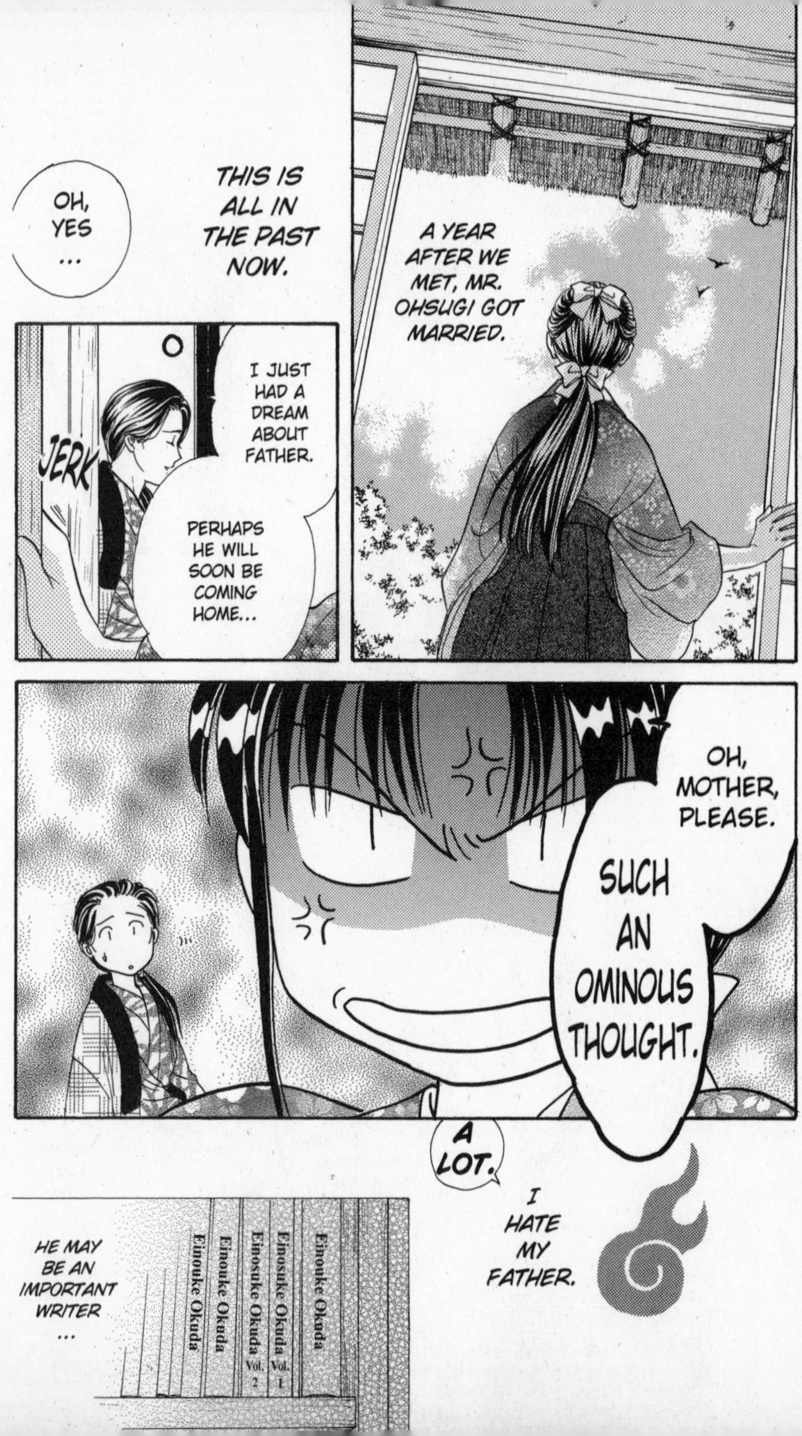
A YEAR AFTER WE MET, MR. OHSUGI GOT MARRIED.
THIS IS ALL IN THE PAST NOW.
OH, YES ...
JERK
I JUST HAD A DREAM ABOUT FATHER.
PERHAPS HE WILL SOON BE COMING HOME...
OH, MOTHER, PLEASE.
SUCH AN OMINOUS THOUGHT.
A LOT.
I HATE MY FATHER.
Einouke Okuda
Einosuke Okuda Vol. 1
Einosuke Okuda Vol. 2
Einouke Okuda
Einouke Okuda
HE MAY BE AN IMPORTANT WRITER ...

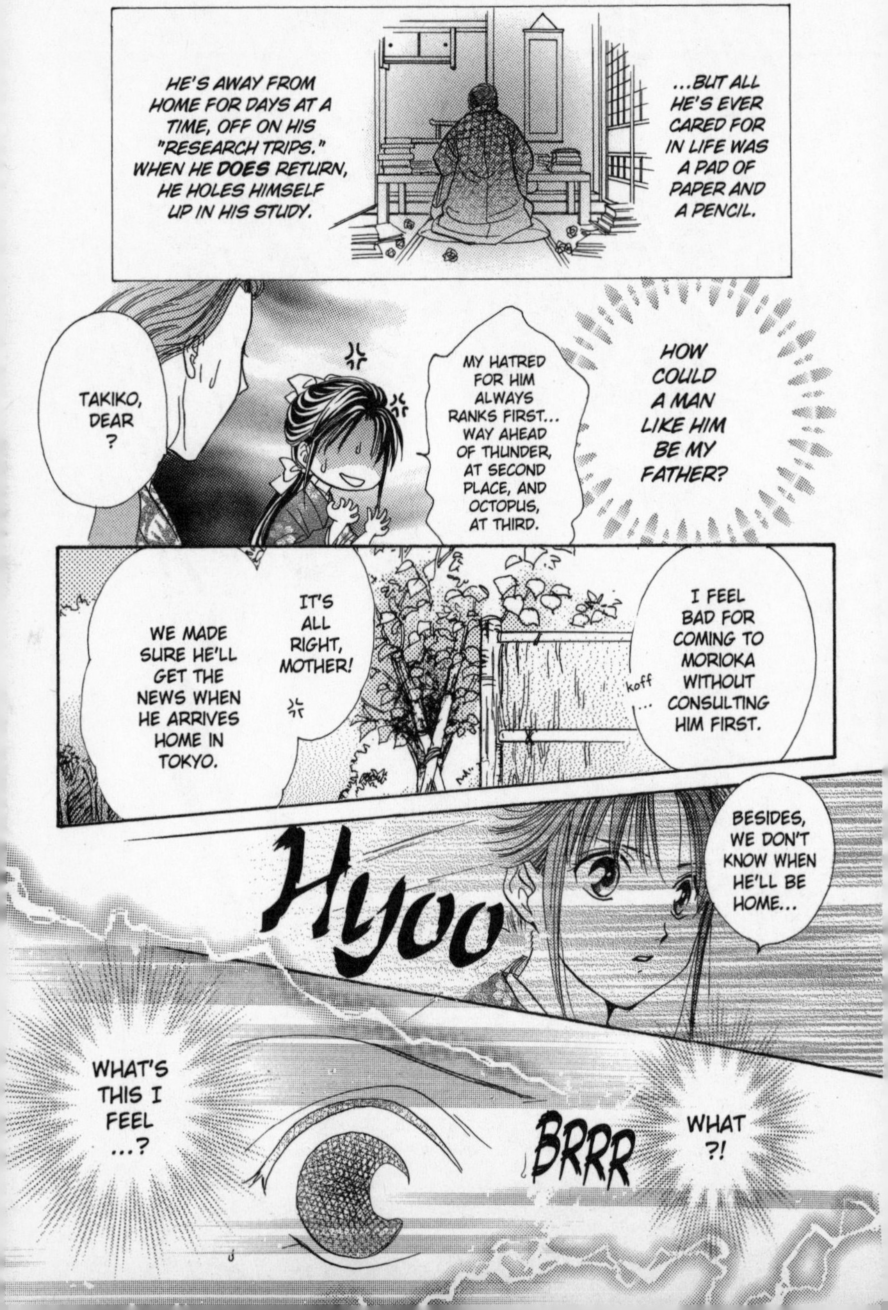
HE'S AWAY FROM HOME FOR DAYS AT A TIME, OFF ON HIS "RESEARCH TRIPS." WHEN HE DOES RETURN, HE HOLES HIMSELF UP IN HIS STUDY.
...BUT ALL HE'S EVER CARED FOR IN LIFE WAS A PAD OF PAPER AND A PENCIL.
HOW COULD A MAN LIKE HIM BE MY FATHER?
MY HATRED FOR HIM ALWAYS RANKS FIRST... WAY AHEAD OF THUNDER, AT SECOND PLACE, AND OCTOPUS, AT THIRD.
TAKIKO, DEAR ?
I FEEL BAD FOR COMING TO MORIOKA WITHOUT CONSULTING HIM FIRST.
koff ...
IT'S ALL RIGHT, MOTHER!
WE MADE SURE HE'LL GET THE NEWS WHEN HE ARRIVES HOME IN TOKYO.
BESIDES, WE DON'T KNOW WHEN HE'LL BE HOME...
Hyoo
WHAT ?!
BRRR
WHAT'S THIS I FEEL ...?

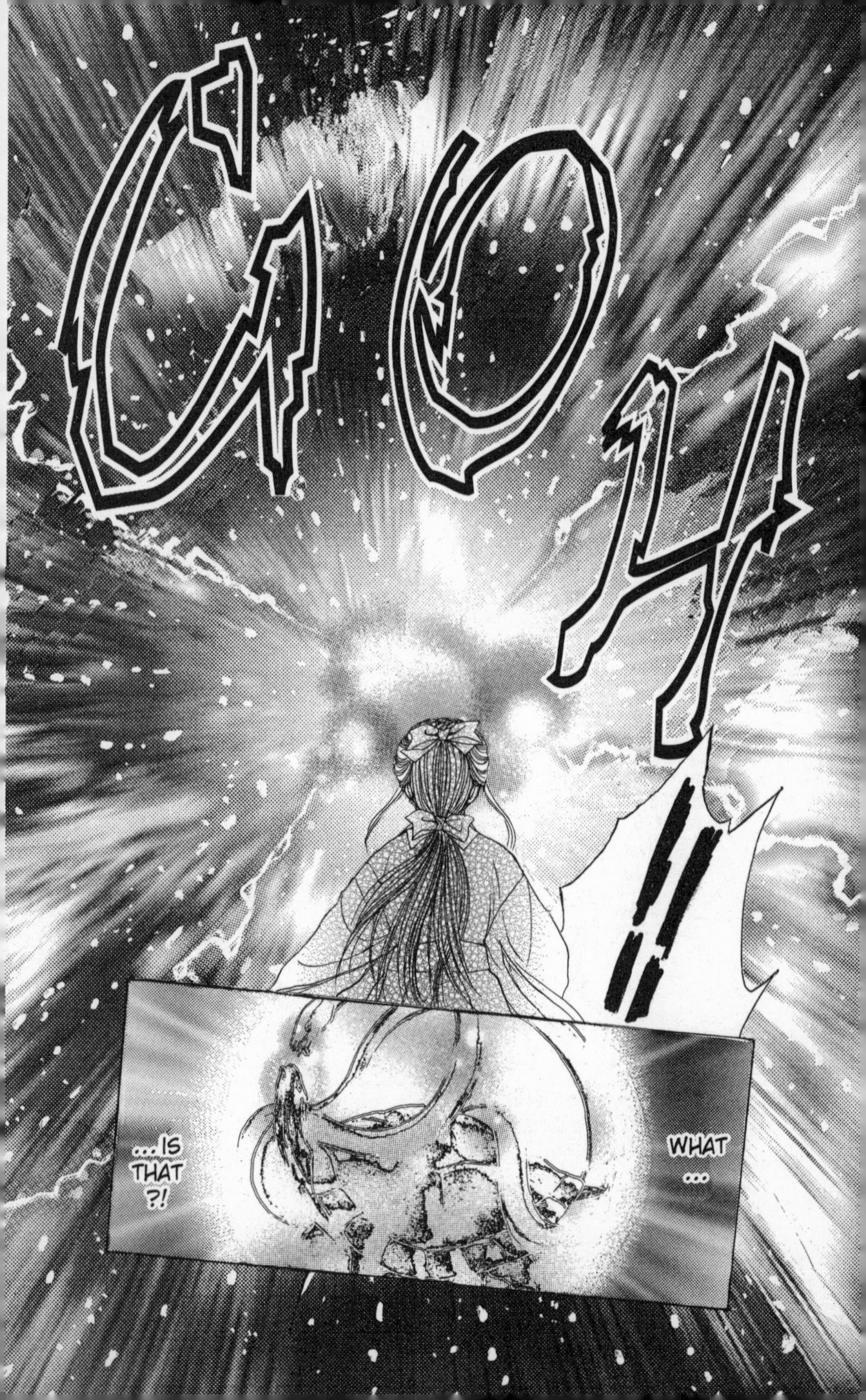
WHAT ...
...IS THAT ?!

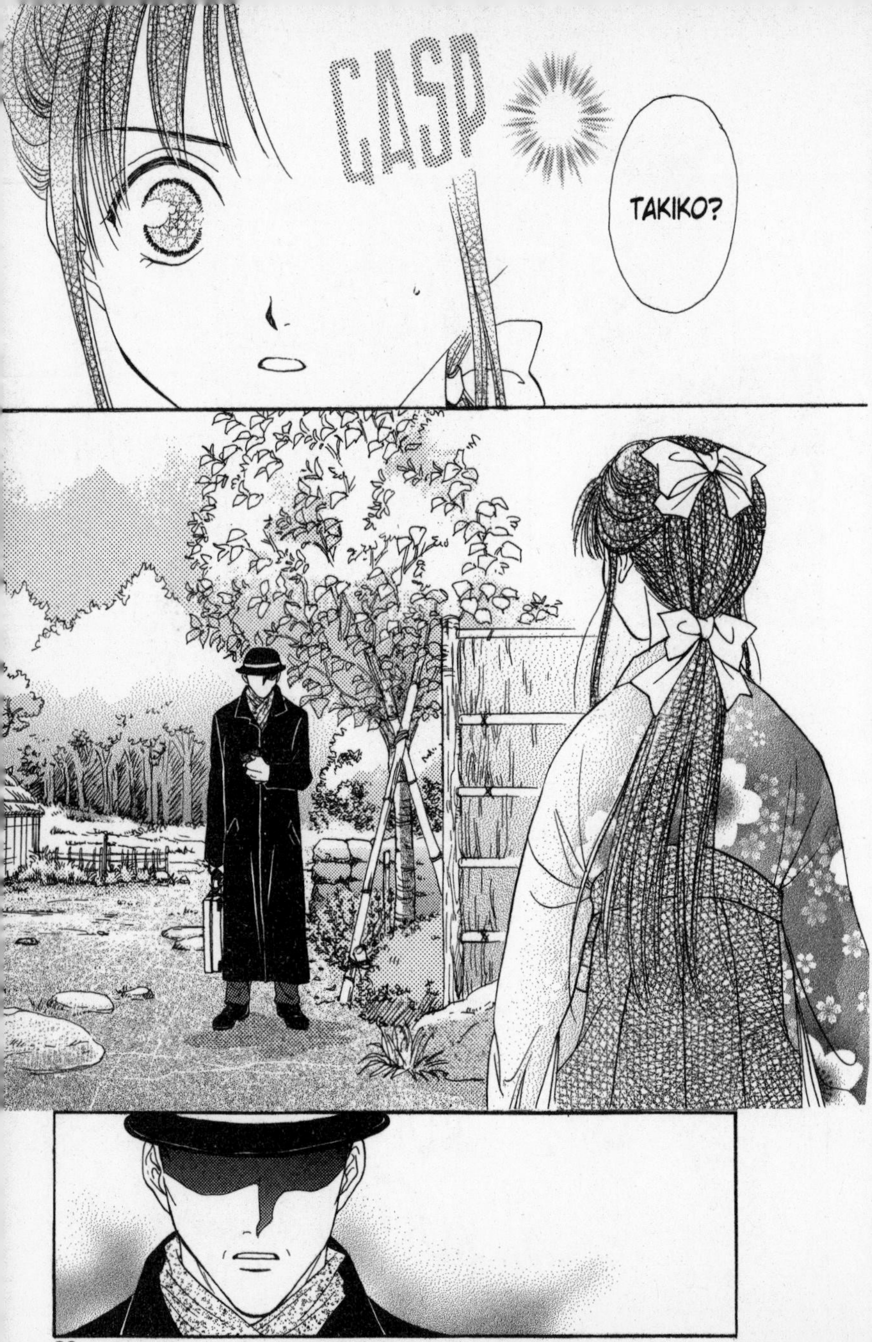
GASP
TAKIKO?

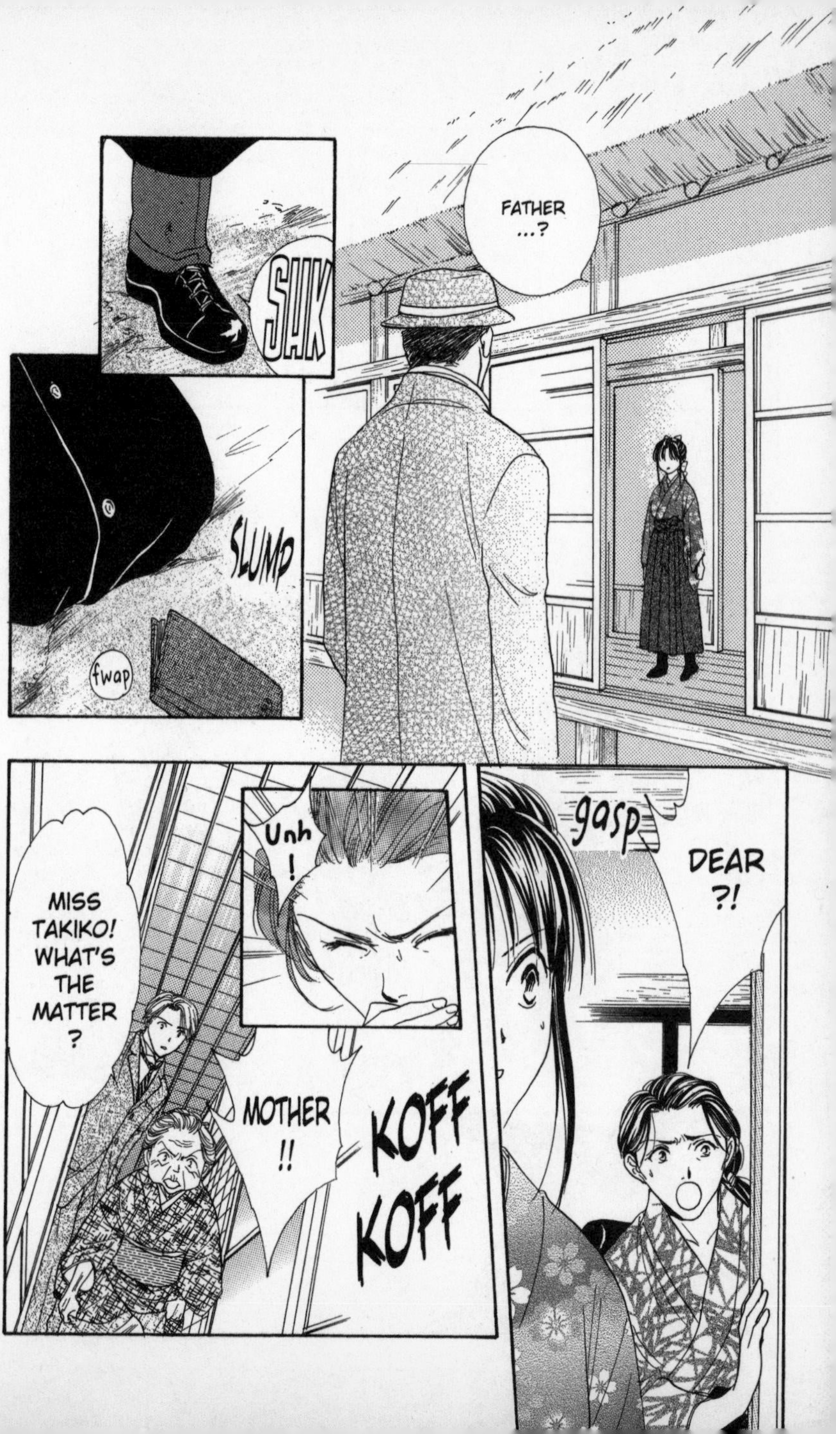
FATHER ...?
SHK
SLUMP
fwap
gasp
DEAR ?!
Unh !
KOFF KOFF
MOTHER !!
MISS TAKIKO! WHAT'S THE MATTER ?

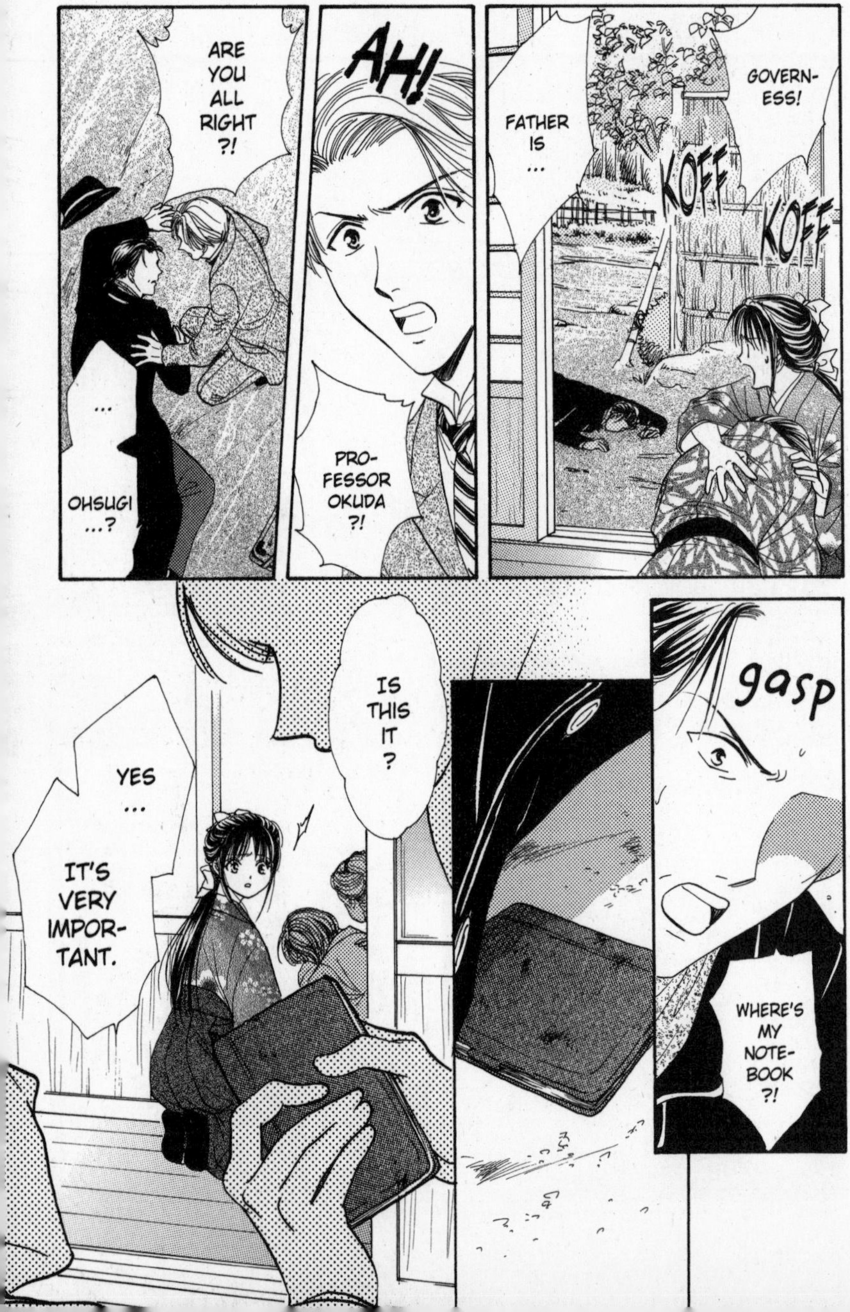
GOVERN-ESS!
FATHER IS ...
KOFF
KOFF
AH!
PRO-FESSOR OKUDA ?!
ARE YOU ALL RIGHT ?!
...
OHSUGI ...?
gasp
WHERE'S MY NOTE-BOOK ?!
IS THIS IT ?
YES ...
IT'S VERY IMPOR-TANT.

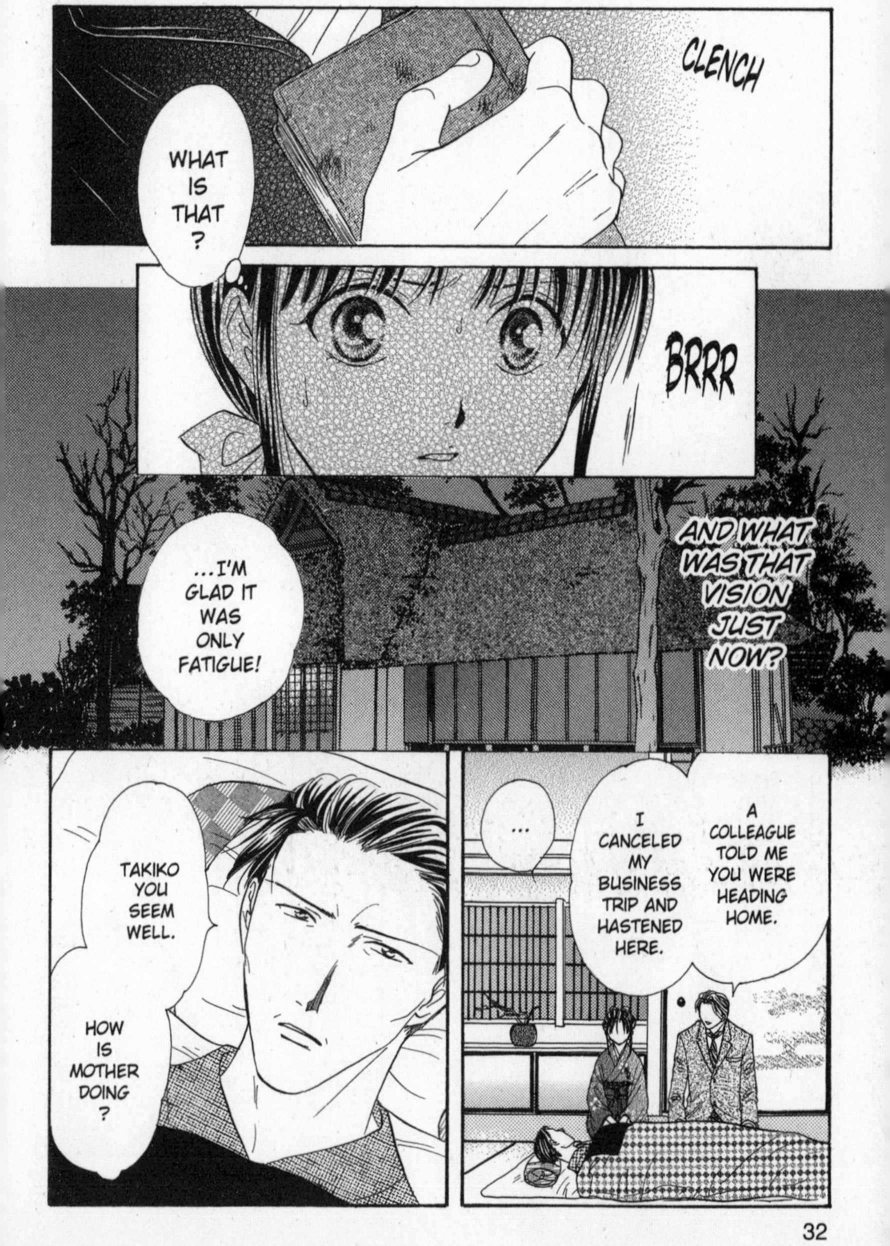
CLENCH
WHAT IS THAT?
BRRR
AND WHAT WAS THAT VISION JUST NOW?
...I'M GLAD IT WAS ONLY FATIGUE!
A COLLEAGUE TOLD ME YOU WERE HEADING HOME.
I CANCELED MY BUSINESS TRIP AND HASTENED HERE.
...
TAKIKO YOU SEEM WELL.
HOW IS MOTHER DOING?

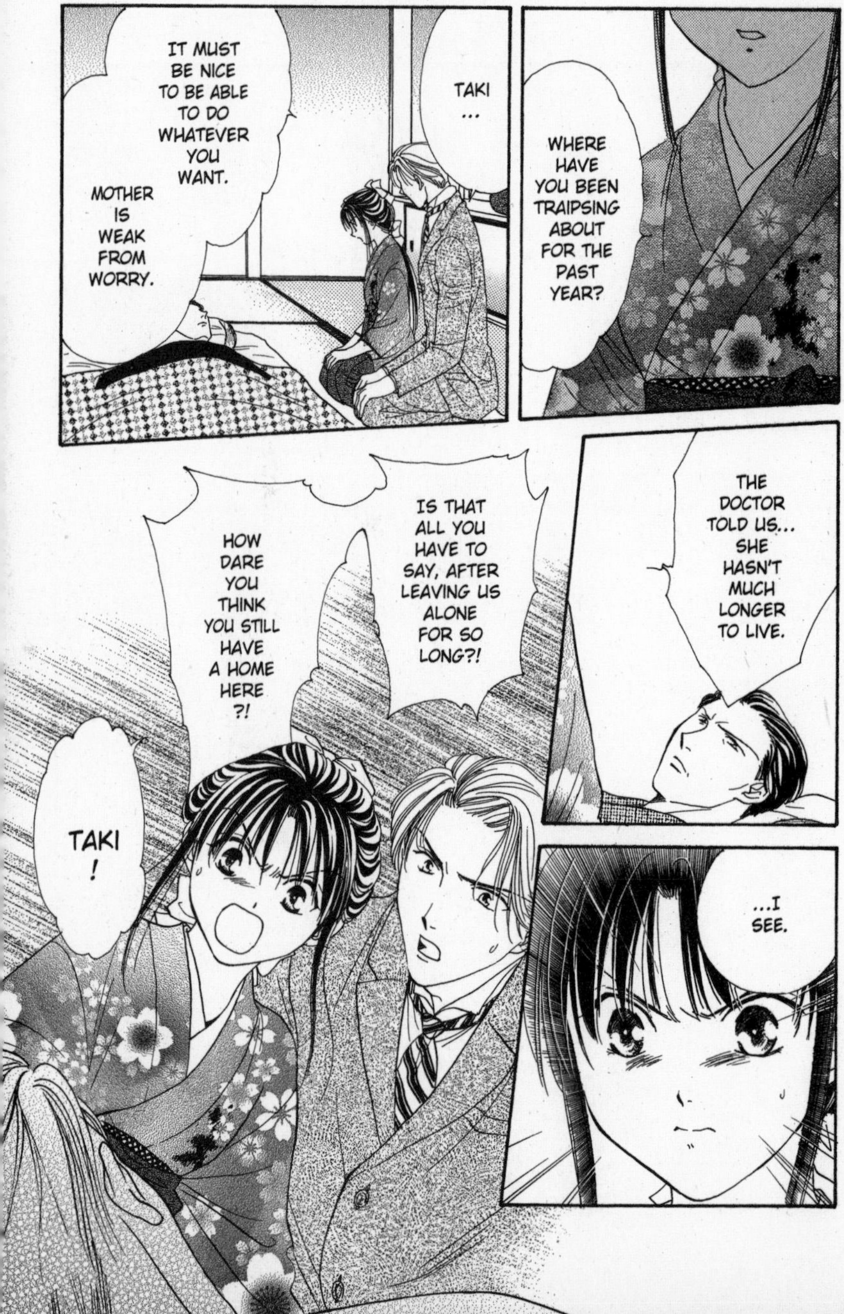
WHERE HAVE YOU BEEN TRAIPSING ABOUT FOR THE PAST YEAR?
TAKI ...
IT MUST BE NICE TO BE ABLE TO DO WHATEVER YOU WANT.
MOTHER IS WEAK FROM WORRY.
THE DOCTOR TOLD US... SHE HASN'T MUCH LONGER TO LIVE.
...I SEE.
IS THAT ALL YOU HAVE TO SAY, AFTER LEAVING US ALONE FOR SO LONG?!
HOW DARE YOU THINK YOU STILL HAVE A HOME HERE ?!
TAKI !

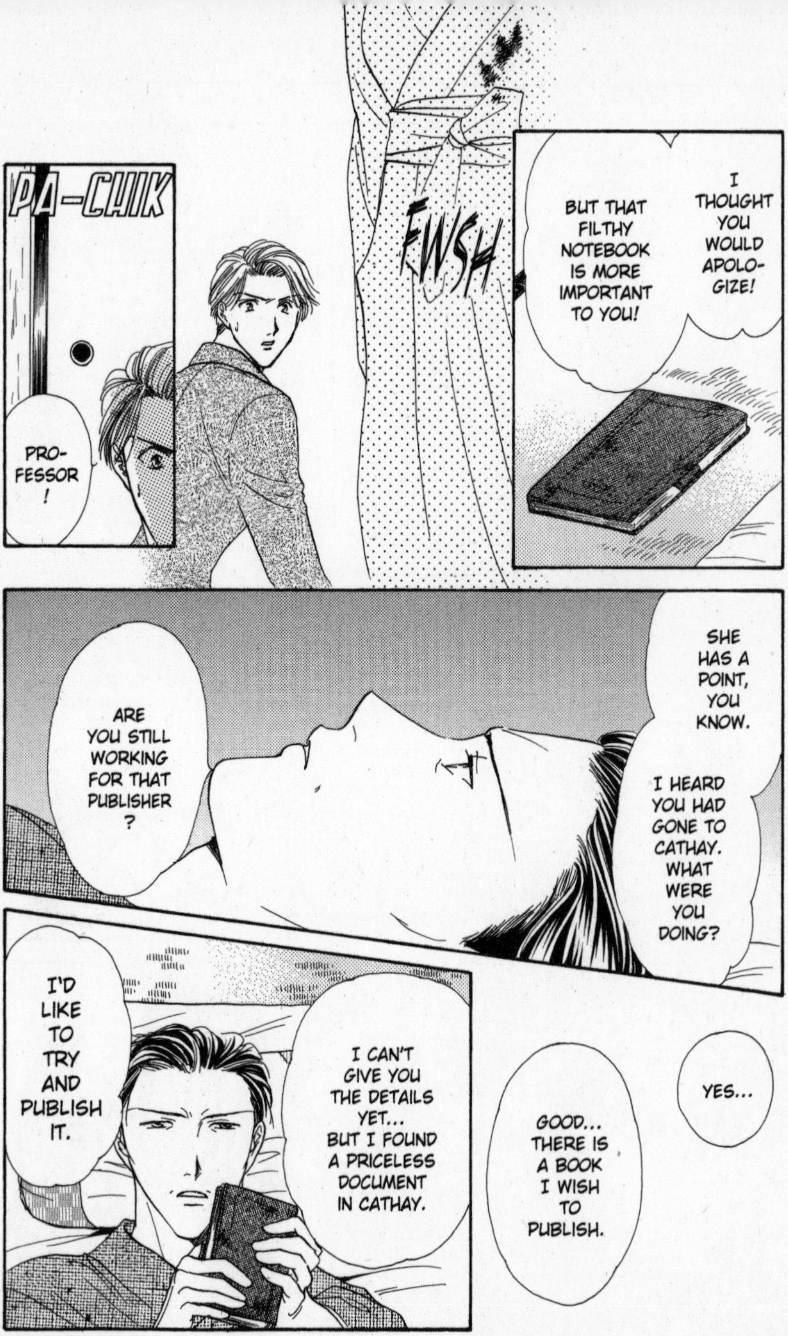
I THOUGHT YOU WOULD APOLOGIZE!
BUT THAT FILTHY NOTEBOOK IS MORE IMPORTANT TO YOU!
FWSH
PA-CHIK
PRO-FESSOR!
SHE HAS A POINT, YOU KNOW.
I HEARD YOU HAD GONE TO CATHAY. WHAT WERE YOU DOING?
ARE YOU STILL WORKING FOR THAT PUBLISHER?
YES...
GOOD... THERE IS A BOOK I WISH TO PUBLISH.
I CAN'T GIVE YOU THE DETAILS YET... BUT I FOUND A PRICELESS DOCUMENT IN CATHAY.
I'D LIKE TO TRY AND PUBLISH IT.

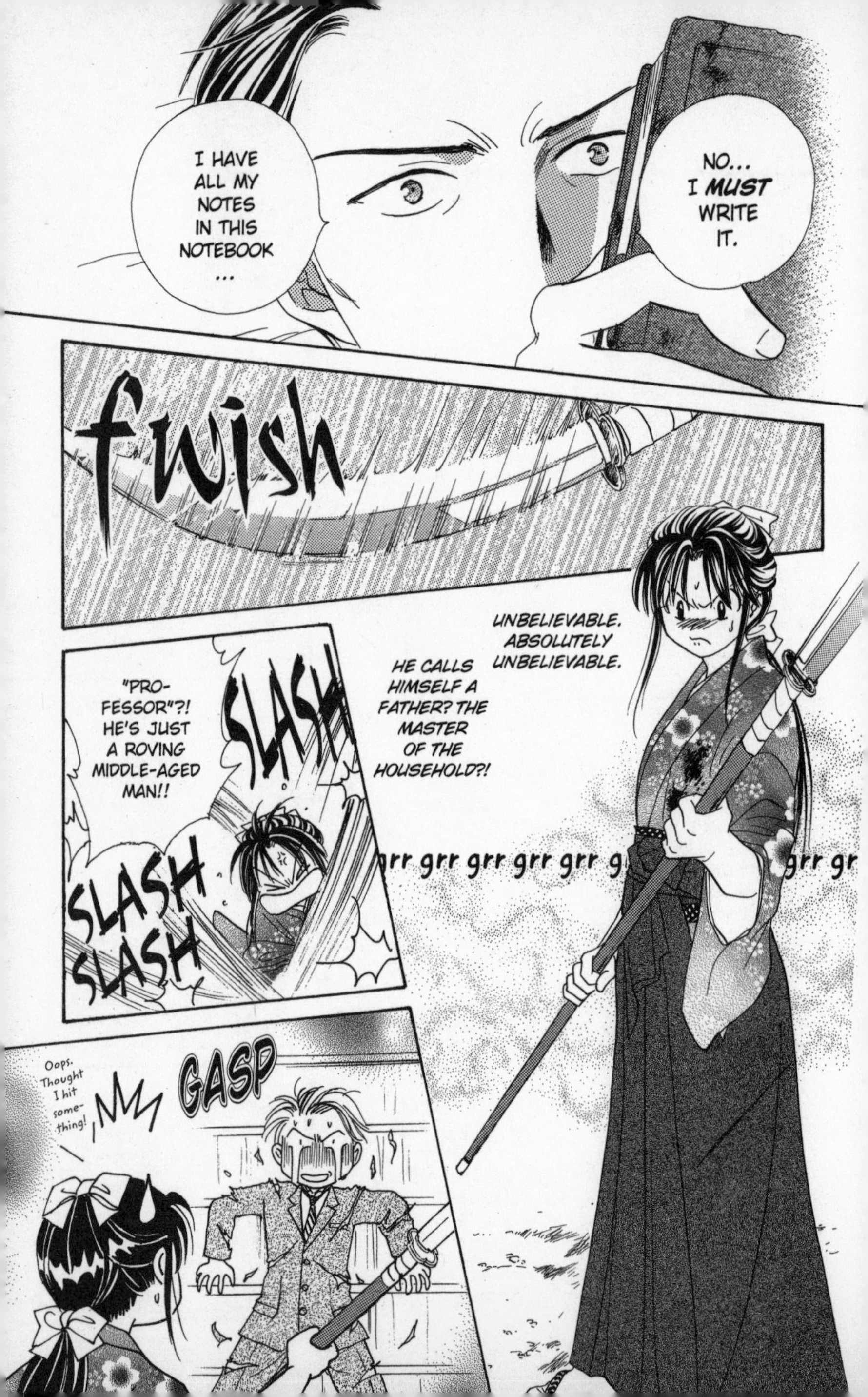
NO... I MUST WRITE IT.
I HAVE ALL MY NOTES IN THIS NOTEBOOK ...
fwish
UNBELIEVABLE. ABSOLUTELY UNBELIEVABLE.
HE CALLS HIMSELF A FATHER? THE MASTER OF THE HOUSEHOLD?!
grr grr grr grr grr g grr gr
"PRO-FESSOR"?! HE'S JUST A ROVING MIDDLE-AGED MAN!!
SLASH
SLASH SLASH SLASH
GASP
Oops. Thought I hit some-thing!

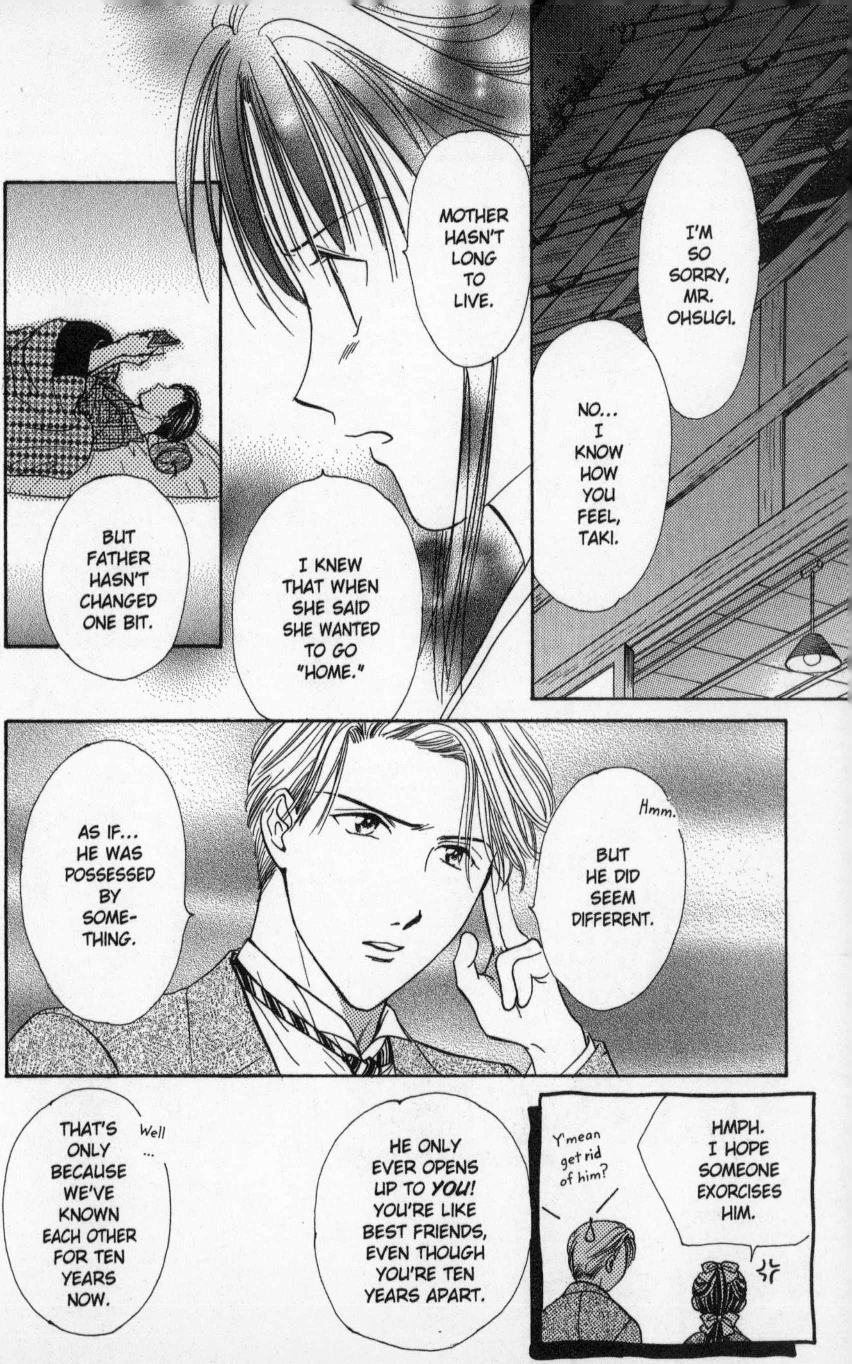
I'M SO SORRY, MR. OHSUGI.
NO... I KNOW HOW YOU FEEL, TAKI.
MOTHER HASN'T LONG TO LIVE.
I KNEW THAT WHEN SHE SAID SHE WANTED TO GO "HOME."
BUT FATHER HASN'T CHANGED ONE BIT.
Hmm.
BUT HE DID SEEM DIFFERENT.
AS IF... HE WAS POSSESSED BY SOME-THING.
HMPH. I HOPE SOMEONE EXORCISES HIM.
Y'mean get rid of him?
HE ONLY EVER OPENS UP TO ***YOU***! YOU'RE LIKE BEST FRIENDS, EVEN THOUGH YOU'RE TEN YEARS APART.
Well ...
THAT'S ONLY BECAUSE WE'VE KNOWN EACH OTHER FOR TEN YEARS NOW.

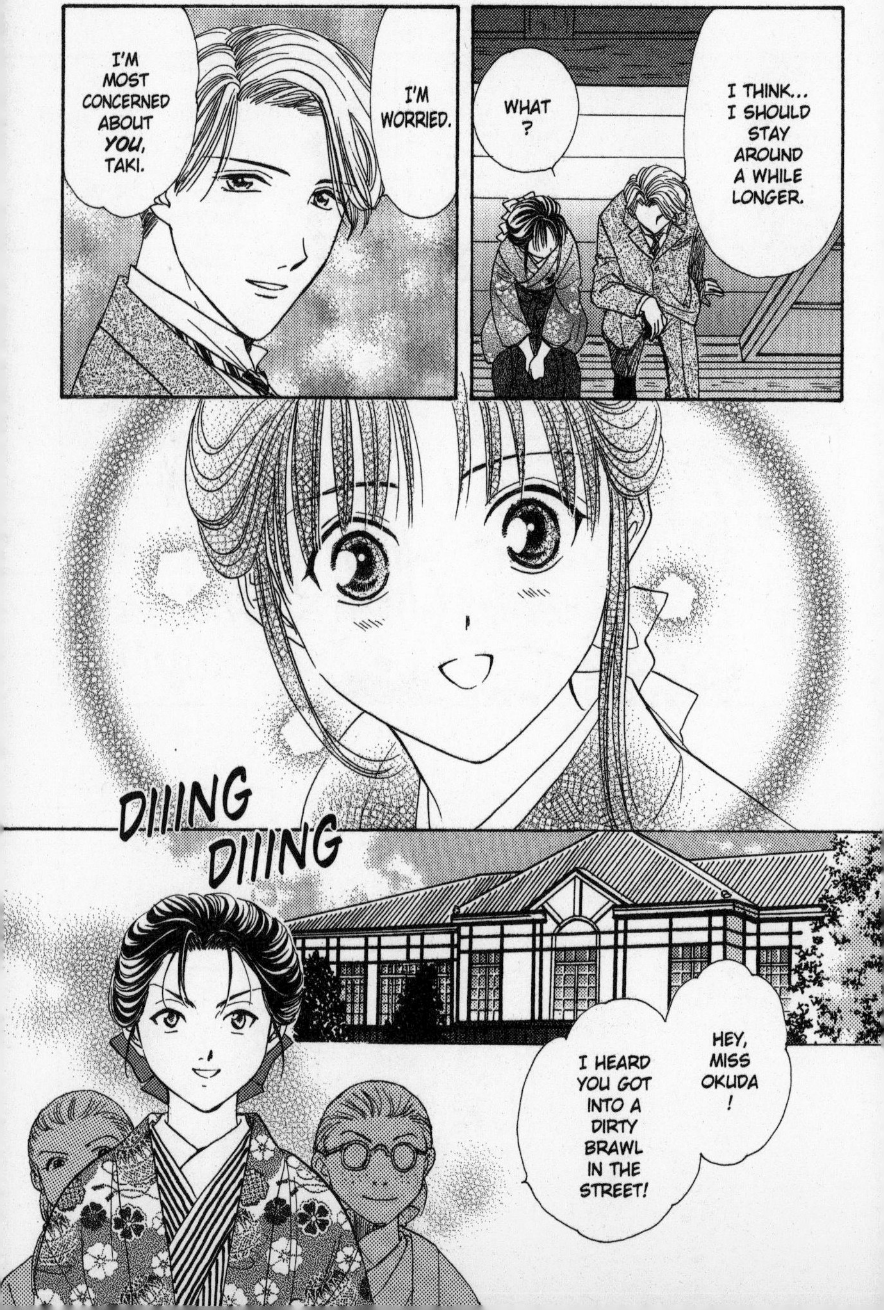
I THINK... I SHOULD STAY AROUND A WHILE LONGER.
WHAT ?
I'M WORRIED.
I'M MOST CONCERNED ABOUT *YOU*, TAKI.
DIIING DIIING
HEY, MISS OKUDA !
I HEARD YOU GOT INTO A DIRTY BRAWL IN THE STREET!

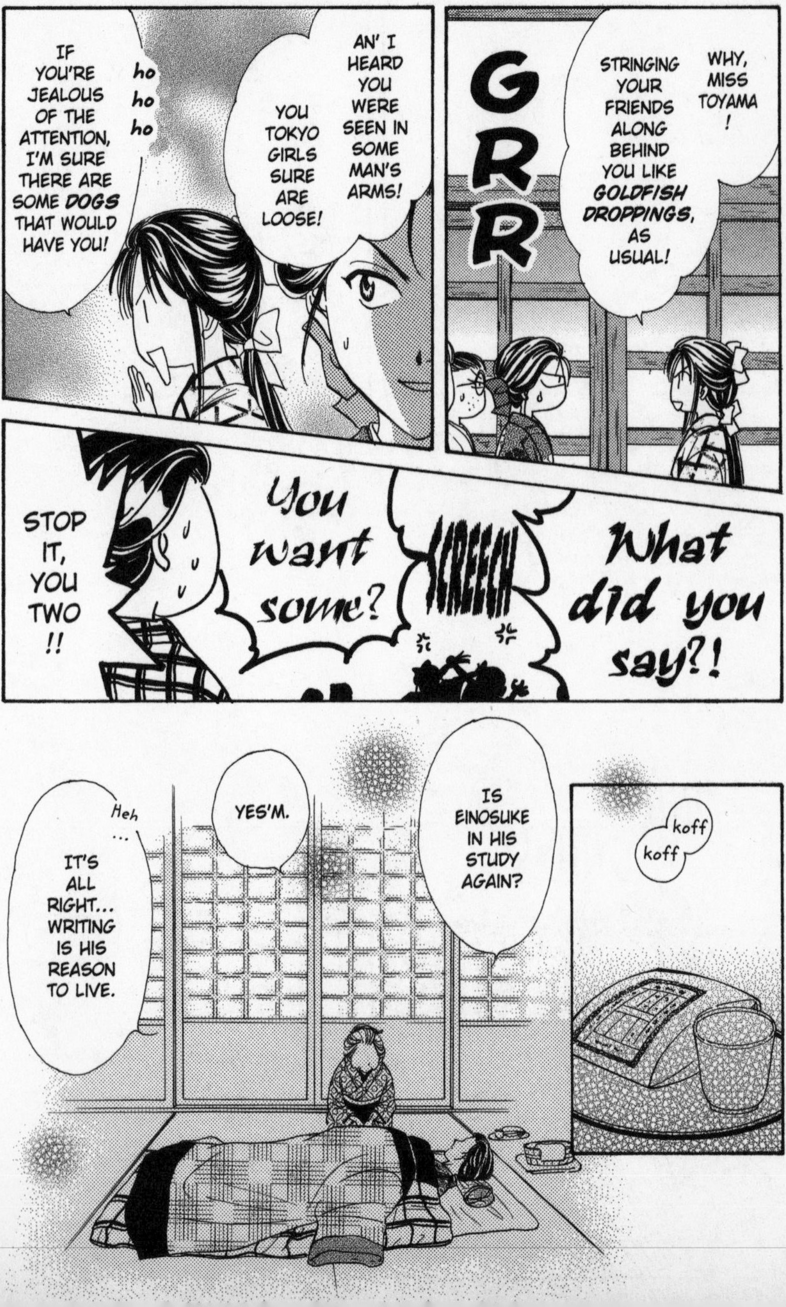
GRR
WHY, MISS TOYAMA!
STRINGING YOUR FRIENDS ALONG BEHIND YOU LIKE GOLDFISH DROPPINGS, AS USUAL!
AN' I HEARD YOU WERE SEEN IN SOME MAN'S ARMS!
YOU TOKYO GIRLS SURE ARE LOOSE!
ho ho ho
IF YOU'RE JEALOUS OF THE ATTENTION, I'M SURE THERE ARE SOME DOGS THAT WOULD HAVE YOU!
What did you say?!
SCREECH
You want some?
STOP IT, YOU TWO!!
koff koff
IS EINOSUKE IN HIS STUDY AGAIN?
YES'M.
Heh...
IT'S ALL RIGHT... WRITING IS HIS REASON TO LIVE.

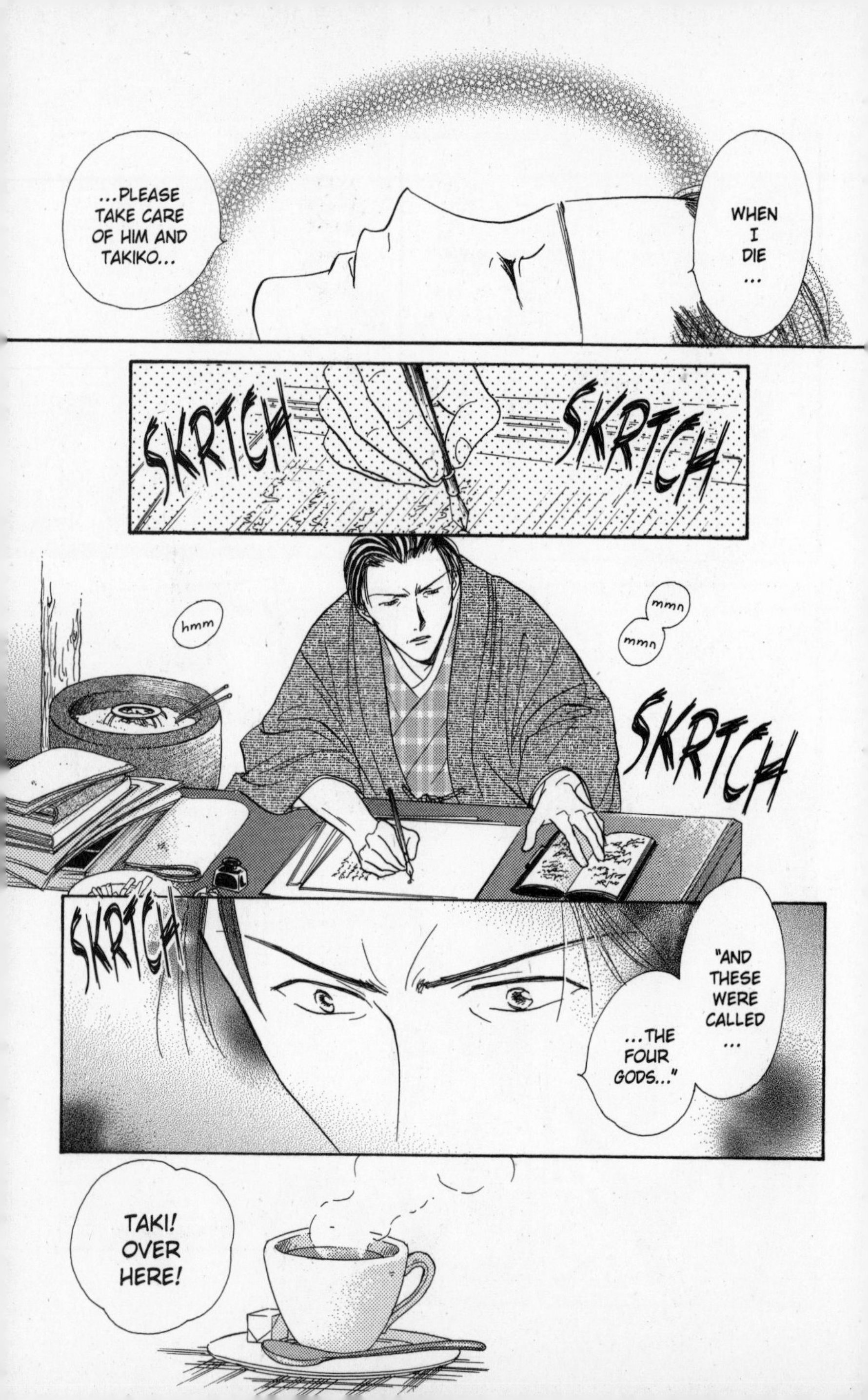
WHEN I DIE ...
...PLEASE TAKE CARE OF HIM AND TAKIKO...
SKRTCH
SKRTCH
mmn
mmn
SKRTCH
hmm
"AND THESE WERE CALLED ...
...THE FOUR GODS..."
SKRTCH
TAKI! OVER HERE!

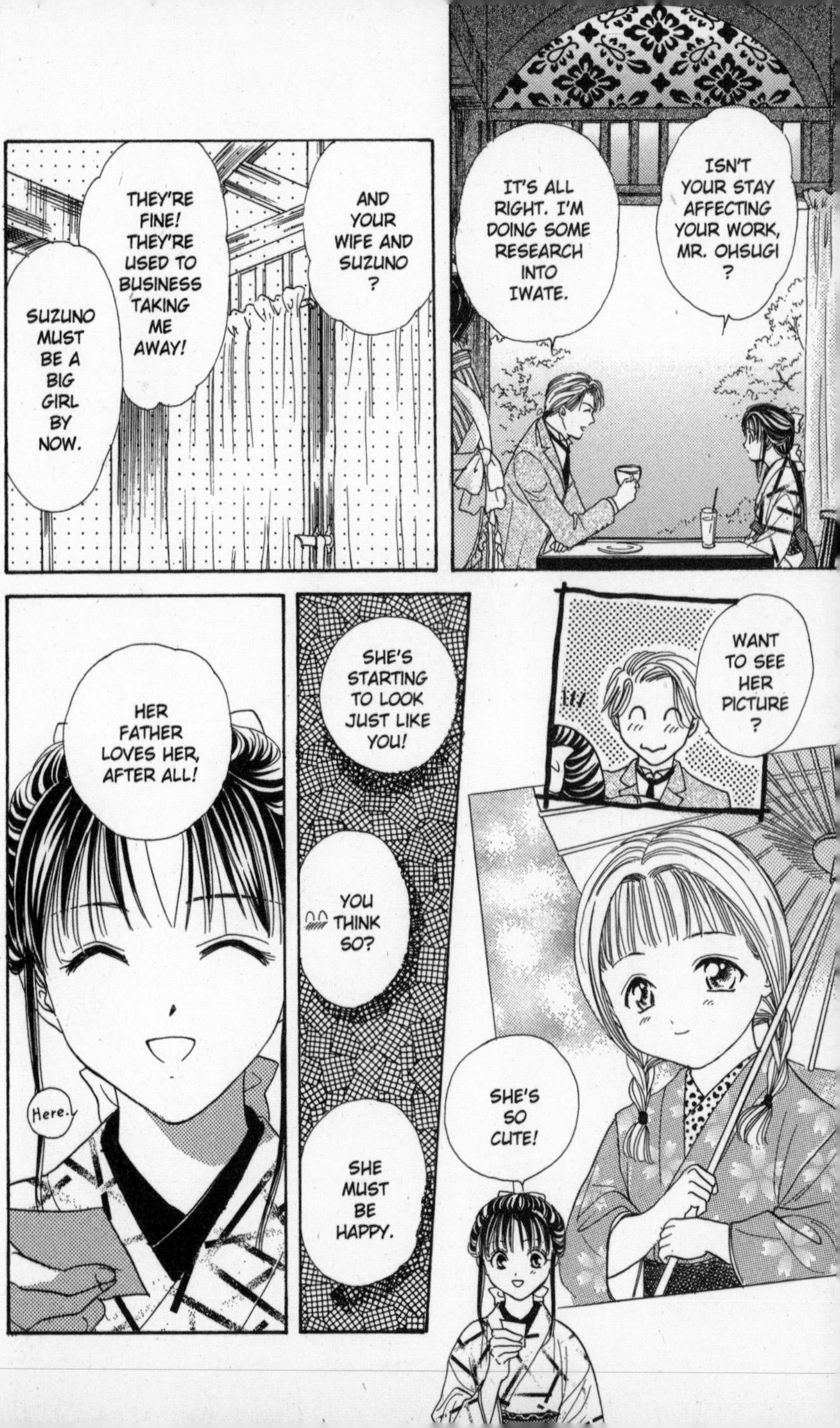
ISN'T YOUR STAY AFFECTING YOUR WORK, MR. OHSUGI ?
IT'S ALL RIGHT. I'M DOING SOME RESEARCH INTO IWATE.
AND YOUR WIFE AND SUZUNO ?
THEY'RE FINE! THEY'RE USED TO BUSINESS TAKING ME AWAY!
SUZUNO MUST BE A BIG GIRL BY NOW.
WANT TO SEE HER PICTURE ?
SHE'S SO CUTE!
SHE'S STARTING TO LOOK JUST LIKE YOU!
YOU THINK SO?
SHE MUST BE HAPPY.
HER FATHER LOVES HER, AFTER ALL!
Here.

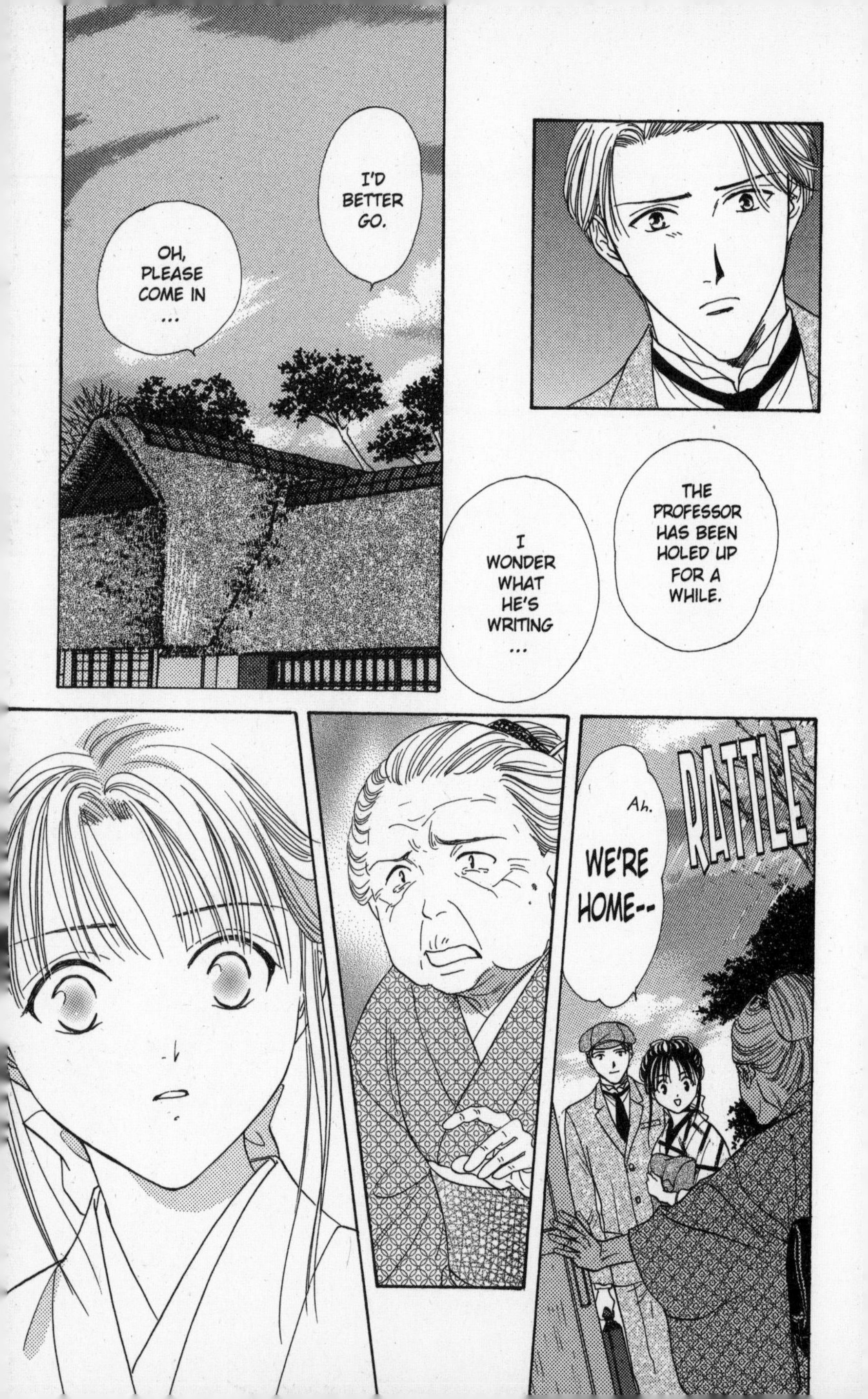
THE PROFESSOR HAS BEEN HOLED UP FOR A WHILE.
I WONDER WHAT HE'S WRITING ...
I'D BETTER GO.
OH, PLEASE COME IN ...
RATTLE
Ah.
WE'RE HOME--

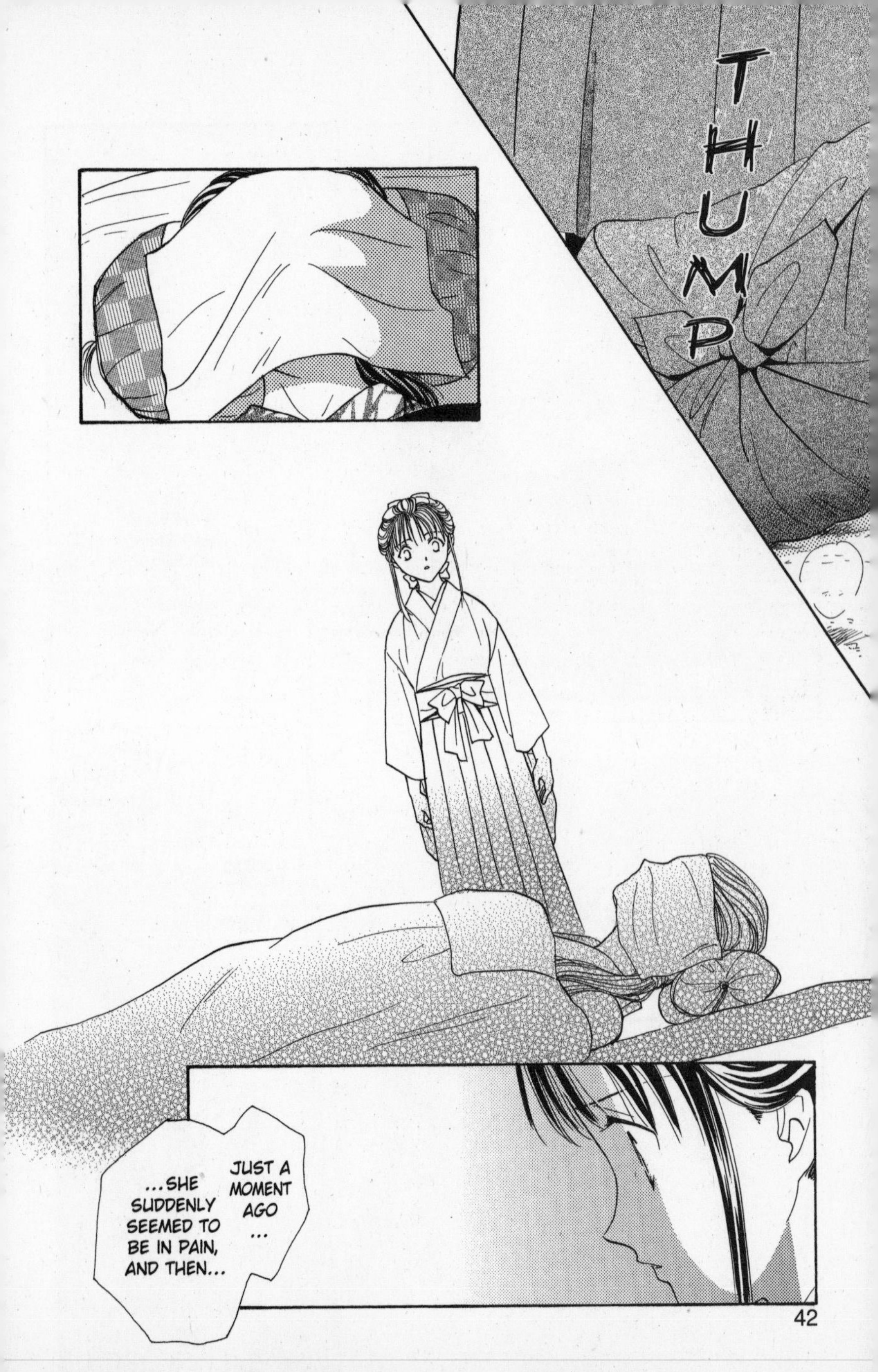
THUMP
JUST A MOMENT AGO ...
...SHE SUDDENLY SEEMED TO BE IN PAIN, AND THEN...

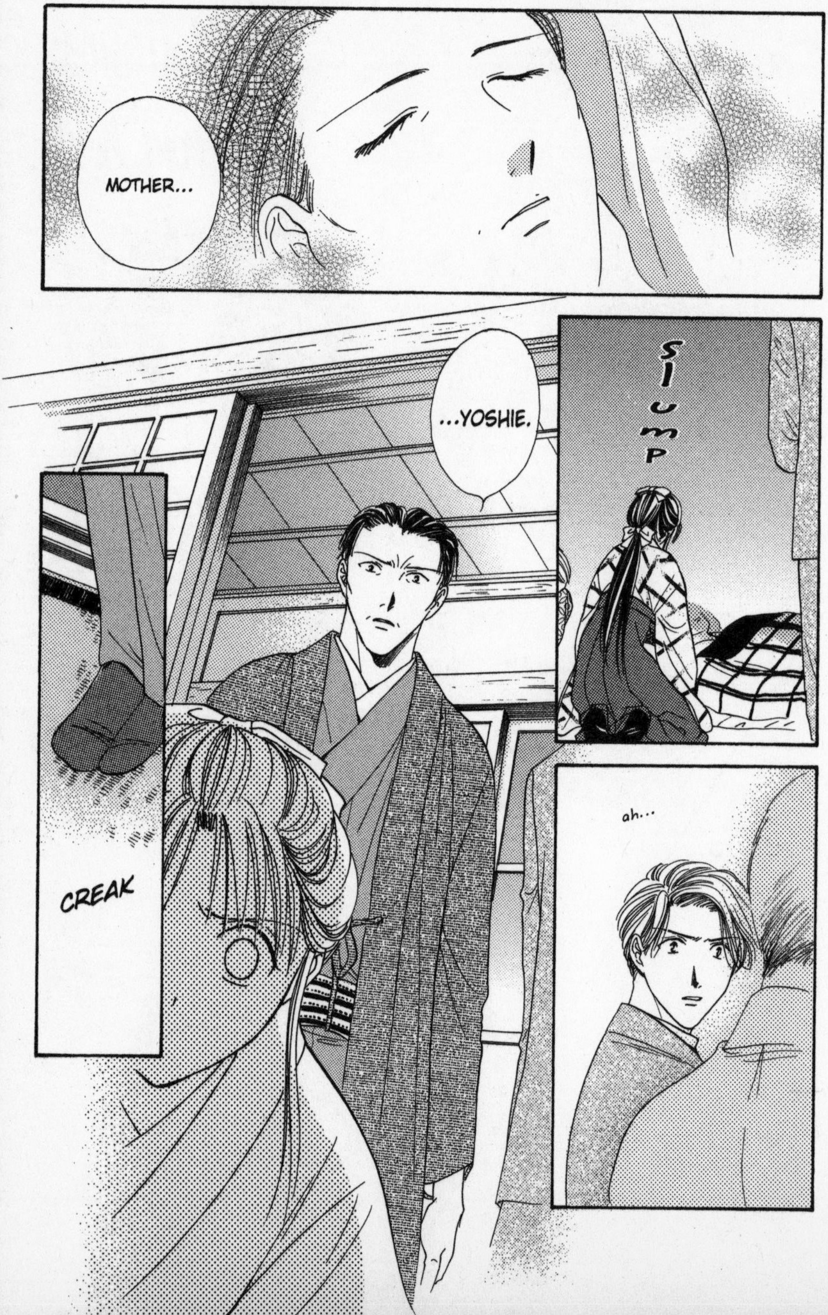
MOTHER...
SLUMP
ah...
...YOSHIE.
CREAK

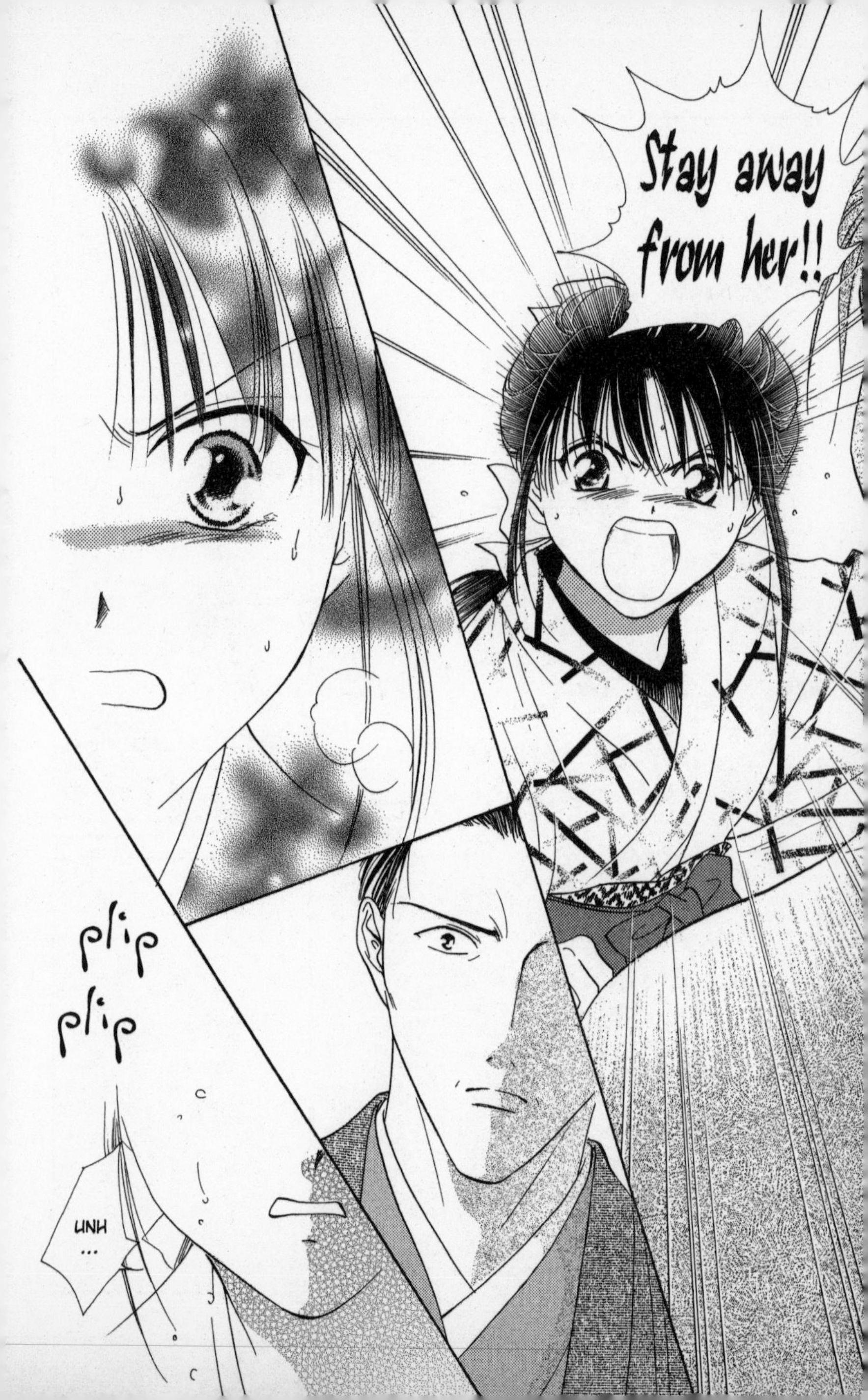
Stay away from her!!
plip plip
UNH ...

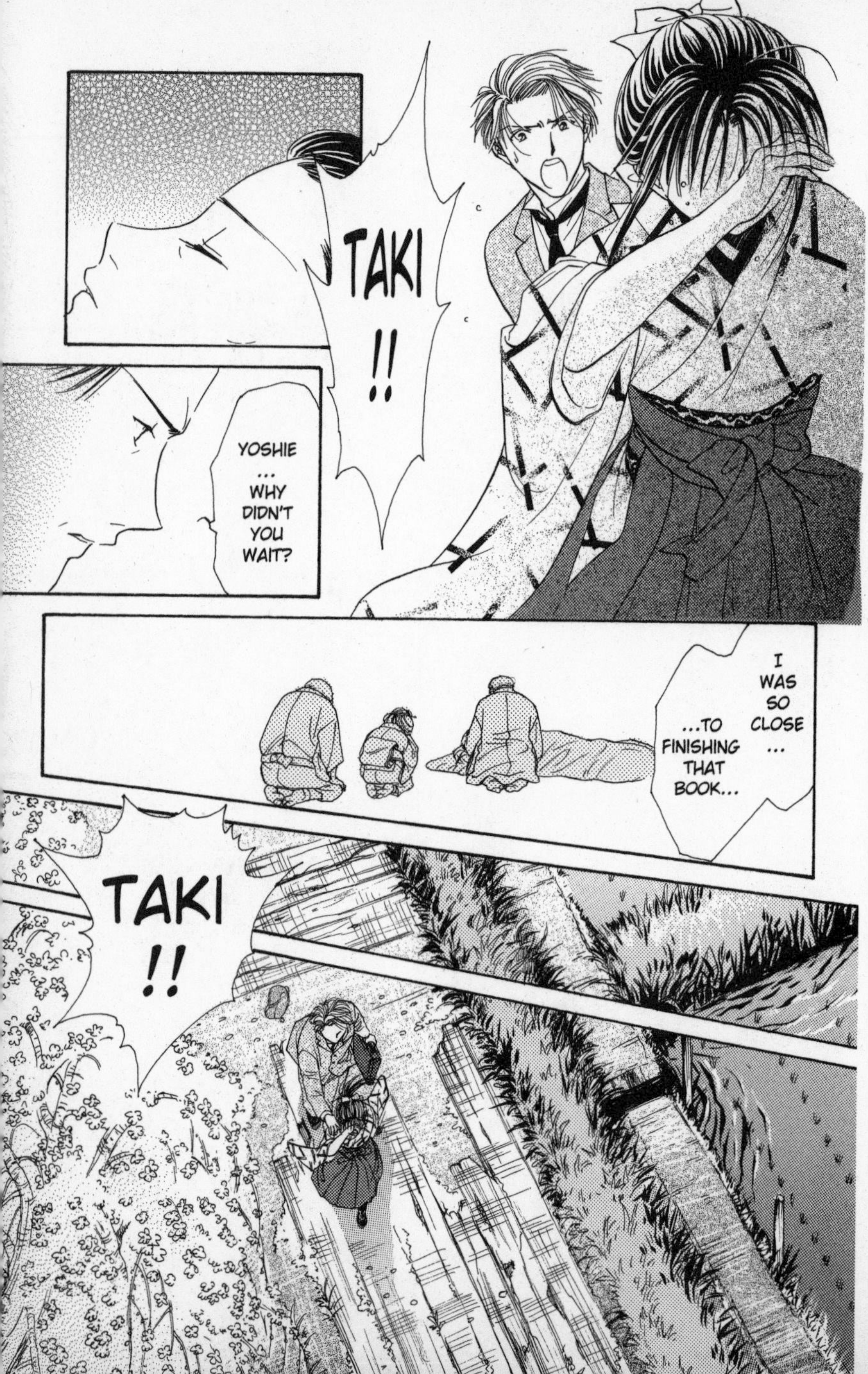
TAKI !!
YOSHIE ... WHY DIDN'T YOU WAIT?
I WAS SO CLOSE ...
...TO FINISHING THAT BOOK...
TAKI !!

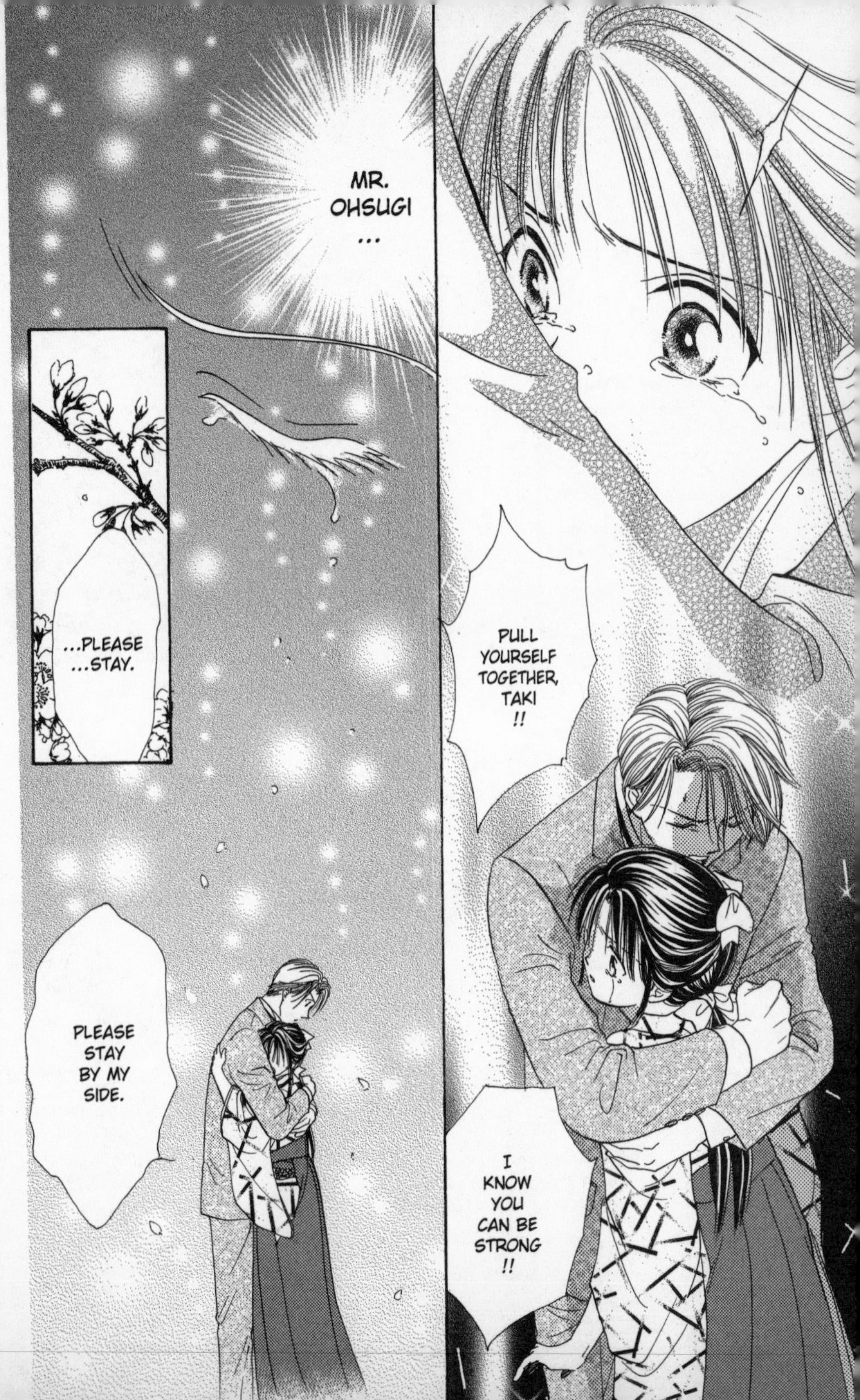
PULL YOURSELF TOGETHER, TAKI !!
I KNOW YOU CAN BE STRONG !!
MR. OHSUGI ...
...PLEASE ...STAY.
PLEASE STAY BY MY SIDE.

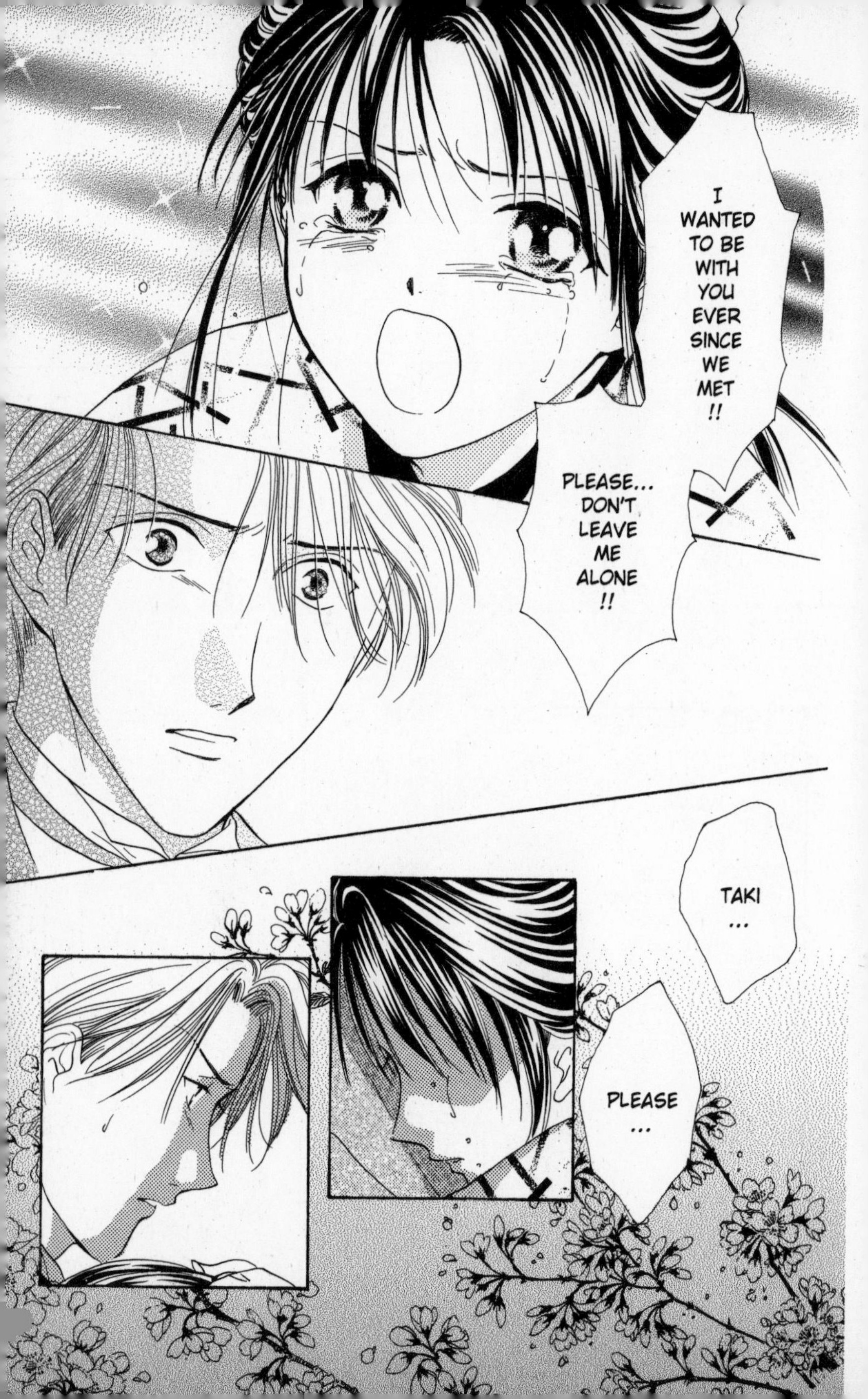
I WANTED TO BE WITH YOU EVER SINCE WE MET !!
PLEASE... DON'T LEAVE ME ALONE !!
TAKI ...
PLEASE ...

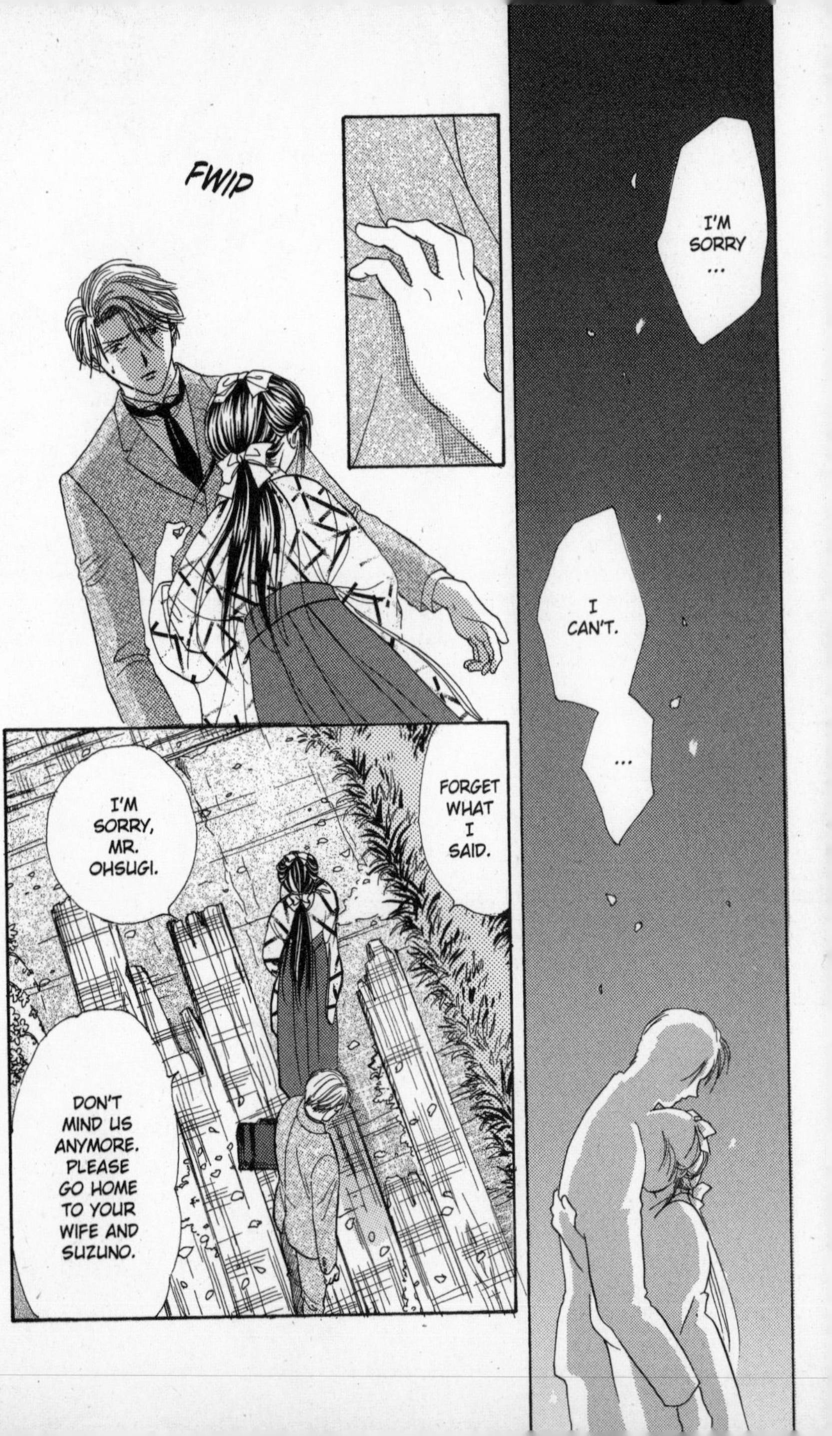
I'M SORRY ...
I CAN'T.
...
FWIP
FORGET WHAT I SAID.
I'M SORRY, MR. OHSUGI.
DON'T MIND US ANYMORE. PLEASE GO HOME TO YOUR WIFE AND SUZUNO.

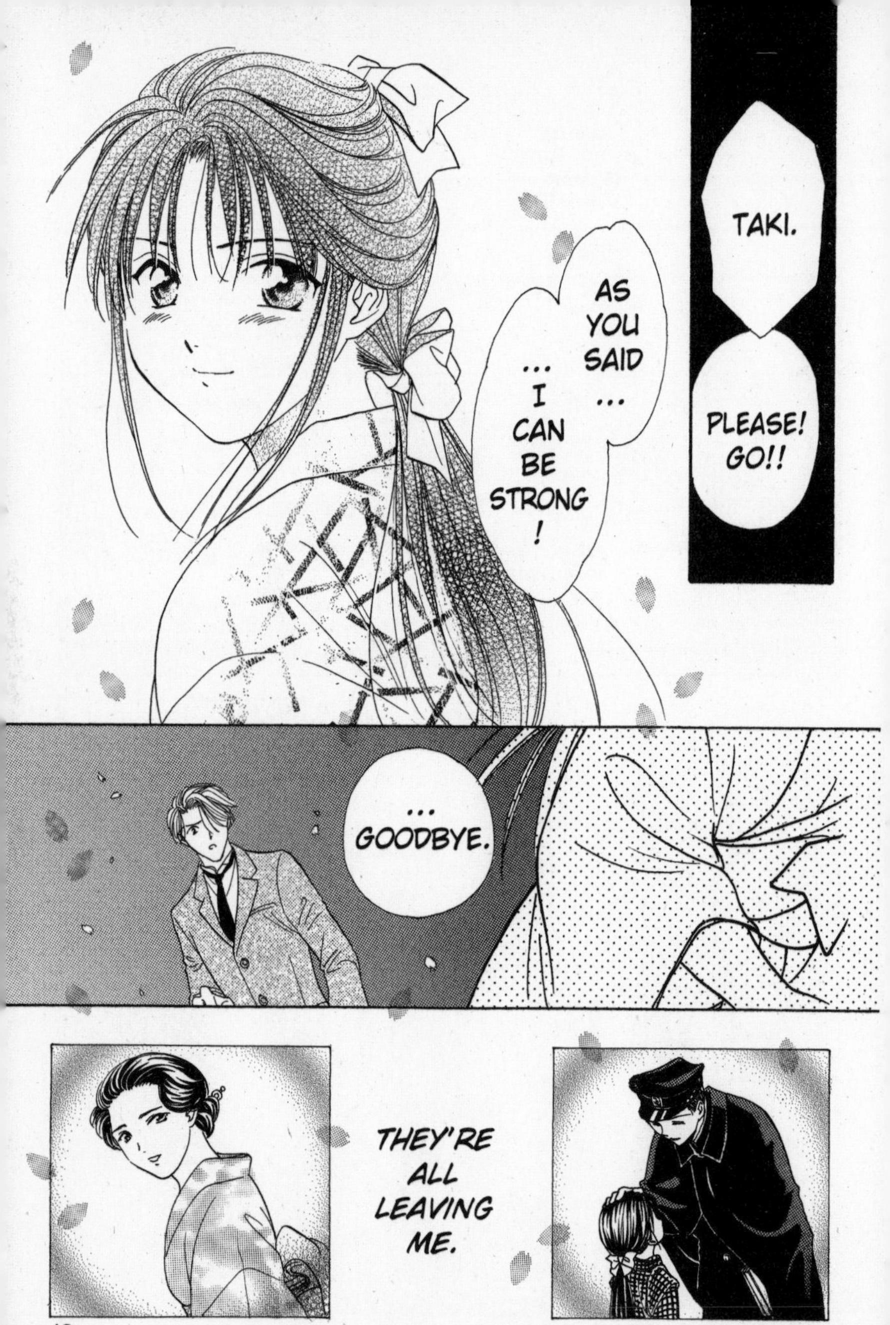
TAKI.
PLEASE! GO!!
AS YOU SAID ...
... I CAN BE STRONG!
... GOODBYE.
THEY'RE ALL LEAVING ME.

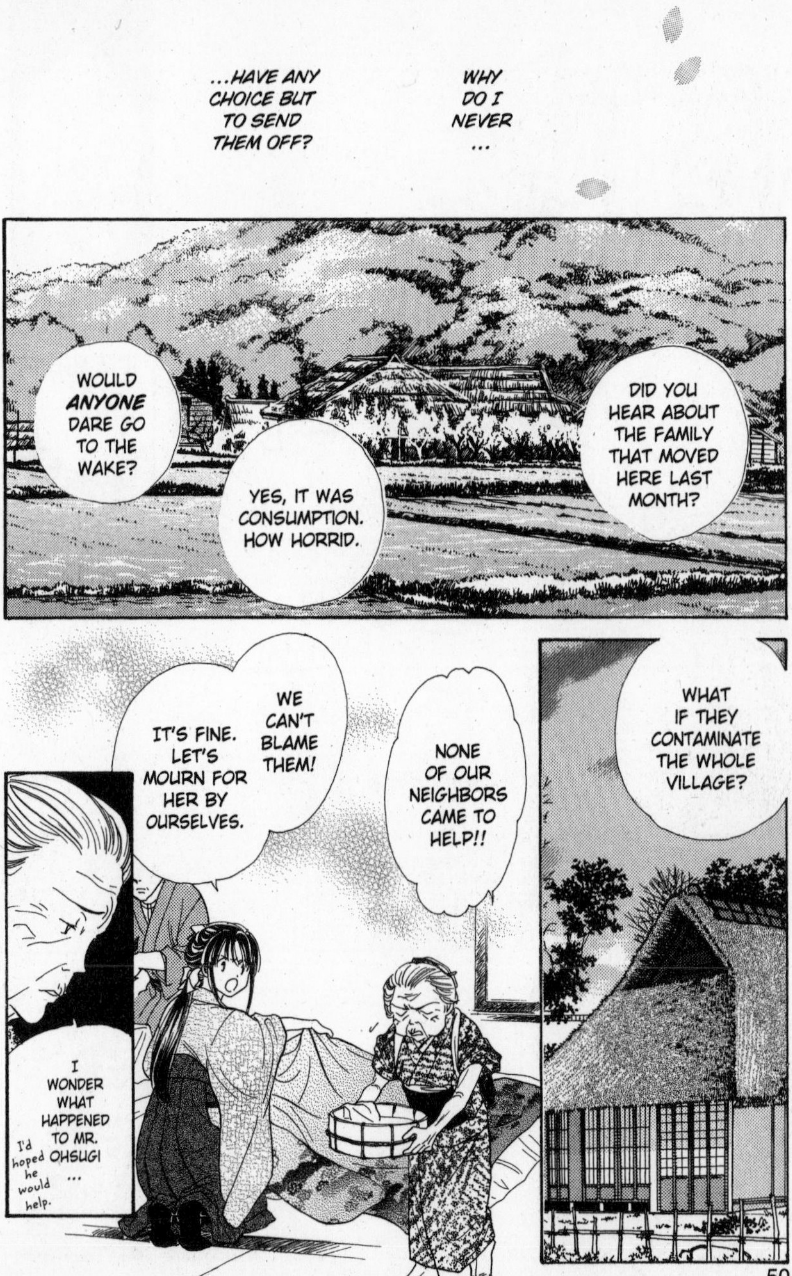
WHY DO I NEVER ...
...HAVE ANY CHOICE BUT TO SEND THEM OFF?
DID YOU HEAR ABOUT THE FAMILY THAT MOVED HERE LAST MONTH?
YES, IT WAS CONSUMPTION. HOW HORRID.
WOULD ANYONE DARE GO TO THE WAKE?
WHAT IF THEY CONTAMINATE THE WHOLE VILLAGE?
NONE OF OUR NEIGHBORS CAME TO HELP!!
WE CAN'T BLAME THEM!
IT'S FINE. LET'S MOURN FOR HER BY OURSELVES.
I WONDER WHAT HAPPENED TO MR. OHSUGI ...
I'd hoped he would help.

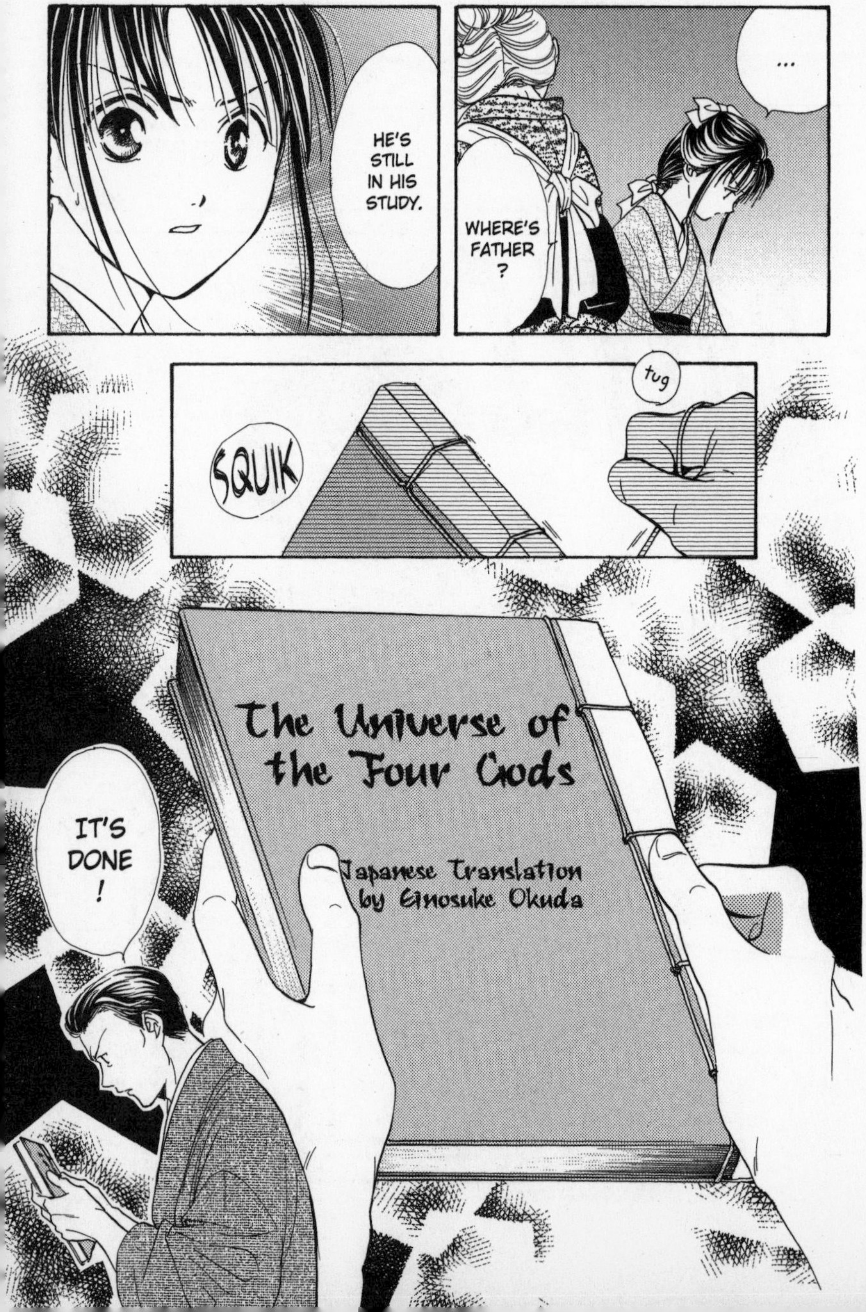
...
WHERE'S FATHER ?
HE'S STILL IN HIS STUDY.
tug
SQUIK
The Universe of the Four Gods
Japanese Translation by Einosuke Okuda
IT'S DONE !

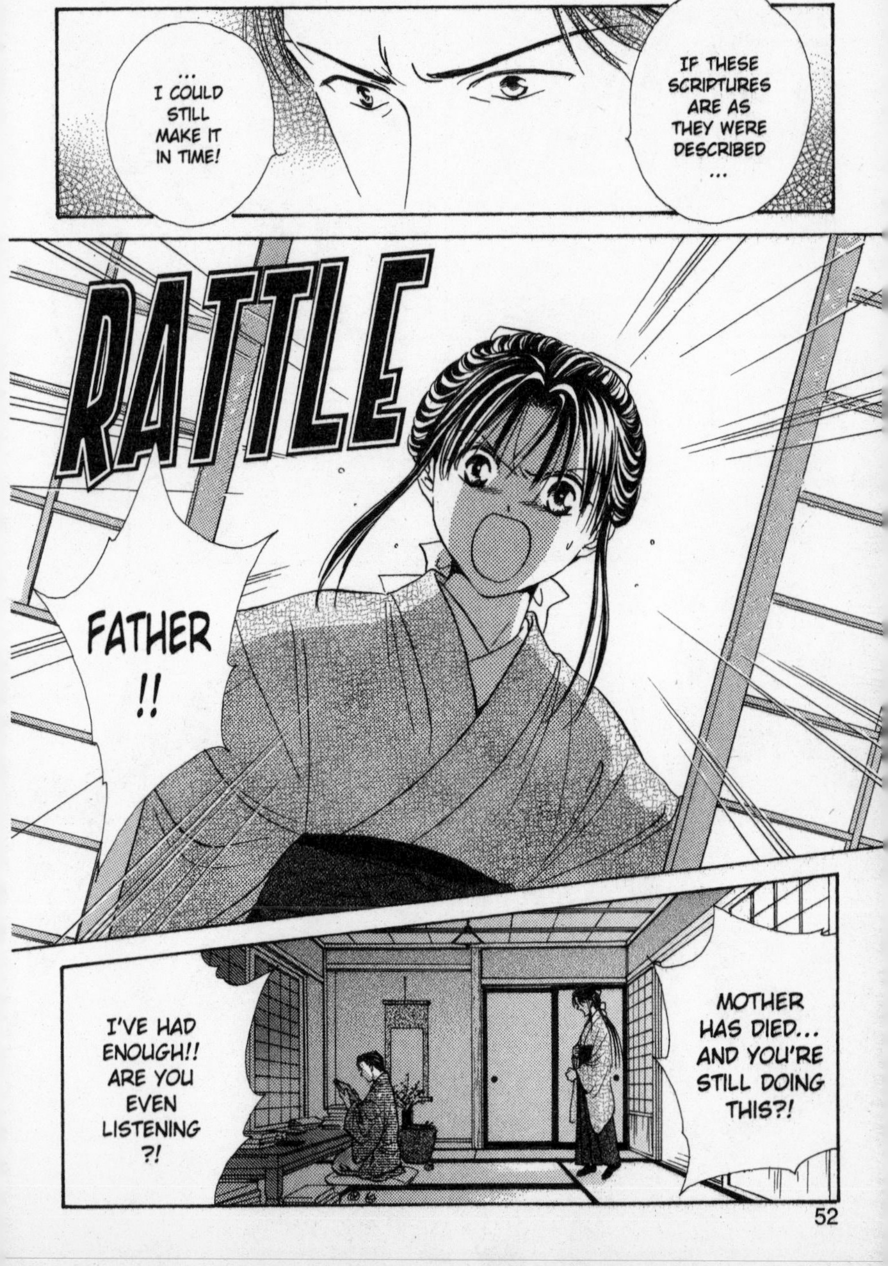
IF THESE SCRIPTURES ARE AS THEY WERE DESCRIBED ...
... I COULD STILL MAKE IT IN TIME!
RATTLE
FATHER !!
MOTHER HAS DIED... AND YOU'RE STILL DOING THIS?!
I'VE HAD ENOUGH!! ARE YOU EVEN LISTENING ?!

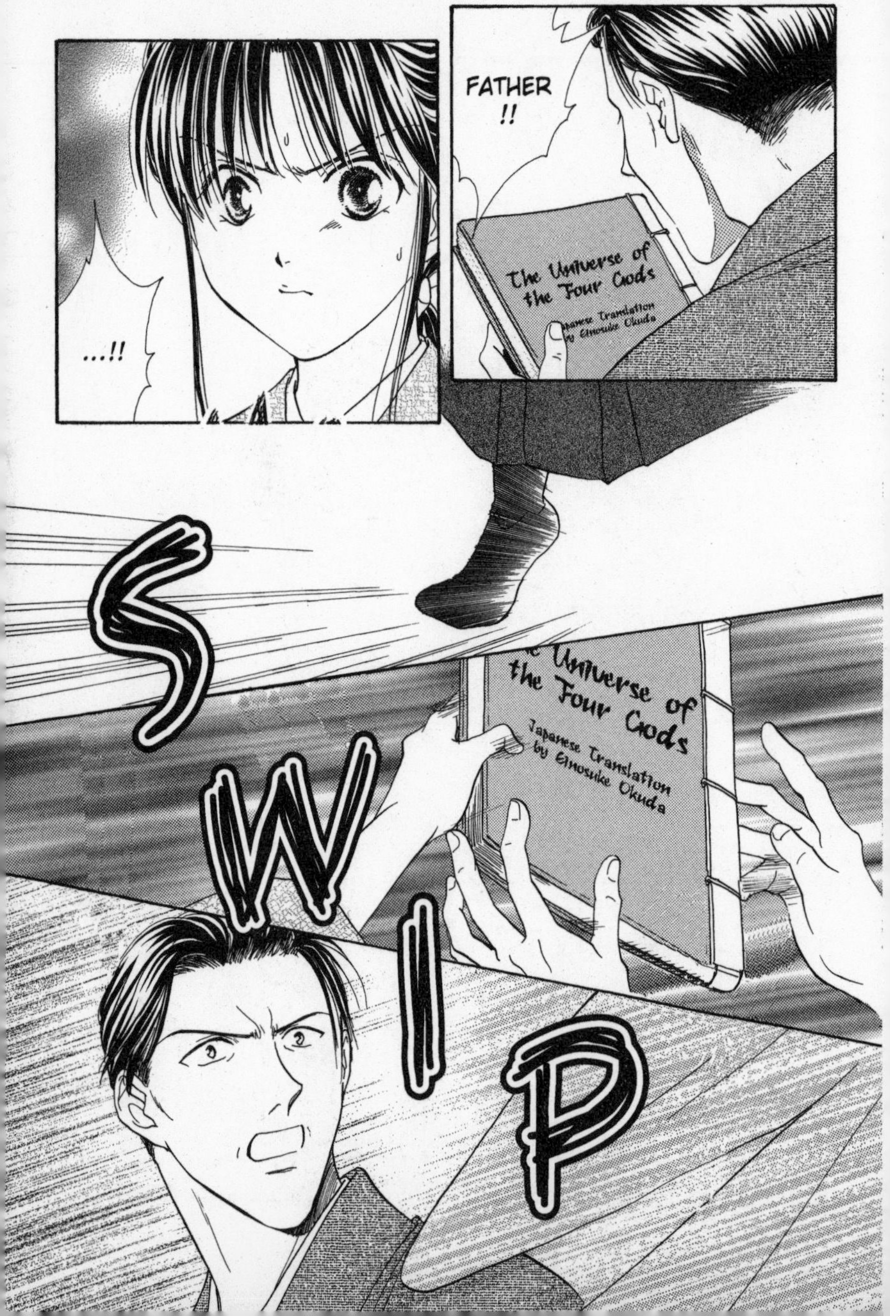
FATHER !!
The Universe of the Four Gods
apanese Translation by Einosuke Okuda
...!!
e Universe of the Four Gods
Japanese Translation by Einosuke Okuda
SWIP

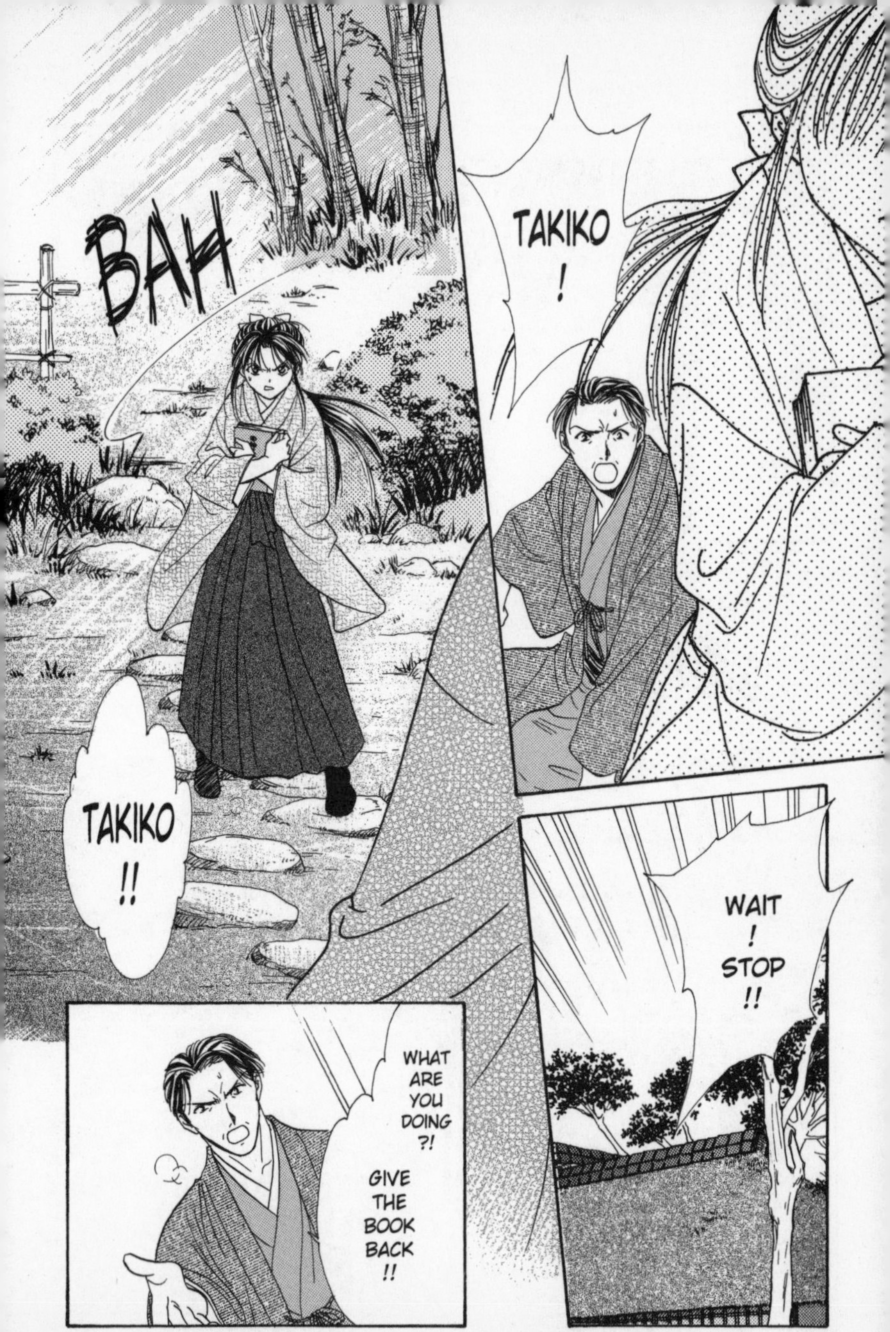
TAKIKO!
BAH
TAKIKO!!
WAIT! STOP!!
WHAT ARE YOU DOING?!
GIVE THE BOOK BACK!!

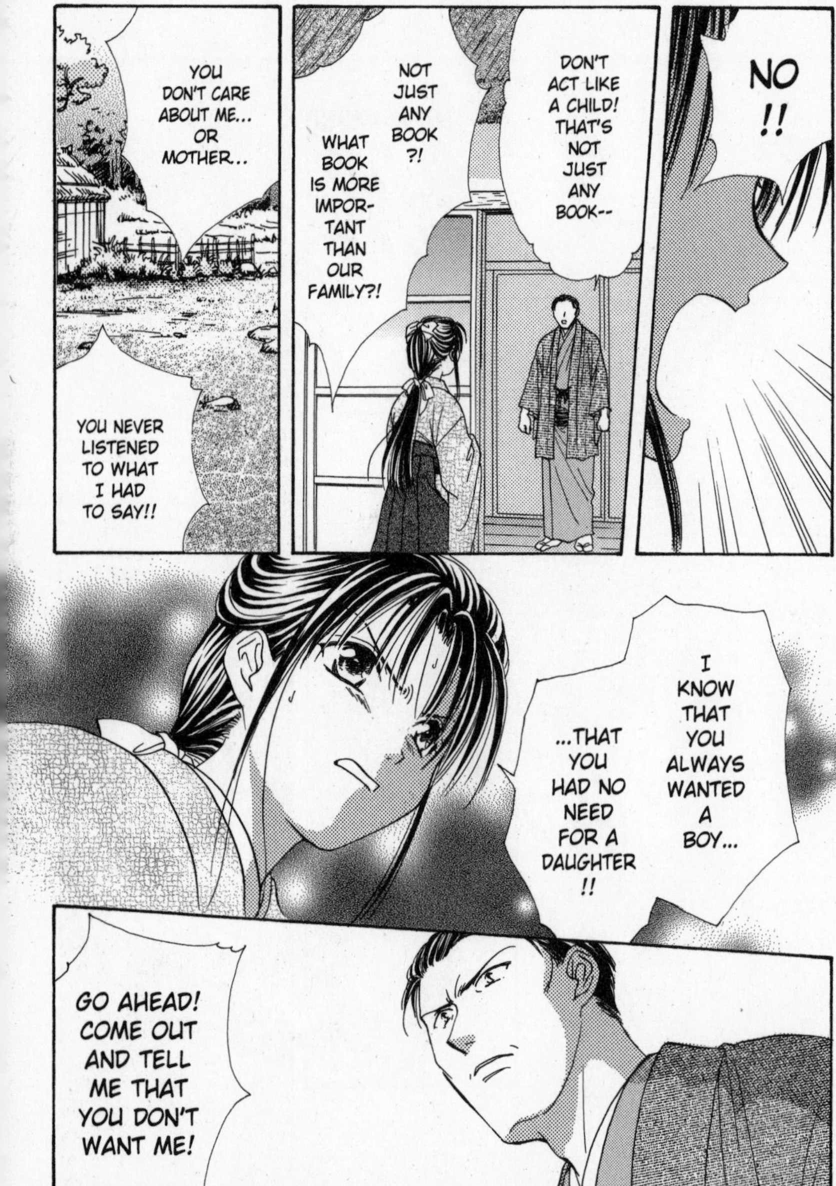
NO !!
DON'T ACT LIKE A CHILD! THAT'S NOT JUST ANY BOOK--
NOT JUST ANY BOOK?!
WHAT BOOK IS MORE IMPOR-TANT THAN OUR FAMILY?!
YOU DON'T CARE ABOUT ME... OR MOTHER...
YOU NEVER LISTENED TO WHAT I HAD TO SAY!!
I KNOW THAT YOU ALWAYS WANTED A BOY...
...THAT YOU HAD NO NEED FOR A DAUGHTER!!
GO AHEAD! COME OUT AND TELL ME THAT YOU DON'T WANT ME!

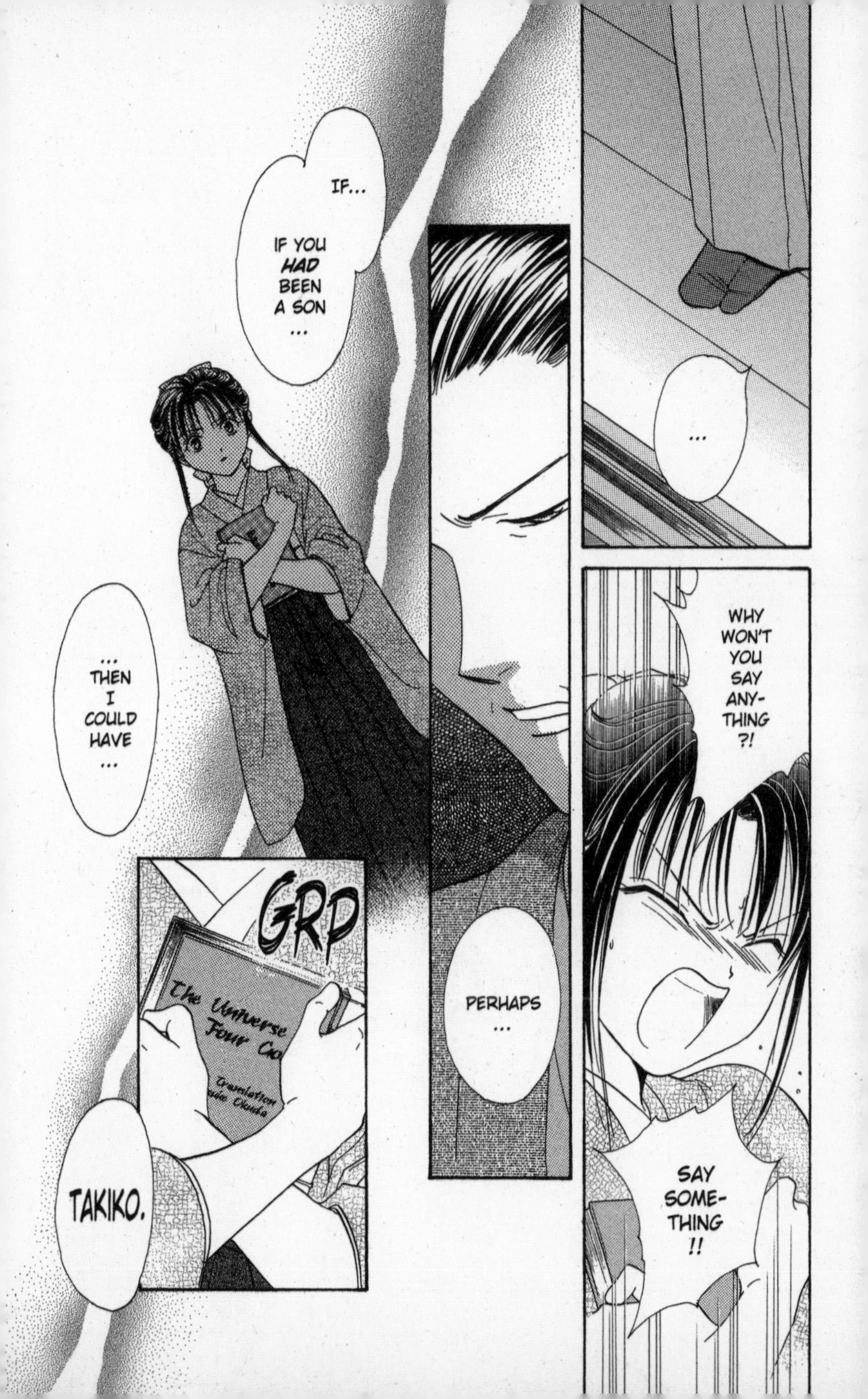
...
WHY WON'T YOU SAY ANYTHING?!
SAY SOMETHING!!
PERHAPS...
IF...
IF YOU HAD BEEN A SON...
...THEN I COULD HAVE...
GRP
TAKIKO.

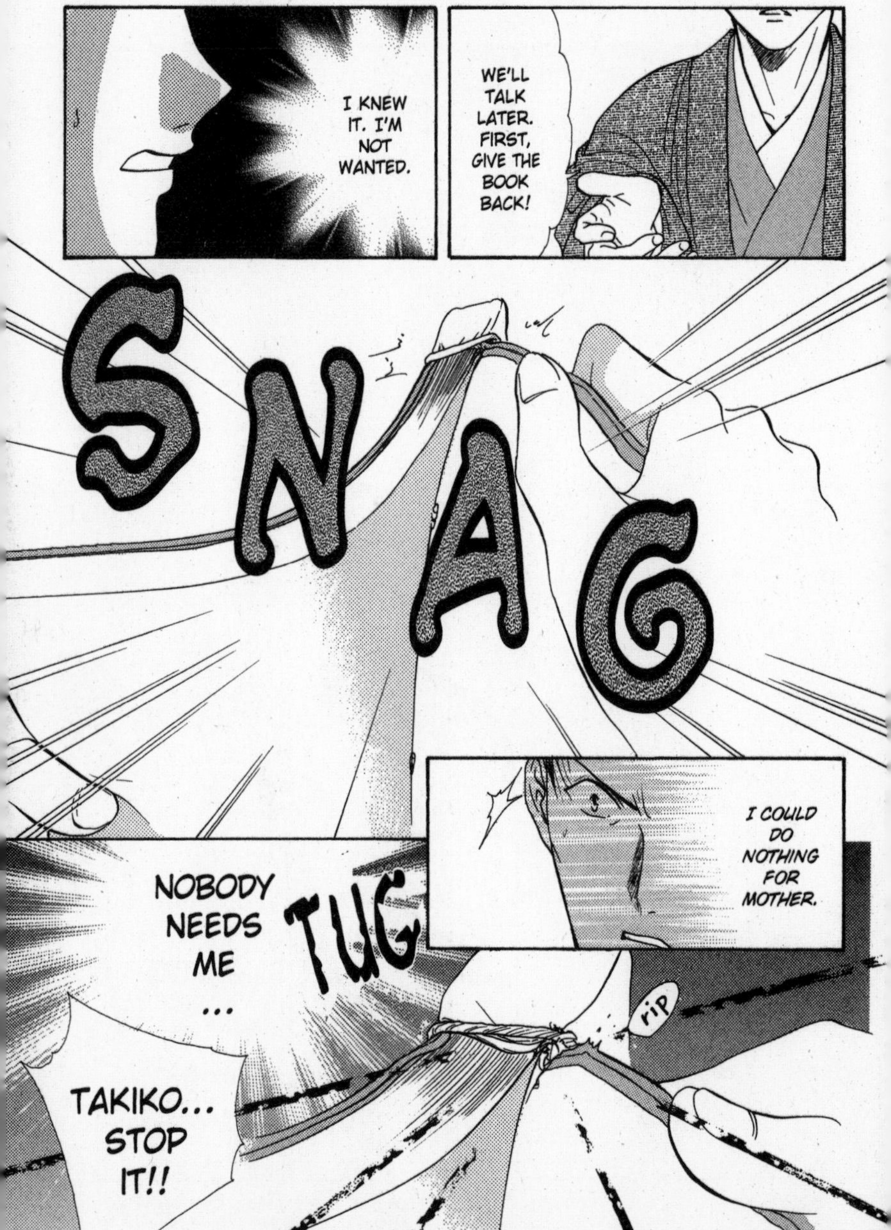
WE'LL TALK LATER. FIRST, GIVE THE BOOK BACK!
I KNEW IT. I'M NOT WANTED.
SNAG
I COULD DO NOTHING FOR MOTHER.
rip
TUG
NOBODY NEEDS ME ...
TAKIKO... STOP IT!!

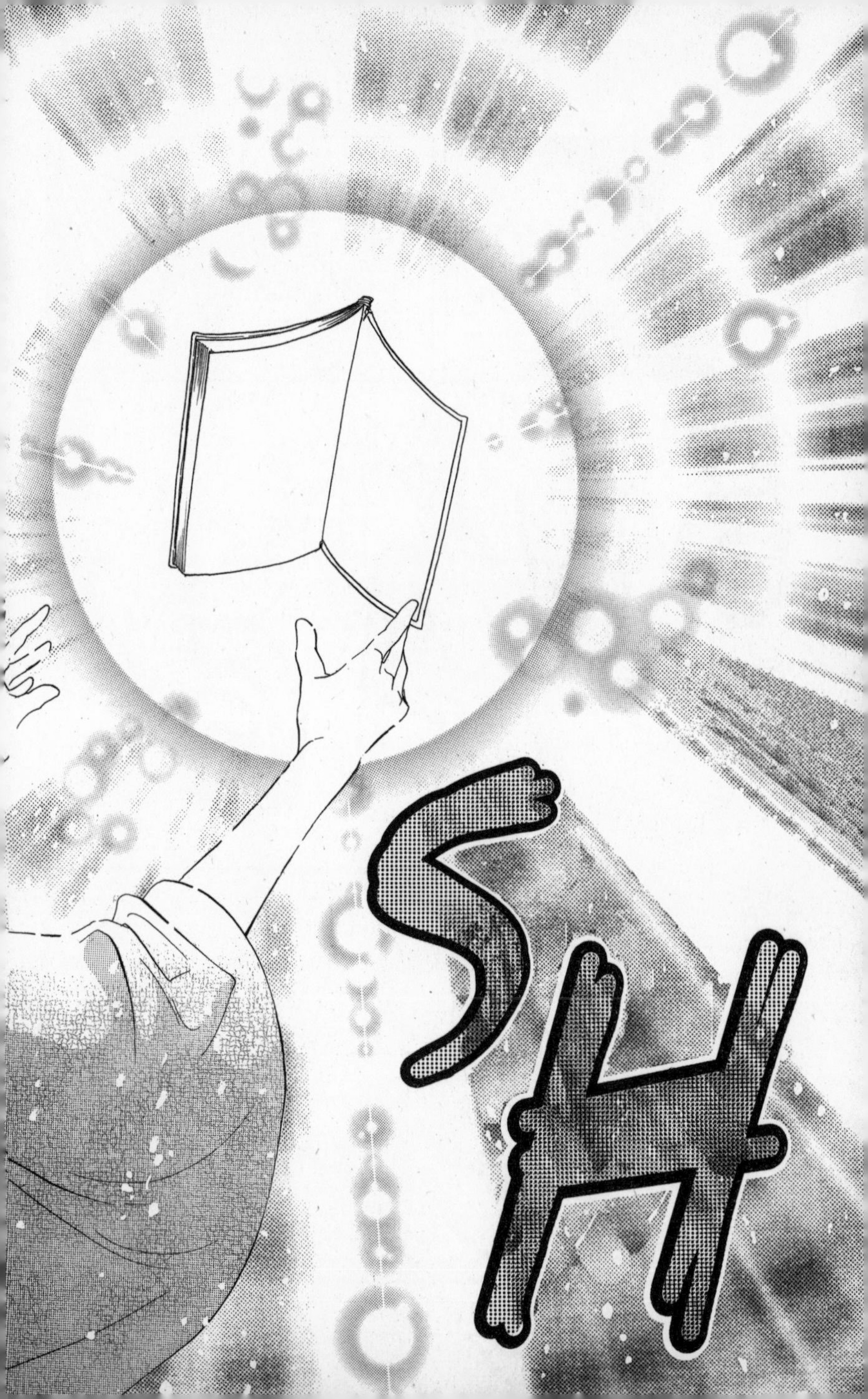
SH

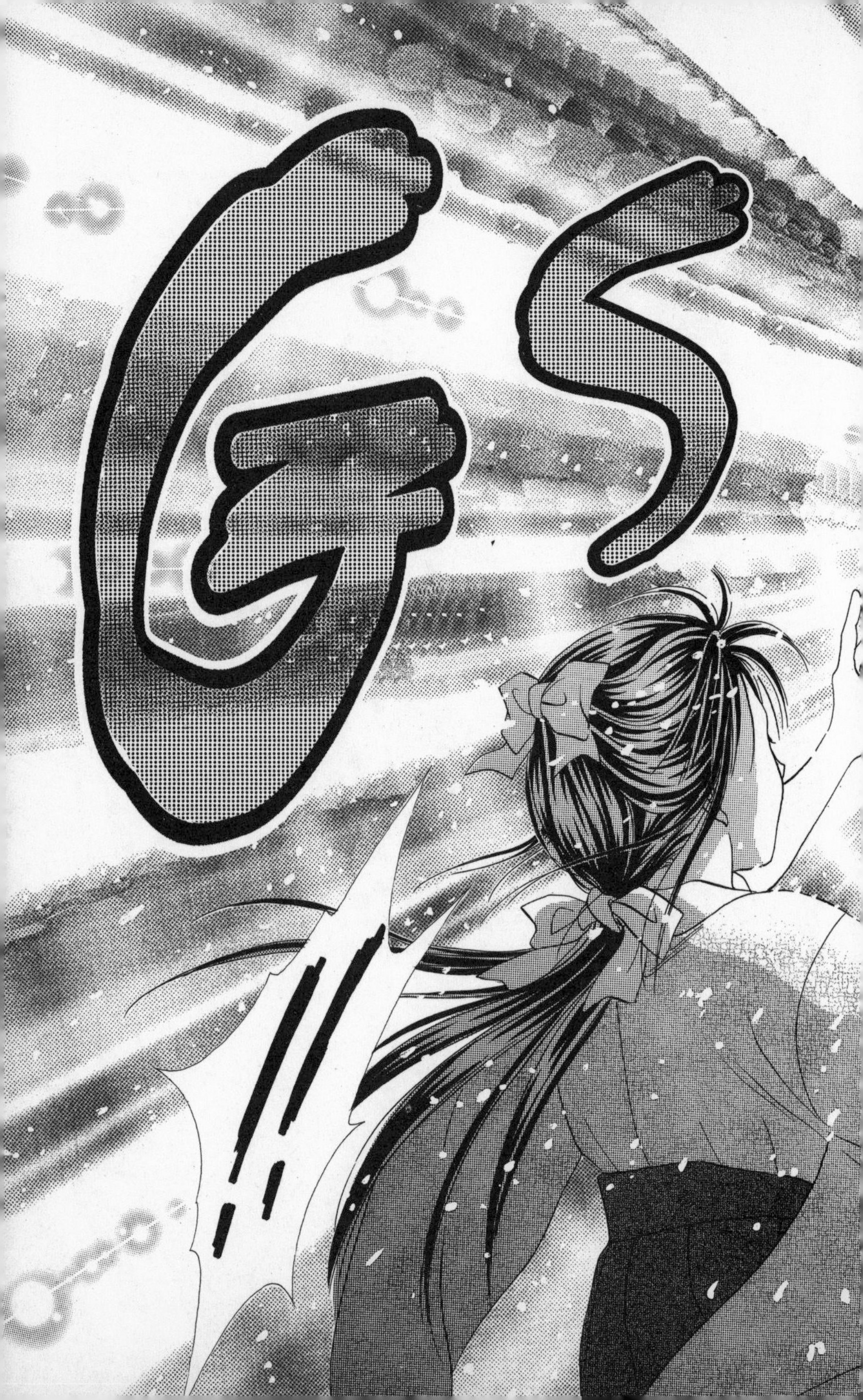

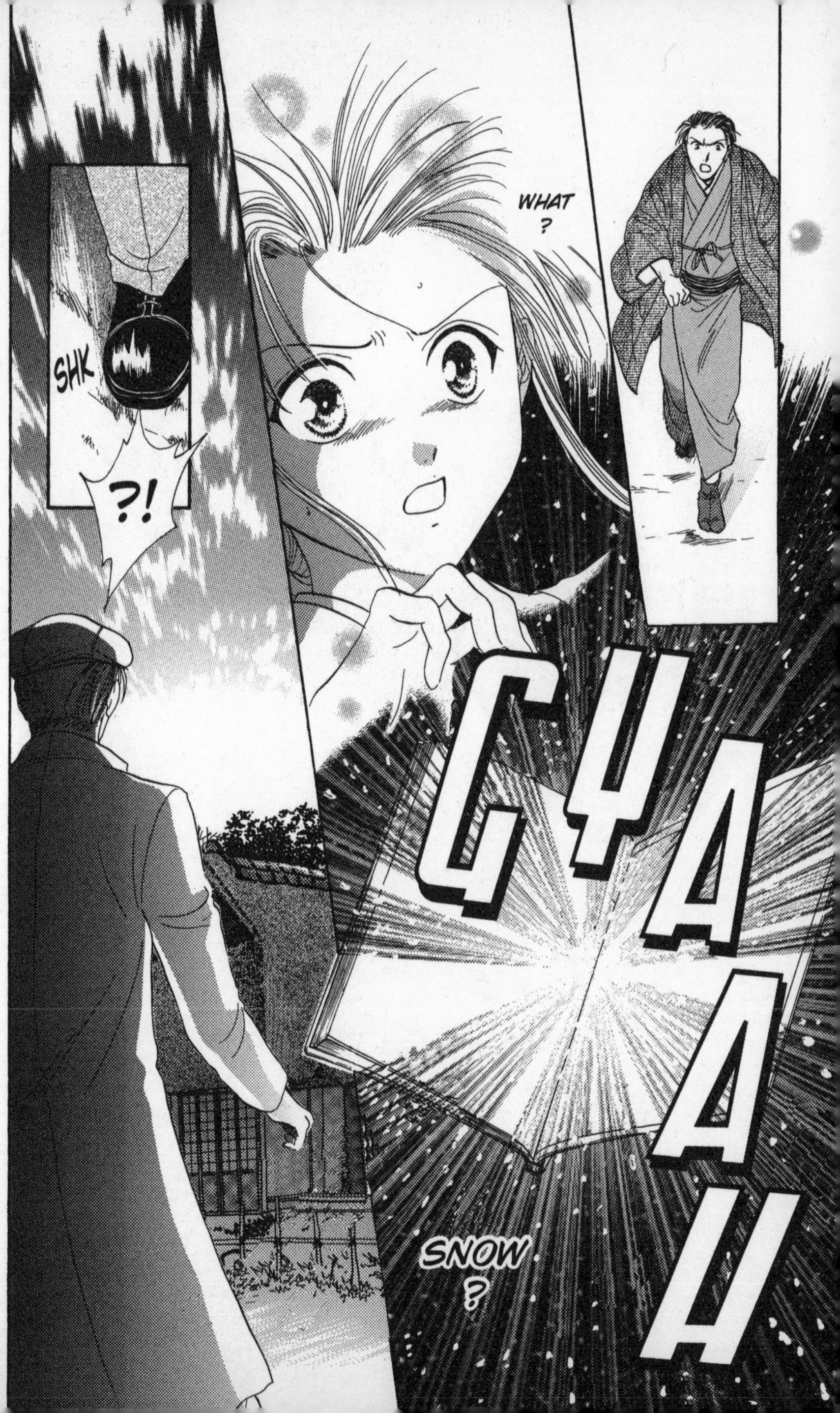
WHAT ?
GYAAAH
SNOW ?
SHK
?!

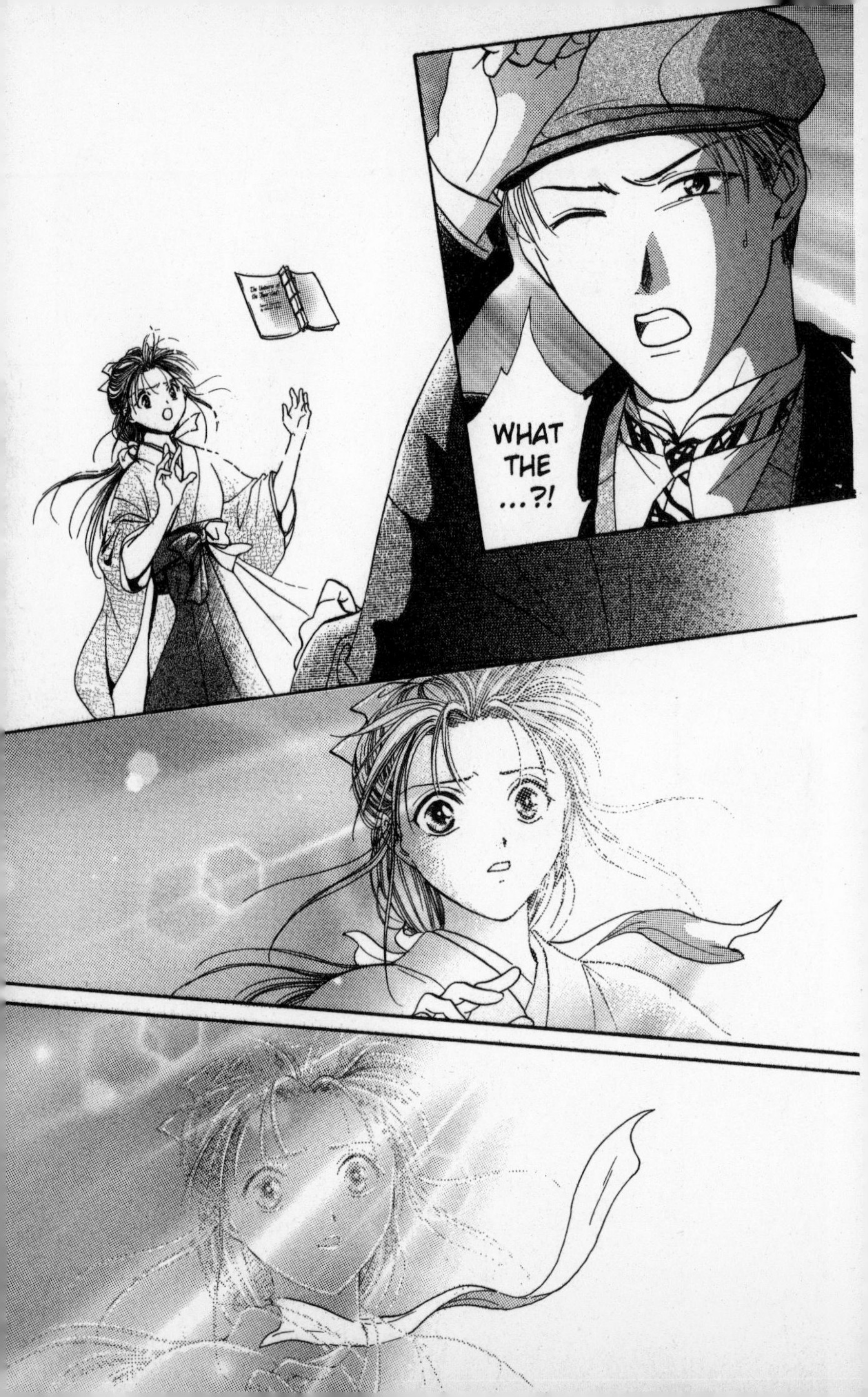
WHAT THE ...?!

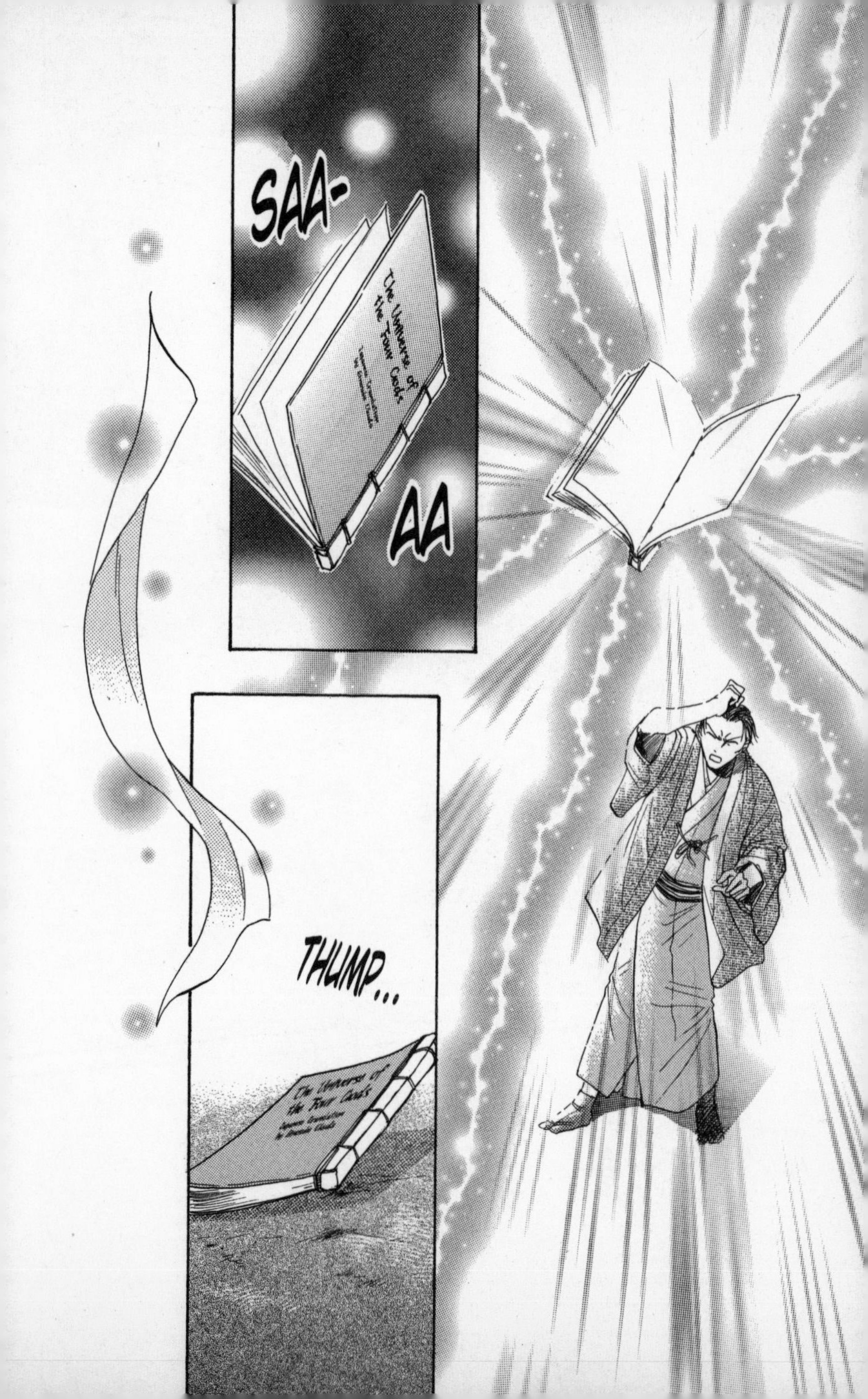
SAA-
AA
The Universe of the Four Gods
THUMP...
The Universe of the Four Gods

TAKIKO ?!

The Universe of Four Gods

BRR

MM...

M-MASTER!! WHAT WAS THAT LIGHT?

TA--

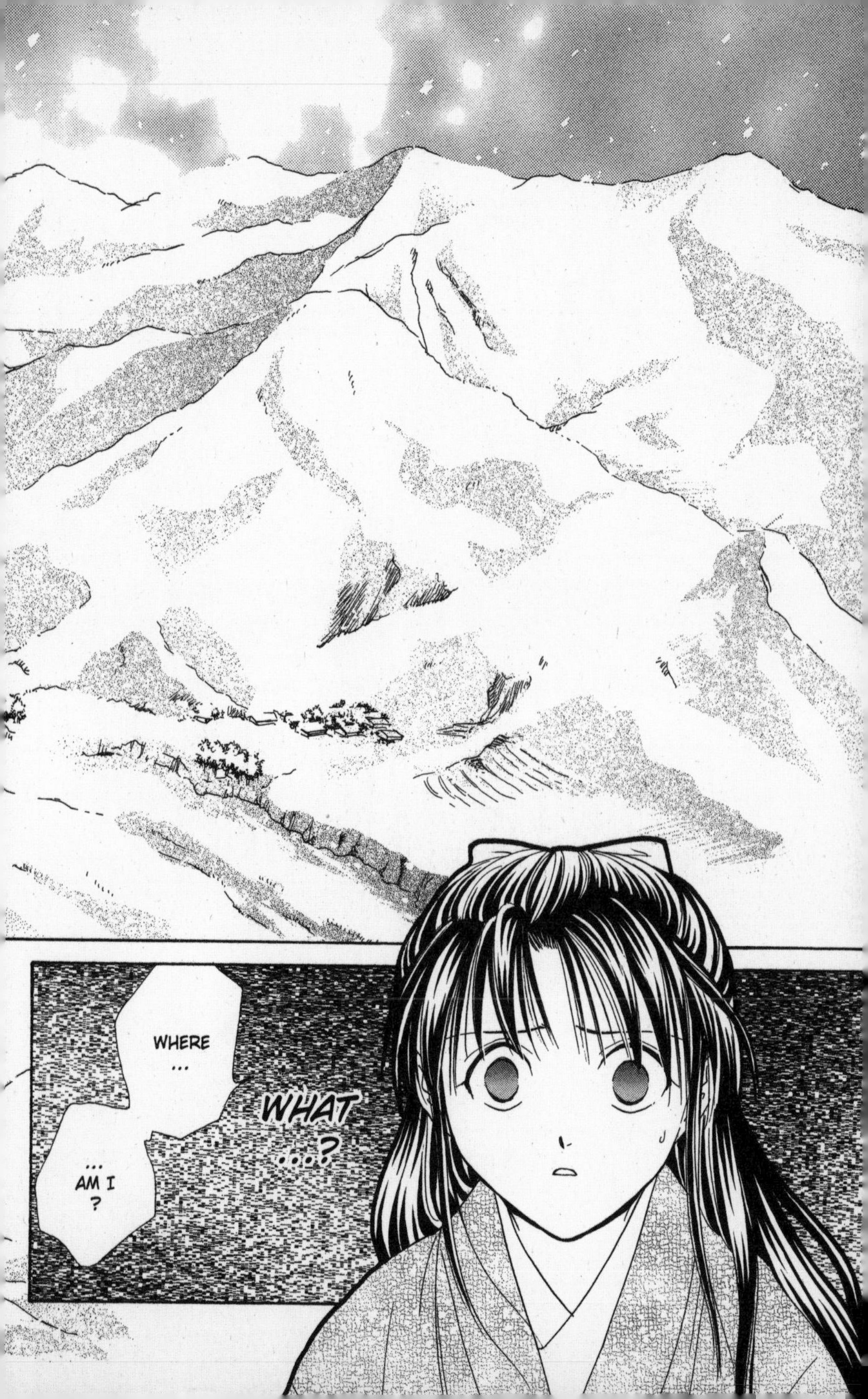

WHAT ...?
WHERE ...
... AM I ?

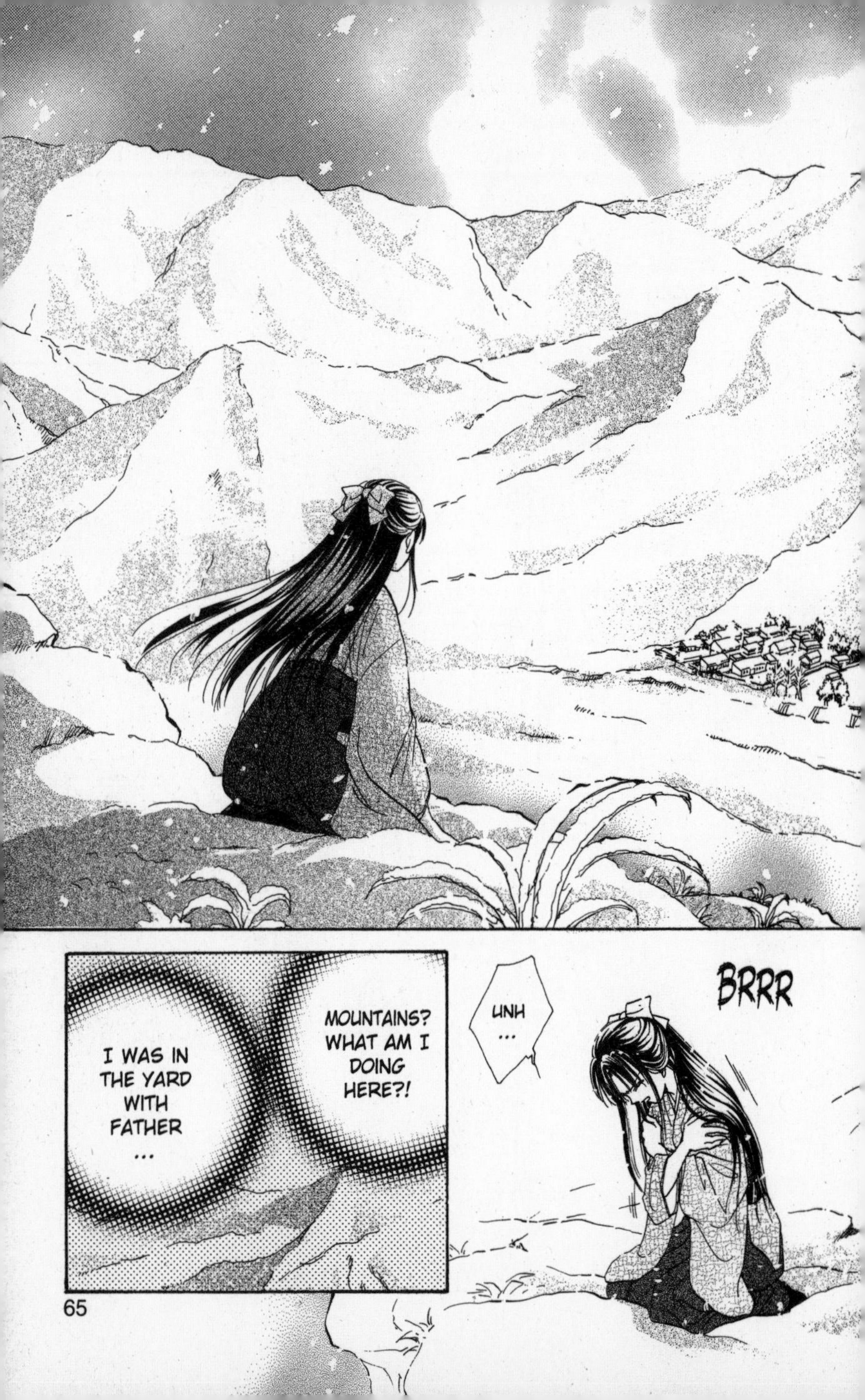
BRRR
UNH ...
MOUNTAINS? WHAT AM I DOING HERE?!
I WAS IN THE YARD WITH FATHER ...

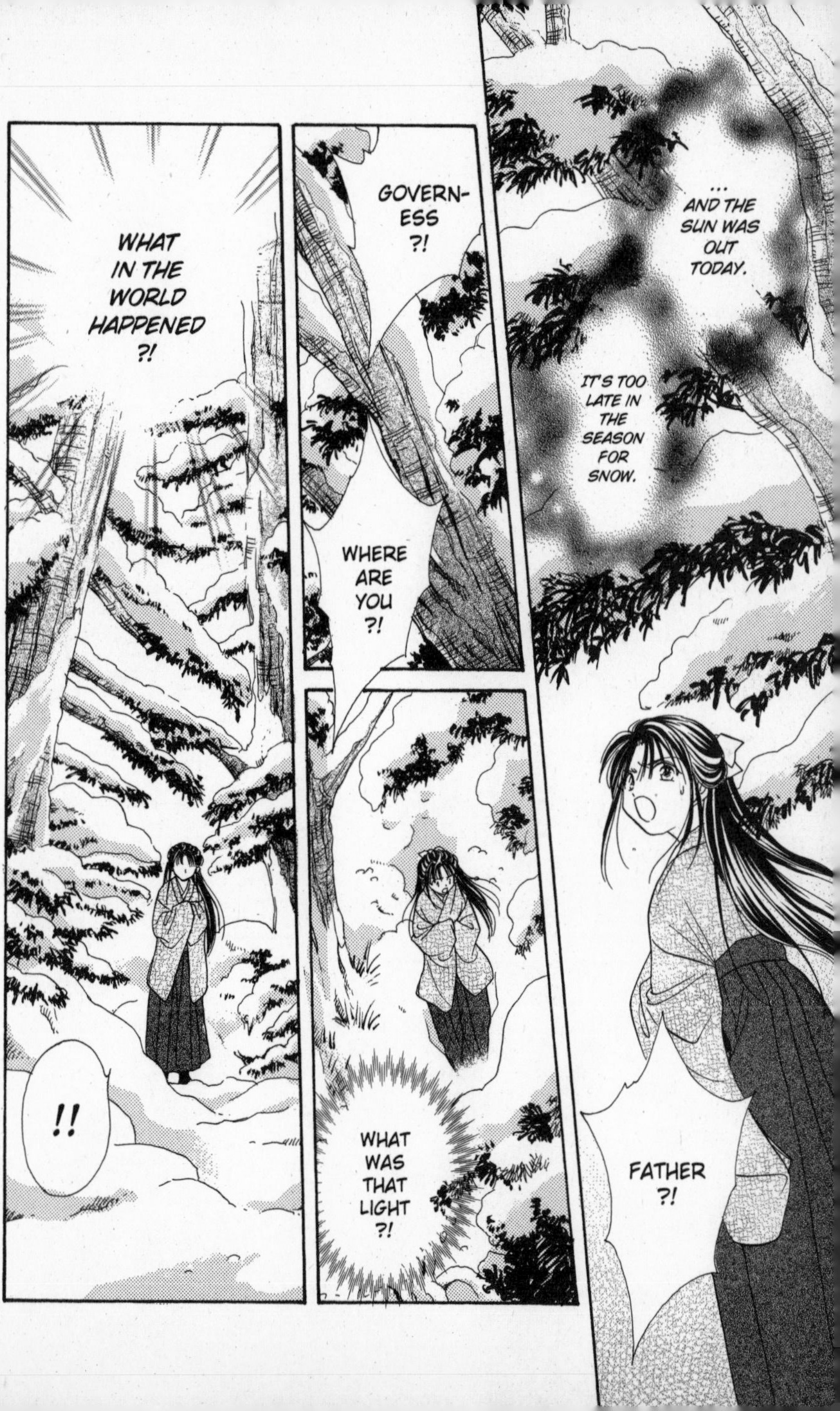
... AND THE SUN WAS OUT TODAY.
IT'S TOO LATE IN THE SEASON FOR SNOW.
FATHER ?!
GOVERN-ESS ?!
WHERE ARE YOU ?!
WHAT WAS THAT LIGHT ?!
WHAT IN THE WORLD HAPPENED ?!
!!

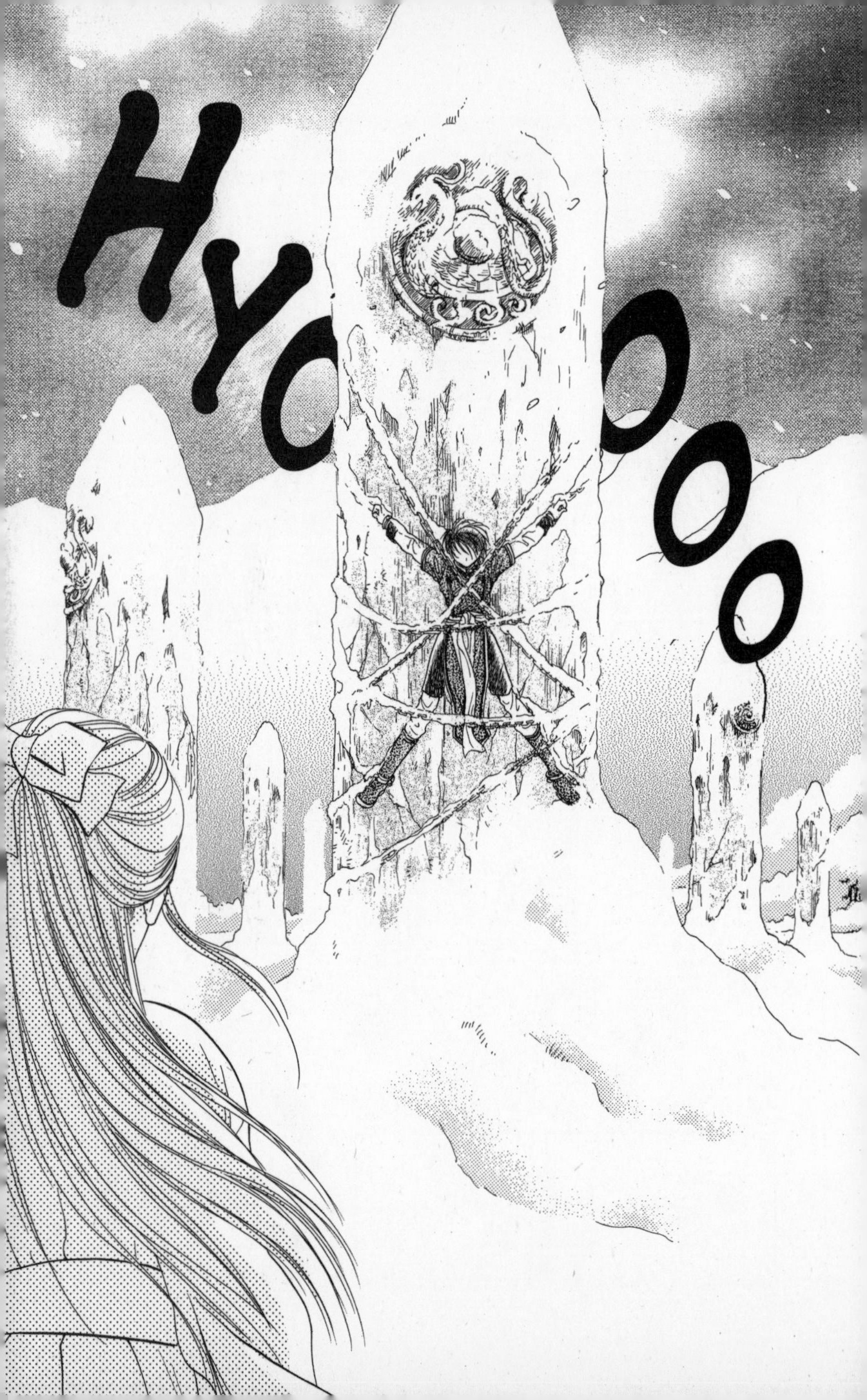
HYOOOOO

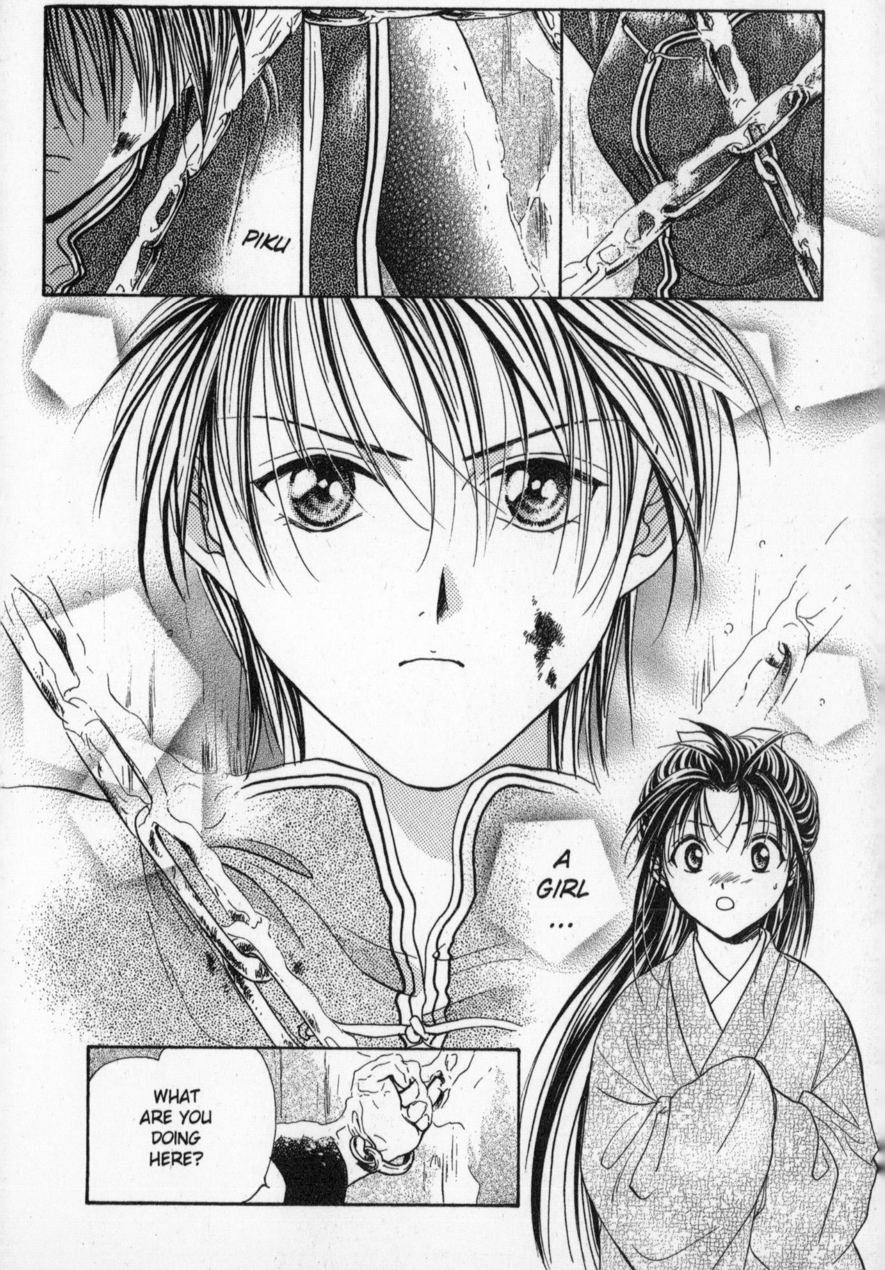
PIKU
A GIRL ...
WHAT ARE YOU DOING HERE?

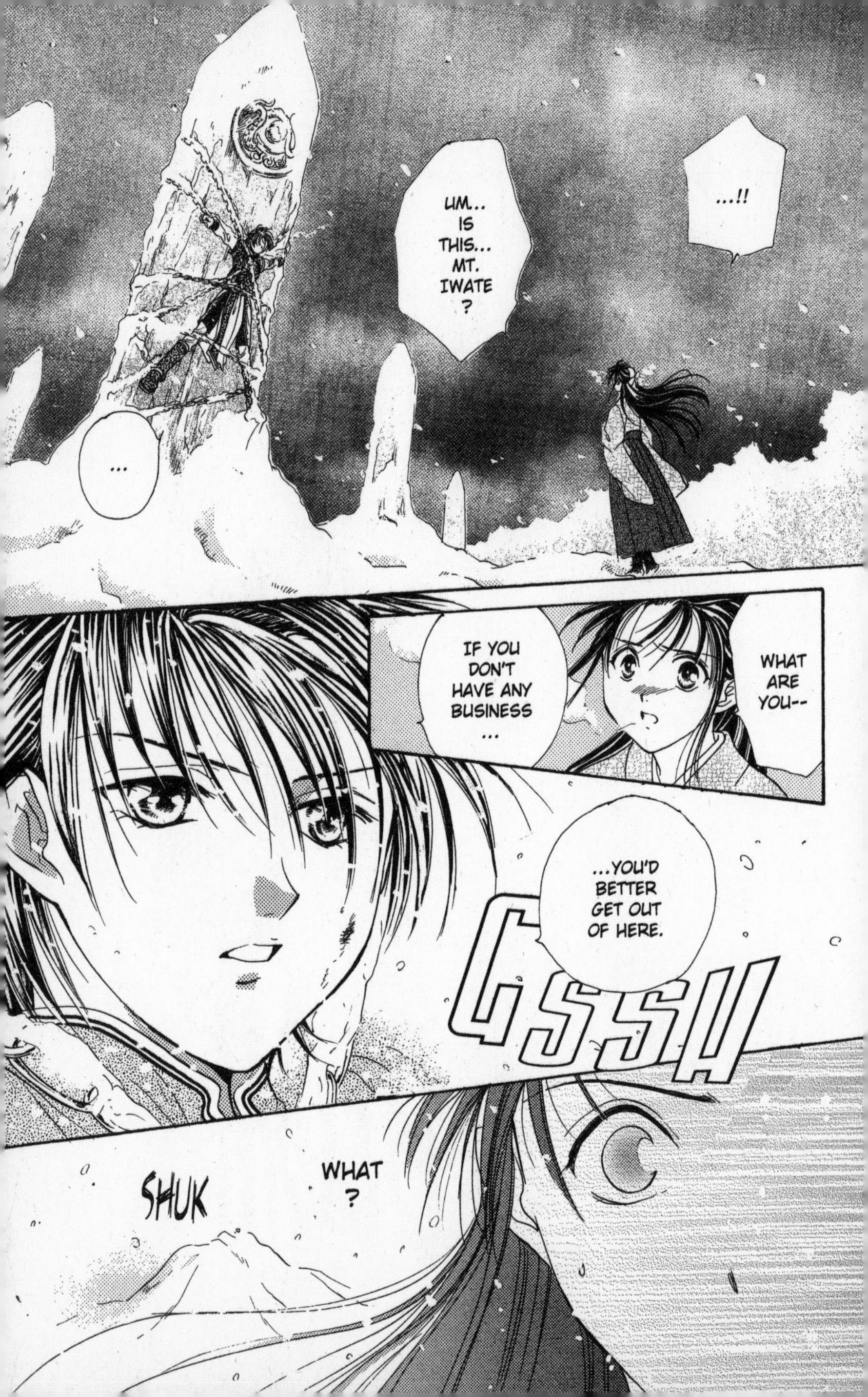
...!!
UM... IS THIS... MT. IWATE?
...
WHAT ARE YOU--
IF YOU DON'T HAVE ANY BUSINESS ...
...YOU'D BETTER GET OUT OF HERE.
GSSH
WHAT?
SHUK

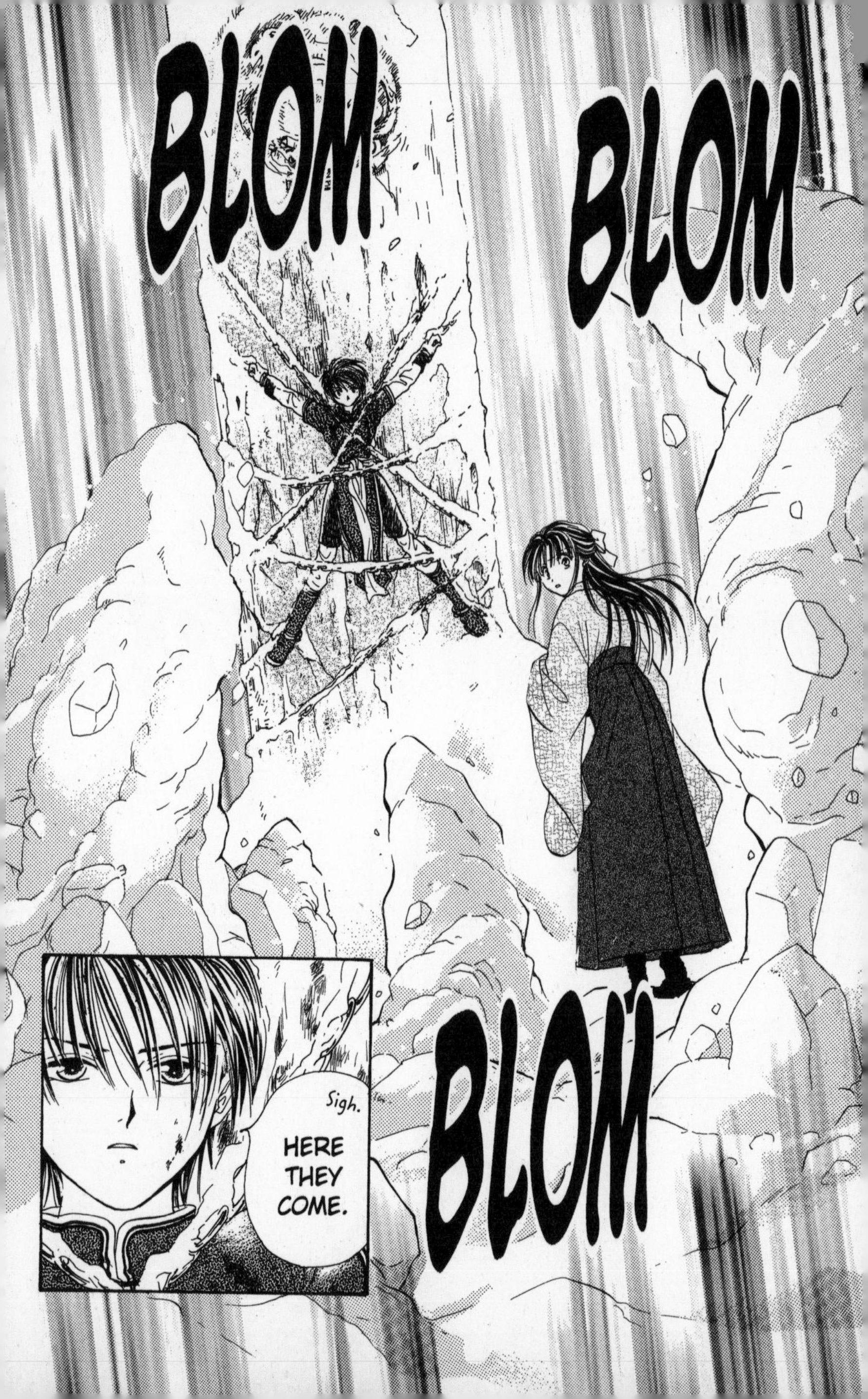
BLOM
BLOM
BLOM
Sigh.
HERE THEY COME.

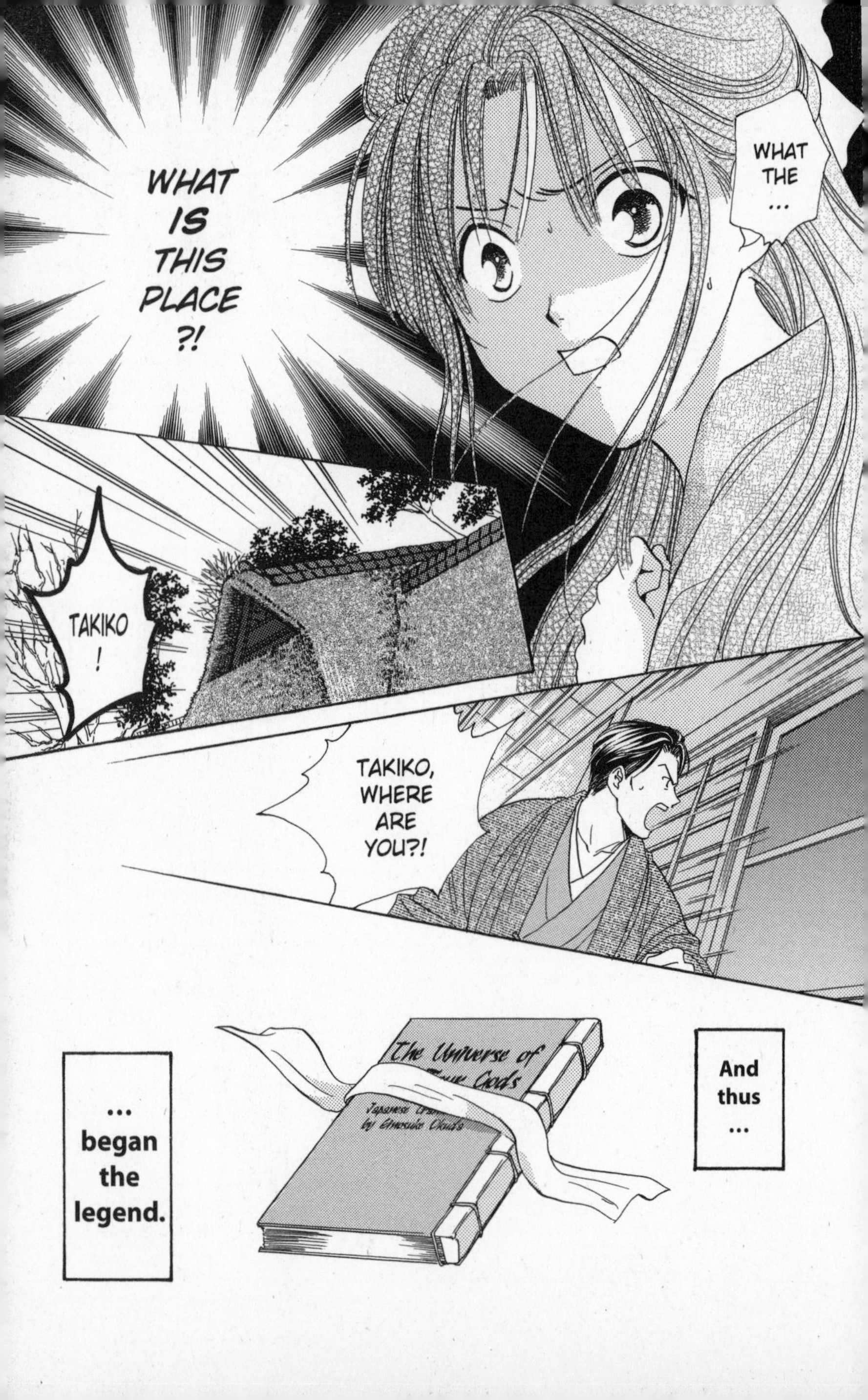
WHAT THE ...
WHAT IS THIS PLACE ?!
TAKIKO !
TAKIKO, WHERE ARE YOU?!
The Universe of
And thus ...
... began the legend.

Tidbits To Better Enjoy Genbu Kaiden

The Taisho Era

I'm sure a lot of people have no clue about what it was like 80 years ago in Japan, so I'd like to write about it here a bit.

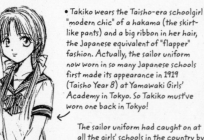

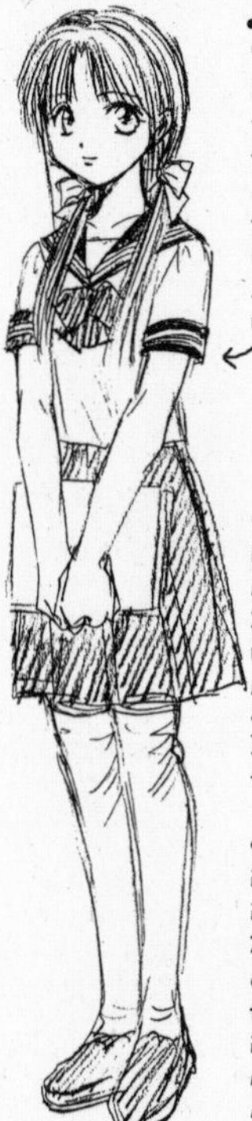

• Takiko wears the Taisho-era schoolgirl "modern chic" of a hakama (the skirt-like pants) and a big ribbon in her hair, the Japanese equivalent of "flapper" fashion. Actually, the sailor uniform now worn in so many Japanese schools first made its appearance in 1919 (Taisho Year 8) at Yamawaki Girls' Academy in Tokyo. So Takiko must've worn one back in Tokyo!

The sailor uniform had caught on at all the girls' schools in the country by the end of the Taisho era (1925).

• I debated about this, but decided to keep Takiko in her hakama. I wanted her to stand apart from Suzuno. Taisho 12 would be the year Western clothes were permitted in girls' high schools in Akita prefecture. I'm just barely historically accurate...
If I could start over, I would've dated this story a bit earlier... but it's too late.

• I used Morioka as the setting because it was used in the FY anime. :) It was interesting! Especially around episodes 29 and 30... You can consider the anime and the novels to be separate entities from the manga... But I'll borrow interesting ideas. I went there on a research trip a few days ago. :) It's a nice place!!! I'll write more in the next volume...

Tidbits on Girls' Schools

Meiji 39 (1906)

It was a fad to pronounce and write words backwards (Ex: "baka" → "kaba") and call it "the New Esperanto."

Esperanto is an international language.

Meiji 40 (1907)

"Byuburu": the verb form of "beauty." Refers to a guy with ho-hum looks pretending he's hot stuff.
"Shusai": supposed to describe how ugly a guy is.

*These terms were used to pass judgment on boys. How awful. Not very different from modern teenage girls.

By the way, there were female delinquent gangs by the first year of Taisho...

The image of the "genteel ladies" comes crashing down.

Hi, Watase here.

Listening to: "Twelve Girls Band"

I'm back to **Fushigi Yûgi** again. It's been about seven years since I last worked on it in manga form. To people who know the previous FY (which I will refer to as the "Suzaku/Seiryu arc," or FY: SS), and people who are new to the series, thank you for picking this up!

I've always wanted to work on this story, Genbu Kaiden, along with the Byakko story. Oh... when I told people, "I won't do any more **Fushigi Yûgi**," I was talking about doing a sequel to FY:SS. That one's totally finished, at 18 volumes. Fans have always asked for the Genbu and Byakko stories, including the fans overseas... I dreamed of writing them one day, but I figured it was 90% impossible. Well, lots of things have happened since then, and it's now become a reality. I'm very surprised. Actually, it still feels unreal to me.

FY was made into an anime, and even after the manga ended, there were the OVAs, the novels, the boxed set, trading cards, the manga republished as a "Perfect Collection" ... The flow of work has actually never ceased... It's mostly because the anime was rerun on cable. I'm very grateful...
There was never a year when I didn't draw some kind of artwork for FY. Ha ha. Thank you so much, dear readers.

The protagonist this time is a schoolgirl from 80 years in the past, in the Taisho era. Since it doesn't take place in modern times, I took care to depict the historical background in the first episode, to get readers used to the mood back in the day, and to enter the girl's mind.

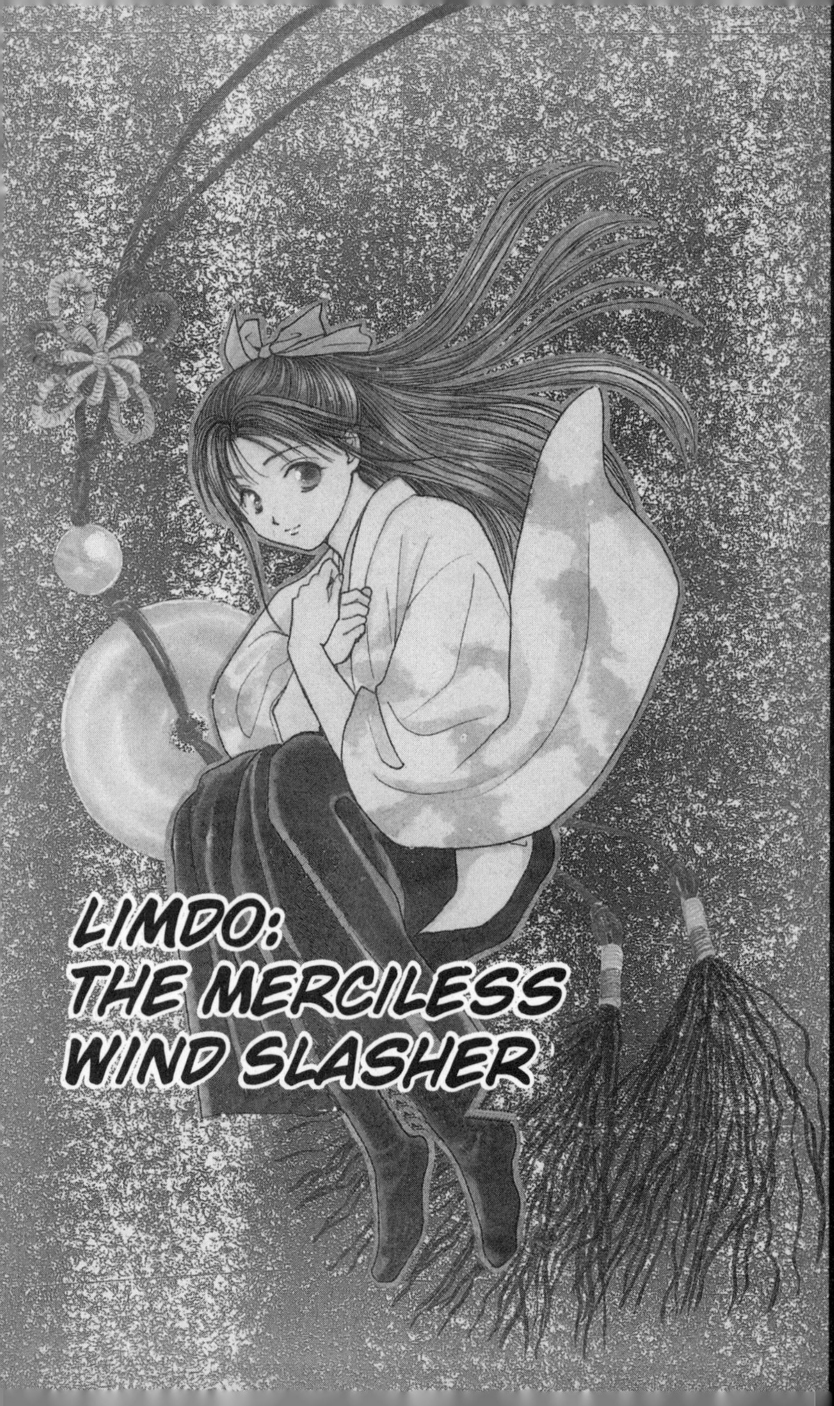
LIMDO:
THE MERCILESS
WIND SLASHER

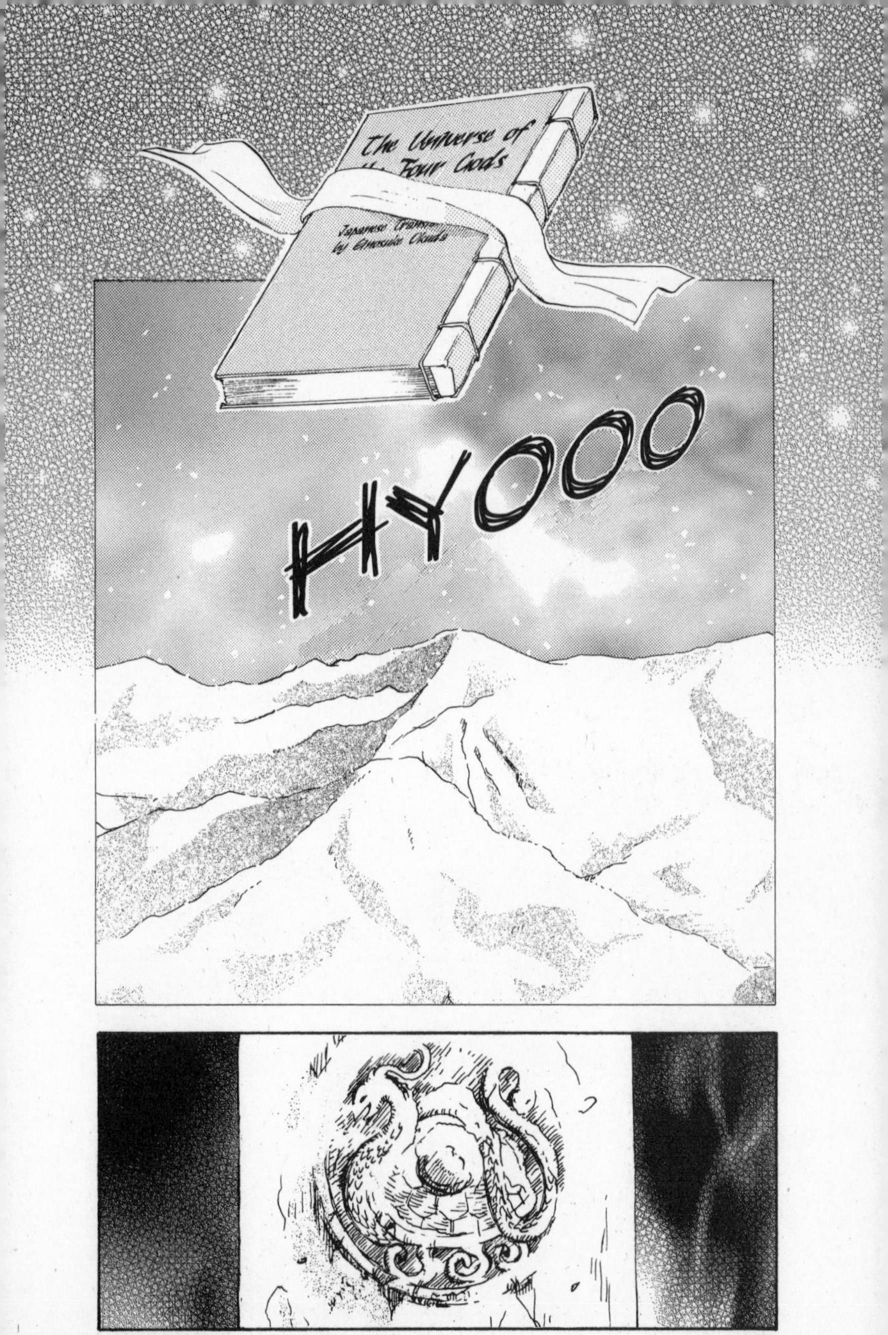

The Universe of
Four Gods
HYOOO

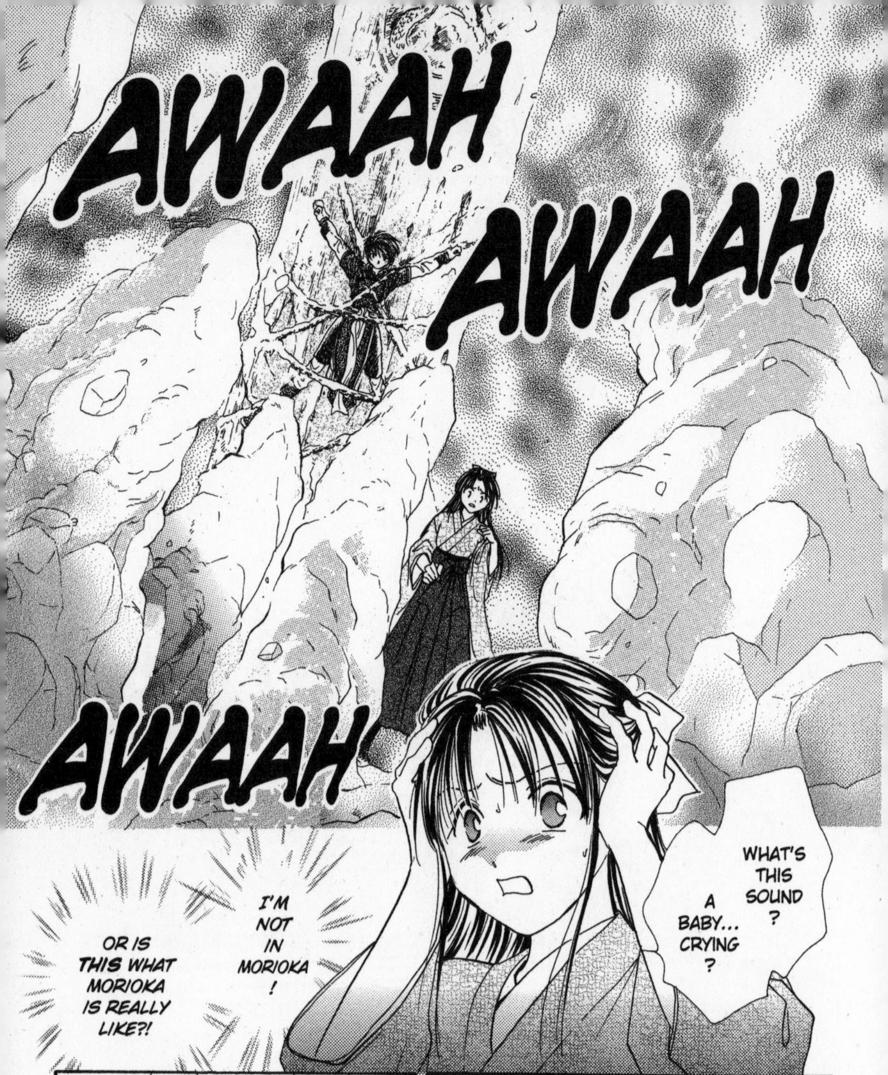
AWAAH
AWAAH
AWAAH
WHAT'S THIS SOUND?
A BABY... CRYING?
I'M NOT IN MORIOKA!
OR IS THIS WHAT MORIOKA IS REALLY LIKE?!

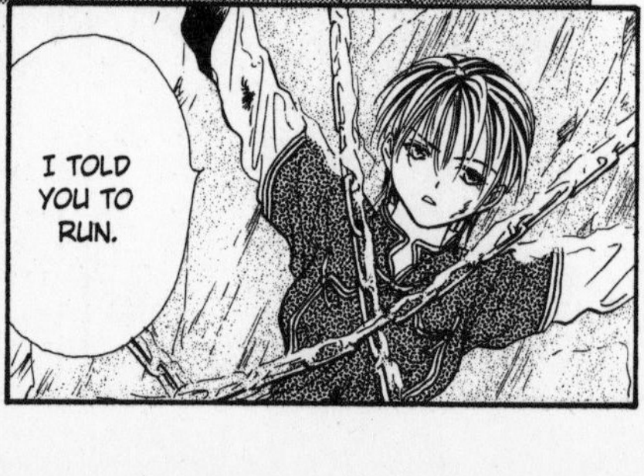
I TOLD YOU TO RUN.

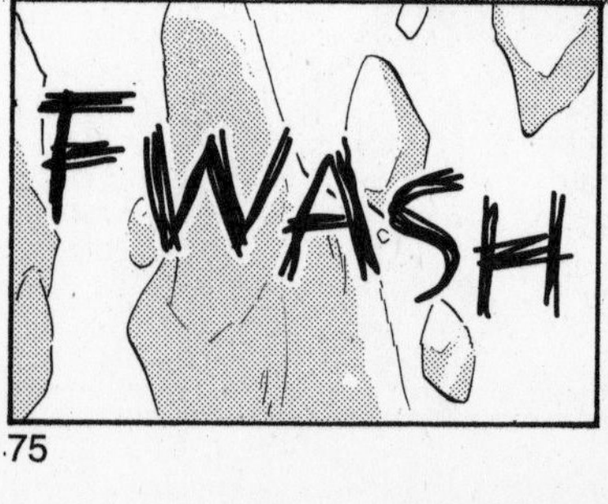
FWASH

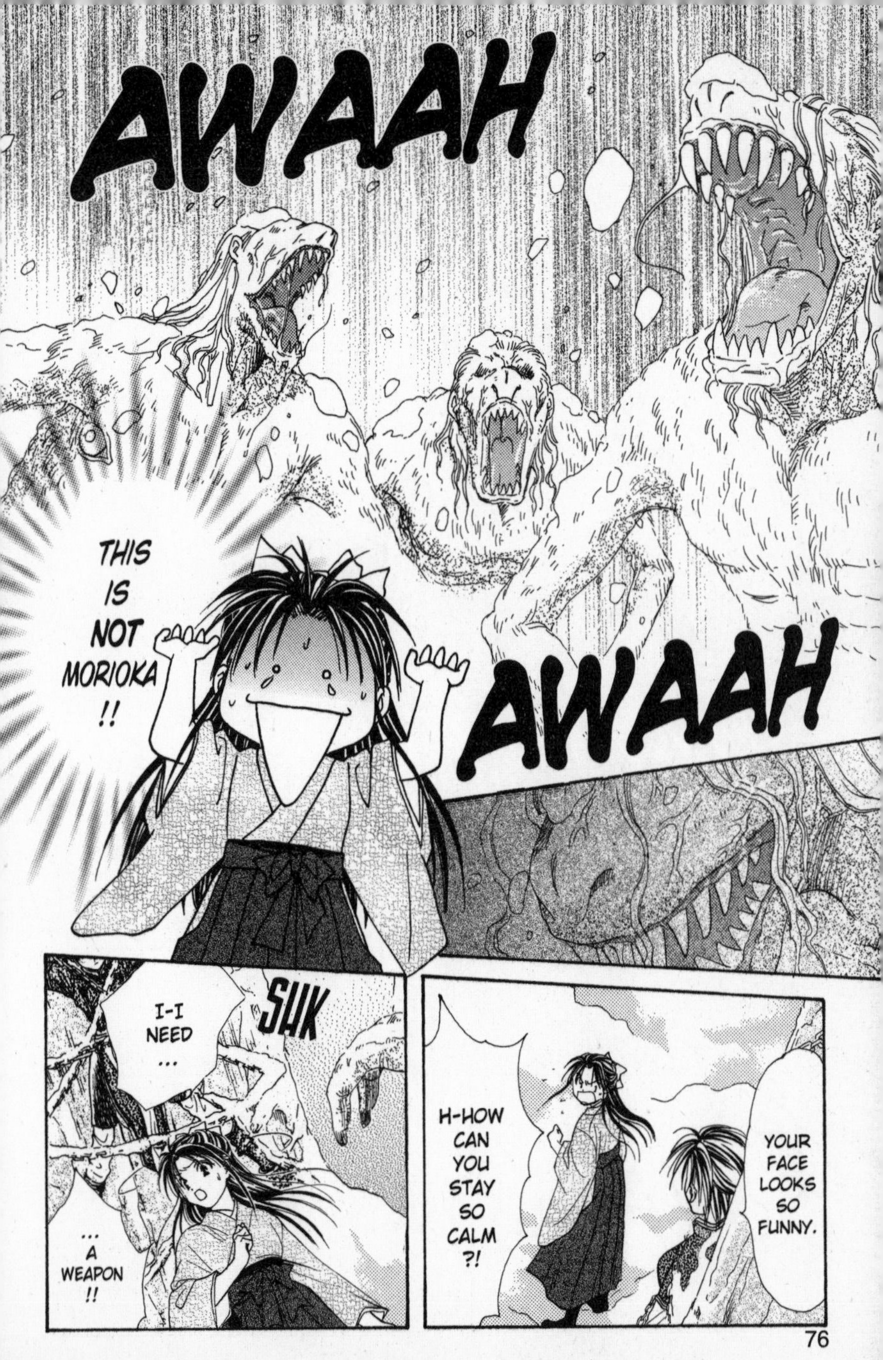
AWAAH
THIS IS NOT MORIOKA!!
AWAAH
YOUR FACE LOOKS SO FUNNY.
H-HOW CAN YOU STAY SO CALM?!
SUK
I-I NEED...
...A WEAPON!!

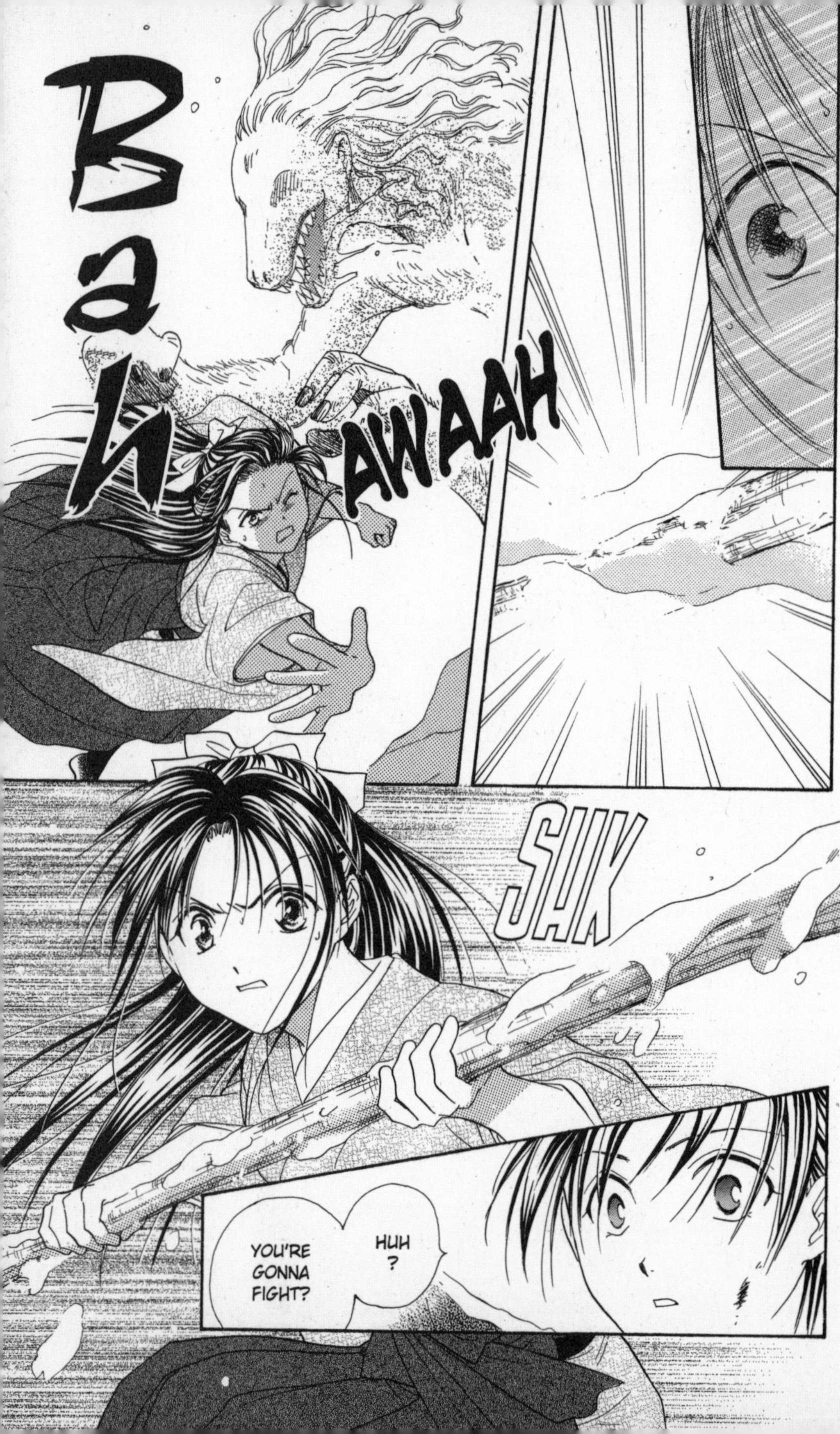
BaW
AWAAH
SHK
HUH ?
YOU'RE GONNA FIGHT?

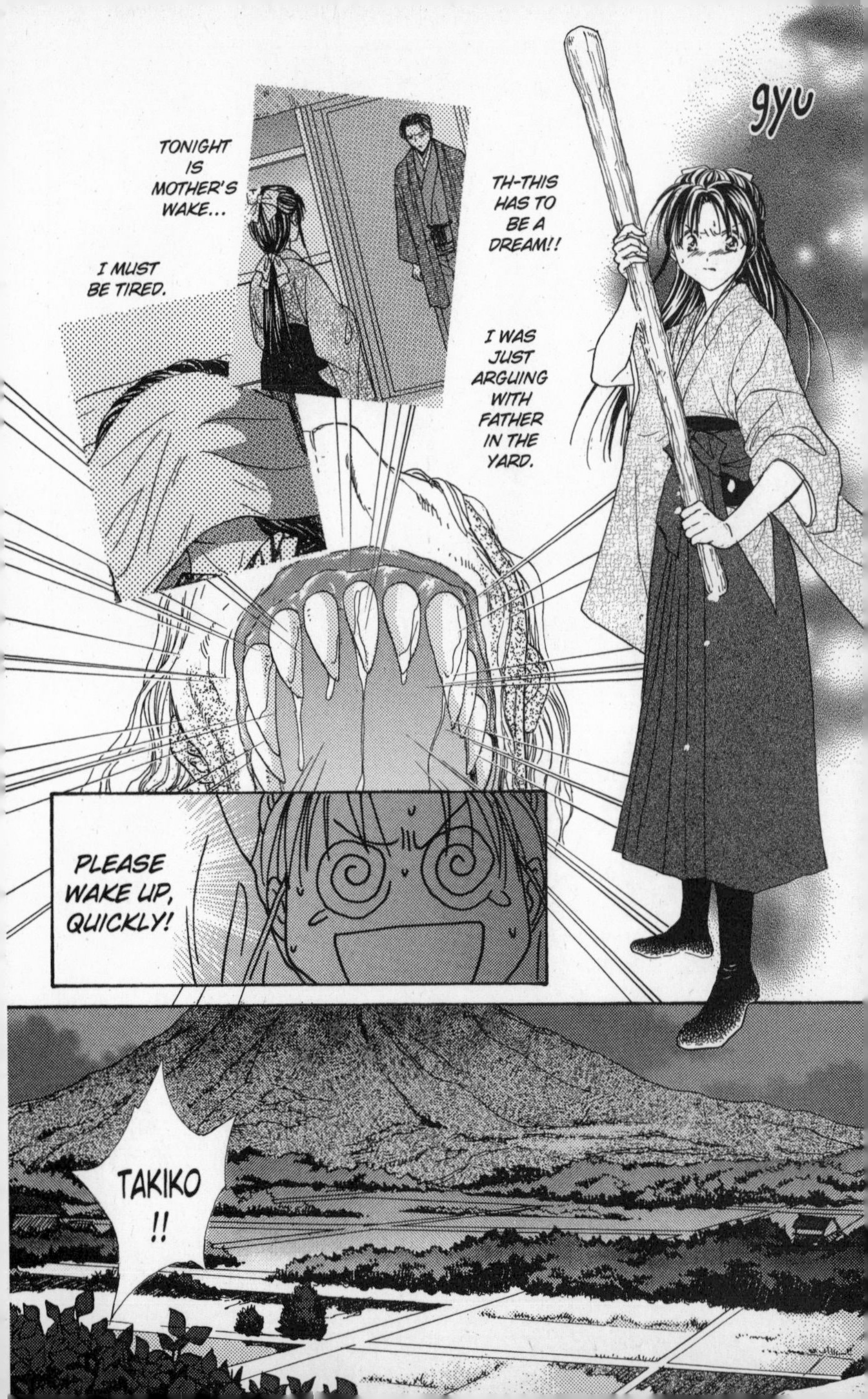
gyu
TH-THIS HAS TO BE A DREAM!!
I WAS JUST ARGUING WITH FATHER IN THE YARD.
TONIGHT IS MOTHER'S WAKE...
I MUST BE TIRED.
PLEASE WAKE UP, QUICKLY!
TAKIKO !!

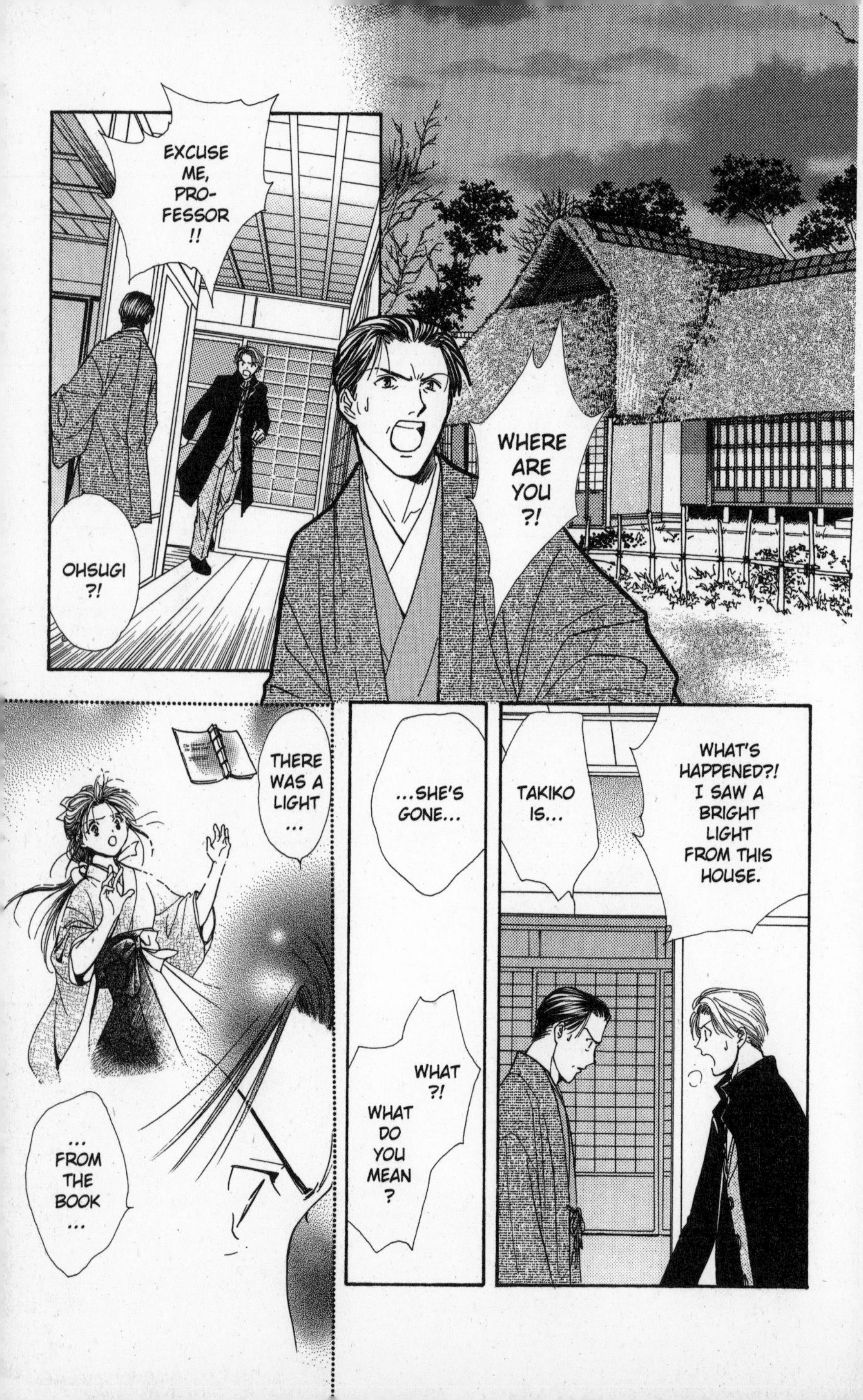
WHERE ARE YOU ?!
EXCUSE ME, PRO-FESSOR !!
OHSUGI ?!
WHAT'S HAPPENED?! I SAW A BRIGHT LIGHT FROM THIS HOUSE.
TAKIKO IS...
...SHE'S GONE...
WHAT ?!
WHAT DO YOU MEAN ?
THERE WAS A LIGHT ...
... FROM THE BOOK ...

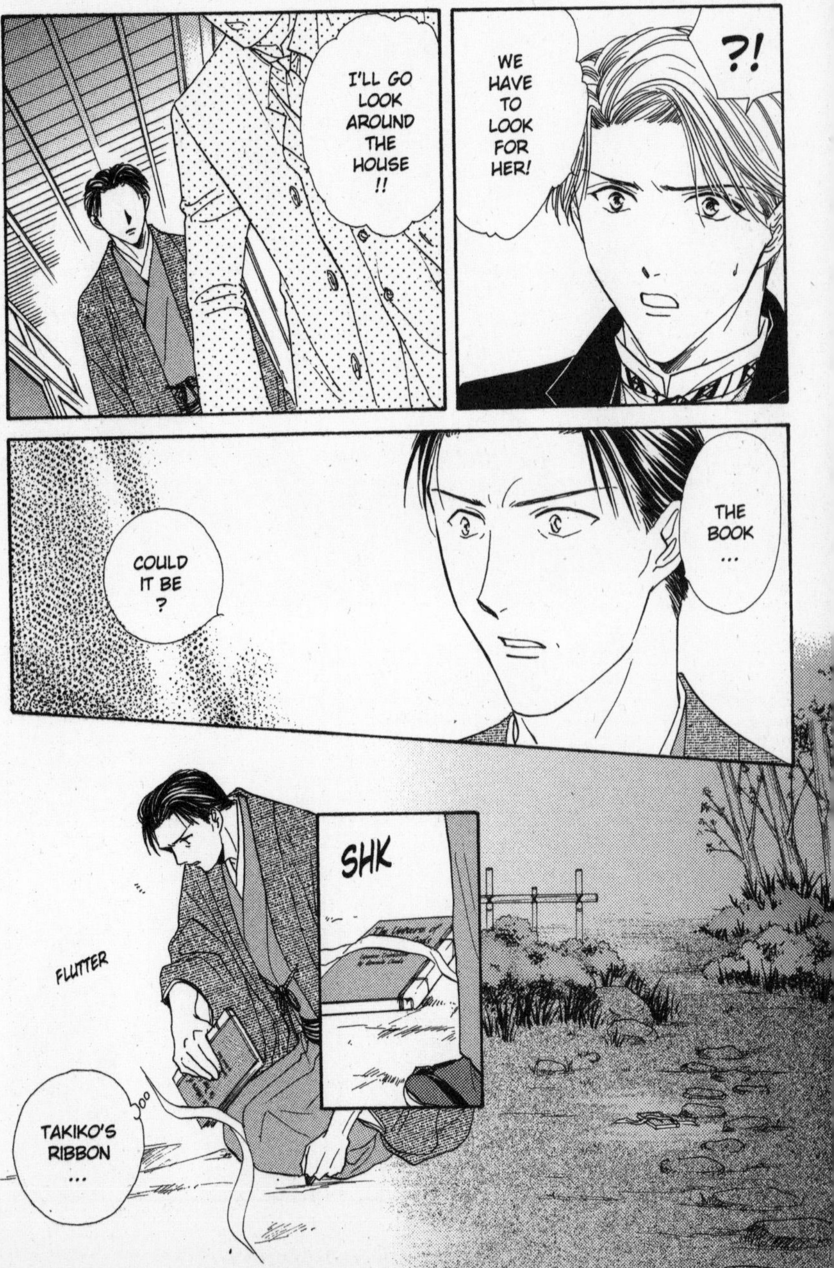
?!
WE HAVE TO LOOK FOR HER!
I'LL GO LOOK AROUND THE HOUSE !!
THE BOOK ...
COULD IT BE ?
SHK
FLUTTER
TAKIKO'S RIBBON ...

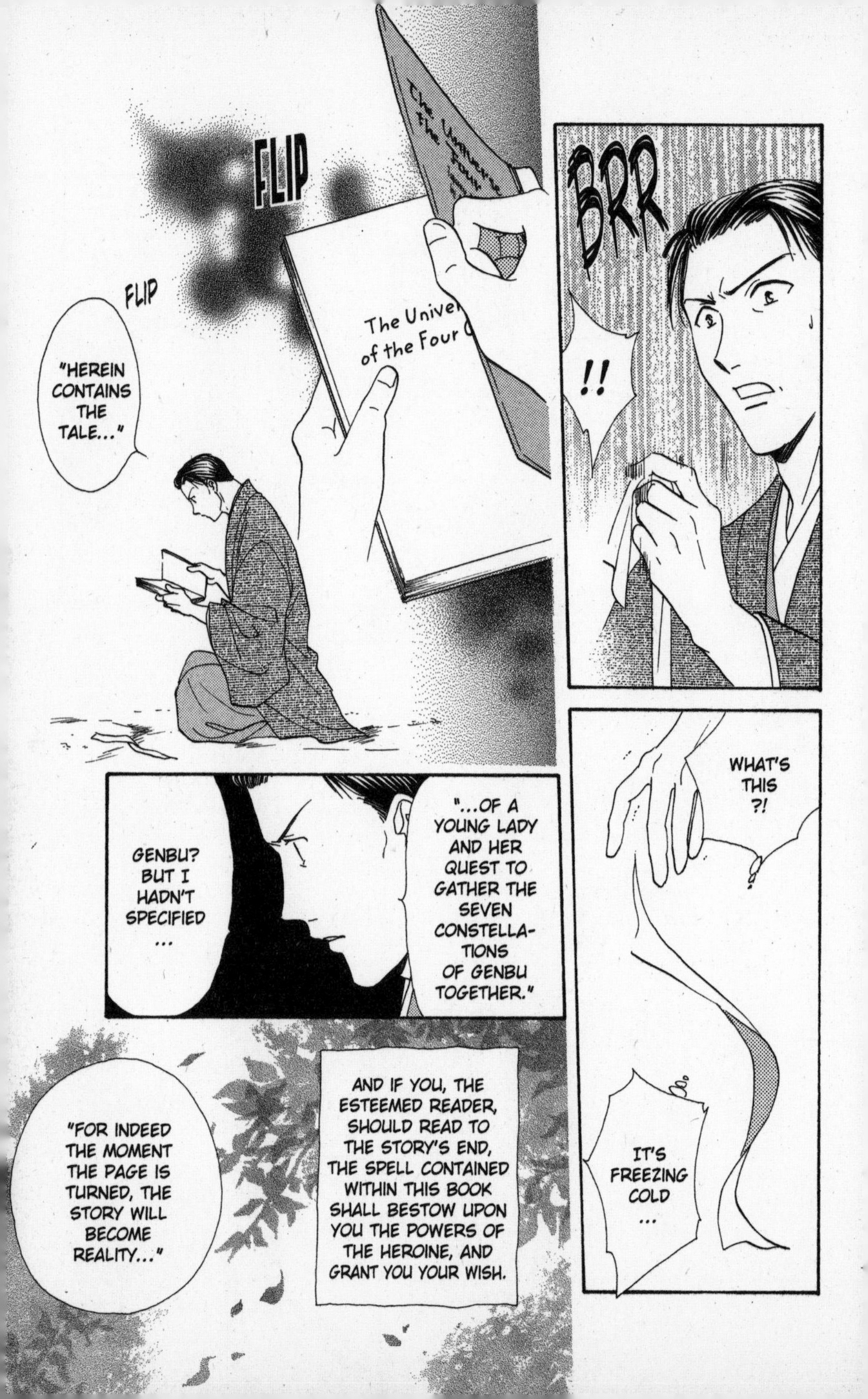
BRR
!!
FLIP
FLIP
"HEREIN CONTAINS THE TALE..."
The Univer
of the Four
WHAT'S THIS?!
IT'S FREEZING COLD...
"...OF A YOUNG LADY AND HER QUEST TO GATHER THE SEVEN CONSTELLATIONS OF GENBU TOGETHER."
GENBU? BUT I HADN'T SPECIFIED...
AND IF YOU, THE ESTEEMED READER, SHOULD READ TO THE STORY'S END, THE SPELL CONTAINED WITHIN THIS BOOK SHALL BESTOW UPON YOU THE POWERS OF THE HEROINE, AND GRANT YOU YOUR WISH.
"FOR INDEED THE MOMENT THE PAGE IS TURNED, THE STORY WILL BECOME REALITY..."

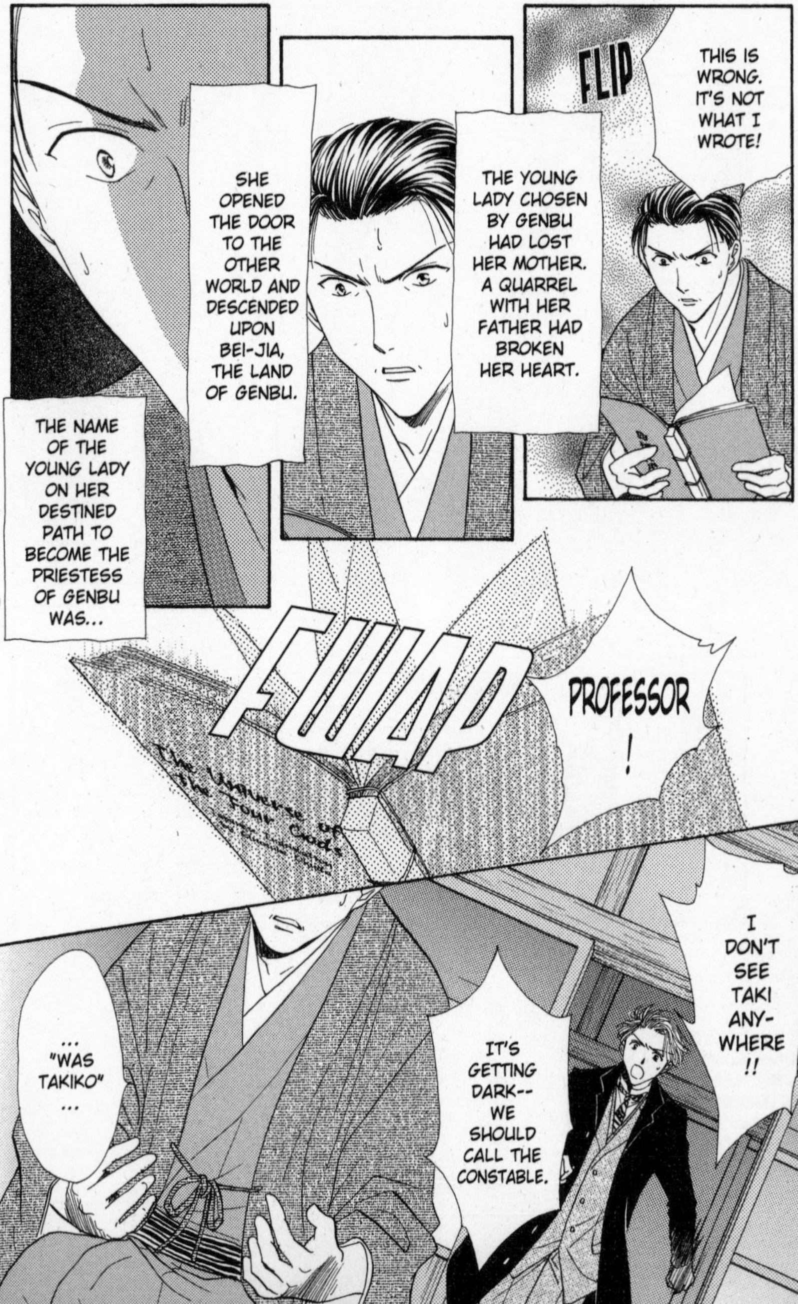
FLIP
THIS IS WRONG. IT'S NOT WHAT I WROTE!
THE YOUNG LADY CHOSEN BY GENBU HAD LOST HER MOTHER. A QUARREL WITH HER FATHER HAD BROKEN HER HEART.
SHE OPENED THE DOOR TO THE OTHER WORLD AND DESCENDED UPON BEI-JIA, THE LAND OF GENBU.
THE NAME OF THE YOUNG LADY ON HER DESTINED PATH TO BECOME THE PRIESTESS OF GENBU WAS...
PROFESSOR!
FWAP
The Universe of The Four Gods
I DON'T SEE TAKI ANY-WHERE!!
IT'S GETTING DARK--WE SHOULD CALL THE CONSTABLE.
..."WAS TAKIKO"...

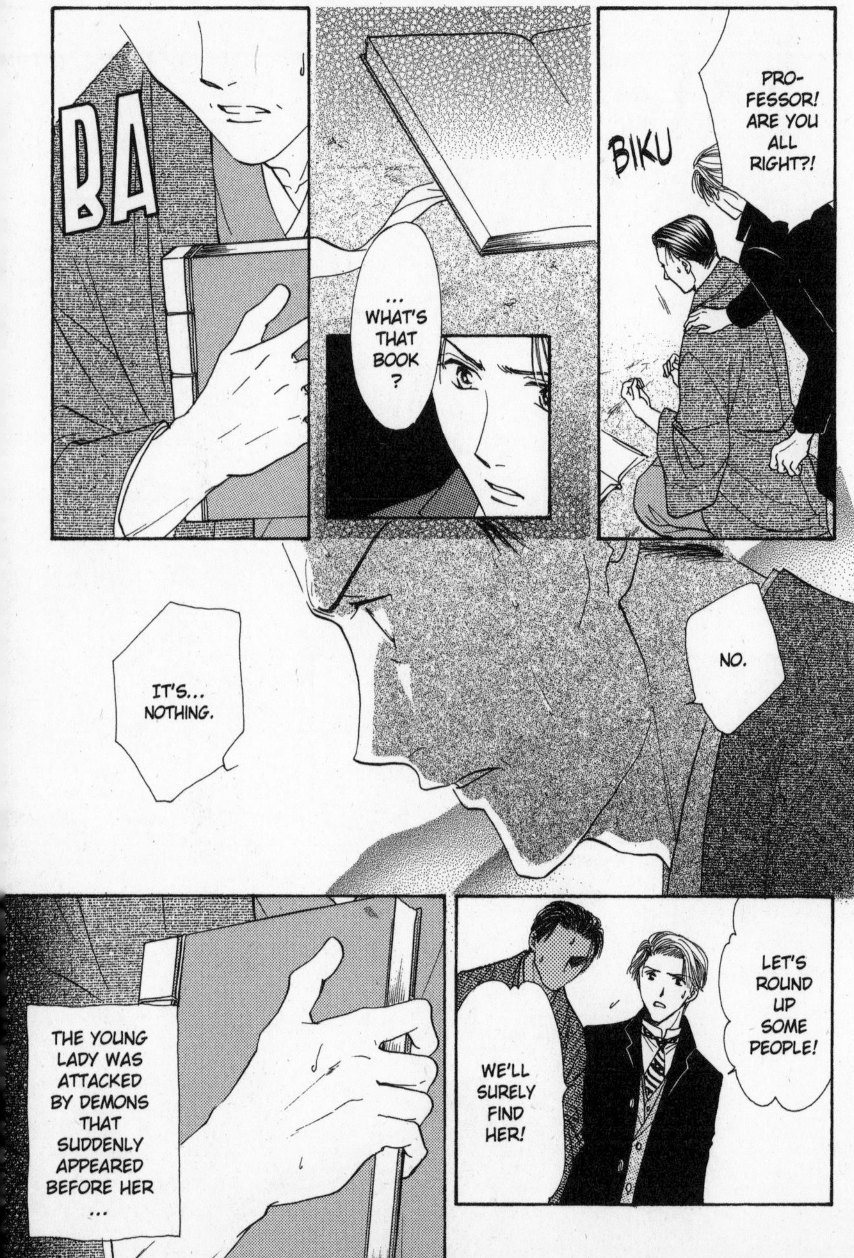
BIKU
PRO-FESSOR! ARE YOU ALL RIGHT?!
... WHAT'S THAT BOOK ?
BA
NO.
IT'S... NOTHING.
LET'S ROUND UP SOME PEOPLE!
WE'LL SURELY FIND HER!
THE YOUNG LADY WAS ATTACKED BY DEMONS THAT SUDDENLY APPEARED BEFORE HER ...

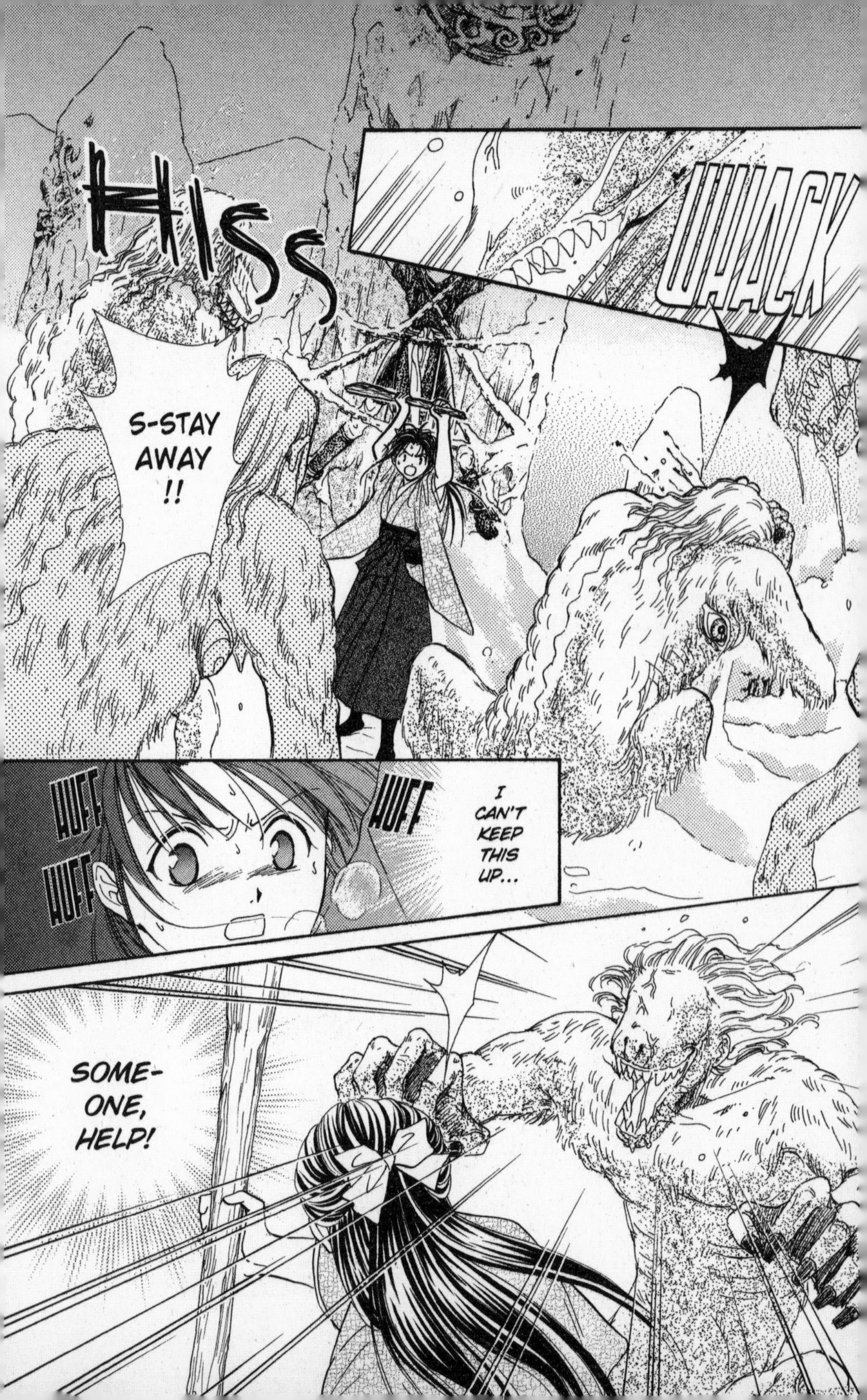
WHACK
HISS
S-STAY AWAY !!
I CAN'T KEEP THIS UP...
HUFF
HUFF HUFF
SOME-ONE, HELP!

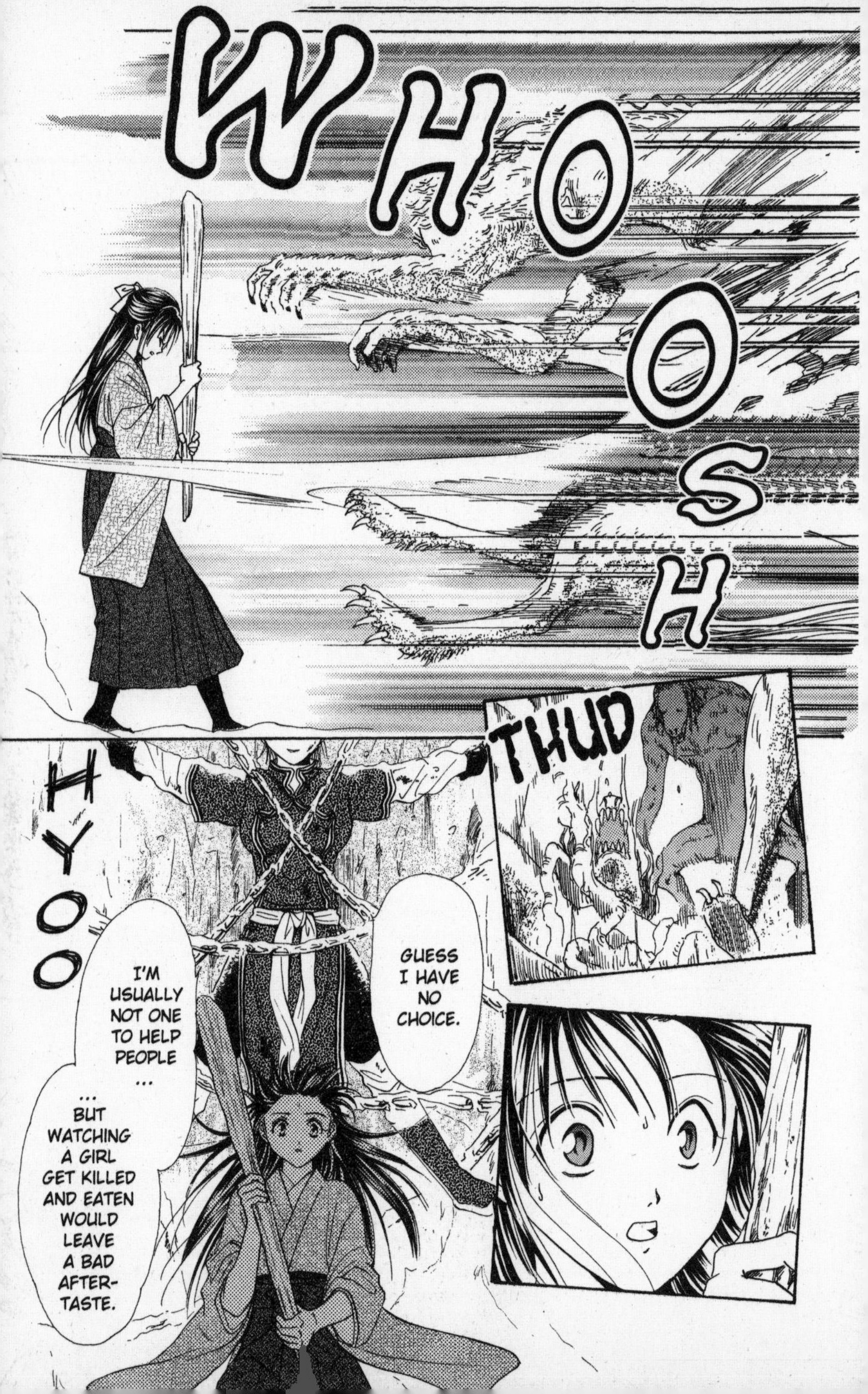
WHOOSH
THUD
HYOOO
GUESS I HAVE NO CHOICE.
I'M USUALLY NOT ONE TO HELP PEOPLE ...
... BUT WATCHING A GIRL GET KILLED AND EATEN WOULD LEAVE A BAD AFTER-TASTE.

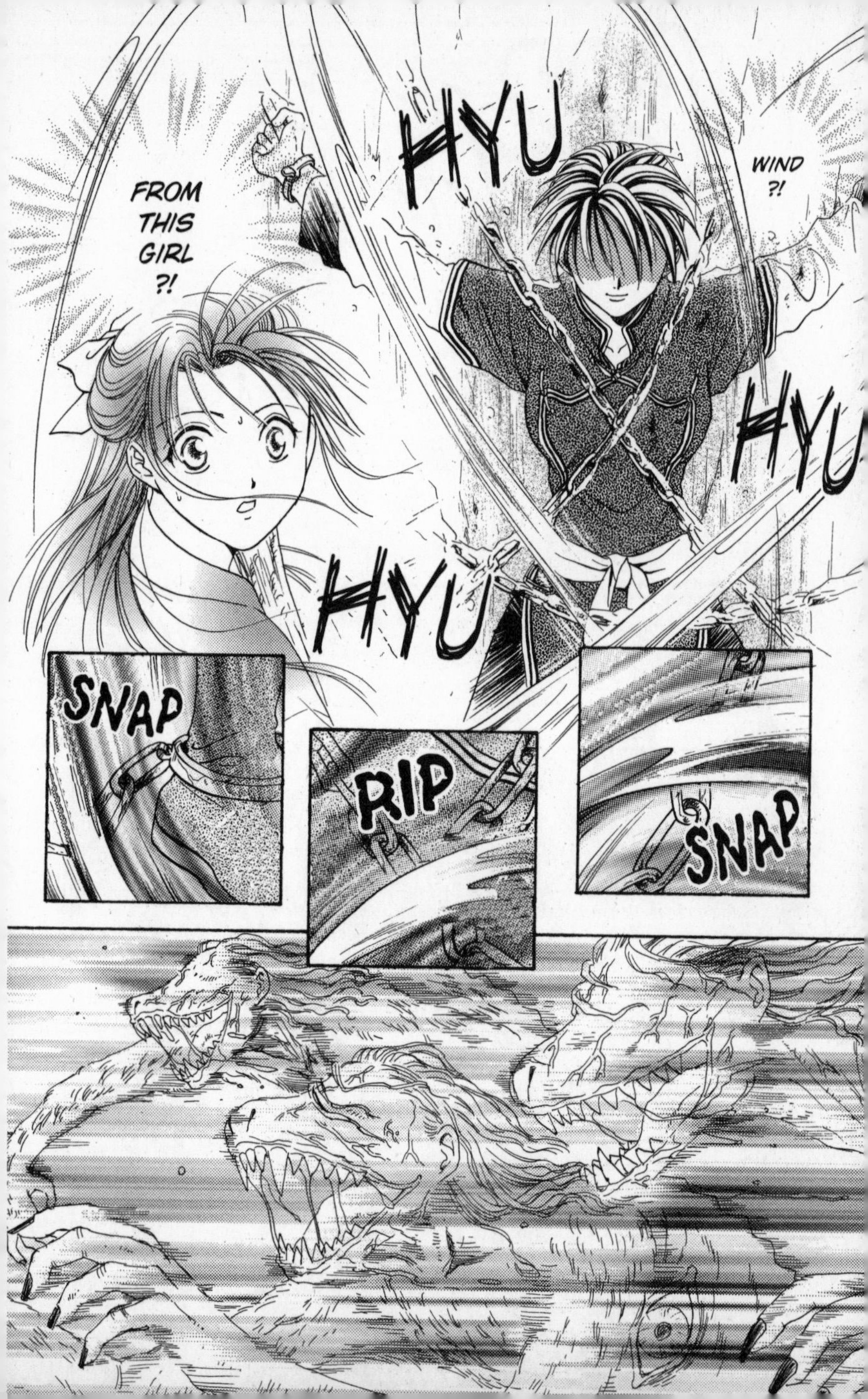
WIND ?!
HYU
FROM THIS GIRL ?!
HYU
HYU
SNAP
RIP
SNAP

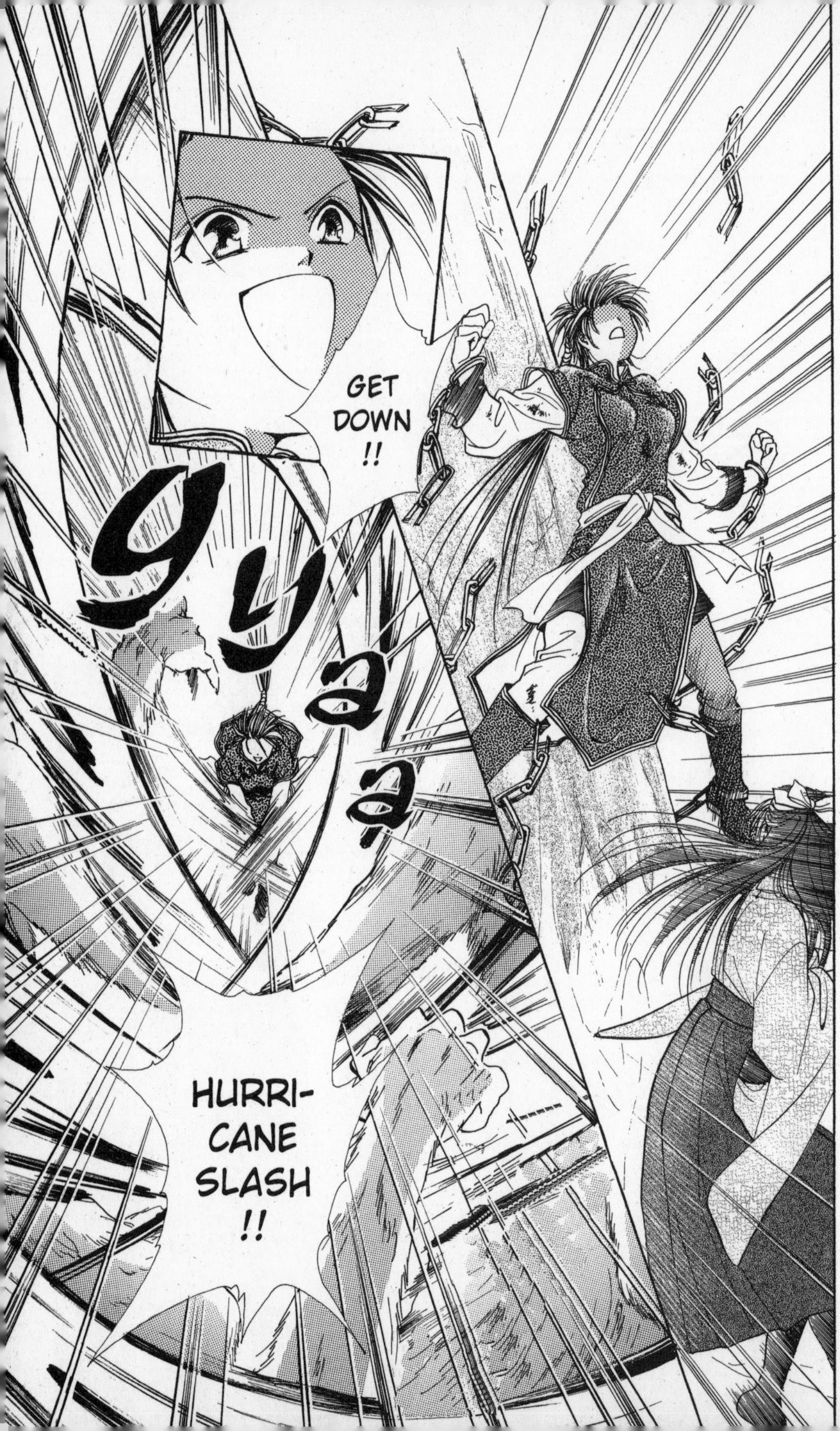
GET DOWN !!
Gyyaaa
HURRI-CANE SLASH !!

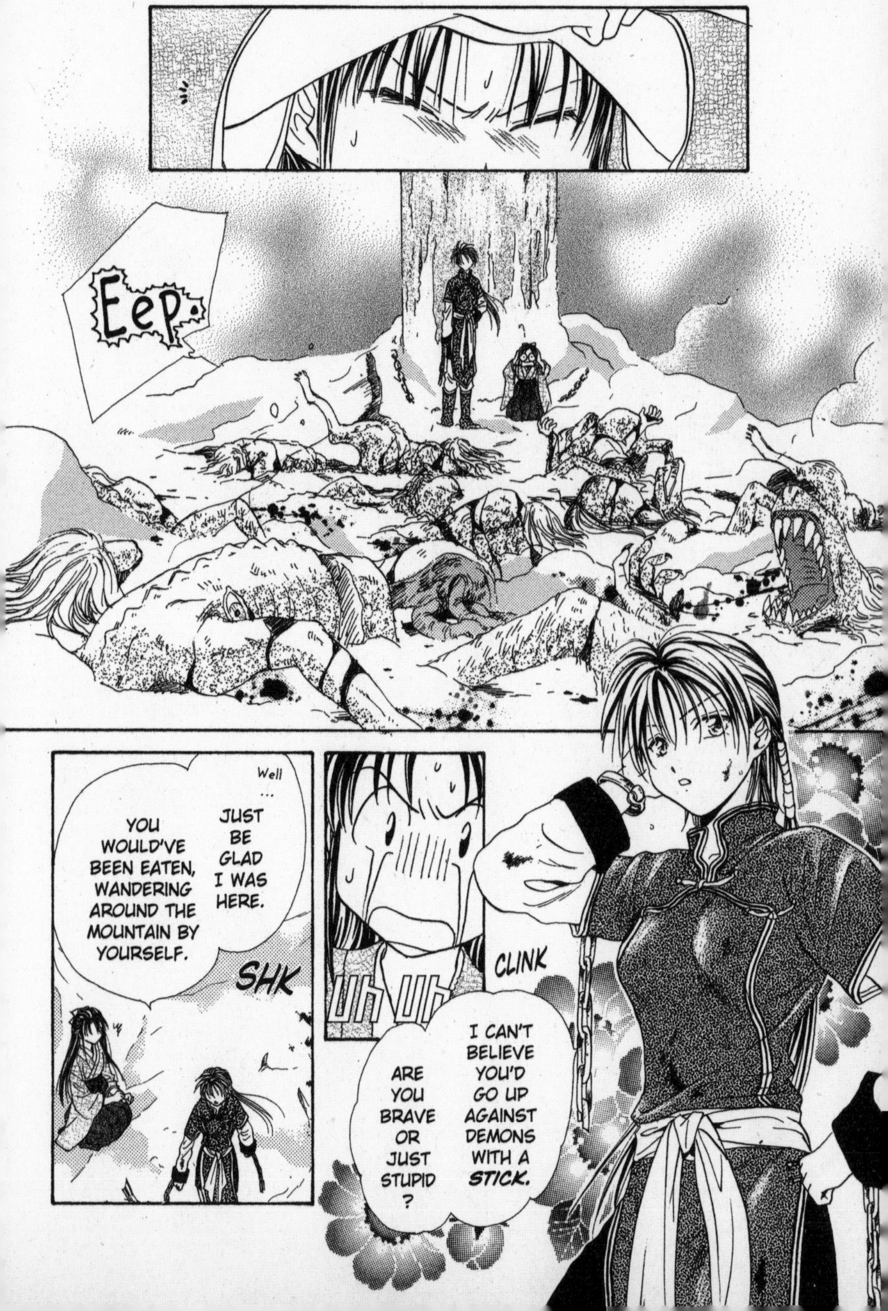
Eep.
CLINK
I CAN'T BELIEVE YOU'D GO UP AGAINST DEMONS WITH A STICK.
ARE YOU BRAVE OR JUST STUPID?
uh uh
Well... JUST BE GLAD I WAS HERE.
YOU WOULD'VE BEEN EATEN, WANDERING AROUND THE MOUNTAIN BY YOURSELF.
SHK

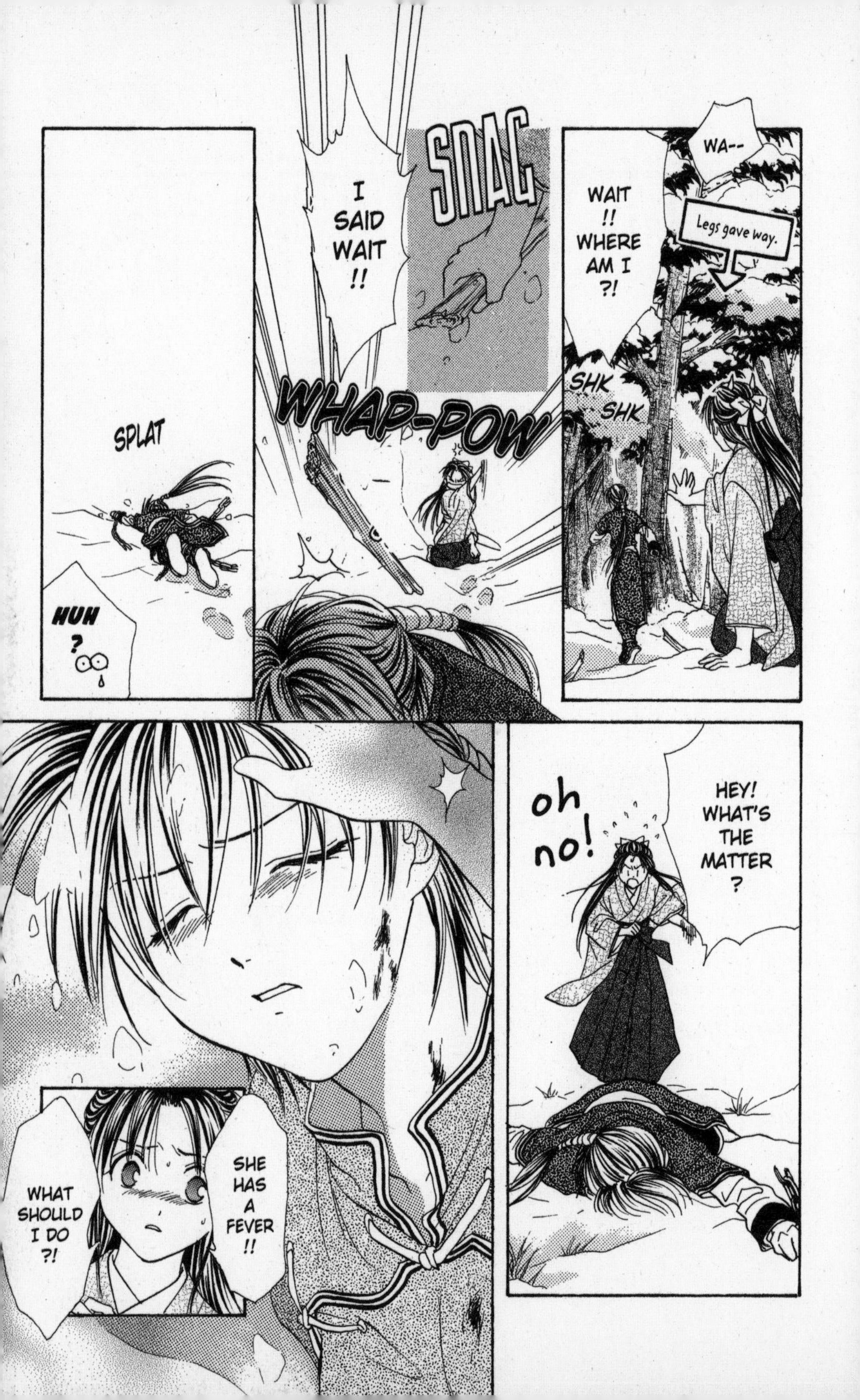
WA--
WAIT !! WHERE AM I ?!
Legs gave way.
SHK SHK
SNAG
I SAID WAIT !!
WHAP-POW
SPLAT
HUH ?
HEY! WHAT'S THE MATTER ?
oh no!
SHE HAS A FEVER !!
WHAT SHOULD I DO ?!

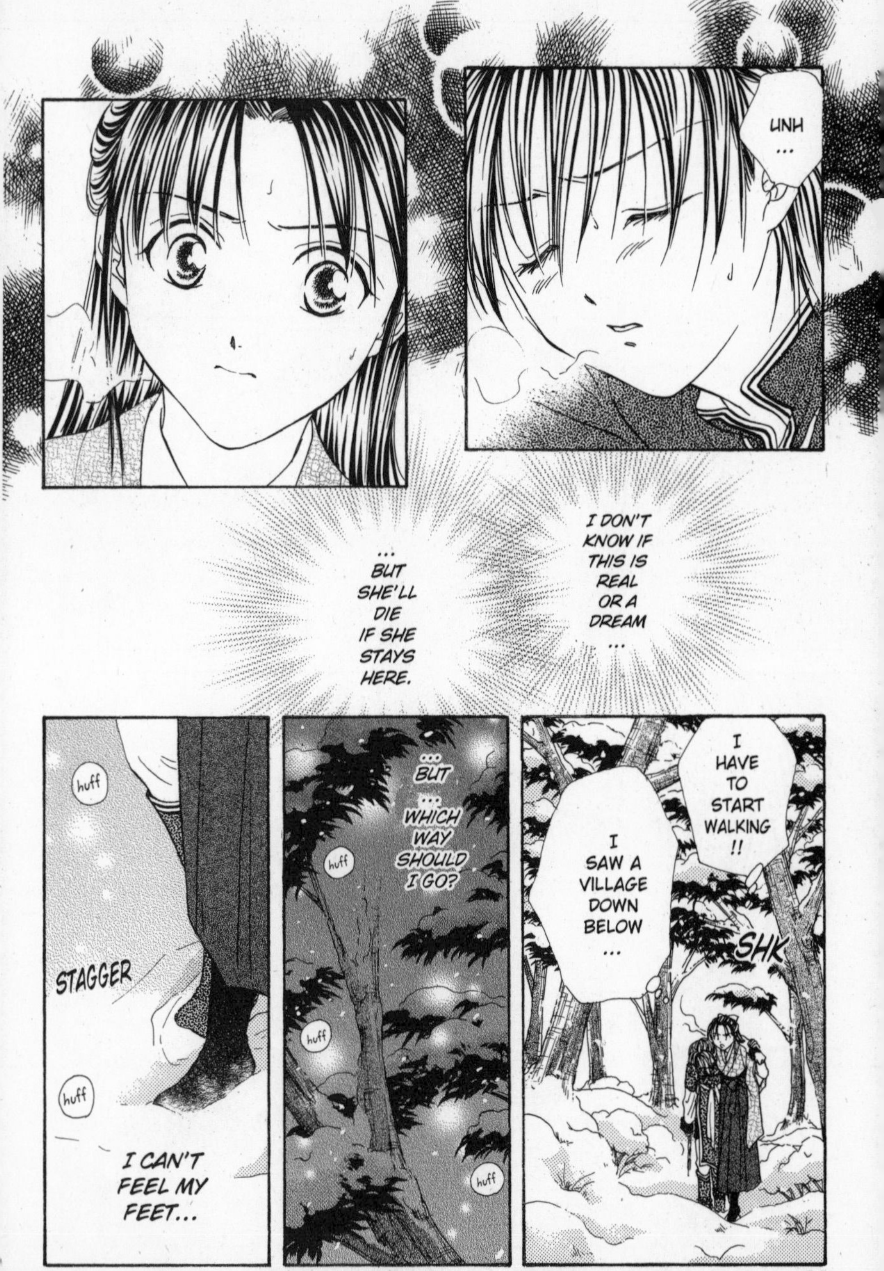
UNH ...
I DON'T KNOW IF THIS IS REAL OR A DREAM ...
... BUT SHE'LL DIE IF SHE STAYS HERE.
I HAVE TO START WALKING !!
I SAW A VILLAGE DOWN BELOW ...
SHK
... BUT ... WHICH WAY SHOULD I GO?
huff
huff
huff
huff
STAGGER
huff
I CAN'T FEEL MY FEET...

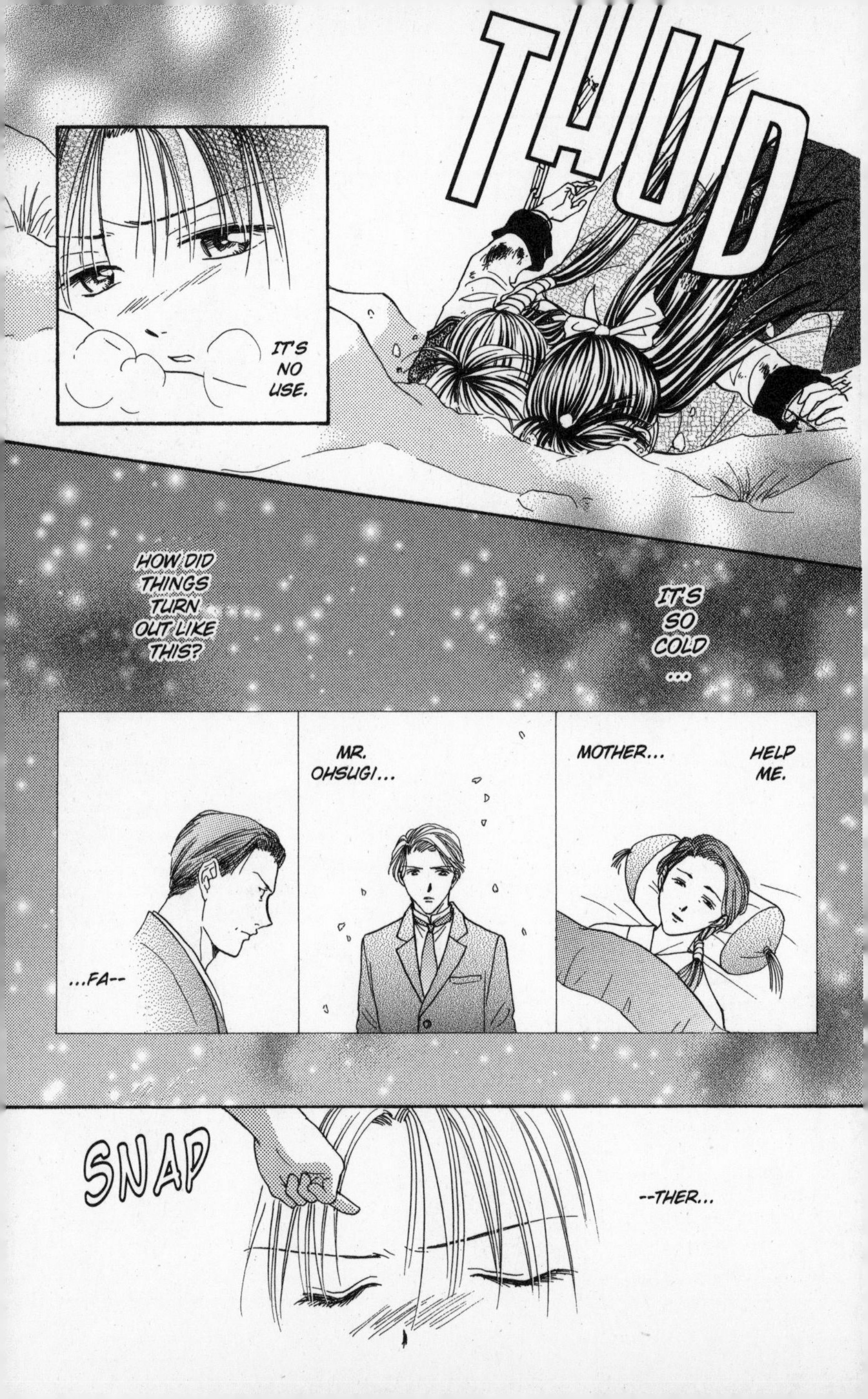
THUD
IT'S NO USE.
IT'S SO COLD...
HOW DID THINGS TURN OUT LIKE THIS?
MOTHER... HELP ME.
MR. OHSUGI...
...FA--
--THER...
SNAP

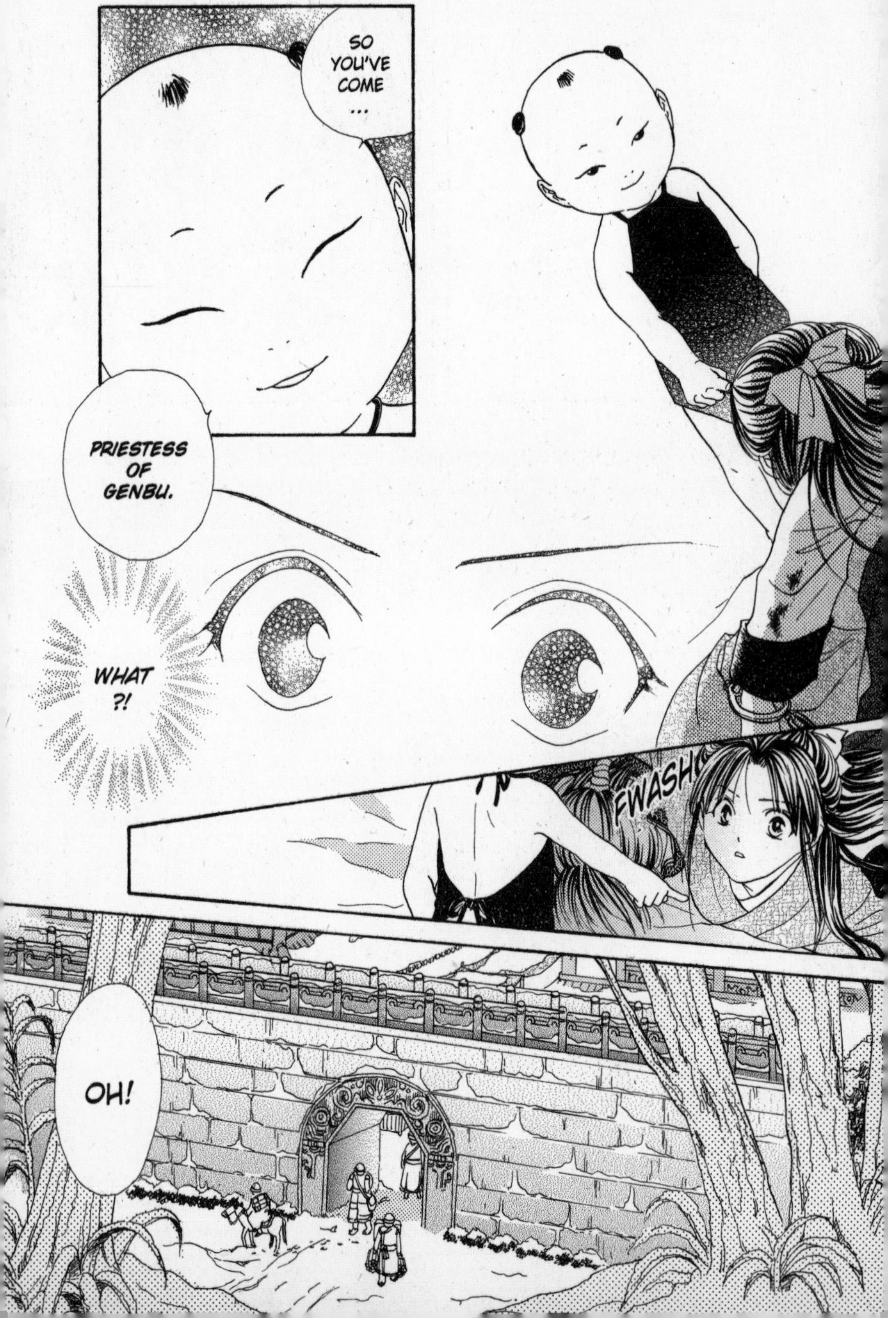
SO YOU'VE COME ...
PRIESTESS OF GENBU.
WHAT ?!
FWASH
OH!

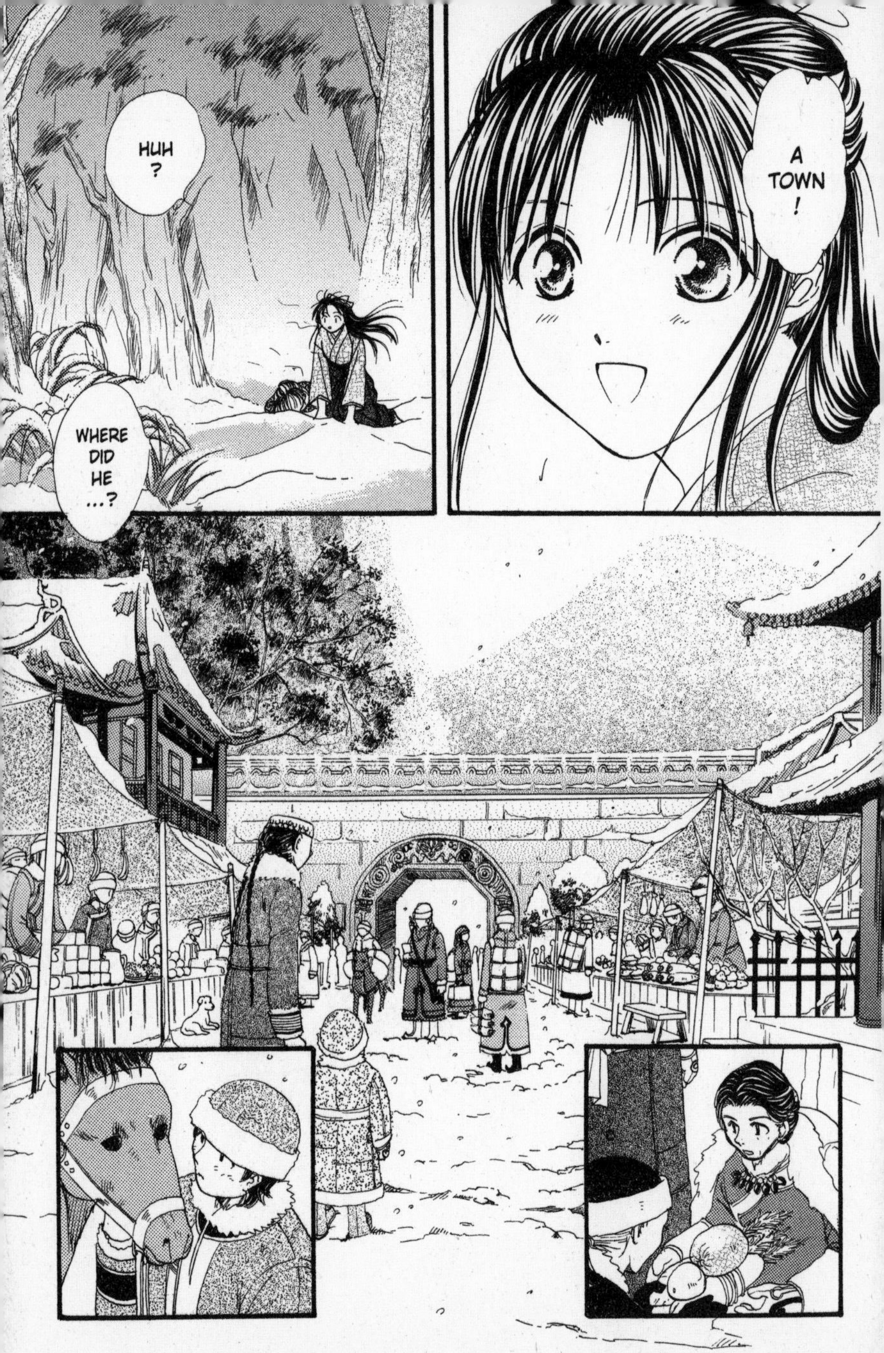
A TOWN!
HUH?
WHERE DID HE ...?

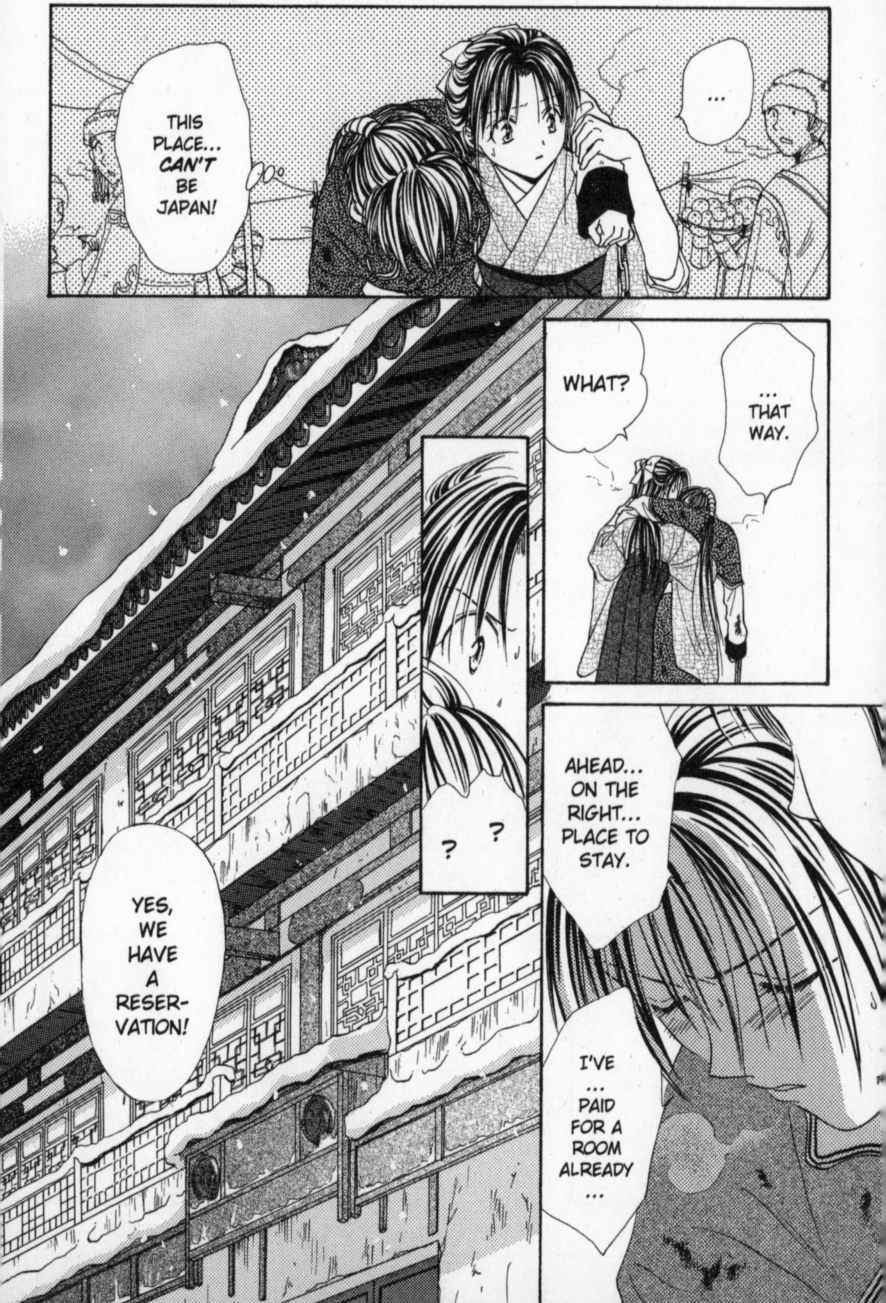
...
THIS PLACE... CAN'T BE JAPAN!
... THAT WAY.
WHAT?
AHEAD... ON THE RIGHT... PLACE TO STAY.
I'VE ... PAID FOR A ROOM ALREADY ...
? ?
YES, WE HAVE A RESERVATION!

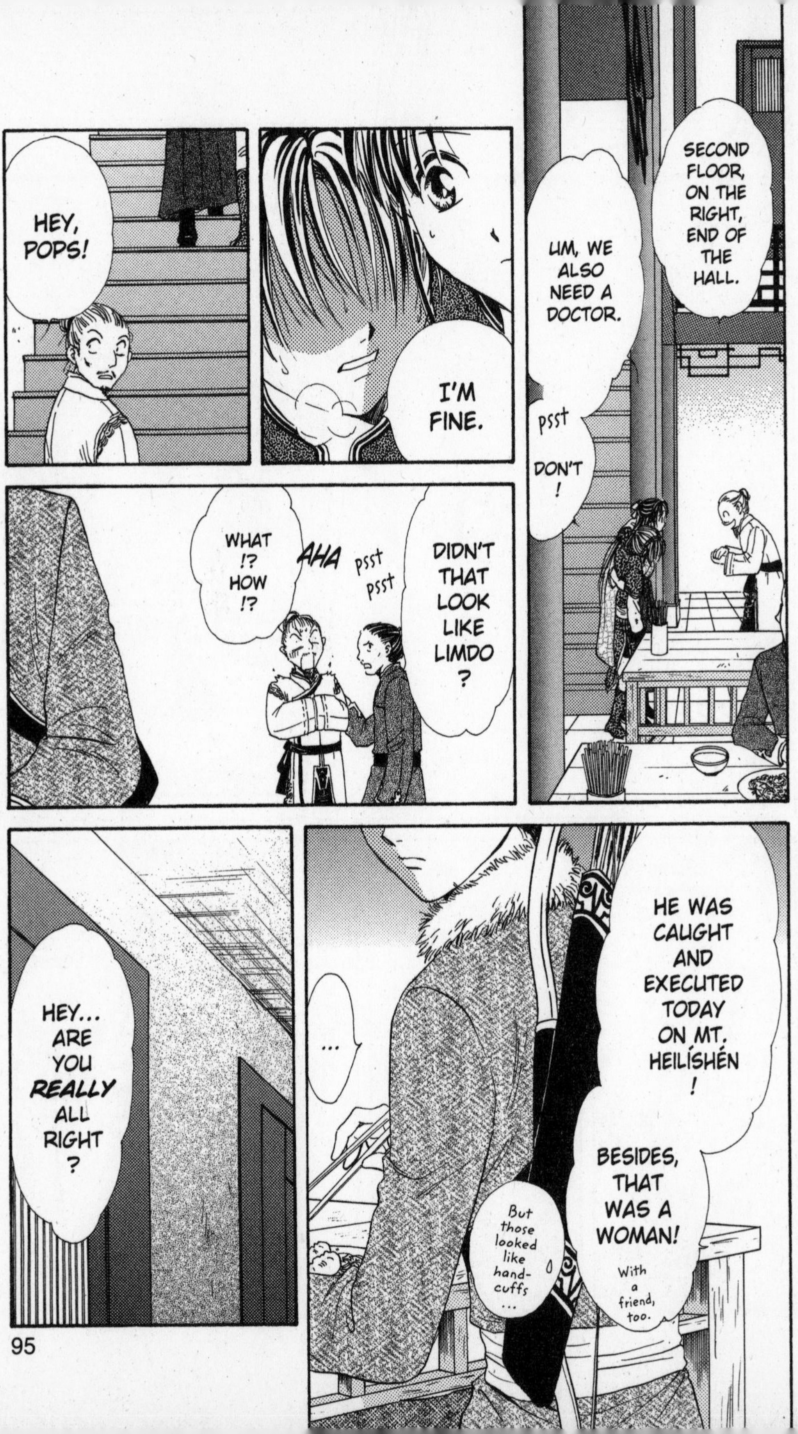
SECOND FLOOR, ON THE RIGHT, END OF THE HALL.
UM, WE ALSO NEED A DOCTOR.
psst
DON'T!
I'M FINE.
HEY, POPS!
DIDN'T THAT LOOK LIKE LIMDO?
psst psst
AHA
WHAT!? HOW!?
HE WAS CAUGHT AND EXECUTED TODAY ON MT. HEILÍSHÉN!
BESIDES, THAT WAS A WOMAN!
With a friend, too.
But those looked like hand-cuffs...
...
HEY... ARE YOU *REALLY* ALL RIGHT?

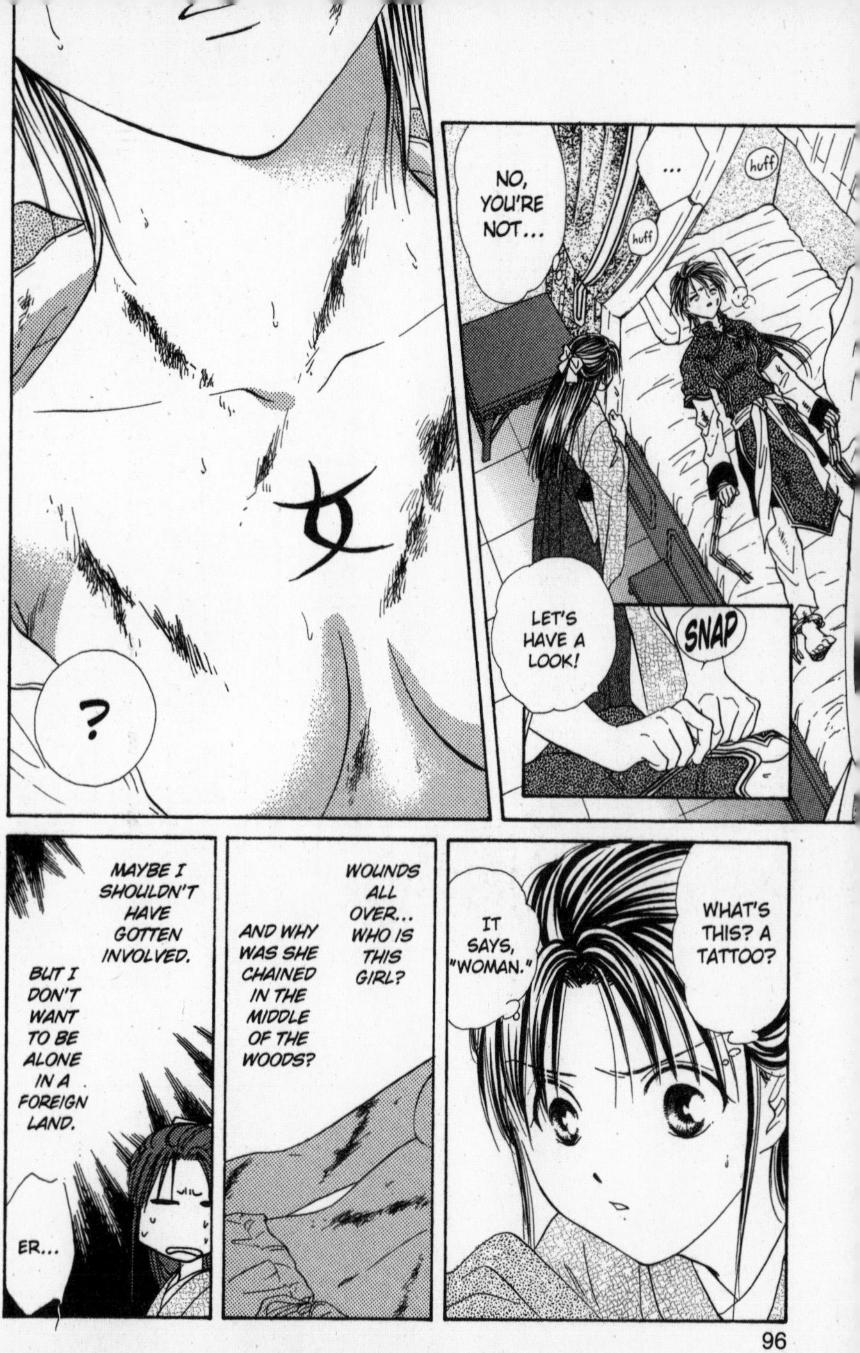
huff
...
huff
NO, YOU'RE NOT...
SNAP
LET'S HAVE A LOOK!
?
WHAT'S THIS? A TATTOO?
IT SAYS, "WOMAN."
WOUNDS ALL OVER... WHO IS THIS GIRL?
AND WHY WAS SHE CHAINED IN THE MIDDLE OF THE WOODS?
MAYBE I SHOULDN'T HAVE GOTTEN INVOLVED.
BUT I DON'T WANT TO BE ALONE IN A FOREIGN LAND.
ER...

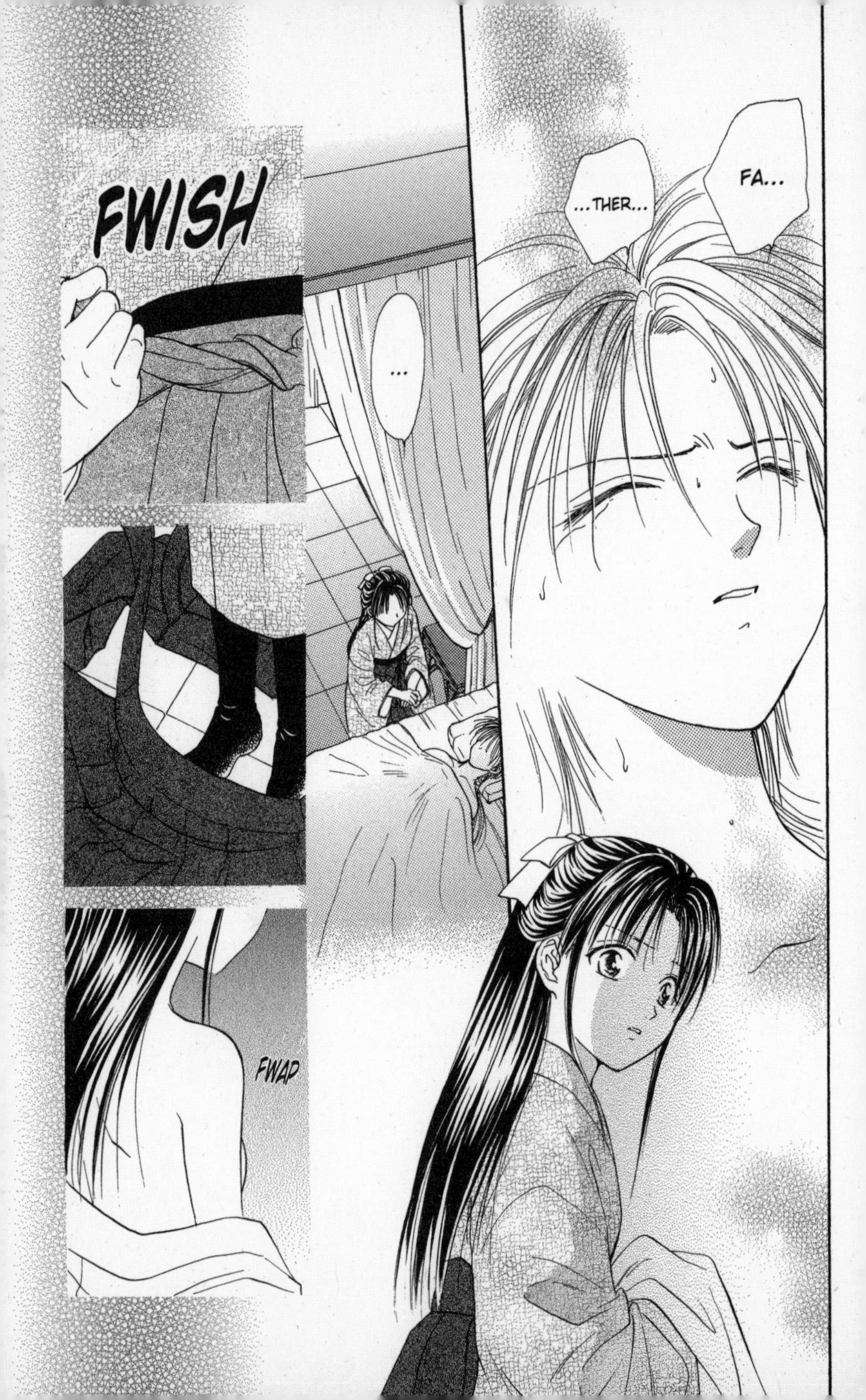
FA...
...THER...
...
FWISH
FWAP

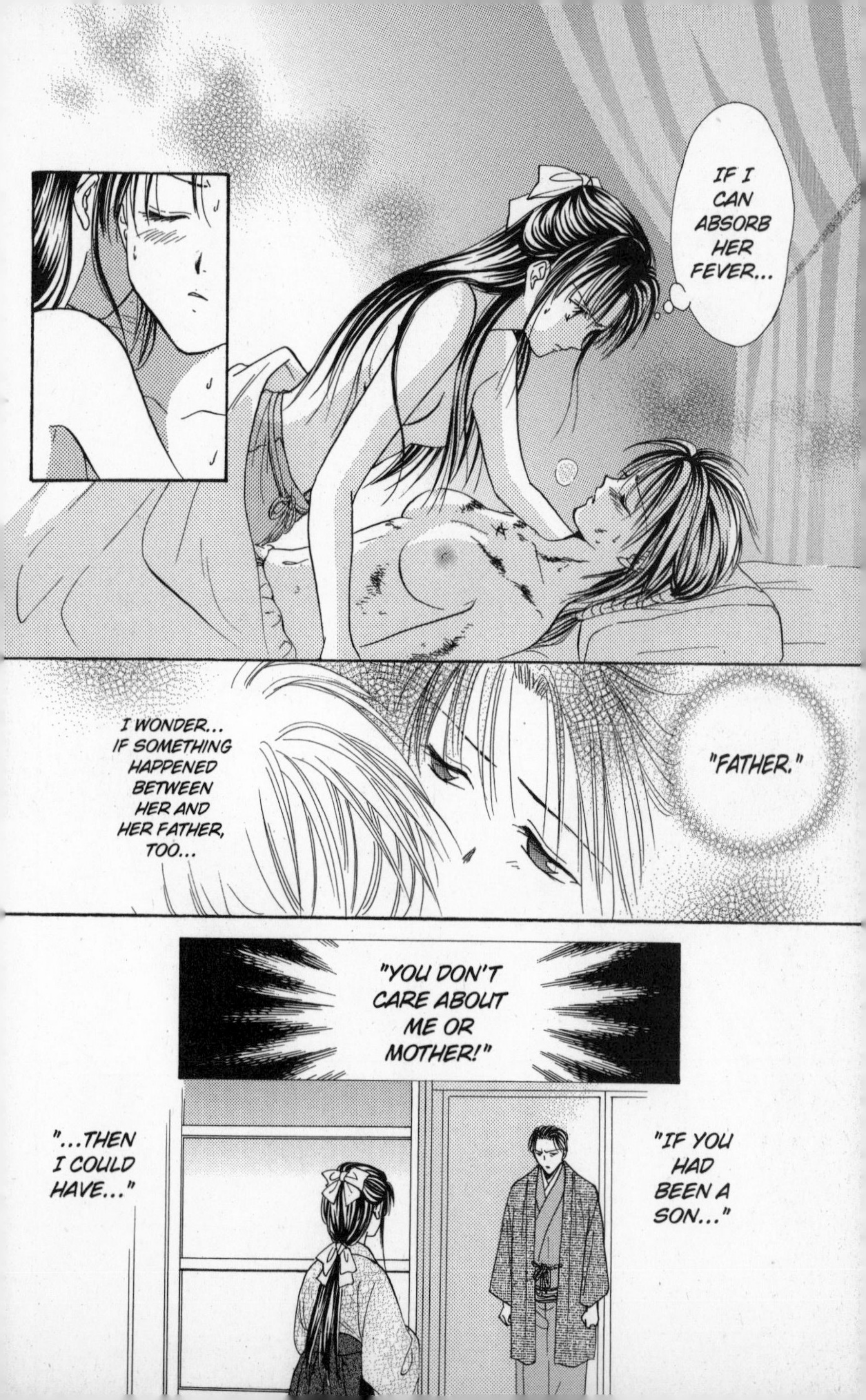
IF I CAN ABSORB HER FEVER...
"FATHER."
I WONDER... IF SOMETHING HAPPENED BETWEEN HER AND HER FATHER, TOO...
"YOU DON'T CARE ABOUT ME OR MOTHER!"
"IF YOU HAD BEEN A SON..."
"...THEN I COULD HAVE..."

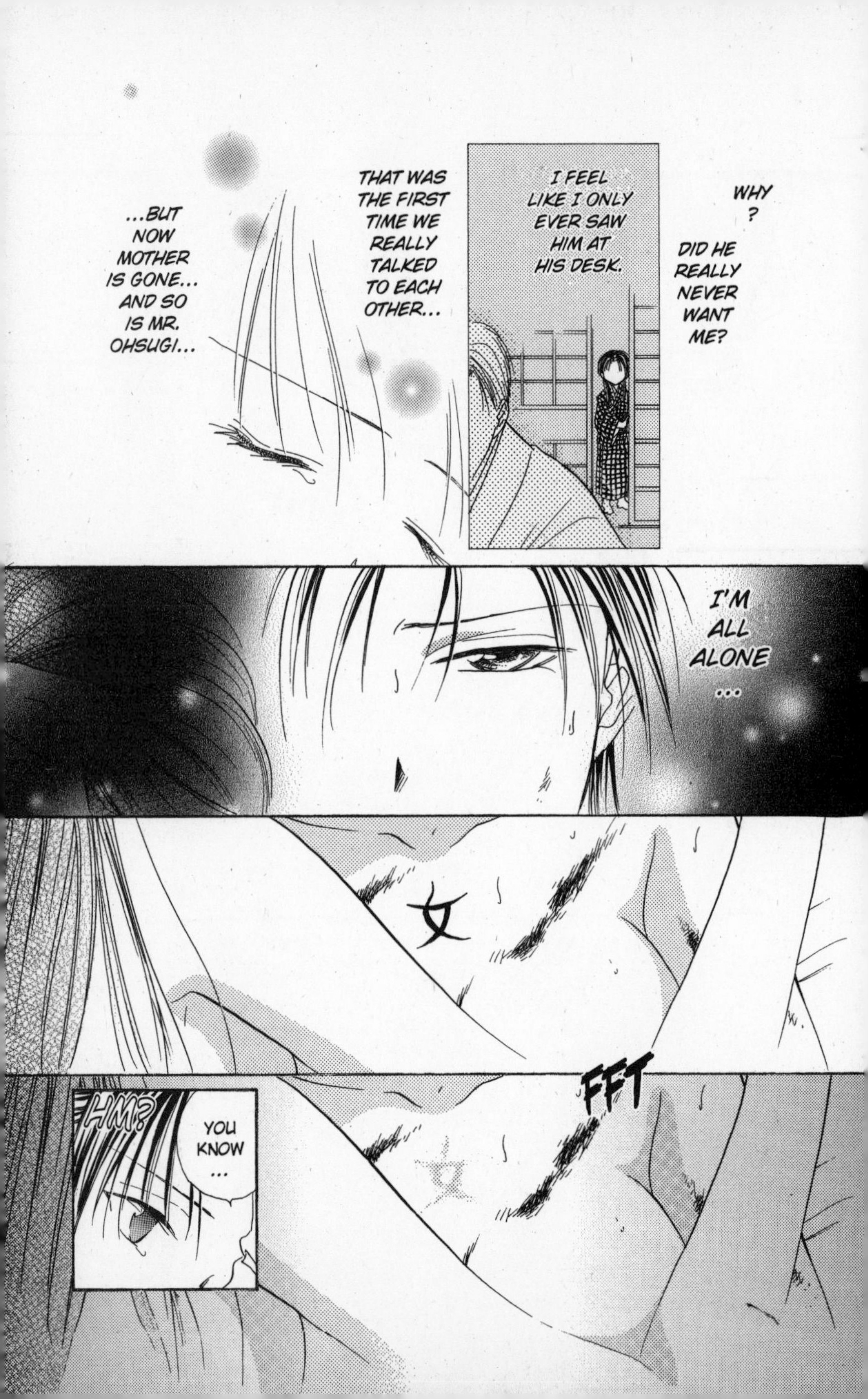
WHY?
DID HE REALLY NEVER WANT ME?
I FEEL LIKE I ONLY EVER SAW HIM AT HIS DESK.
THAT WAS THE FIRST TIME WE REALLY TALKED TO EACH OTHER...
...BUT NOW MOTHER IS GONE... AND SO IS MR. OHSUGI...
I'M ALL ALONE...
FFT
HM?
YOU KNOW...

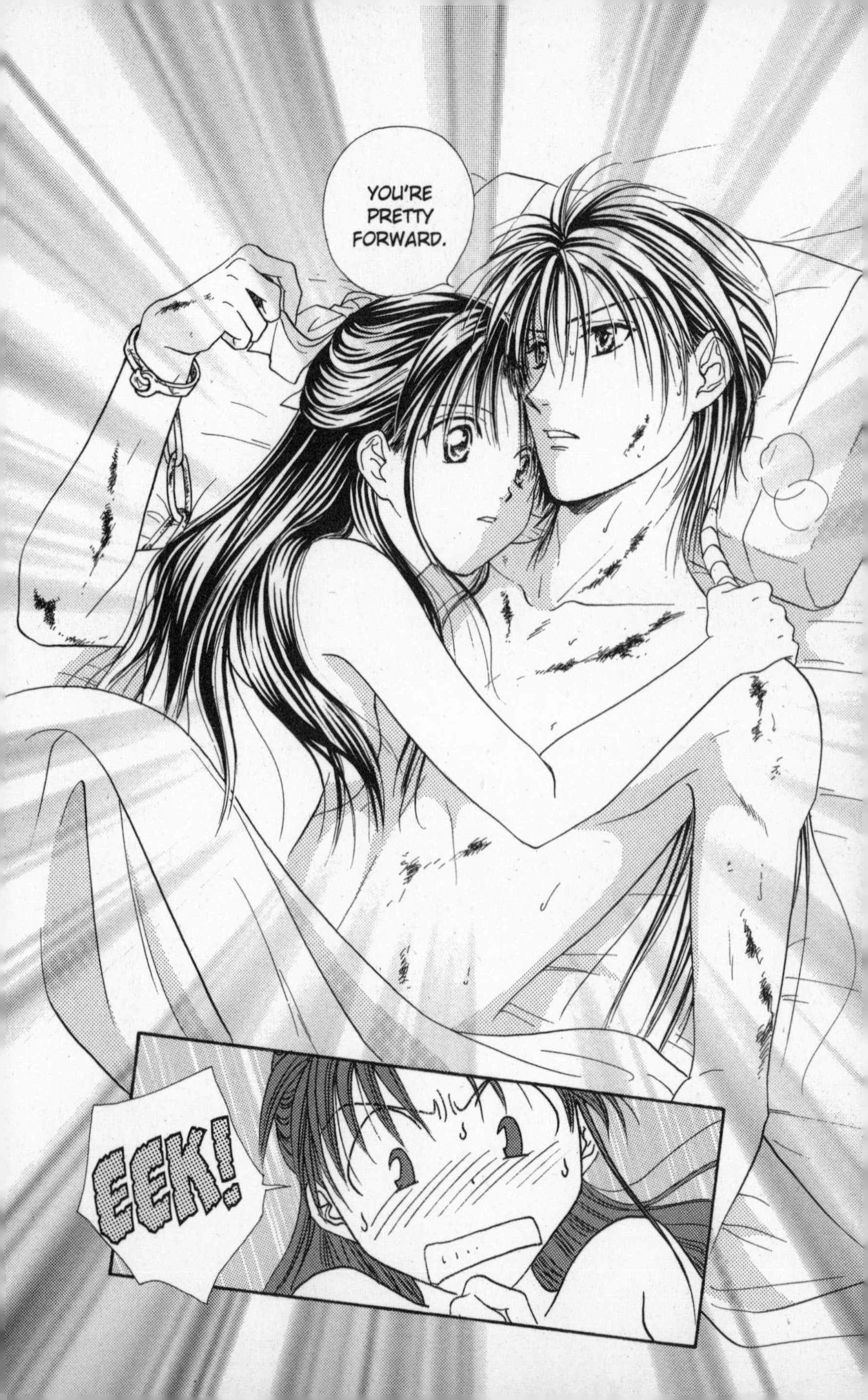

YOU'RE PRETTY FORWARD.
EEK!
...

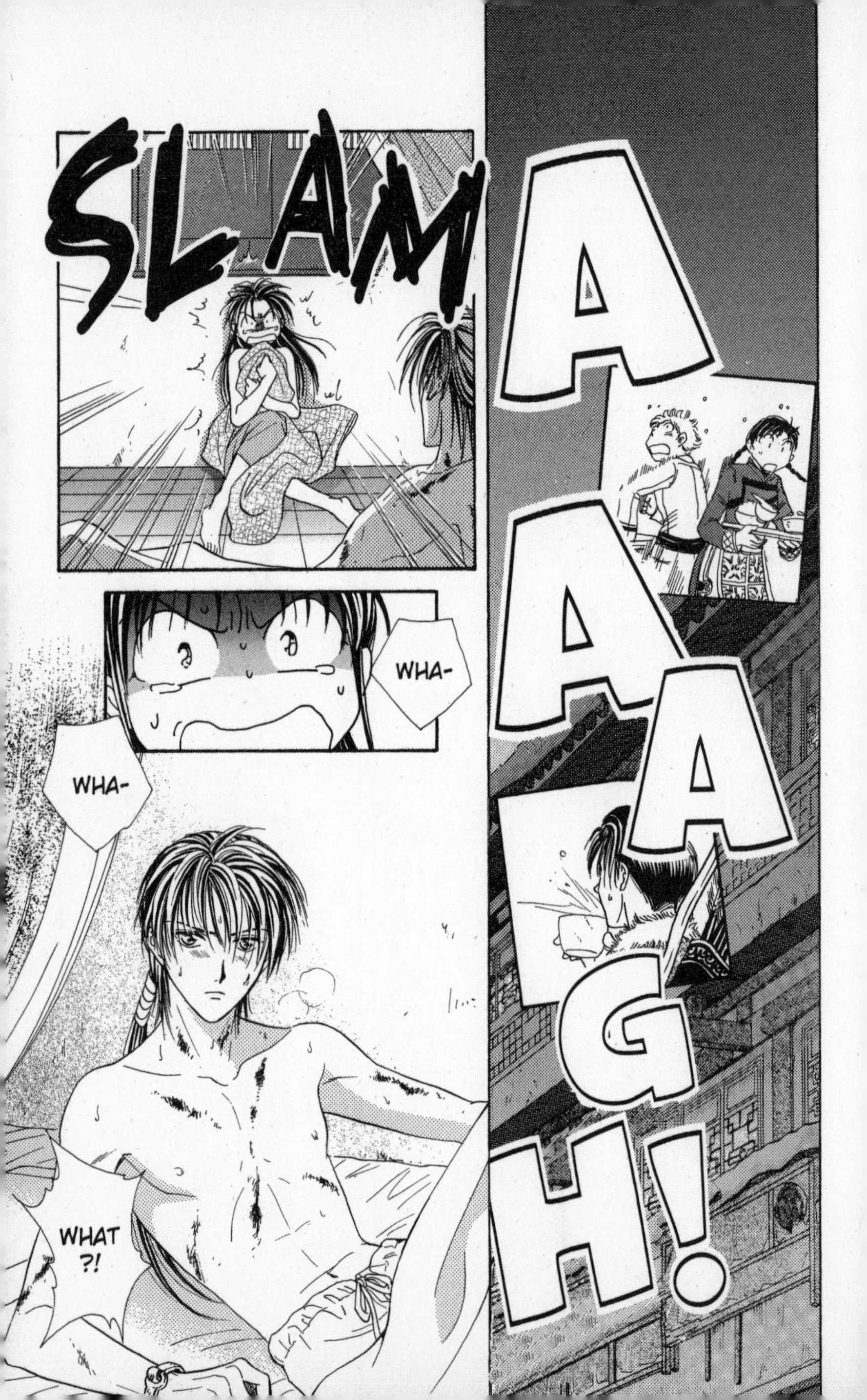
AAAAGH!
SLAM
WHA-
WHA-
WHAT ?!

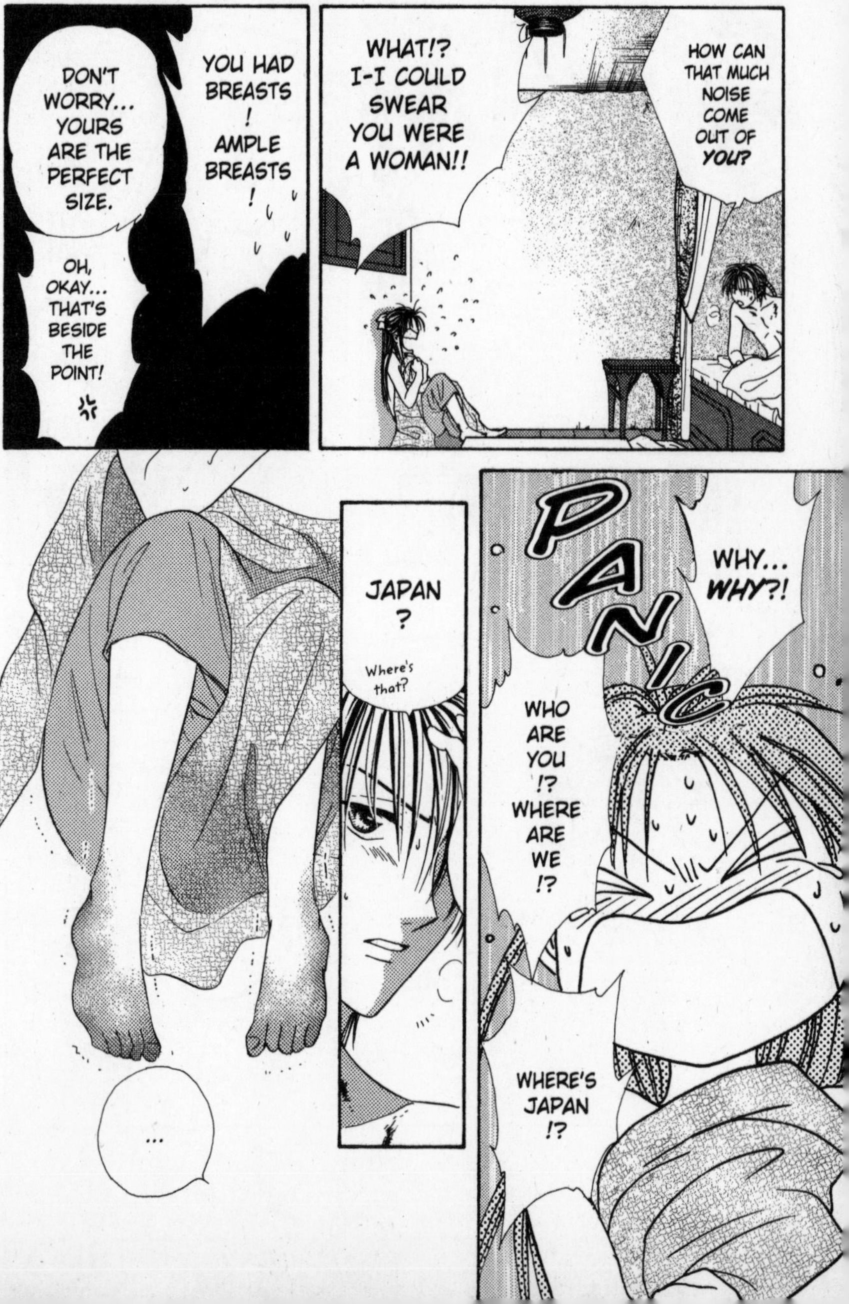
HOW CAN THAT MUCH NOISE COME OUT OF *YOU?*
WHAT!? I-I COULD SWEAR YOU WERE A WOMAN!!
YOU HAD BREASTS! AMPLE BREASTS!
DON'T WORRY... YOURS ARE THE PERFECT SIZE.
OH, OKAY... THAT'S BESIDE THE POINT!
PANIC
WHY... *WHY?!*
WHO ARE YOU!? WHERE ARE WE!?
WHERE'S JAPAN!?
JAPAN?
Where's that?
...

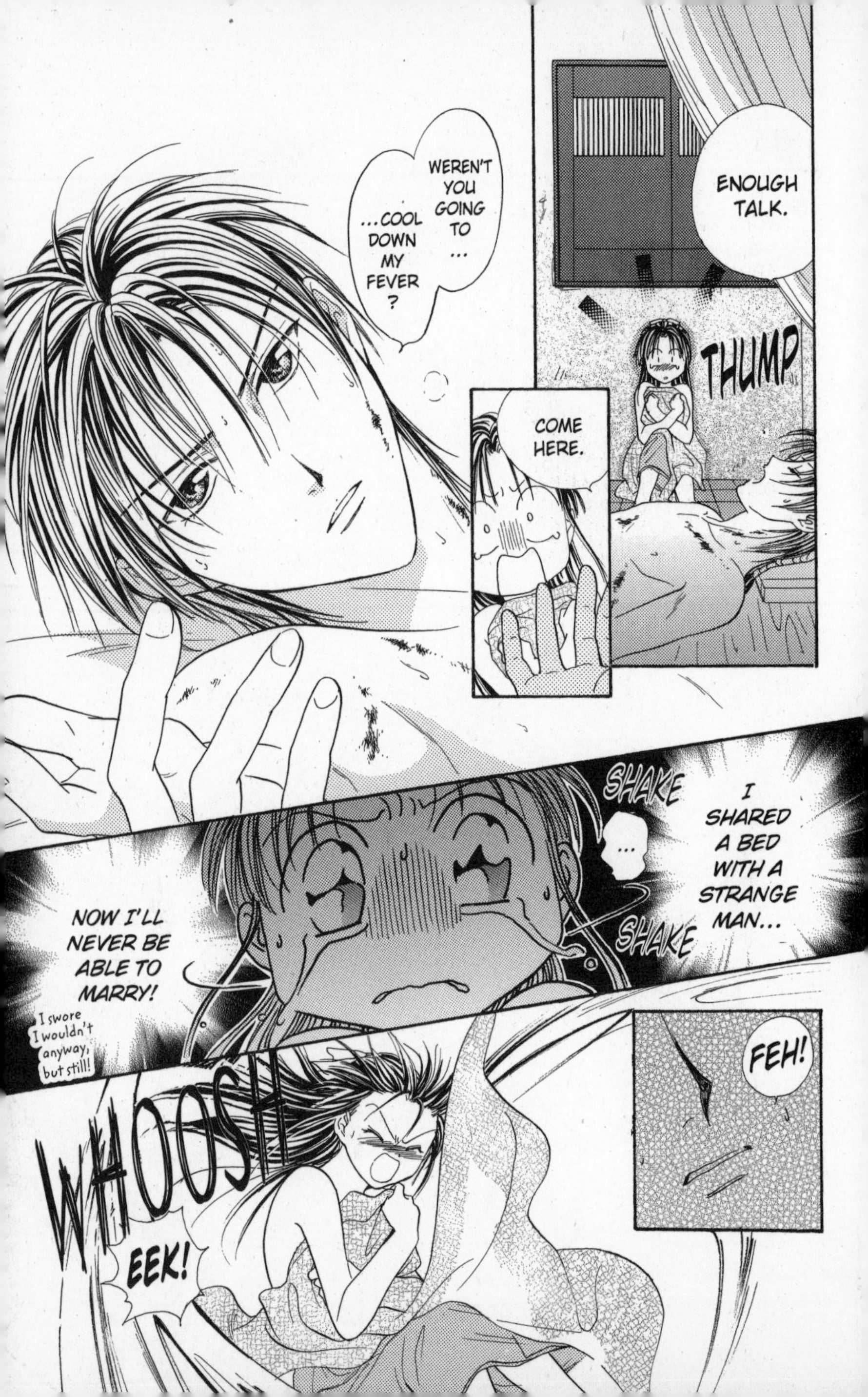
ENOUGH TALK.
THUMP
COME HERE.
WEREN'T YOU GOING TO ...
...COOL DOWN MY FEVER ?
SHAKE
...
I SHARED A BED WITH A STRANGE MAN...
SHAKE
NOW I'LL NEVER BE ABLE TO MARRY!
I swore I wouldn't anyway, but still!
FEH!
WHOOSH
EEK!

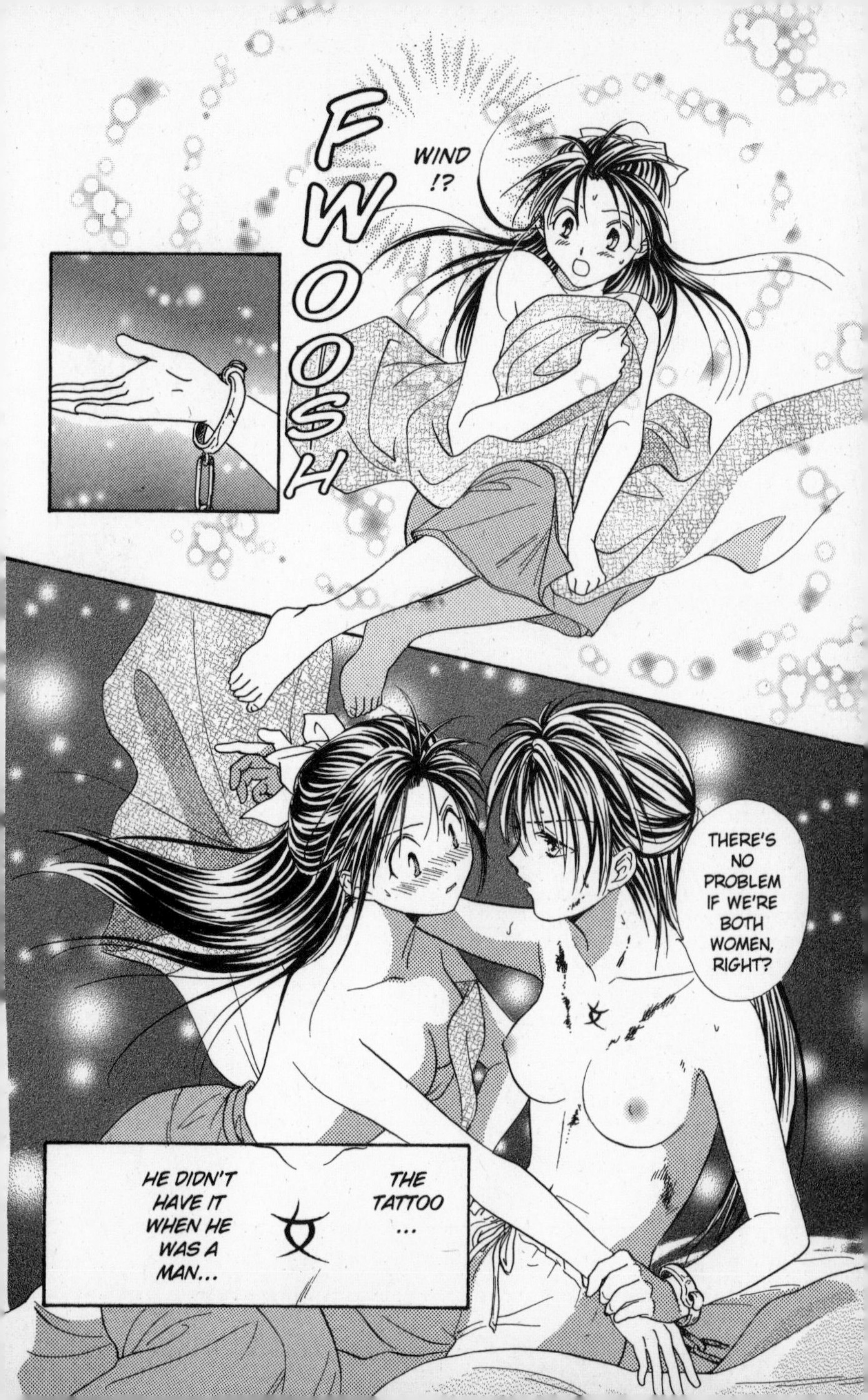
FWOOSH
WIND !?
THERE'S NO PROBLEM IF WE'RE BOTH WOMEN, RIGHT?
THE TATTOO...
HE DIDN'T HAVE IT WHEN HE WAS A MAN...

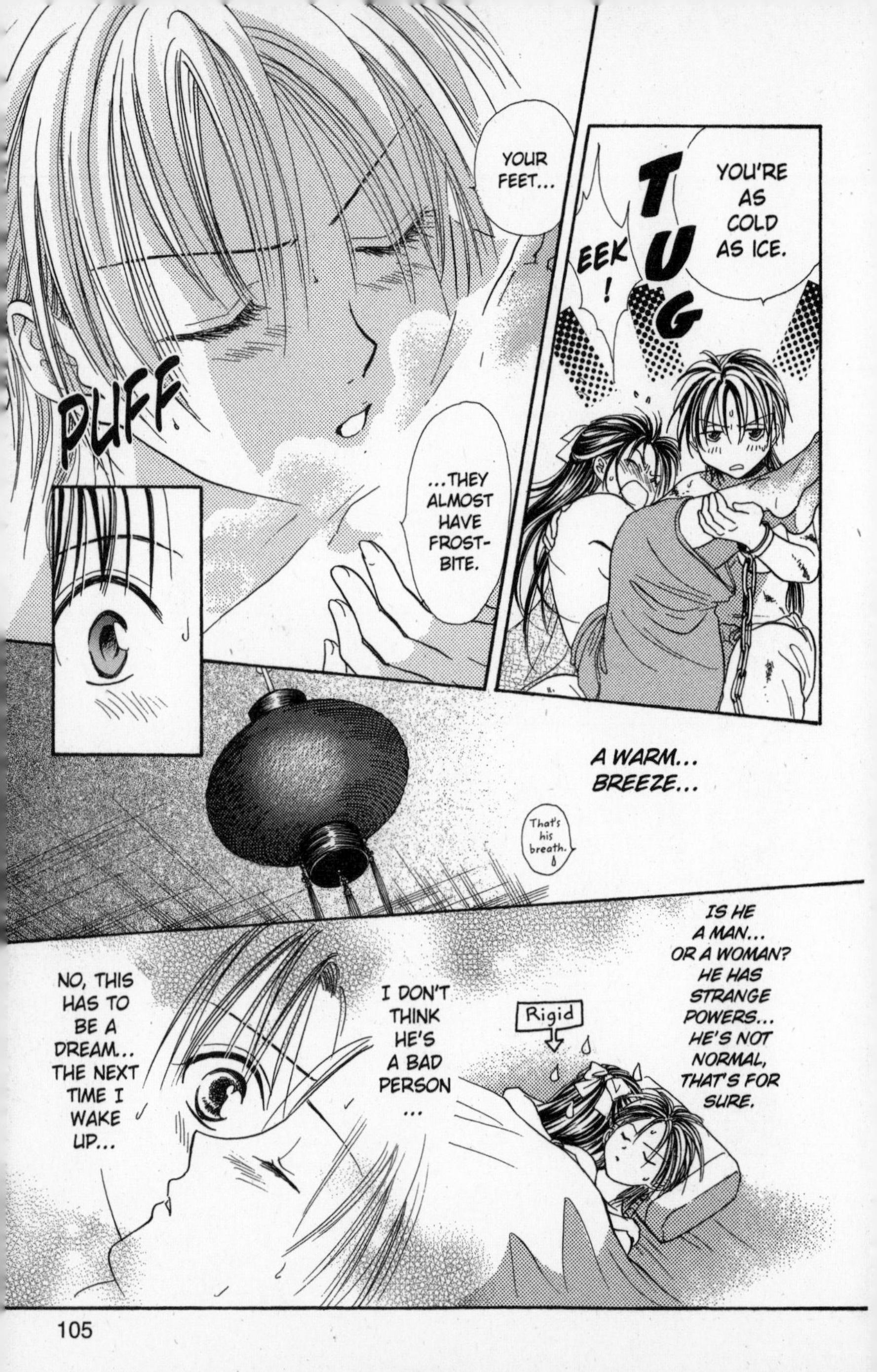
YOU'RE AS COLD AS ICE.
TUG
EEK!
YOUR FEET...
...THEY ALMOST HAVE FROST-BITE.
PUFF
A WARM... BREEZE...
That's his breath.
IS HE A MAN... OR A WOMAN? HE HAS STRANGE POWERS... HE'S NOT NORMAL, THAT'S FOR SURE.
Rigid
I DON'T THINK HE'S A BAD PERSON...
NO, THIS HAS TO BE A DREAM... THE NEXT TIME I WAKE UP...

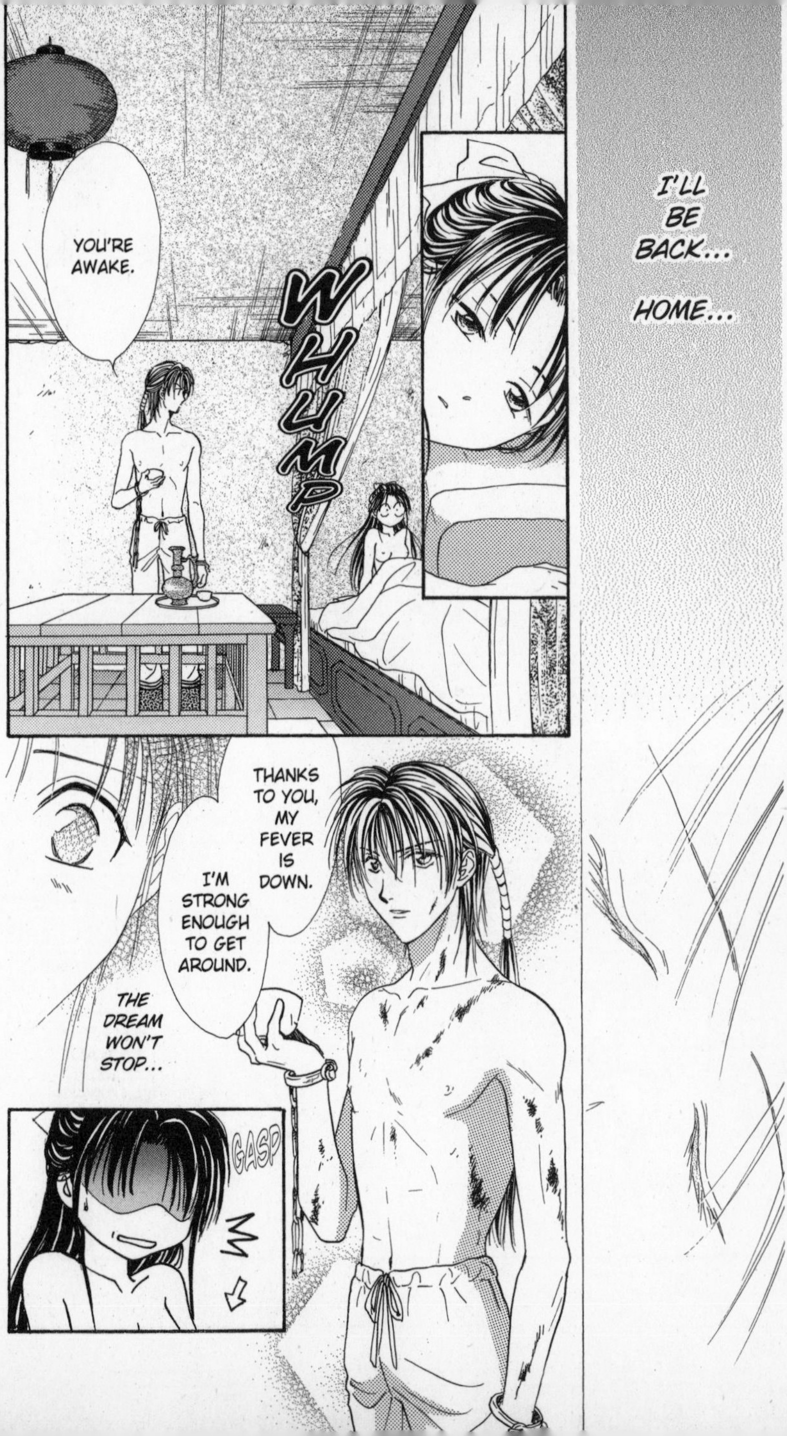
I'LL BE BACK...
HOME...
YOU'RE AWAKE.
WHUMP
THANKS TO YOU, MY FEVER IS DOWN.
I'M STRONG ENOUGH TO GET AROUND.
THE DREAM WON'T STOP...
GASP
M

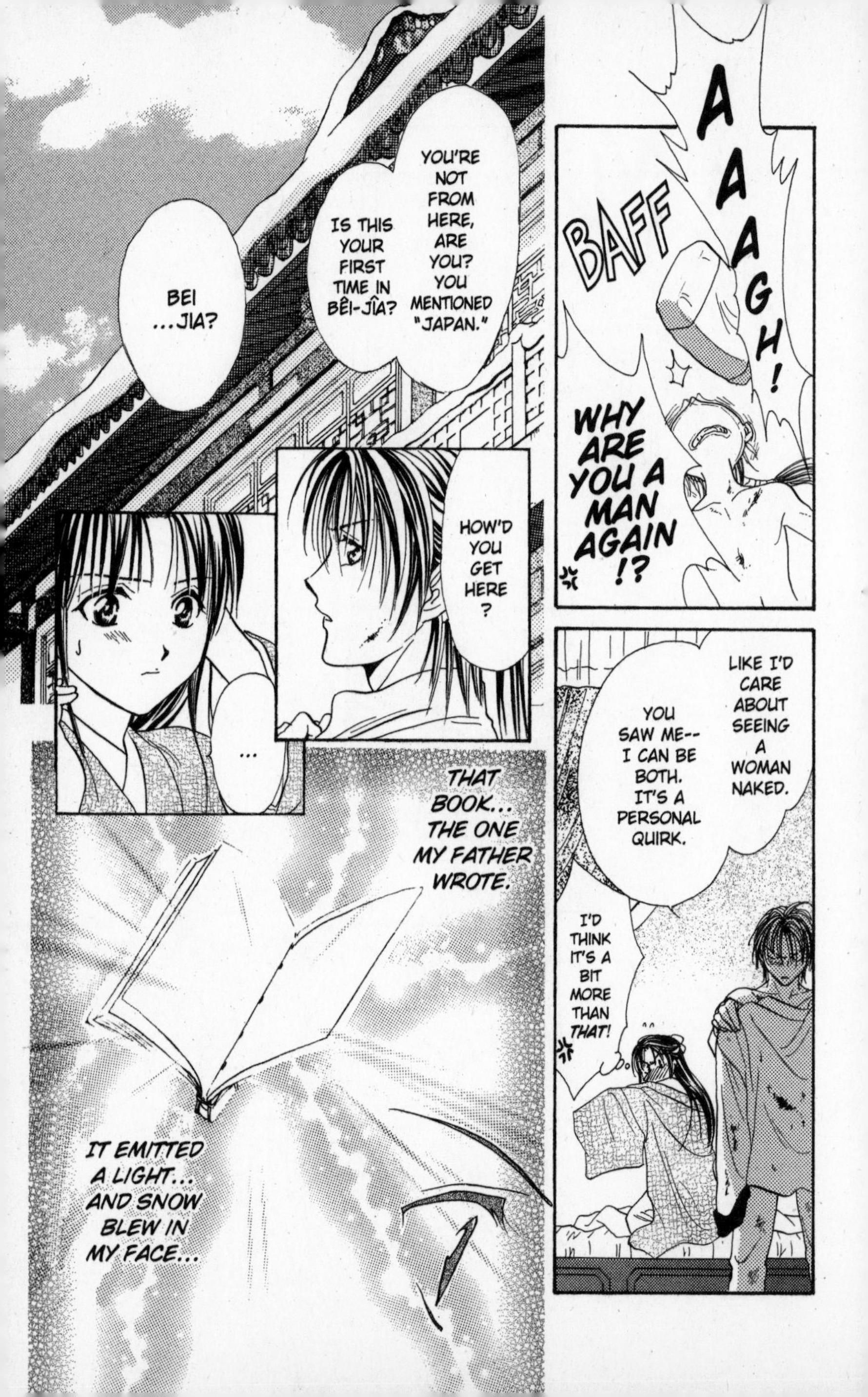
AAAAGH!
BAFF
WHY ARE YOU A MAN AGAIN!?
LIKE I'D CARE ABOUT SEEING A WOMAN NAKED.
YOU SAW ME-- I CAN BE BOTH. IT'S A PERSONAL QUIRK.
I'D THINK IT'S A BIT MORE THAN THAT!
YOU'RE NOT FROM HERE, ARE YOU? YOU MENTIONED "JAPAN."
IS THIS YOUR FIRST TIME IN BÊI-JÎA?
BEI ...JIA?
HOW'D YOU GET HERE?
...
THAT BOOK... THE ONE MY FATHER WROTE.
IT EMITTED A LIGHT... AND SNOW BLEW IN MY FACE...

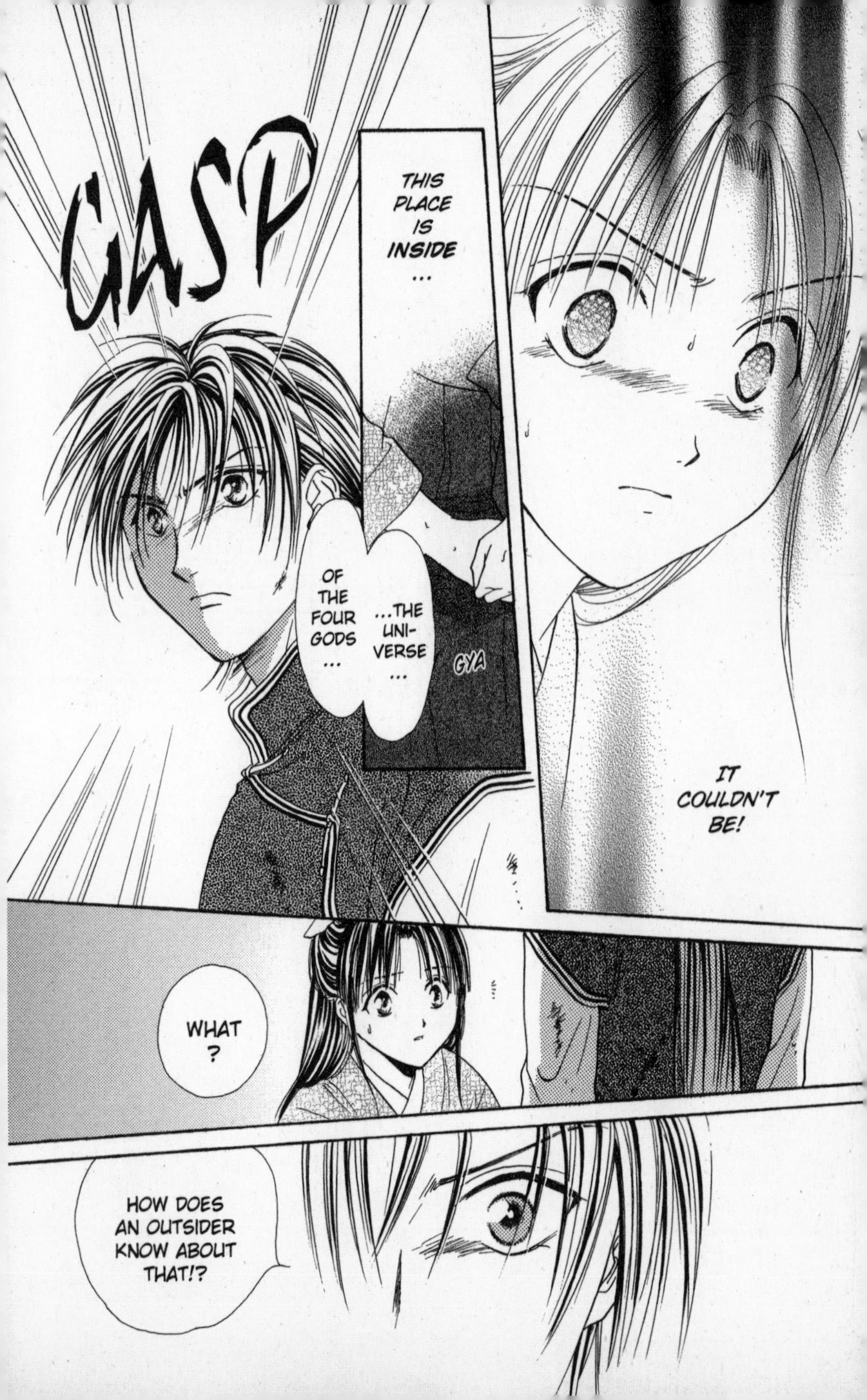
THIS PLACE IS INSIDE ...
...THE UNIVERSE ...
OF THE FOUR GODS ...
GYA
IT COULDN'T BE!
GASP
WHAT?
HOW DOES AN OUTSIDER KNOW ABOUT THAT!?

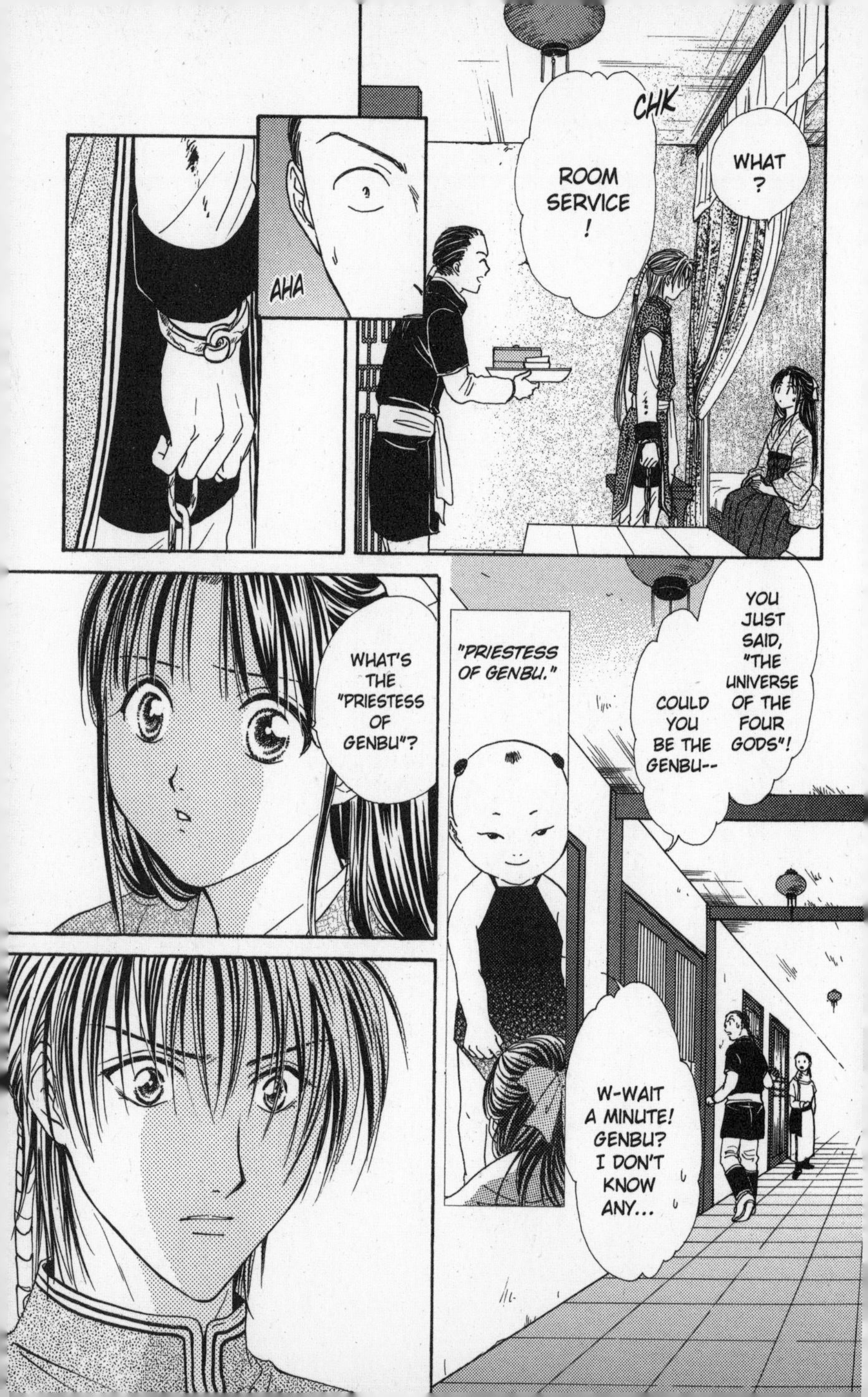
CHK
ROOM SERVICE!
WHAT?
AHA
YOU JUST SAID, "THE UNIVERSE OF THE FOUR GODS"!
COULD YOU BE THE GENBU--
W-WAIT A MINUTE! GENBU? I DON'T KNOW ANY...
"PRIESTESS OF GENBU."
WHAT'S THE "PRIESTESS OF GENBU"?

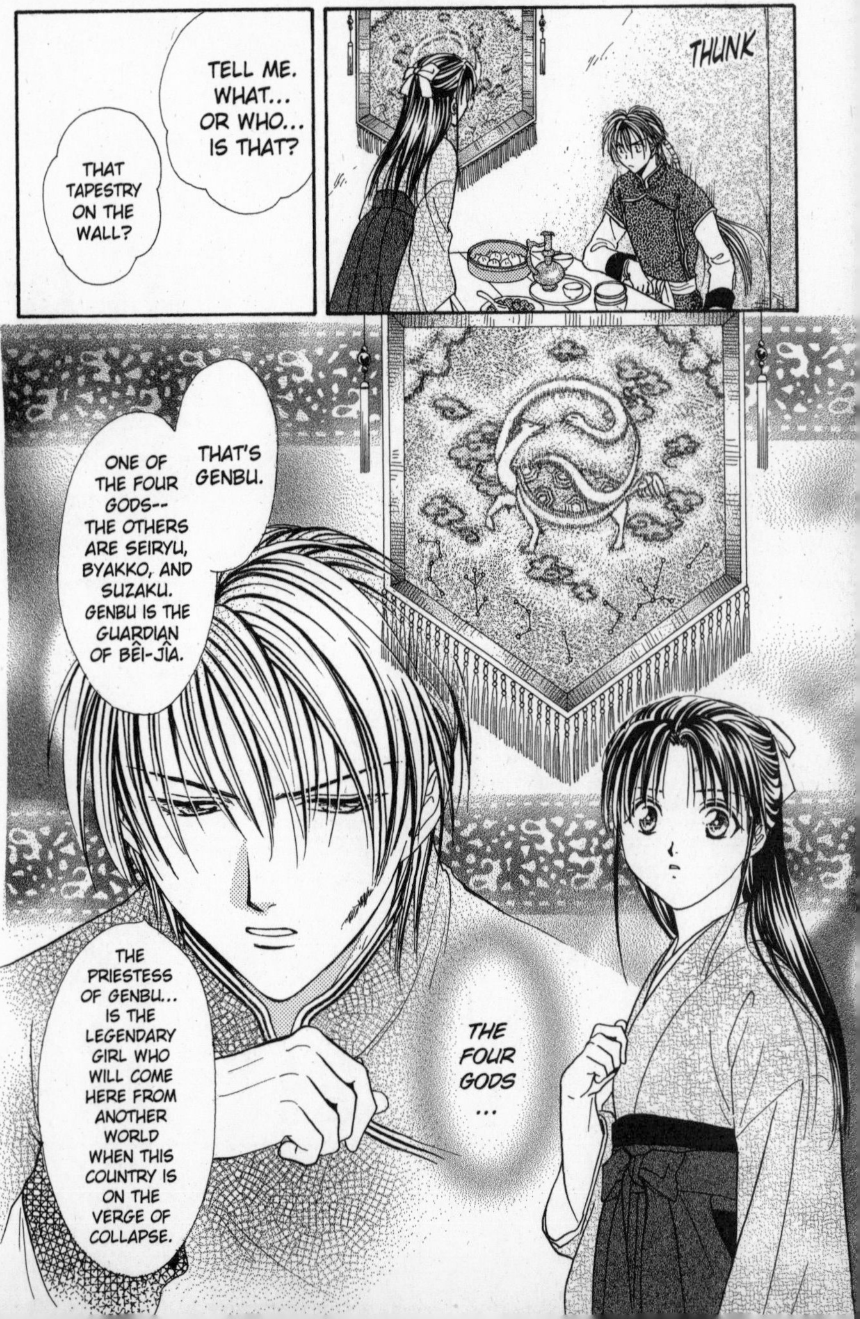
THUNK
TELL ME. WHAT... OR WHO... IS THAT?
THAT TAPESTRY ON THE WALL?
THAT'S GENBU.
ONE OF THE FOUR GODS-- THE OTHERS ARE SEIRYU, BYAKKO, AND SUZAKU. GENBU IS THE GUARDIAN OF BÊI-JÎA.
THE PRIESTESS OF GENBU... IS THE LEGENDARY GIRL WHO WILL COME HERE FROM ANOTHER WORLD WHEN THIS COUNTRY IS ON THE VERGE OF COLLAPSE.
THE FOUR GODS ...

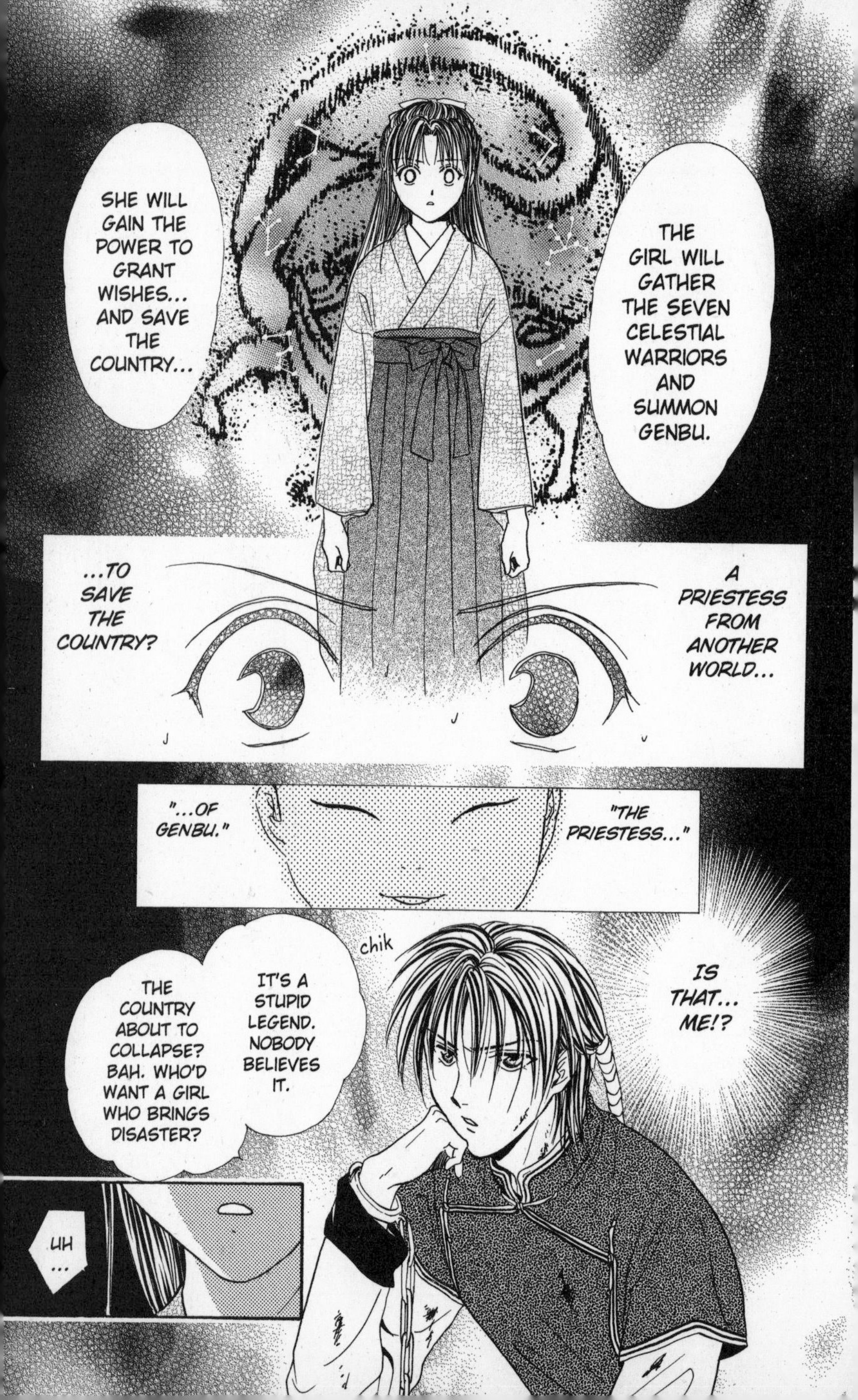
THE GIRL WILL GATHER THE SEVEN CELESTIAL WARRIORS AND SUMMON GENBU.
SHE WILL GAIN THE POWER TO GRANT WISHES... AND SAVE THE COUNTRY...
A PRIESTESS FROM ANOTHER WORLD...
...TO SAVE THE COUNTRY?
"THE PRIESTESS..."
"...OF GENBU."
IS THAT... ME!?
chik
IT'S A STUPID LEGEND. NOBODY BELIEVES IT.
THE COUNTRY ABOUT TO COLLAPSE? BAH. WHO'D WANT A GIRL WHO BRINGS DISASTER?
UH ...

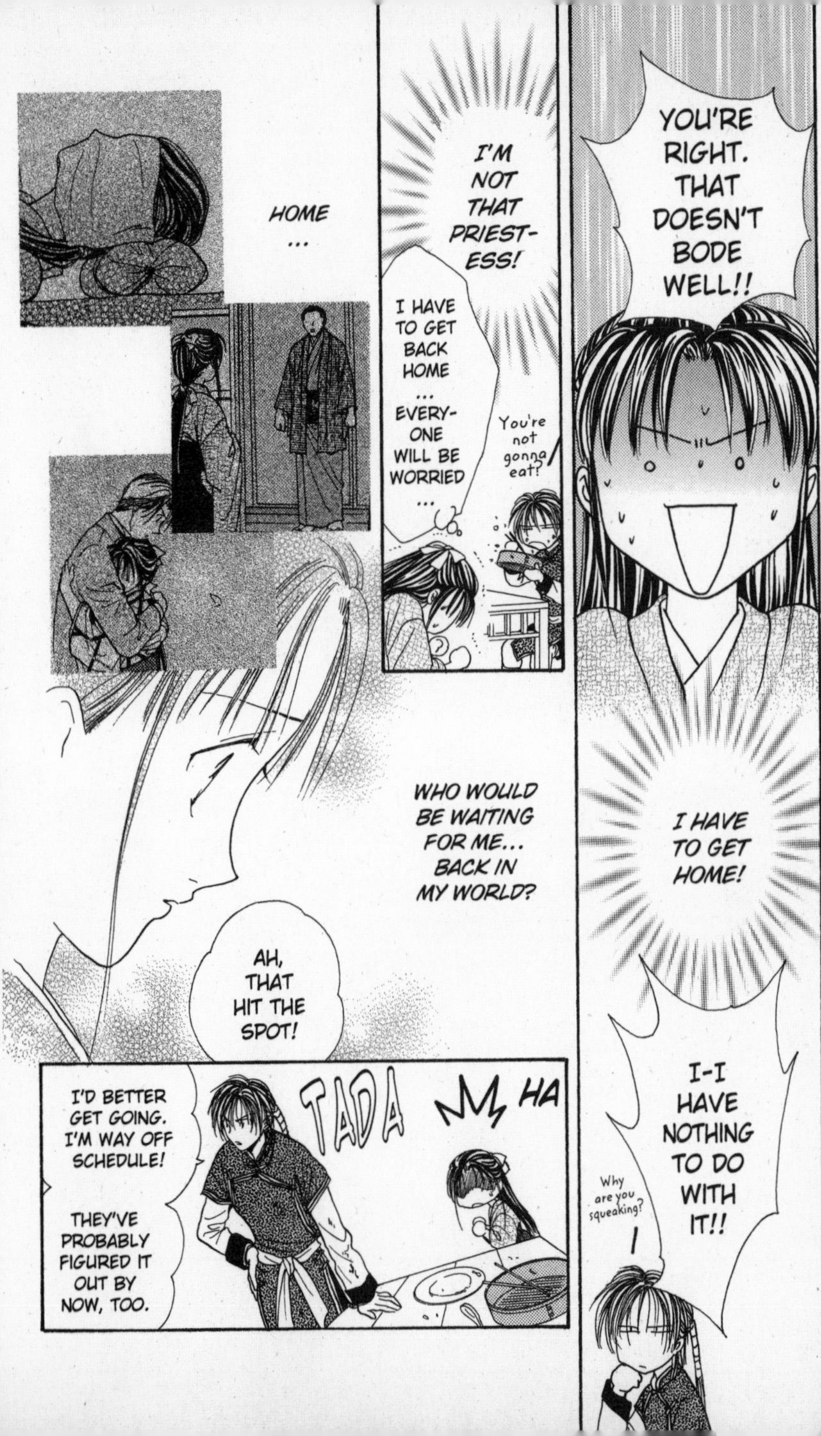
YOU'RE RIGHT. THAT DOESN'T BODE WELL!!
I HAVE TO GET HOME!
I-I HAVE NOTHING TO DO WITH IT!!
Why are you squeaking?
I'M NOT THAT PRIEST-ESS!
I HAVE TO GET BACK HOME ... EVERY-ONE WILL BE WORRIED ...
You're not gonna eat?
HOME ...
WHO WOULD BE WAITING FOR ME... BACK IN MY WORLD?
AH, THAT HIT THE SPOT!
HA
TADA
I'D BETTER GET GOING. I'M WAY OFF SCHEDULE!
THEY'VE PROBABLY FIGURED IT OUT BY NOW, TOO.

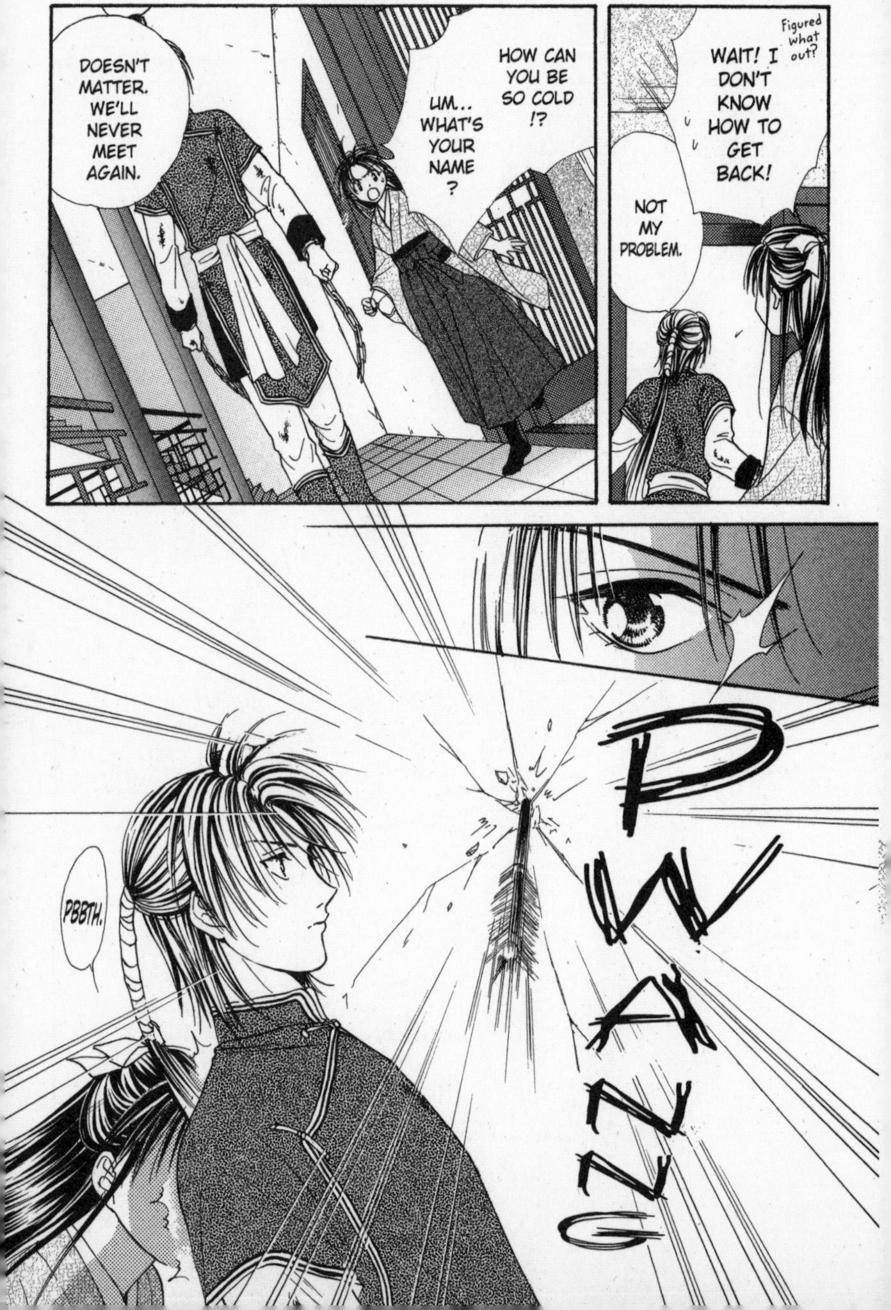
Figured what out?
WAIT! I DON'T KNOW HOW TO GET BACK!
NOT MY PROBLEM.
HOW CAN YOU BE SO COLD !?
UM... WHAT'S YOUR NAME ?
DOESN'T MATTER. WE'LL NEVER MEET AGAIN.
PWANNG
PBBTH.

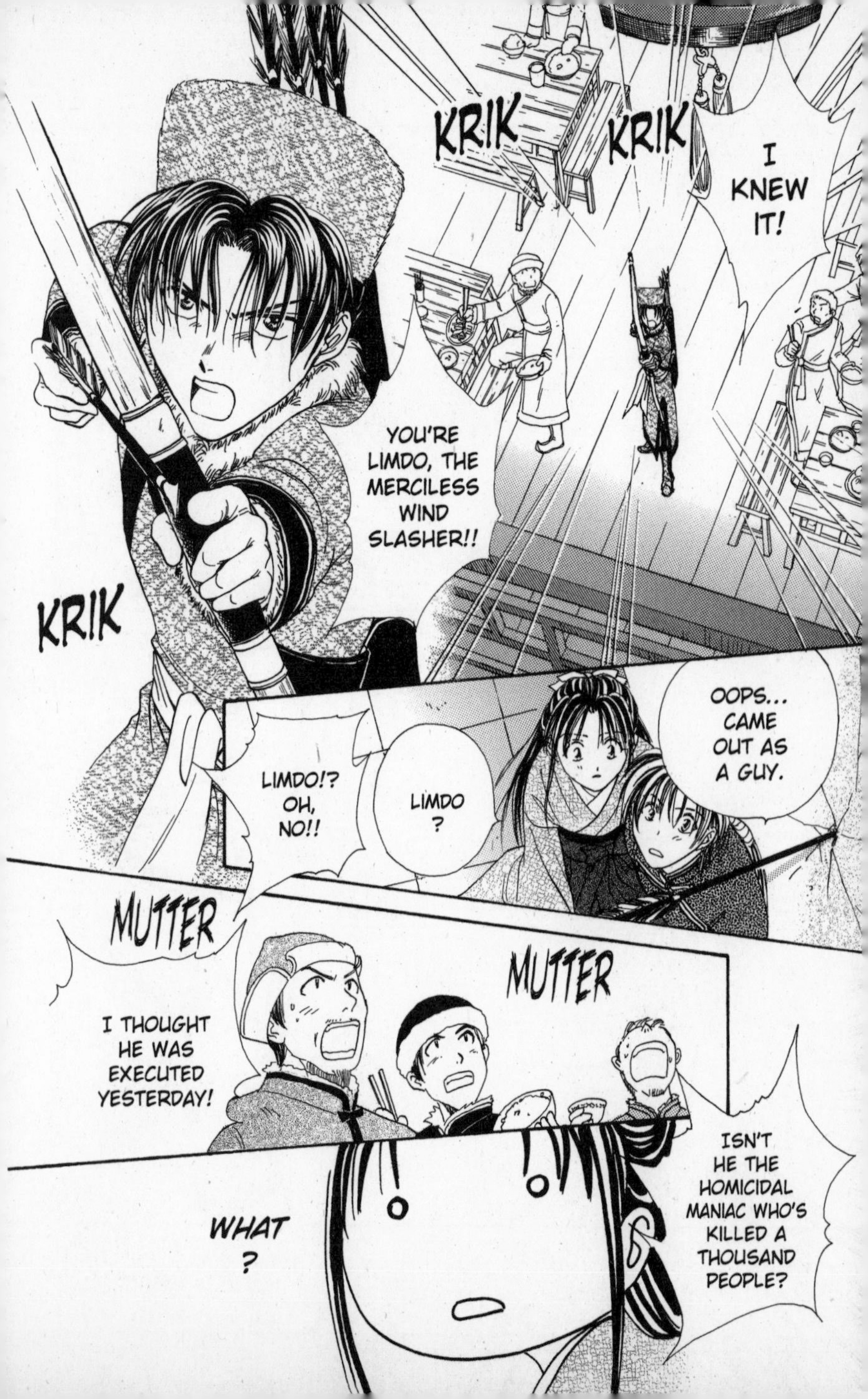
KRIK
KRIK
I KNEW IT!
YOU'RE LIMDO, THE MERCILESS WIND SLASHER!!
KRIK
OOPS... CAME OUT AS A GUY.
LIMDO ?
LIMDO!? OH, NO!!
MUTTER
MUTTER
I THOUGHT HE WAS EXECUTED YESTERDAY!
ISN'T HE THE HOMICIDAL MANIAC WHO'S KILLED A THOUSAND PEOPLE?
WHAT ?

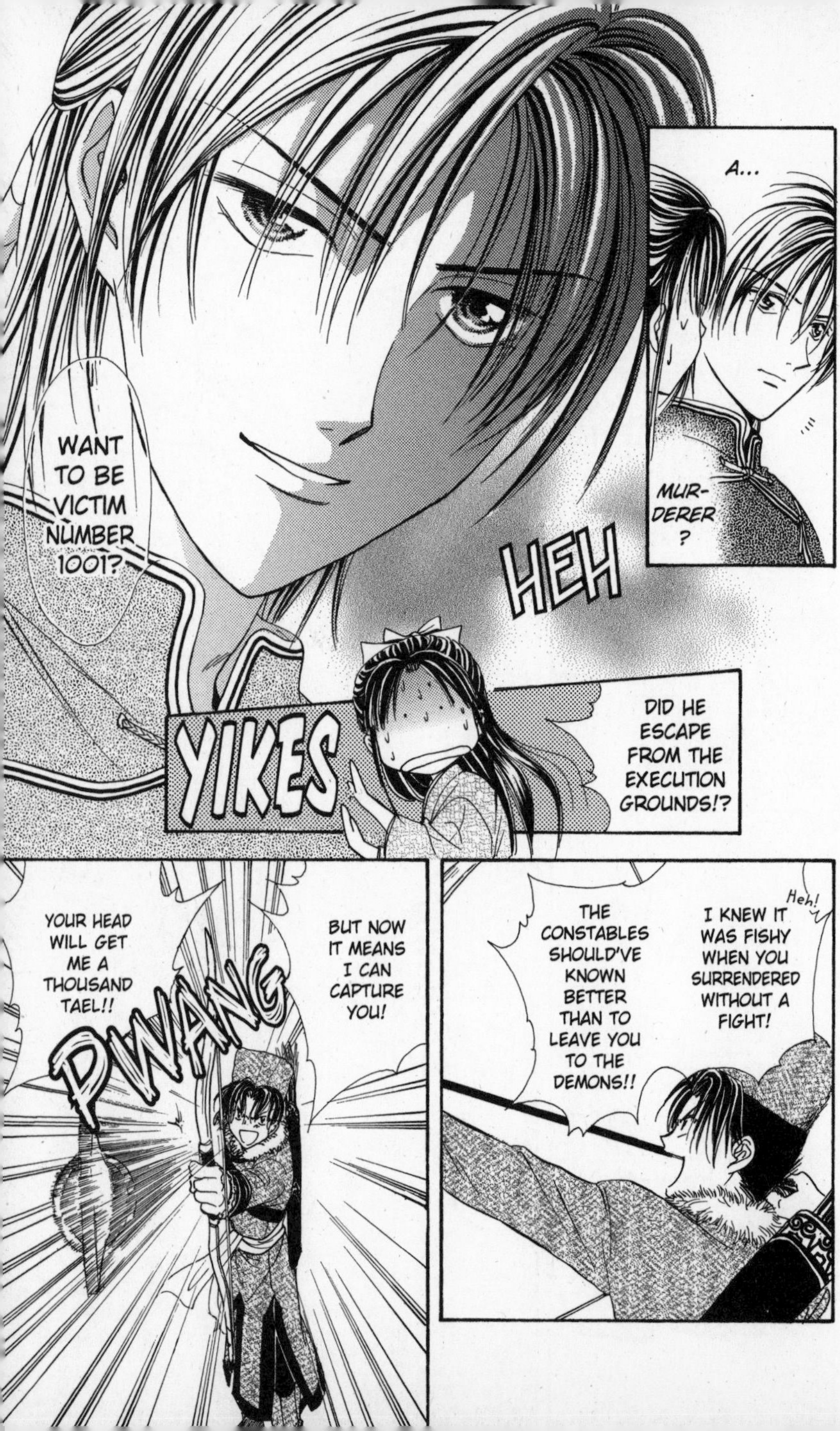
A...
MURDERER?
WANT TO BE VICTIM NUMBER 1001?
HEH
DID HE ESCAPE FROM THE EXECUTION GROUNDS!?
YIKES
Heh!
I KNEW IT WAS FISHY WHEN YOU SURRENDERED WITHOUT A FIGHT!
THE CONSTABLES SHOULD'VE KNOWN BETTER THAN TO LEAVE YOU TO THE DEMONS!!
BUT NOW IT MEANS I CAN CAPTURE YOU!
YOUR HEAD WILL GET ME A THOUSAND TAEL!!
DWANG

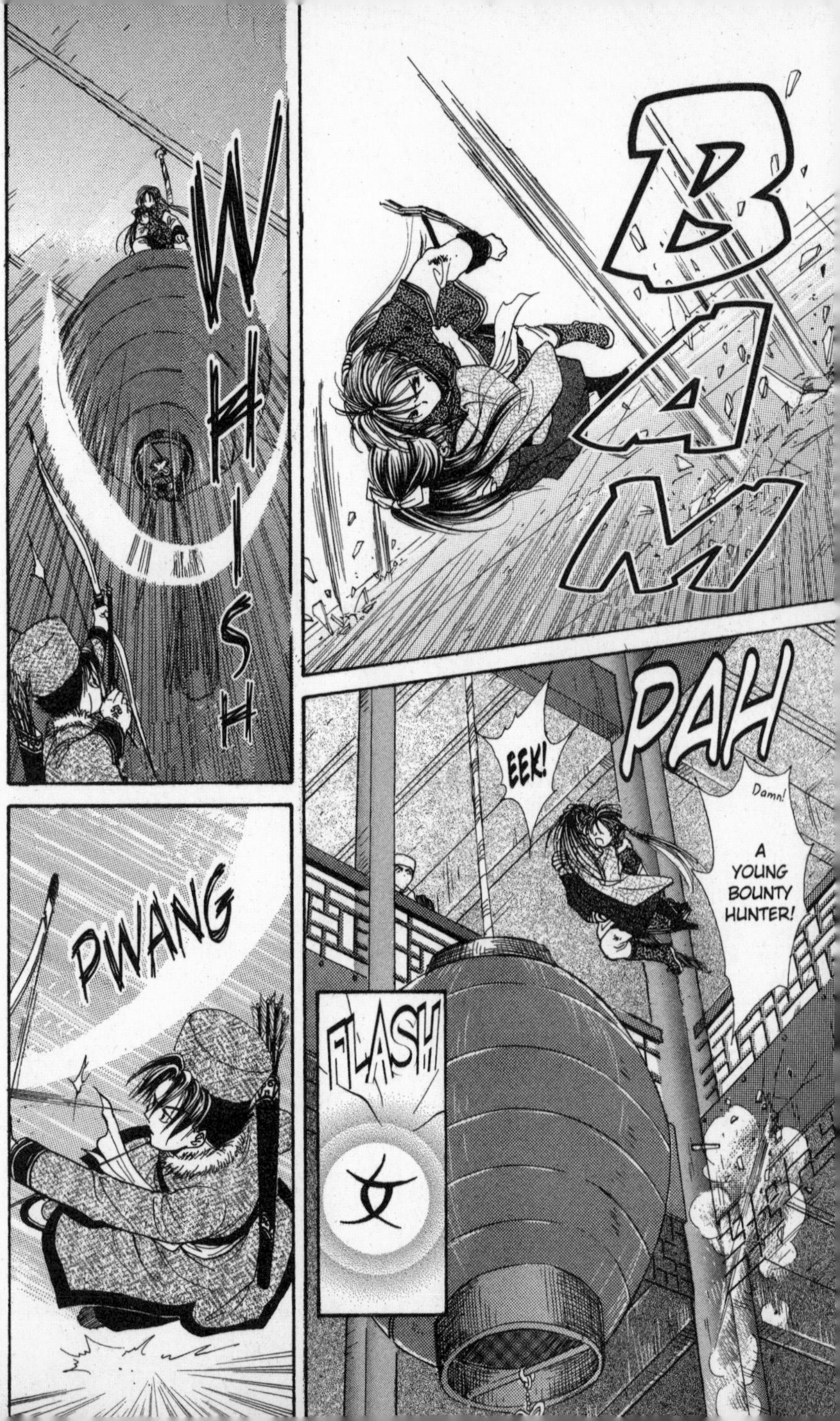
BAM
WHISH
PAH
EEK!
Damn!
A YOUNG BOUNTY HUNTER!
FLASH
PWANG

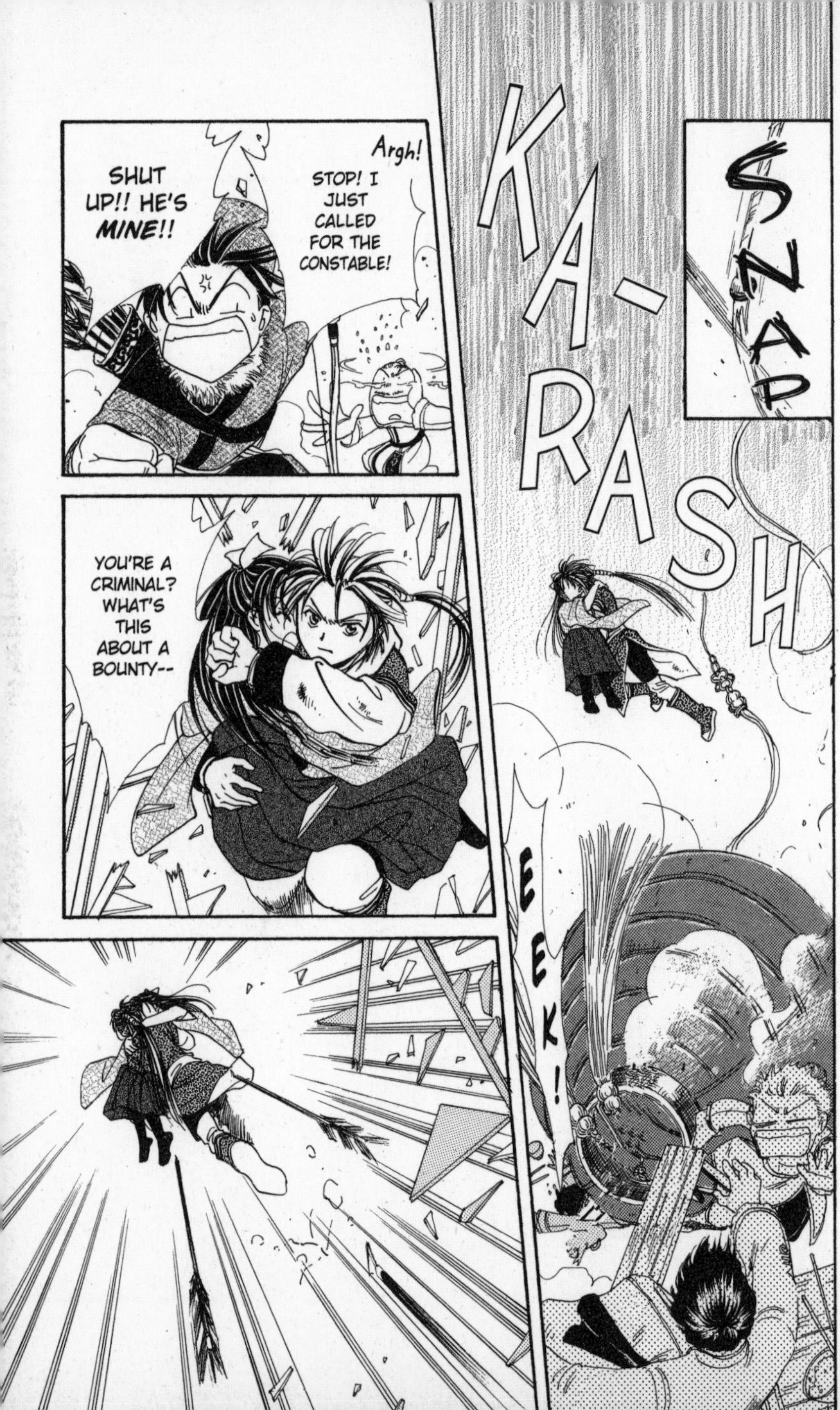
SNAP
KA-RASH
EEEK!
Argh!
STOP! I JUST CALLED FOR THE CONSTABLE!
SHUT UP!! HE'S *MINE*!!
YOU'RE A CRIMINAL? WHAT'S THIS ABOUT A BOUNTY--

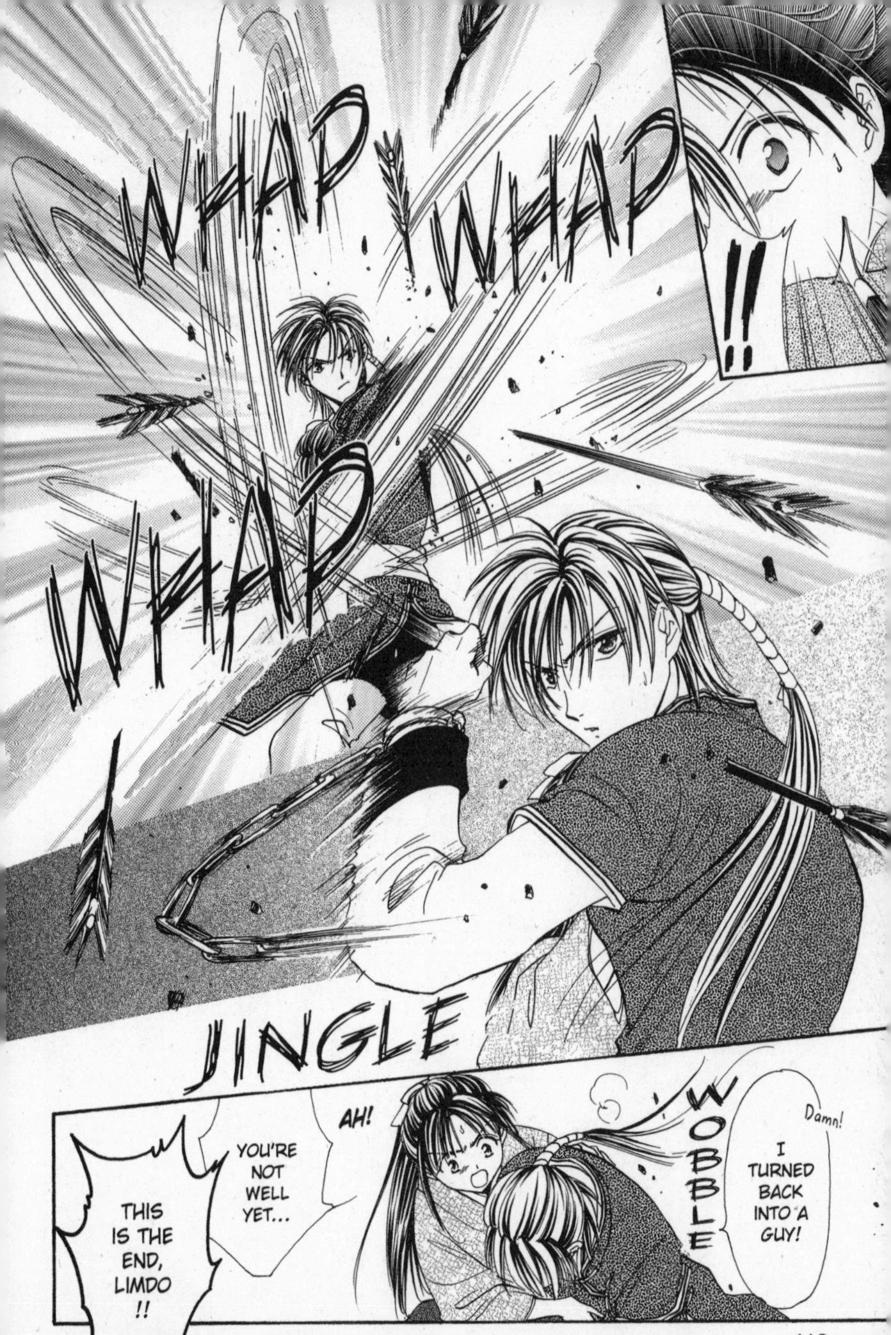
!!
WHAP
WHAP
WHAP
JINGLE
Damn!
I TURNED BACK INTO A GUY!
WOBBLE
AH!
YOU'RE NOT WELL YET...
THIS IS THE END, LIMDO !!

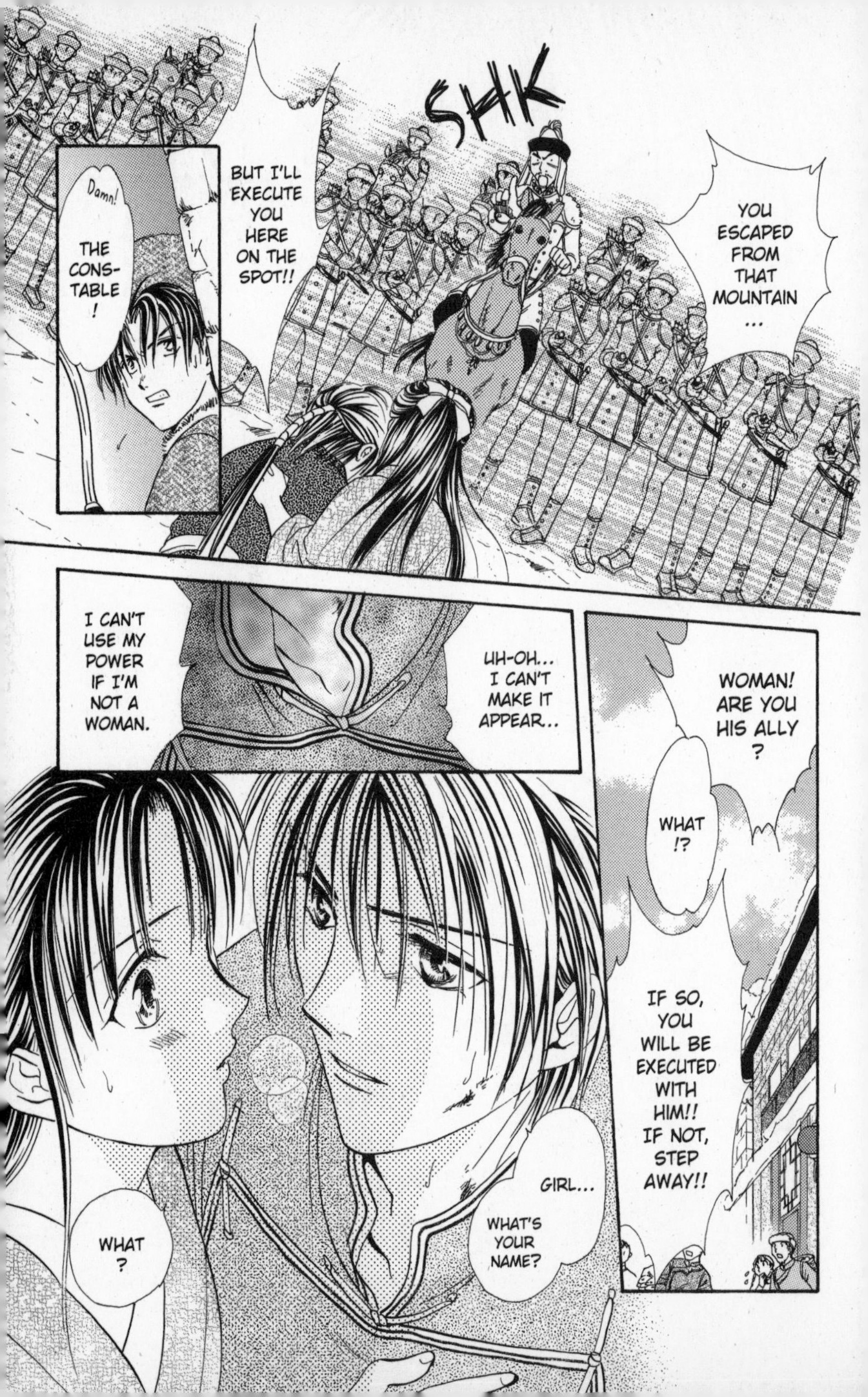
YOU ESCAPED FROM THAT MOUNTAIN...
SHK
BUT I'LL EXECUTE YOU HERE ON THE SPOT!!
Damn!
THE CONSTABLE!
WOMAN! ARE YOU HIS ALLY?
WHAT!?
IF SO, YOU WILL BE EXECUTED WITH HIM!! IF NOT, STEP AWAY!!
UH-OH... I CAN'T MAKE IT APPEAR...
I CAN'T USE MY POWER IF I'M NOT A WOMAN.
GIRL...
WHAT'S YOUR NAME?
WHAT?

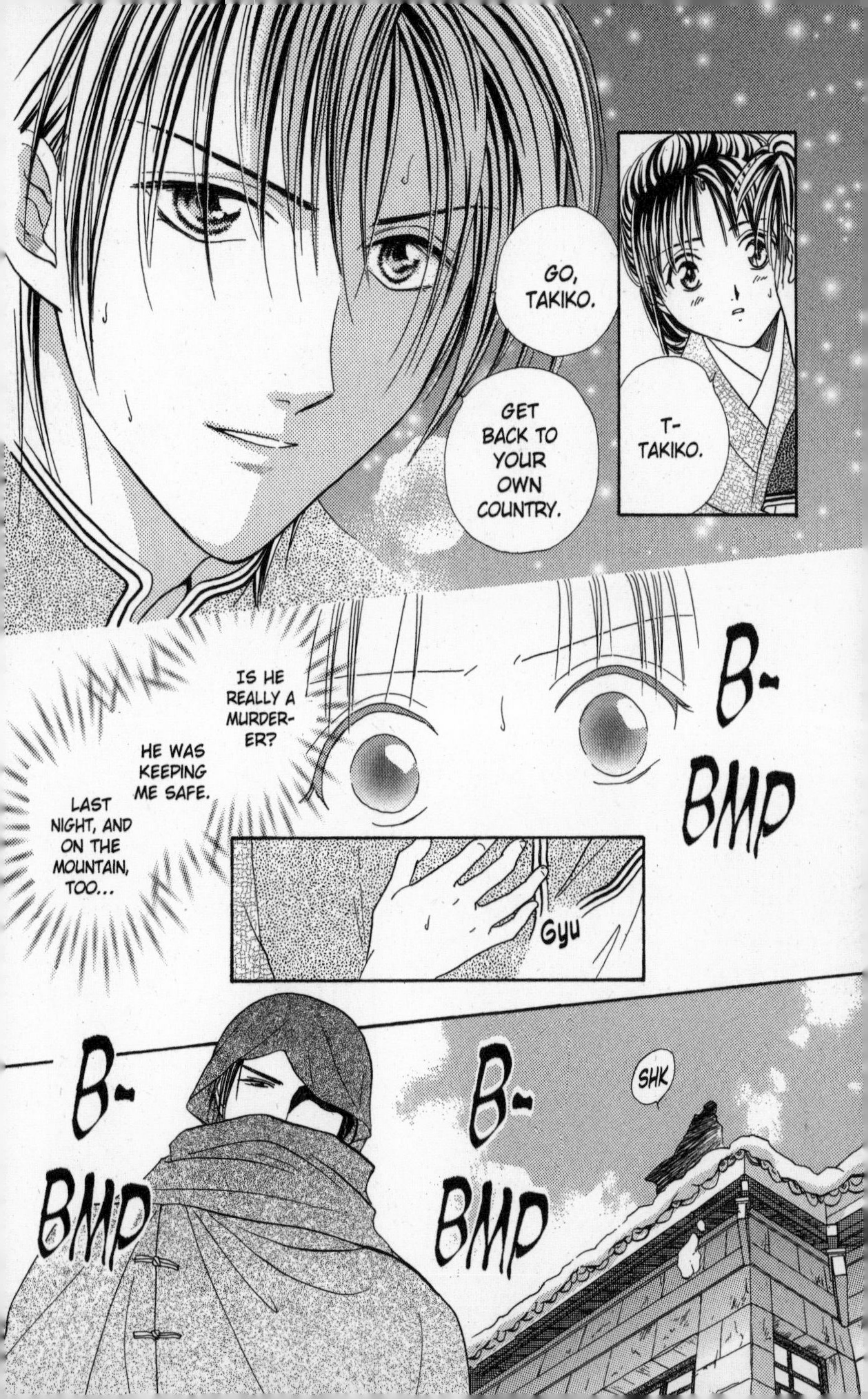
T-TAKIKO.
GO, TAKIKO.
GET BACK TO YOUR OWN COUNTRY.
B-BMP
IS HE REALLY A MURDERER?
HE WAS KEEPING ME SAFE.
LAST NIGHT, AND ON THE MOUNTAIN, TOO...
Gyu
SHK
B-BMP
B-BMP

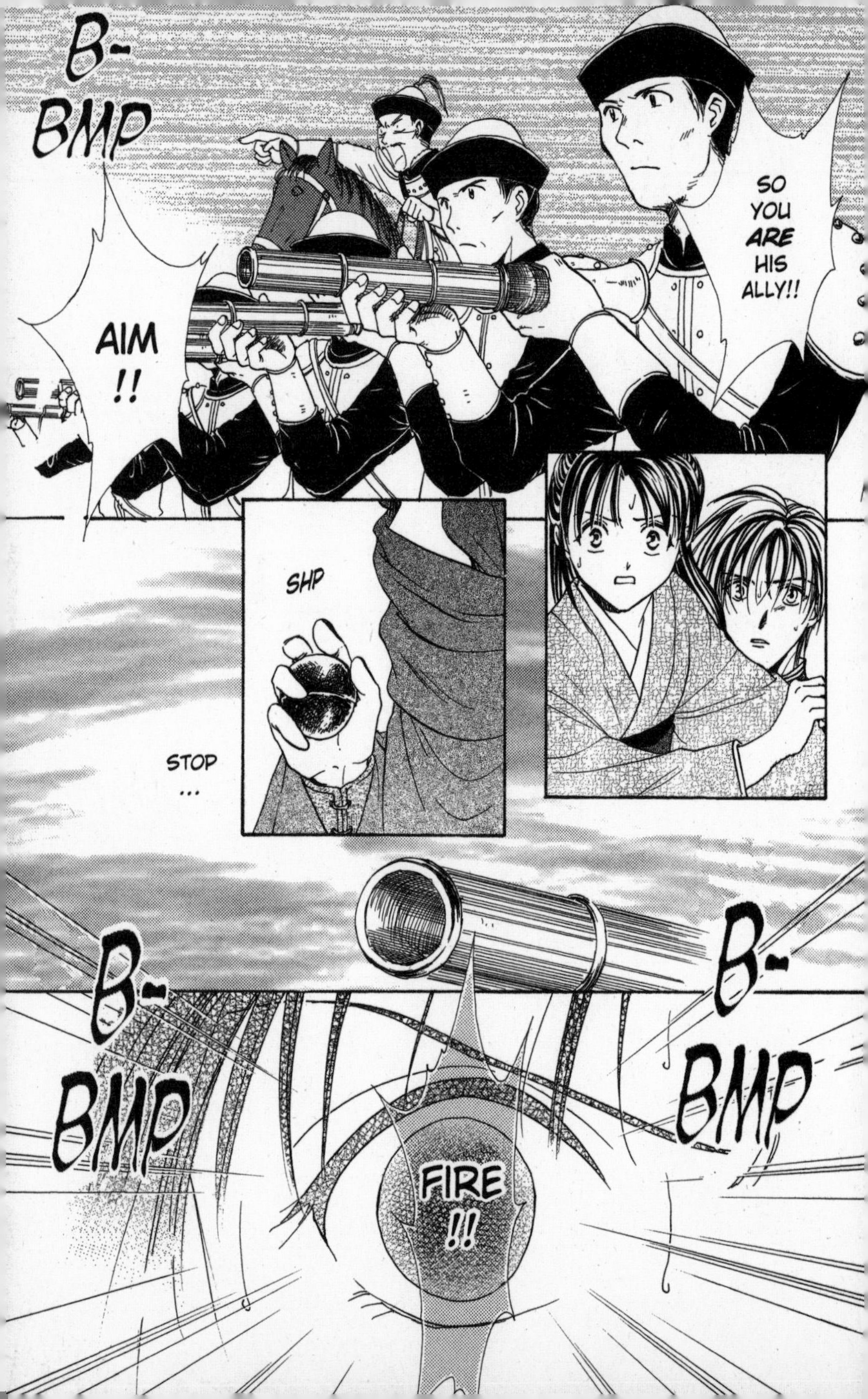
SO YOU ARE HIS ALLY!!
B-BMP
AIM !!
SHP
STOP ...
B-BMP
FIRE !!
B-BMP

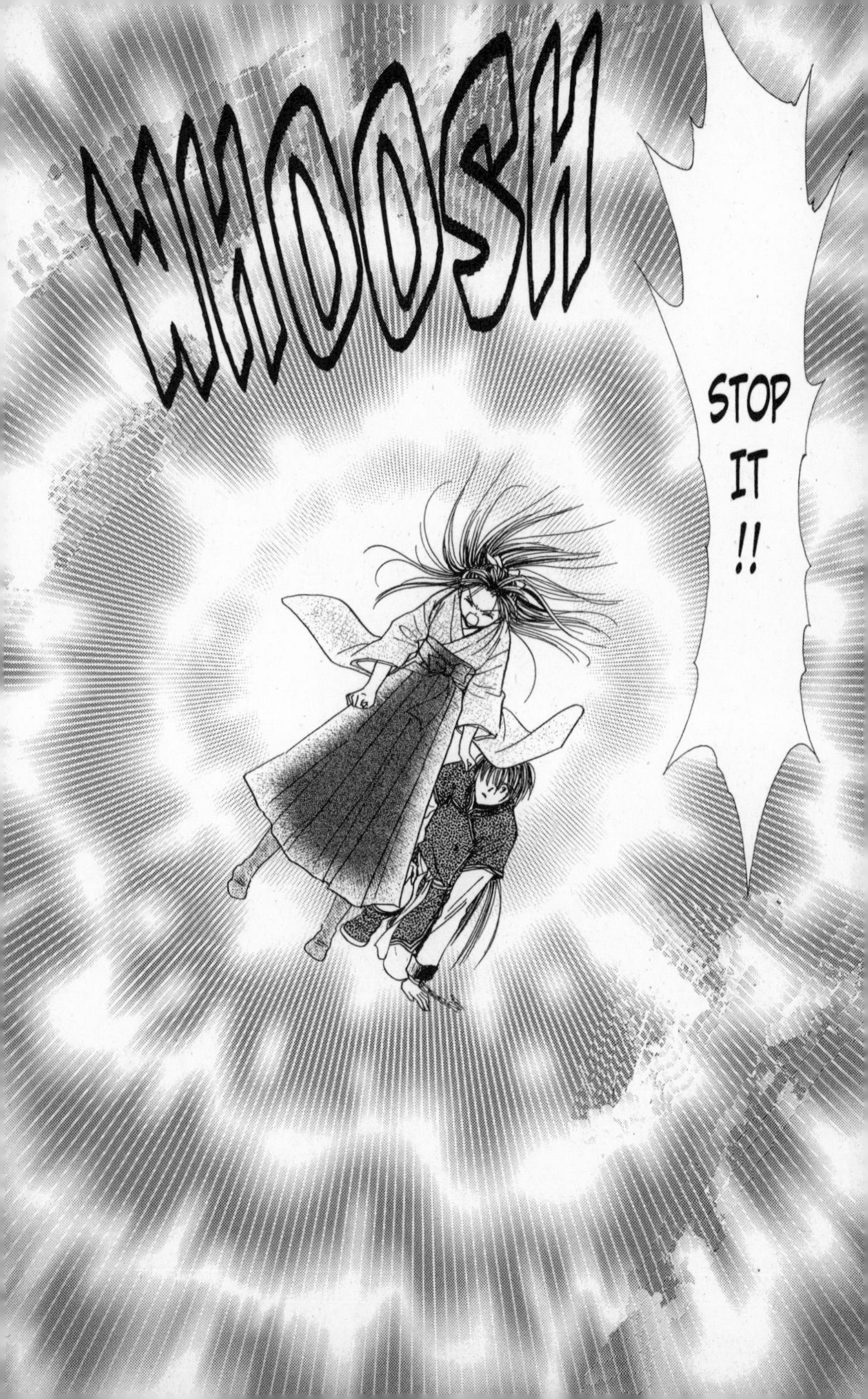
STOP IT !!
WHOOSH

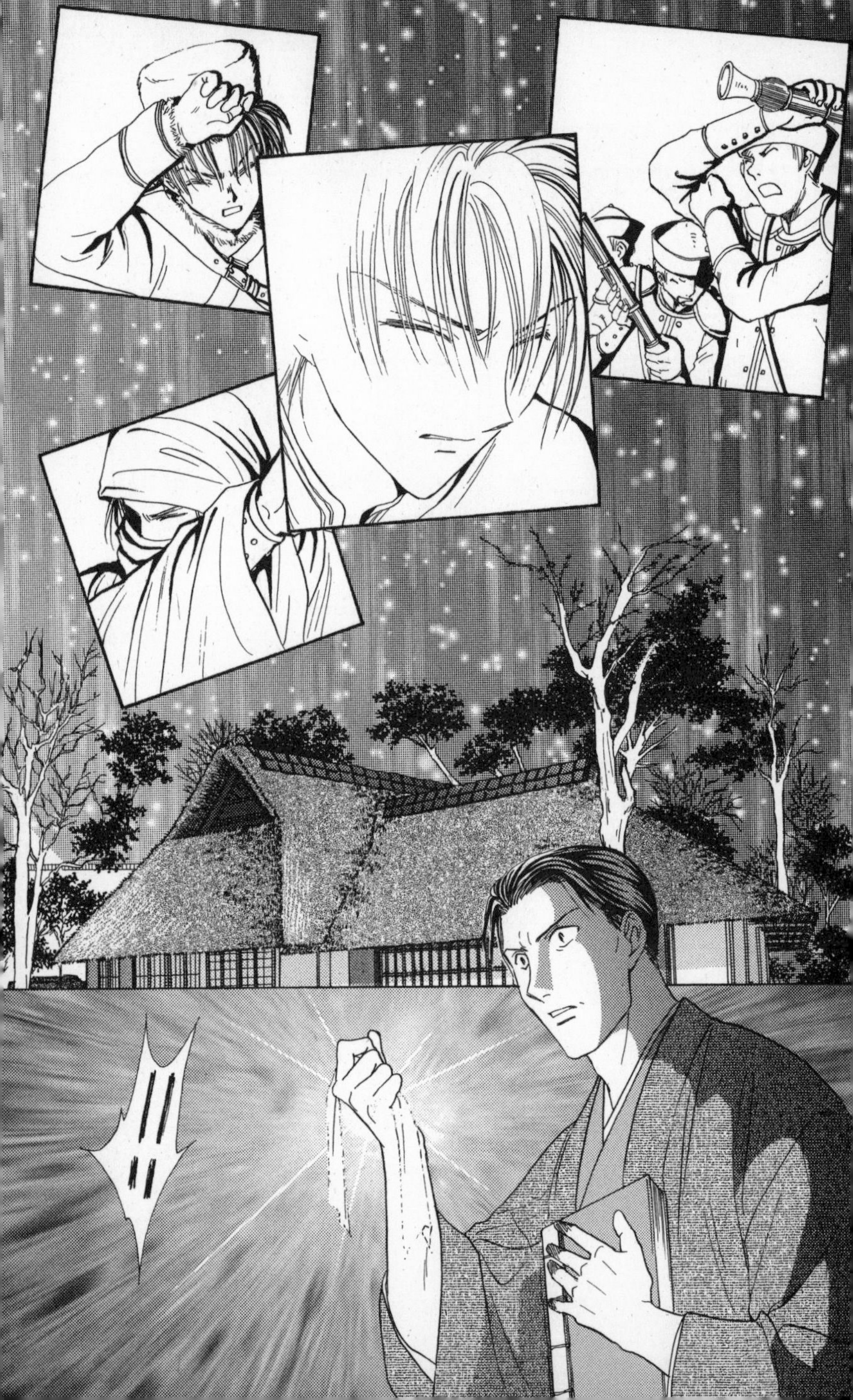

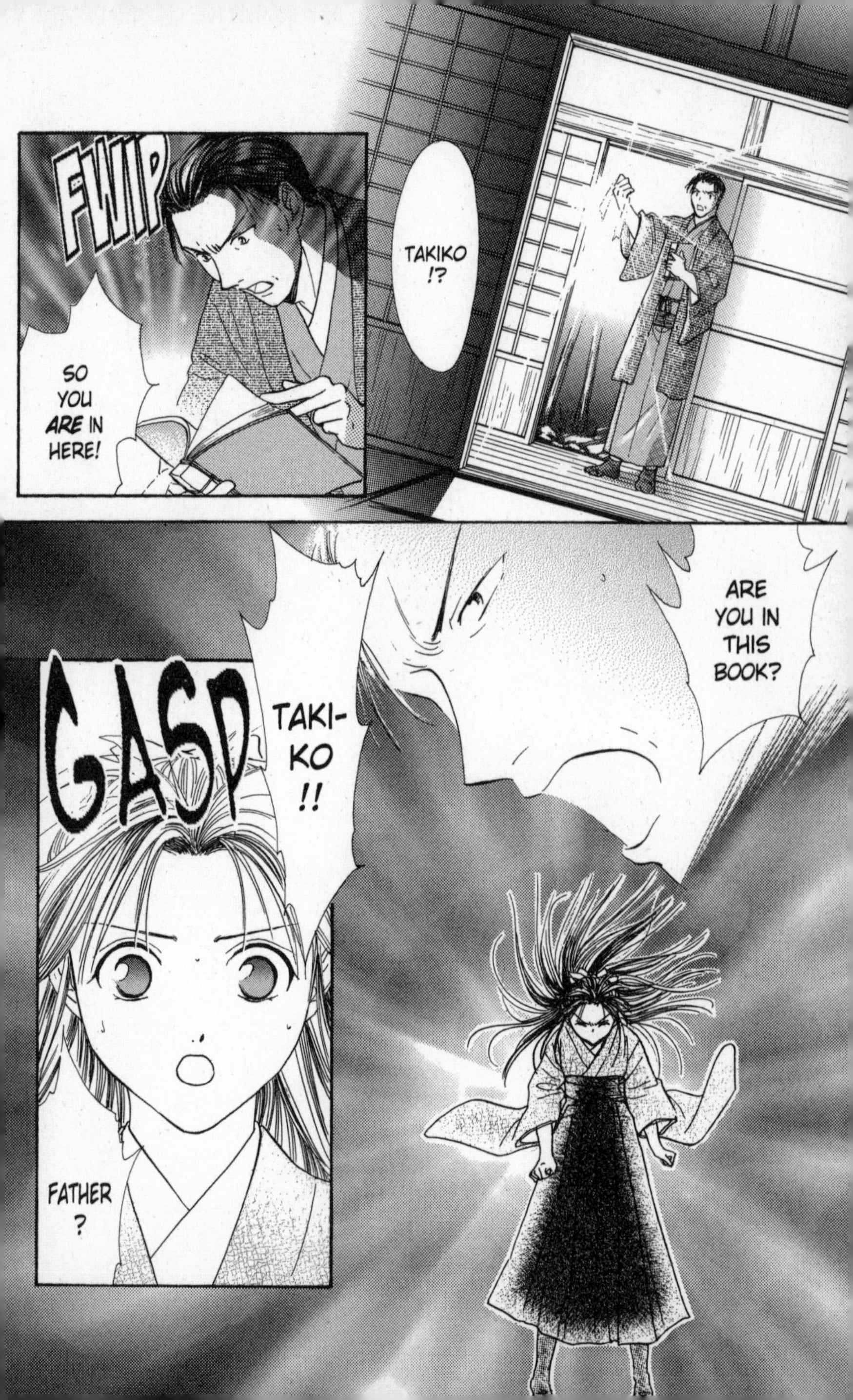
TAKIKO !?
FWIP
SO YOU ARE IN HERE!
ARE YOU IN THIS BOOK?
TAKI-KO !!
GASP
FATHER ?

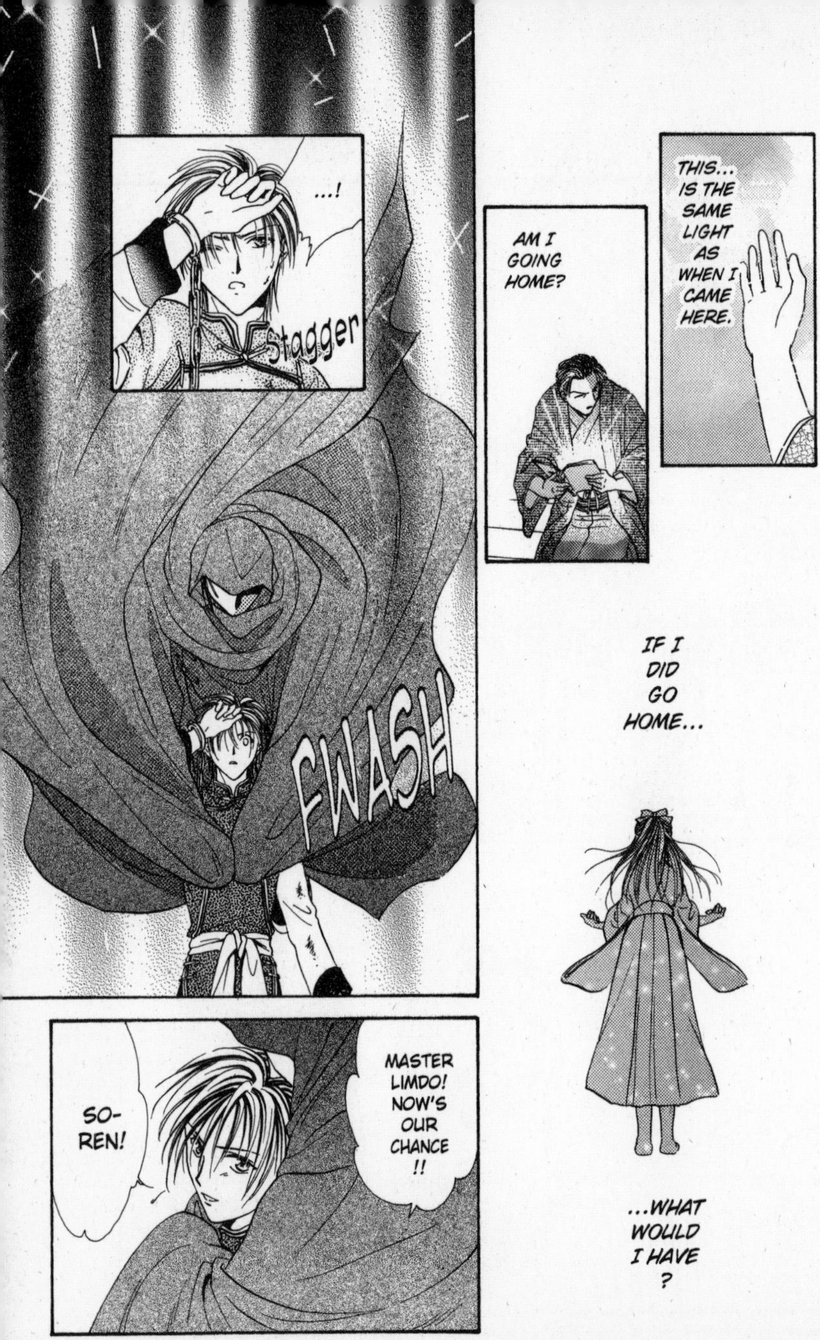
THIS... IS THE SAME LIGHT AS WHEN I CAME HERE.
AM I GOING HOME?
IF I DID GO HOME...
...WHAT WOULD I HAVE ?
...!
Stagger
FWASH
MASTER LIMDO! NOW'S OUR CHANCE !!
SO-REN!

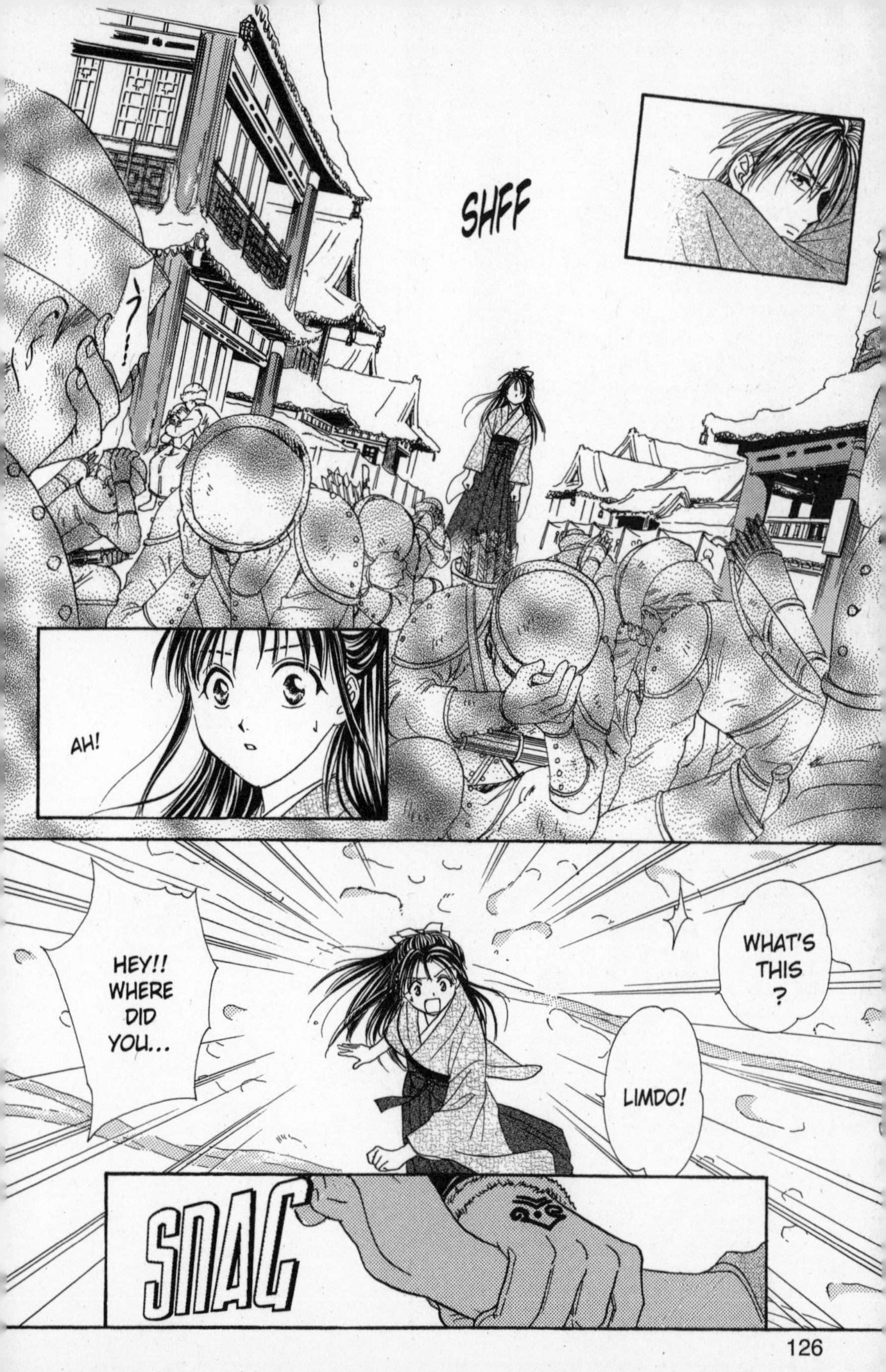
SHFF
?!...
AH!
WHAT'S THIS ?
LIMDO!
HEY!! WHERE DID YOU...
SNAG

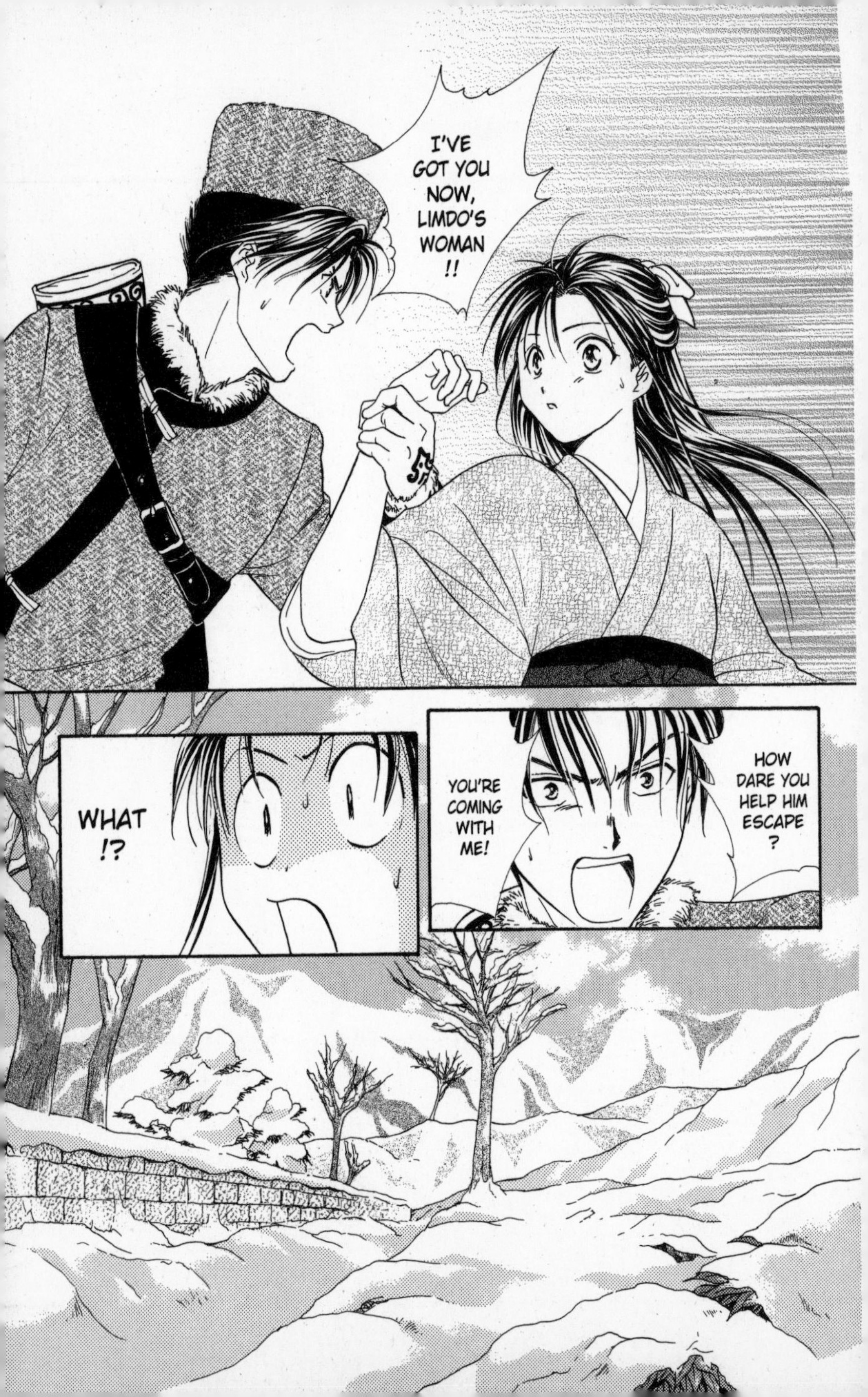
I'VE GOT YOU NOW, LIMDO'S WOMAN !!
HOW DARE YOU HELP HIM ESCAPE ?
YOU'RE COMING WITH ME!
WHAT !?

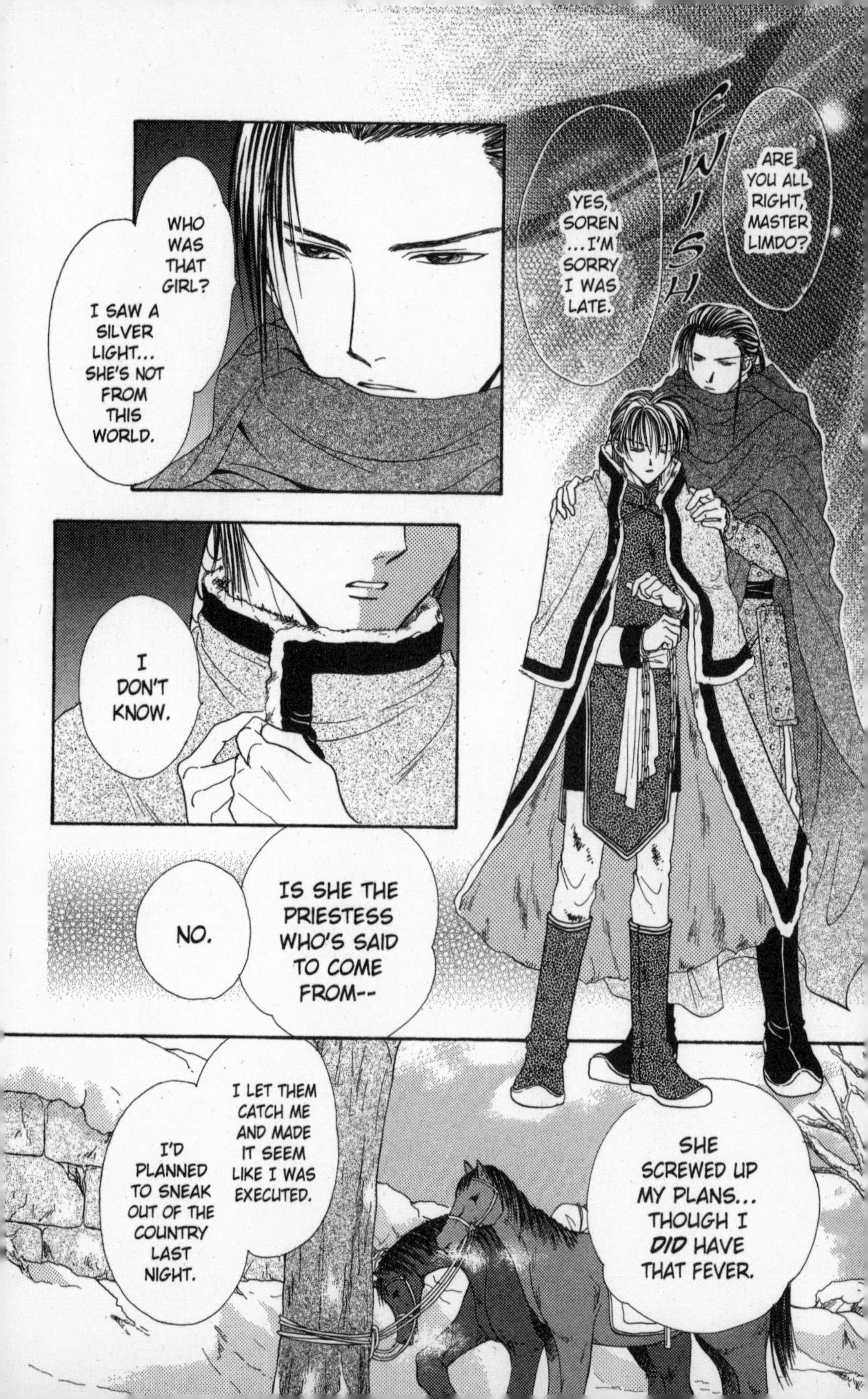
ARE YOU ALL RIGHT, MASTER LIMDO?
FWISH
YES, SOREN ...I'M SORRY I WAS LATE.
WHO WAS THAT GIRL?
I SAW A SILVER LIGHT... SHE'S NOT FROM THIS WORLD.
I DON'T KNOW.
IS SHE THE PRIESTESS WHO'S SAID TO COME FROM--
NO.
SHE SCREWED UP MY PLANS... THOUGH I *DID* HAVE THAT FEVER.
I LET THEM CATCH ME AND MADE IT SEEM LIKE I WAS EXECUTED.
I'D PLANNED TO SNEAK OUT OF THE COUNTRY LAST NIGHT.

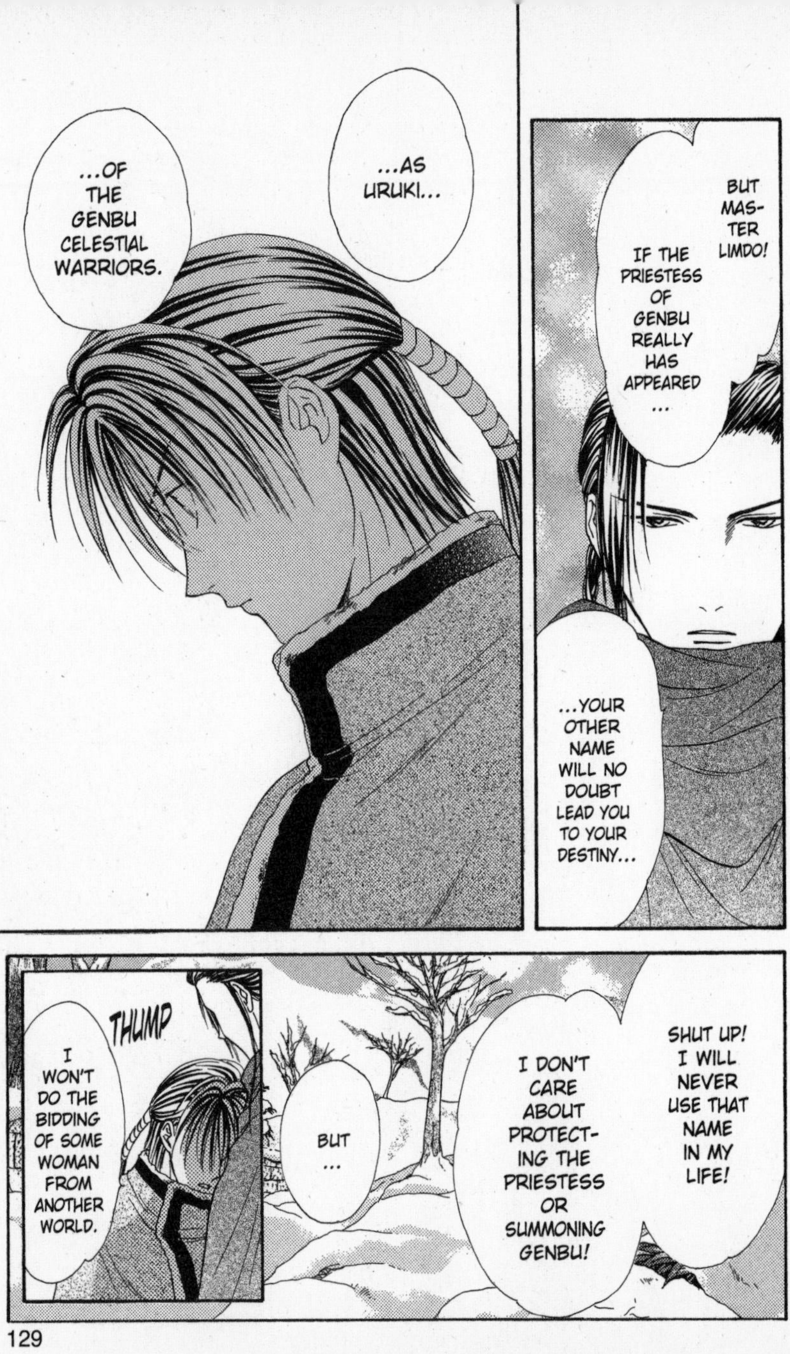
BUT MAS-TER LIMDO!
IF THE PRIESTESS OF GENBU REALLY HAS APPEARED ...
...YOUR OTHER NAME WILL NO DOUBT LEAD YOU TO YOUR DESTINY...
...AS URUKI...
...OF THE GENBU CELESTIAL WARRIORS.
SHUT UP! I WILL NEVER USE THAT NAME IN MY LIFE!
I DON'T CARE ABOUT PROTECT-ING THE PRIESTESS OR SUMMONING GENBU!
BUT ...
THUMP
I WON'T DO THE BIDDING OF SOME WOMAN FROM ANOTHER WORLD.

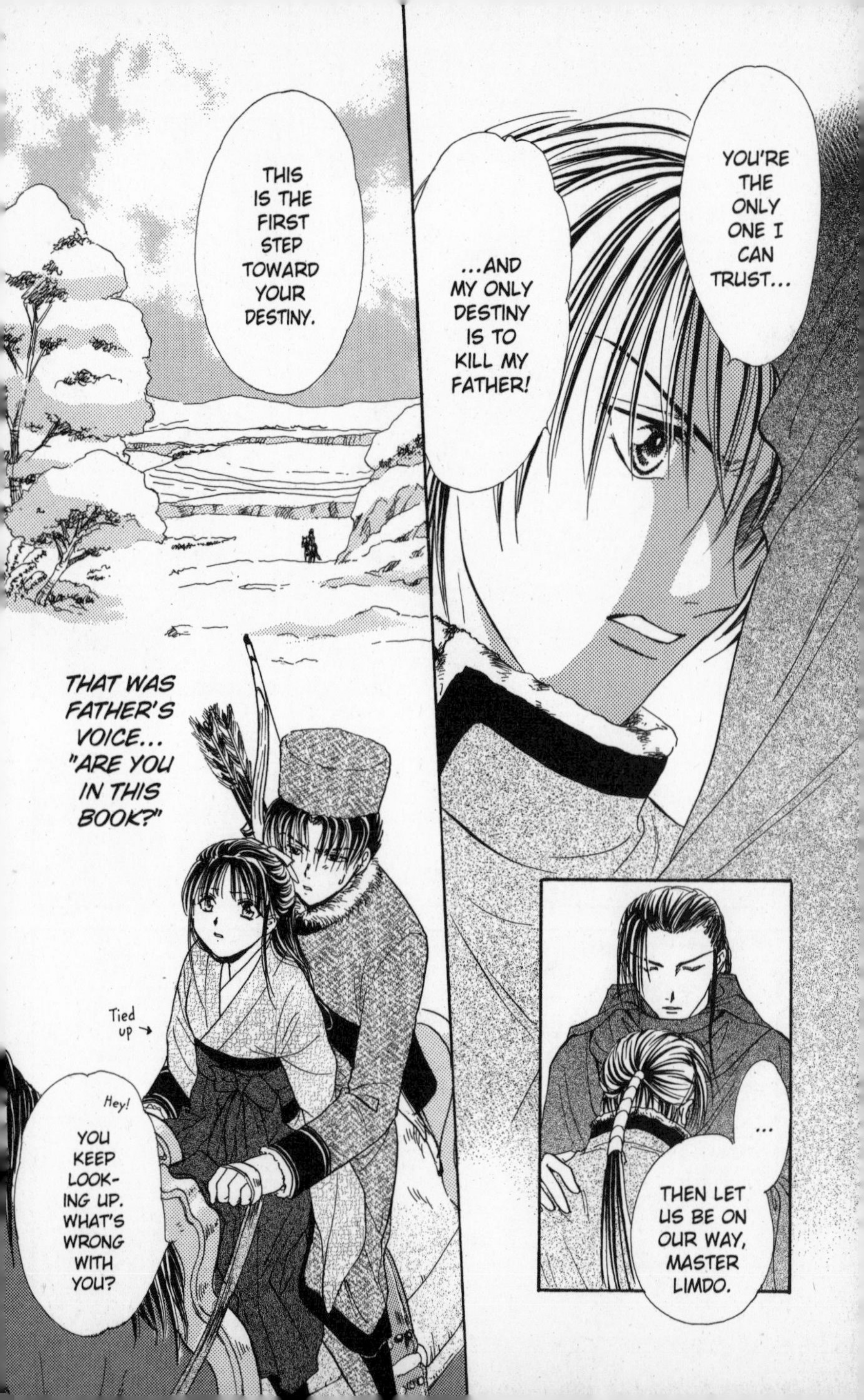
YOU'RE THE ONLY ONE I CAN TRUST...
...AND MY ONLY DESTINY IS TO KILL MY FATHER!
...
THEN LET US BE ON OUR WAY, MASTER LIMDO.
THIS IS THE FIRST STEP TOWARD YOUR DESTINY.
THAT WAS FATHER'S VOICE... "ARE YOU IN THIS BOOK?"
Tied up →
Hey!
YOU KEEP LOOK-ING UP. WHAT'S WRONG WITH YOU?

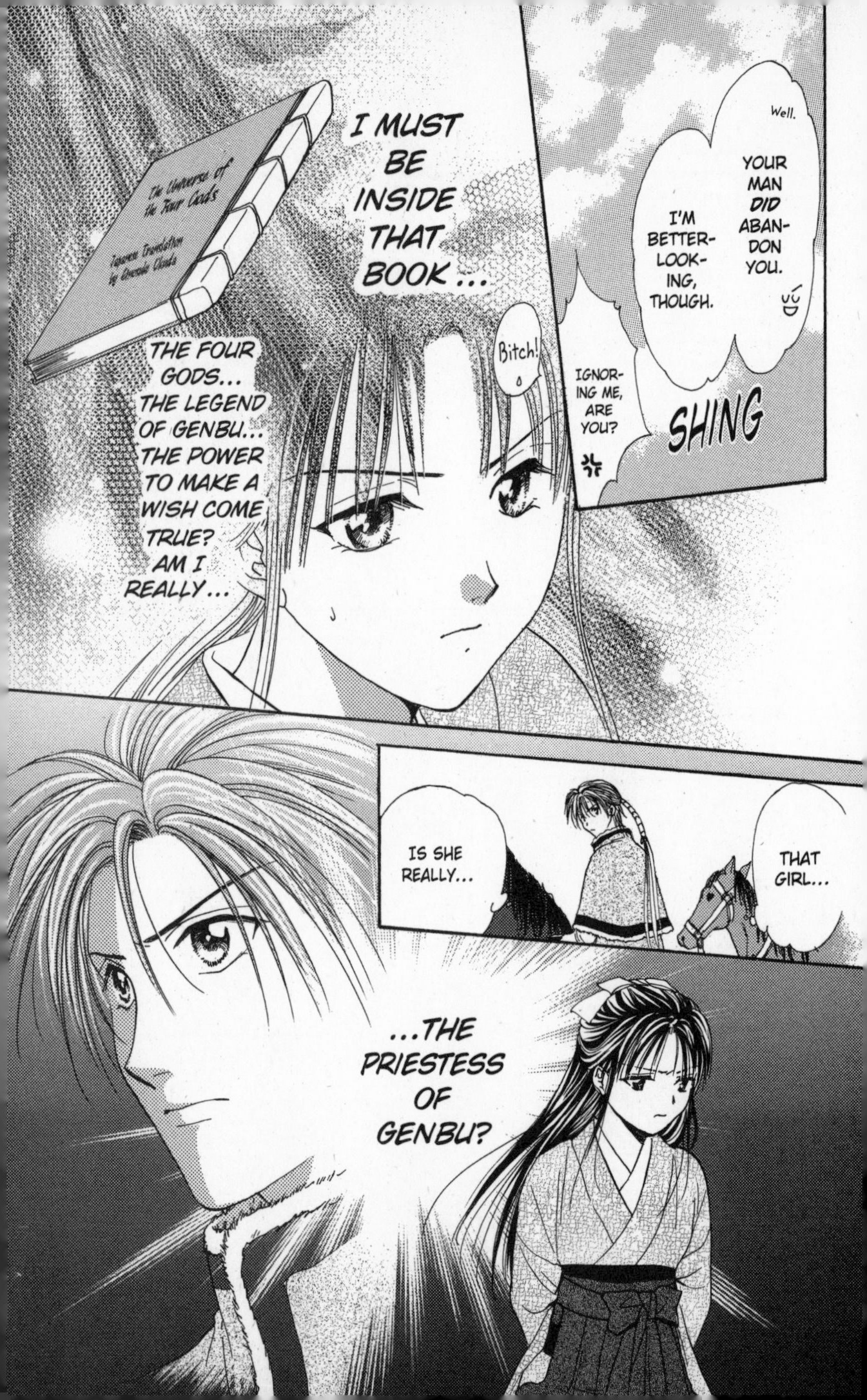

Well.
YOUR MAN DID ABANDON YOU.
I'M BETTER-LOOKING, THOUGH.
SHING
IGNORING ME, ARE YOU?
I MUST BE INSIDE THAT BOOK...
Bitch!
The Universe of the Four Gods
THE FOUR GODS... THE LEGEND OF GENBU... THE POWER TO MAKE A WISH COME TRUE? AM I REALLY...
THAT GIRL...
IS SHE REALLY...
...THE PRIESTESS OF GENBU?

I think the Genbu arc will seem a little bit more mature. There might be parts that will be very different from the first FY. But that's natural - the characters and the time period are different. I've matured ten years, too. :) Art, story, and presentation skills naturally change along with internal growth. I hope you can treat this as a totally new title... But there will still be guidelines I'll follow. I won't forget to include parts that will be a treat to my past readers, where they can go, "Hey! I remember that!" Kind of like *Star Wars: Episode 1.* The scene of silver light in chapter two, for example, was supposed to remind you of Miaka in *FY: SS,* chapter two. Will I be able to keep these guidelines, yet push the envelope and come up with new twists? It might be hard. I didn't think I'd be able to do this story way back then, so I wrote the stuff about Takiko and the Genbu story without much thought (bad girl!). When I read it over, I couldn't believe what I'd written! Will I be able to make everything consistent? I could change some things around to make them more interesting. It depends. Wouldn't it be more interesting to see the story evolve? :) If you've never read *FY:SS,* and don't mind some spoilers about how the Genbu story ends, then please buy the graphic novels (18 volumes), or the Perfect Collection edition (9 volumes), or the pocket-size edition currently being published (10 volumes). Please check out *Absolute Boyfriend Vol. 1,* too!

Write me at:

Yuu Watase
Fushigi Yugi Genbu Kaiden
c/o VIZ, LLC
P.O. Box 77010
San Francisco, CA
U.S.A

My friend's homepage:
http://homepage2.nifty.com/nankou/

I'm planning to sell my 15th anniversary book at the '03 Winter Comic Market. If my application gets accepted, that is.

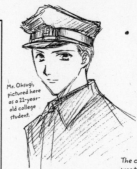

Mr. Ohsugi, pictured here as a 21-year-old college student.

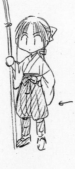

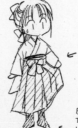

- Women in school back then were super smart (or rich). Some readers were dubious about girls in those days learning English. Au contraire, my friends. Not only English, but German, French, the works. People went to study abroad all the time. High school and college students were much more intellectual than they are now. The cream of the crop was the Imperial University of Tokyo (now Tokyo University). There were so many gifted people there that they were called "the top brains of Japan."

...I doubt this is the case now. They should learn from the past and study more. (Me, too.)

- Back then, people calculated age by the old Japanese system where you're "one year old" at birth, and one year is added each New Year's Day. You basically add two years to your age. So Takiko would technically be 19, but it would get confusing if I wrote that, so I'm going to stick with modern-style ages.

- The naginata was a popular sport in women's athletics. It was one of the sports encouraged for women in Meiji 43 (1910), along with swimming, archery, ice-skating, tennis, and Japanese badminton. It was added to the school curriculum in Taisho 5 (1916).

These are bloomers made by gathering the hakama hem; wide-spread usage began in Taisho 4 (1915).

- Athletics classes began in Meiji 2 (1869), but there were students who protested and withdrew from school in Meiji 15 (1882) because they were outraged that ladies were forced to swing their heads and spread their legs.

By the way, the hakama was originally clothing for men. This style of fashion was controversial at the time, because you were "dressing as a man." There was often a line of color along the hem. So stylish! Students sewed it on to signify which school they attended.

Boots were in style in the first year of Taisho. In mid-Taisho, black socks and black shoes were in vogue.

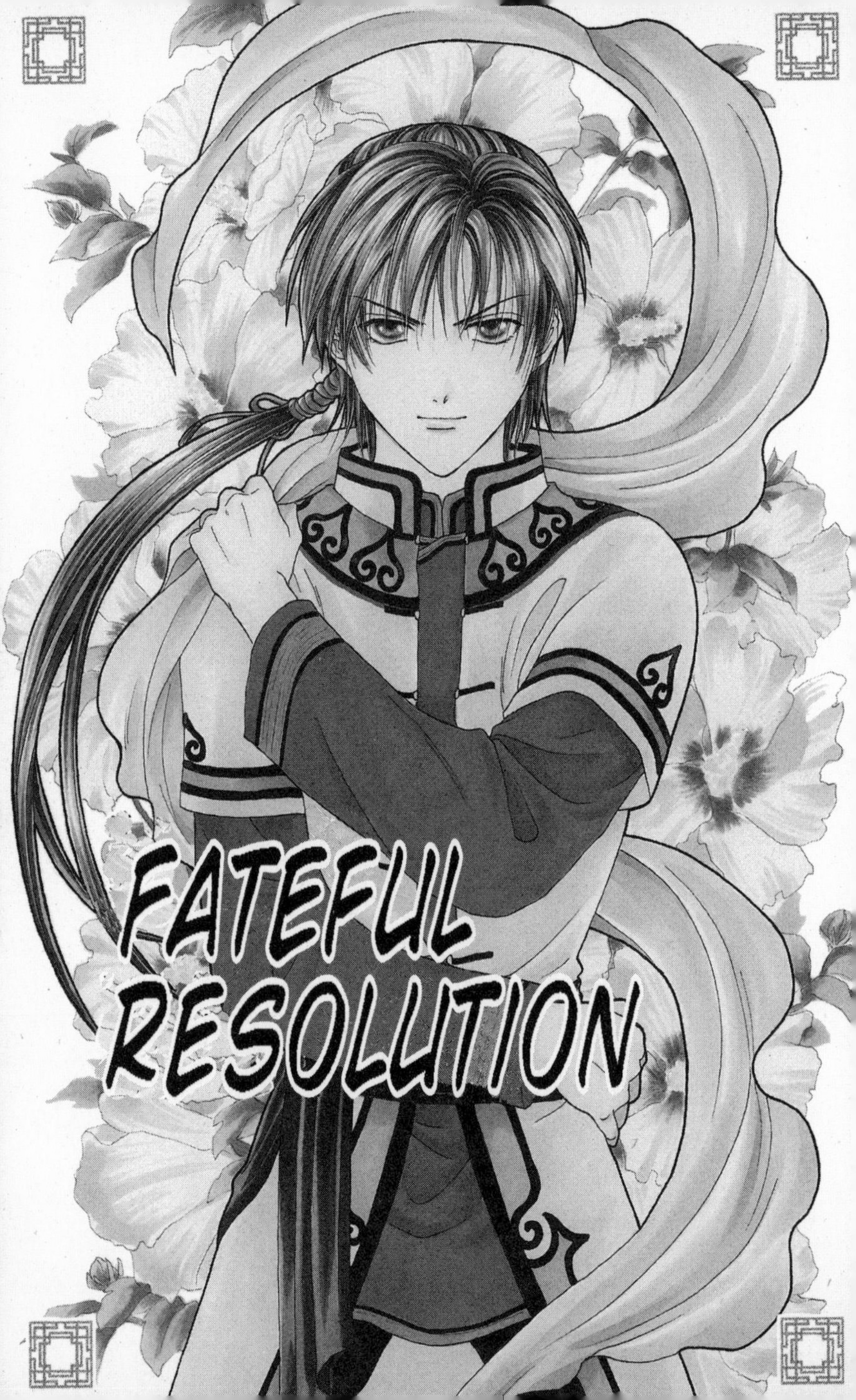
FATEFUL
RESOLUTION

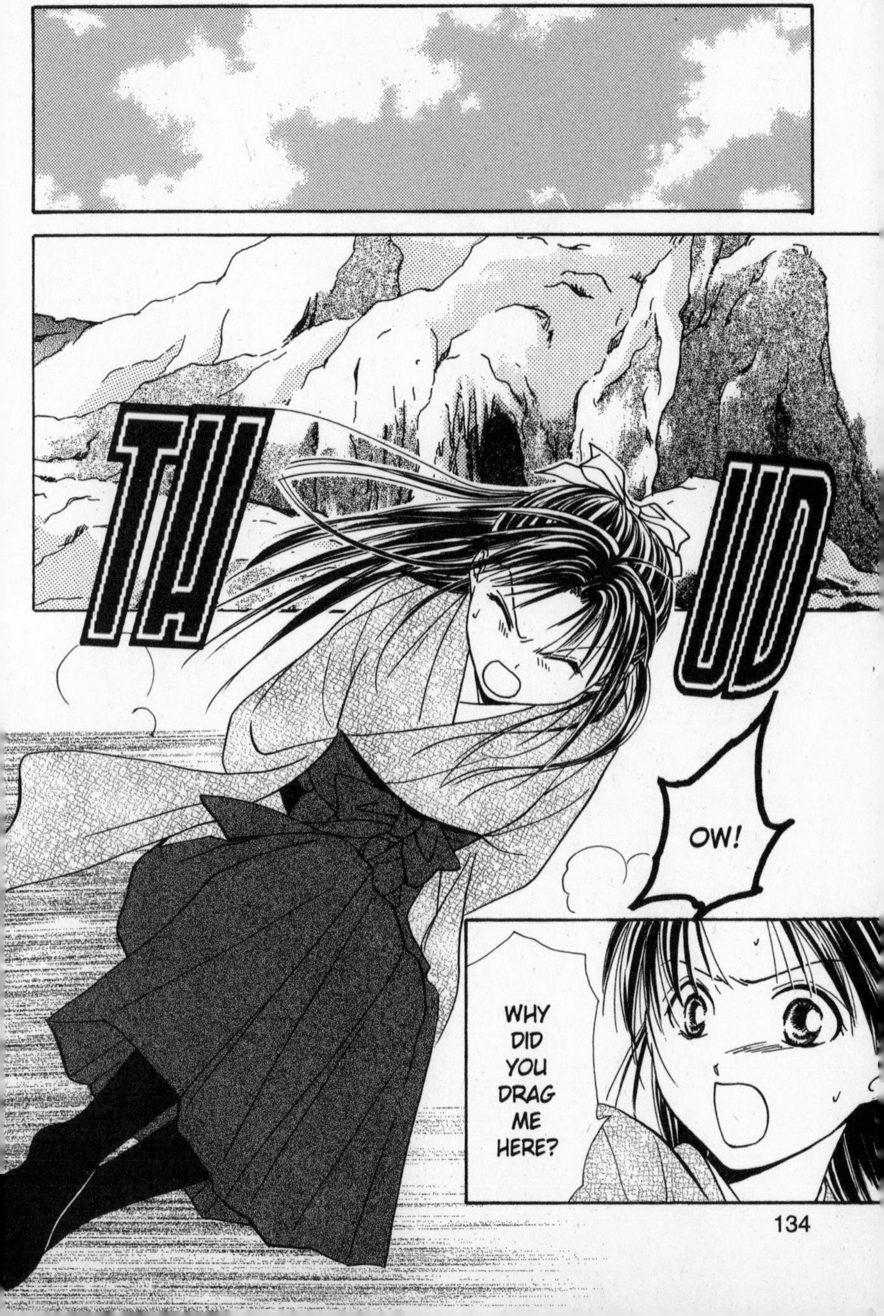
THUD
OW!
WHY DID YOU DRAG ME HERE?

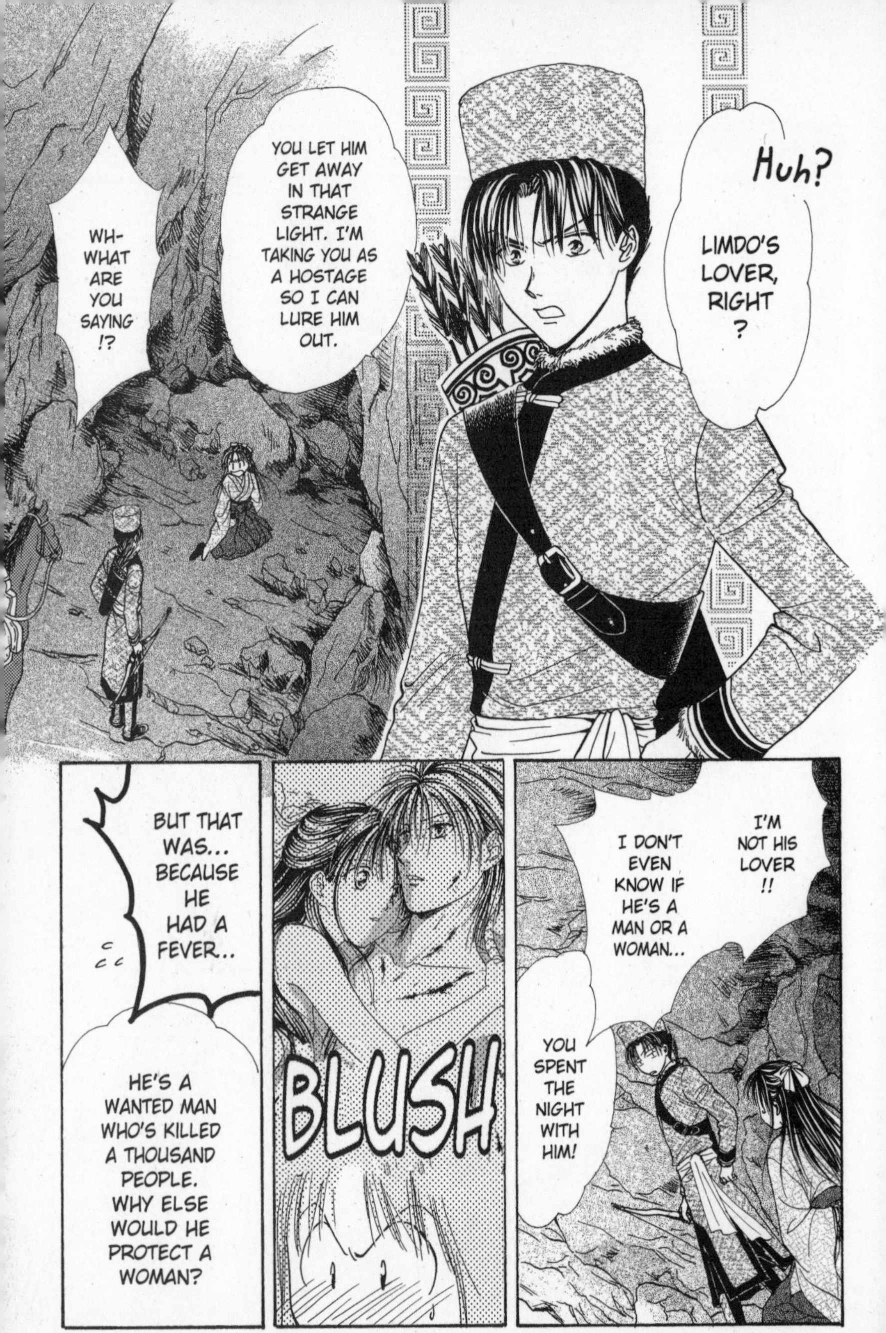
LIMDO'S LOVER, RIGHT?
Huh?
YOU LET HIM GET AWAY IN THAT STRANGE LIGHT. I'M TAKING YOU AS A HOSTAGE SO I CAN LURE HIM OUT.
WH- WHAT ARE YOU SAYING!?
I'M NOT HIS LOVER!!
I DON'T EVEN KNOW IF HE'S A MAN OR A WOMAN...
YOU SPENT THE NIGHT WITH HIM!
BLUSH
BUT THAT WAS... BECAUSE HE HAD A FEVER...
HE'S A WANTED MAN WHO'S KILLED A THOUSAND PEOPLE. WHY ELSE WOULD HE PROTECT A WOMAN?

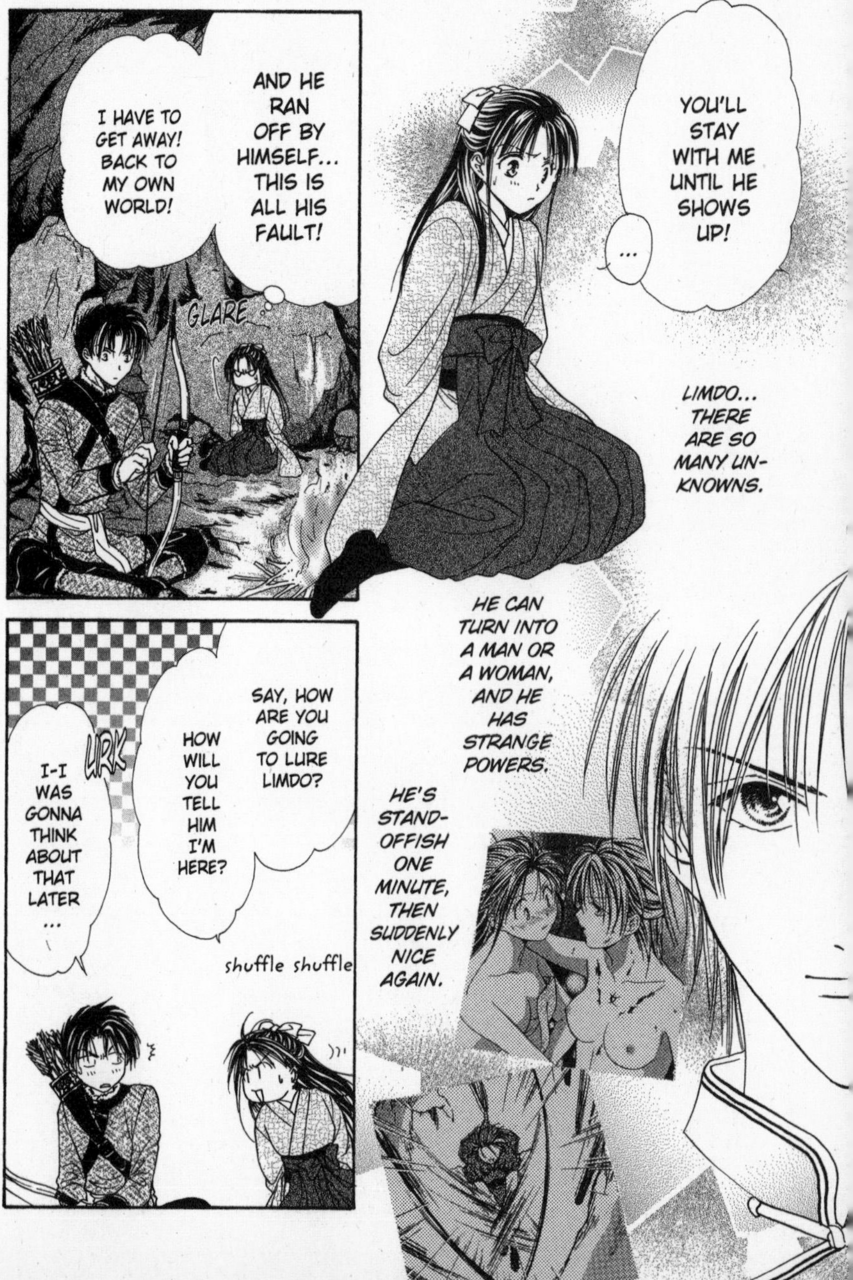
YOU'LL STAY WITH ME UNTIL HE SHOWS UP!
...
AND HE RAN OFF BY HIMSELF... THIS IS ALL HIS FAULT!
I HAVE TO GET AWAY! BACK TO MY OWN WORLD!
GLARE
LIMDO... THERE ARE SO MANY UN-KNOWNS.
HE CAN TURN INTO A MAN OR A WOMAN, AND HE HAS STRANGE POWERS.
HE'S STAND-OFFISH ONE MINUTE, THEN SUDDENLY NICE AGAIN.
SAY, HOW ARE YOU GOING TO LURE LIMDO?
HOW WILL YOU TELL HIM I'M HERE?
URK
I-I WAS GONNA THINK ABOUT THAT LATER ...
shuffle shuffle

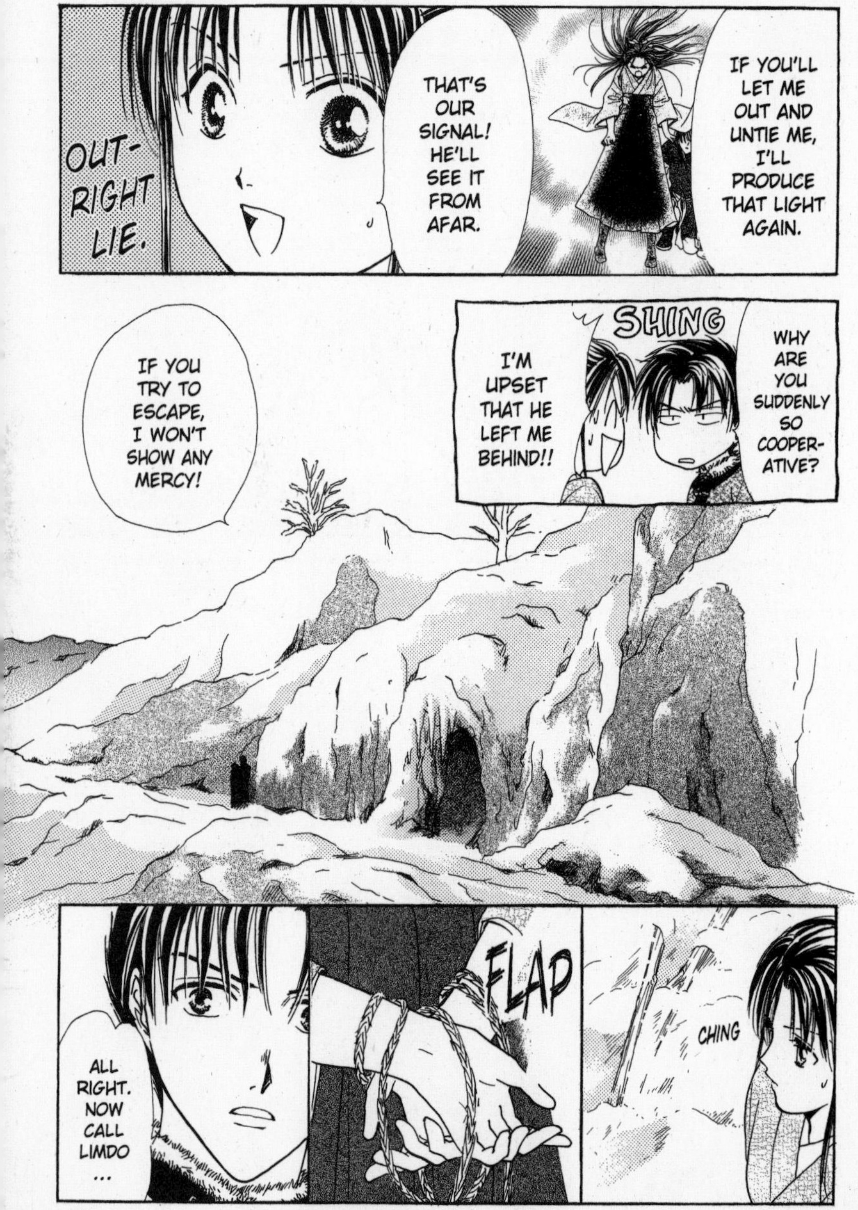
IF YOU'LL LET ME OUT AND UNTIE ME, I'LL PRODUCE THAT LIGHT AGAIN.
THAT'S OUR SIGNAL! HE'LL SEE IT FROM AFAR.
OUT-RIGHT LIE.
WHY ARE YOU SUDDENLY SO COOPER-ATIVE?
SHING
I'M UPSET THAT HE LEFT ME BEHIND!!
IF YOU TRY TO ESCAPE, I WON'T SHOW ANY MERCY!
CHING
FLAP
ALL RIGHT. NOW CALL LIMDO ...

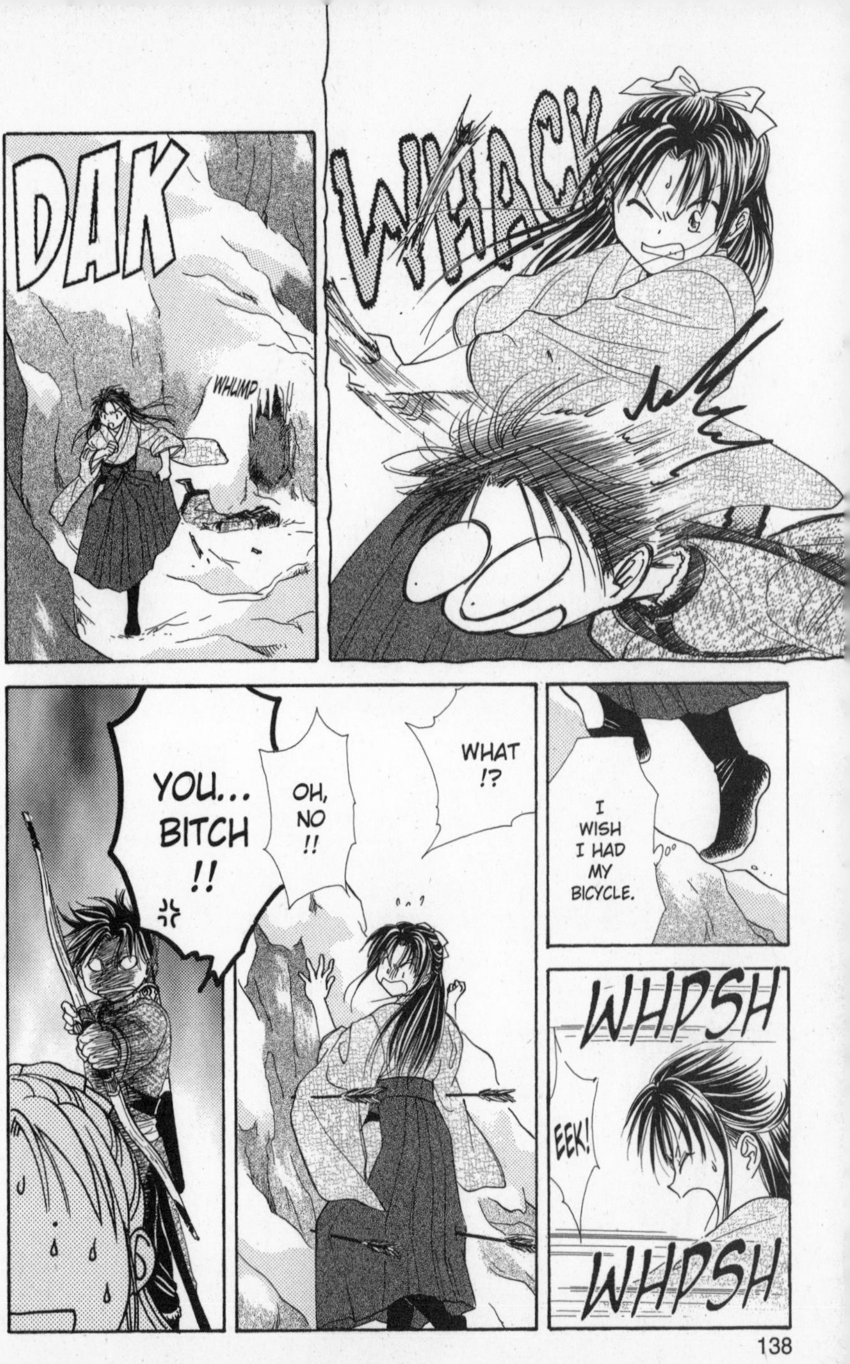
WHACK
DAK
WHUMP
I WISH I HAD MY BICYCLE.
WHPSH
EEK!
WHPSH
WHAT !?
OH, NO !!
YOU... BITCH !!

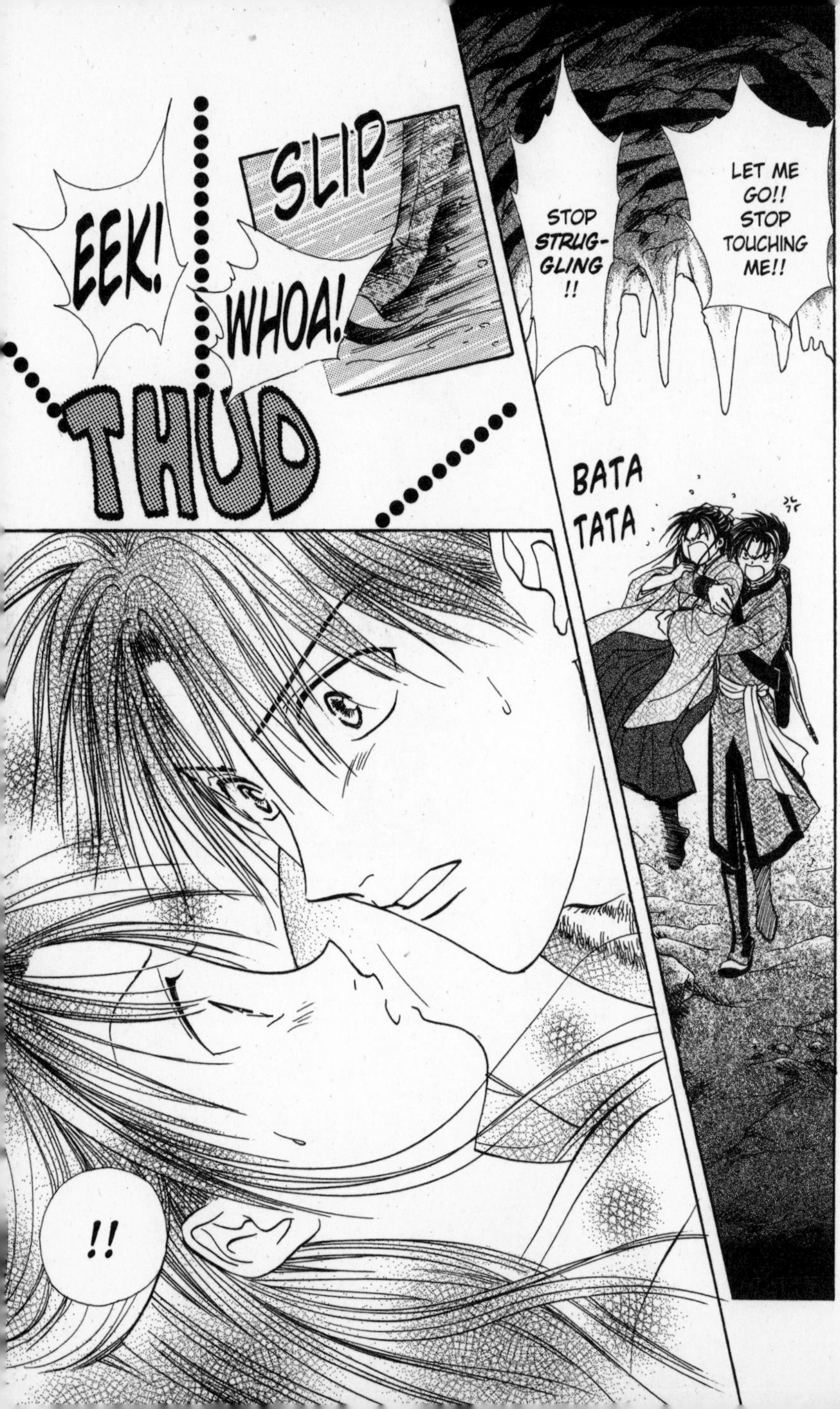
LET ME GO!! STOP TOUCHING ME!!
STOP STRUG- GLING !!
BATA TATA
SLIP
WHOA!
EEK!
THUD
!!

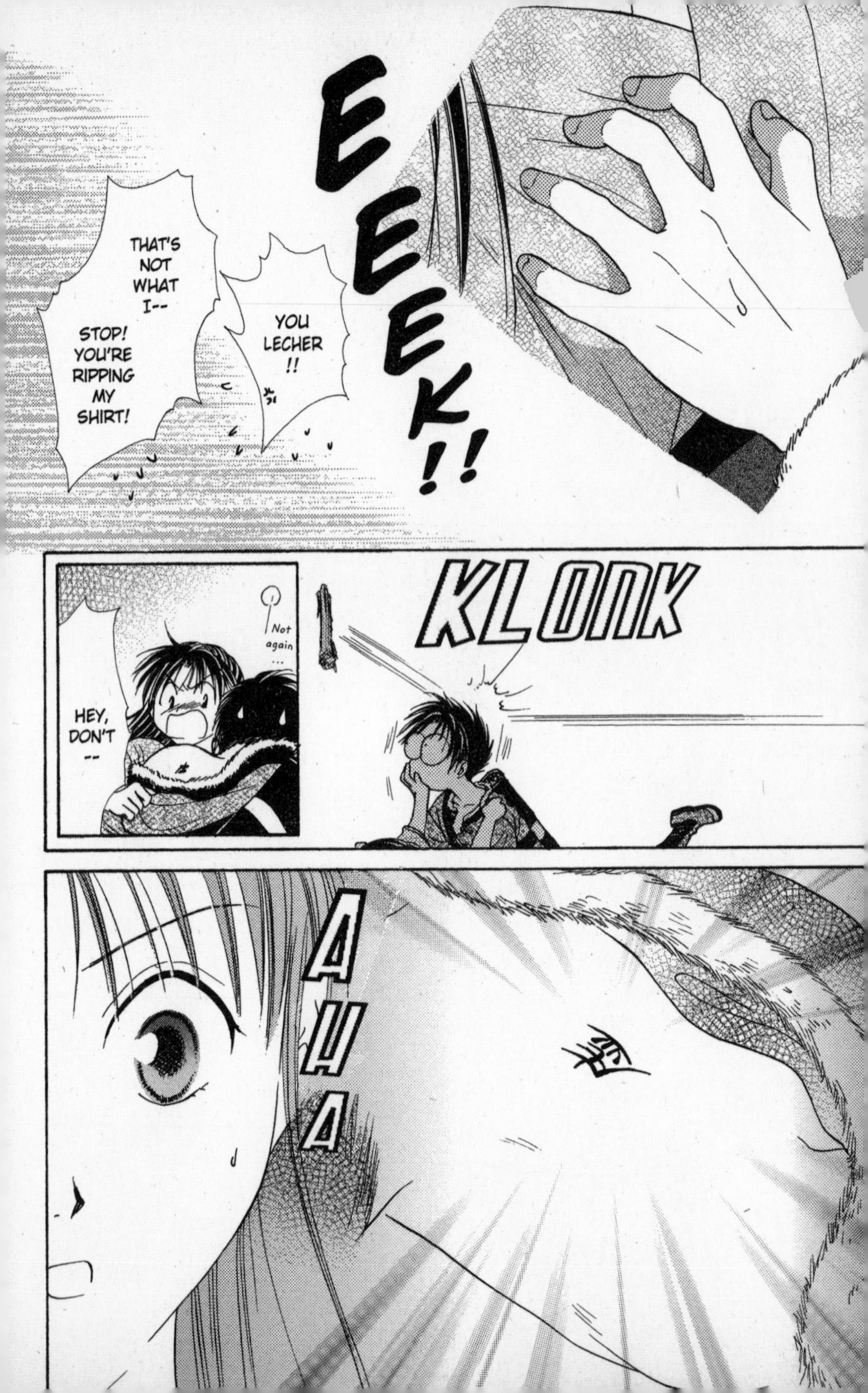
EEEEK!!
YOU LECHER !!
THAT'S NOT WHAT I--
STOP! YOU'RE RIPPING MY SHIRT!
KLONK
Not again ...
HEY, DON'T --
AUA

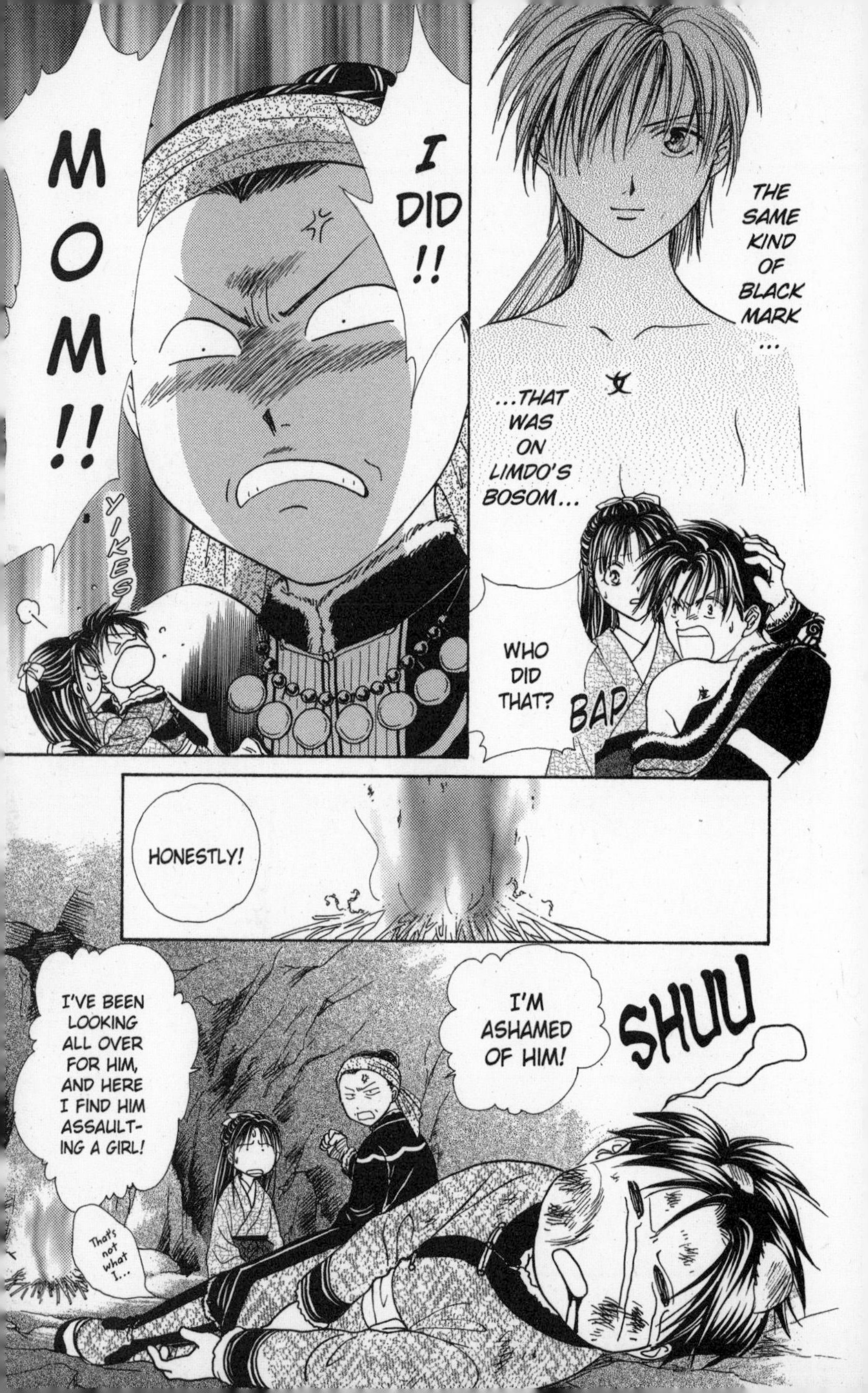
THE SAME KIND OF BLACK MARK...
...THAT WAS ON LIMDO'S BOSOM...
WHO DID THAT?
BAP
I DID!!
MOM!!
YIKES
HONESTLY!
SHUU
I'M ASHAMED OF HIM!
I'VE BEEN LOOKING ALL OVER FOR HIM, AND HERE I FIND HIM ASSAULTING A GIRL!
That's not what I...

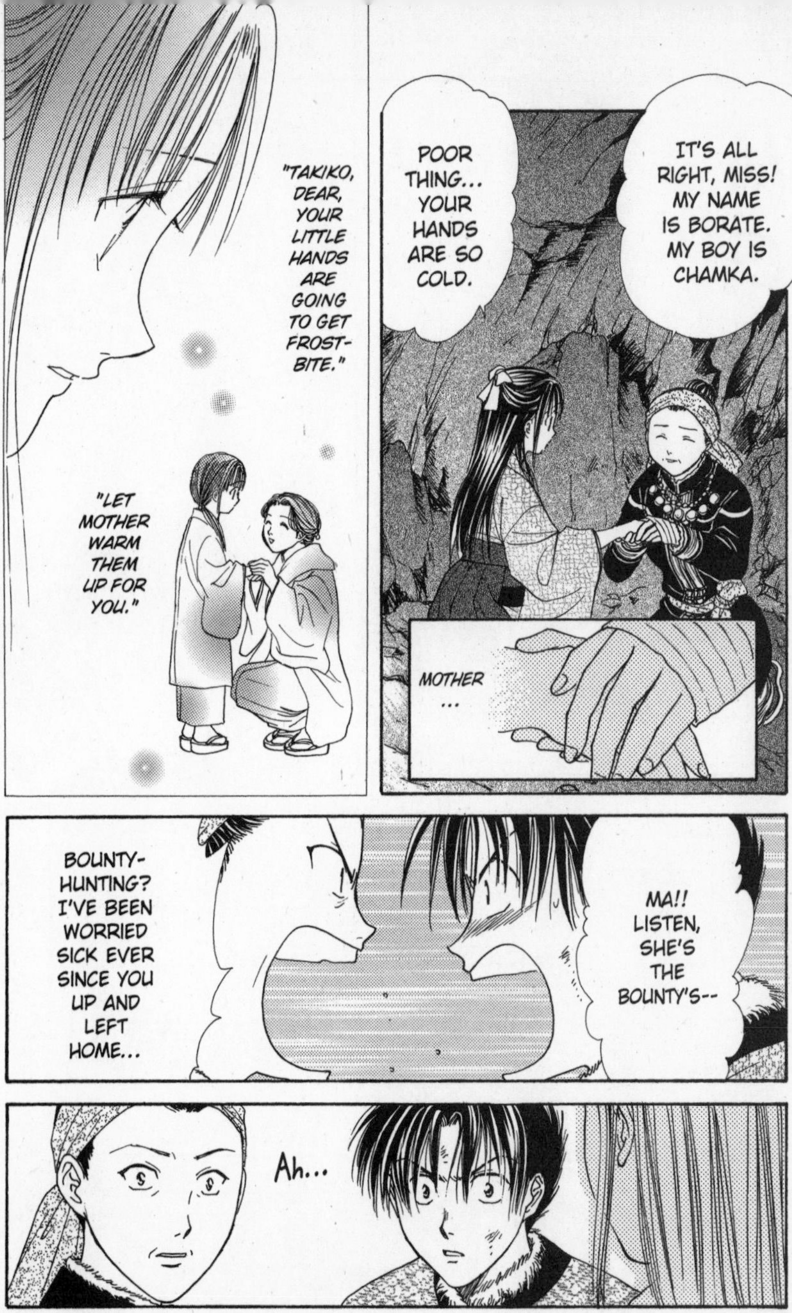
IT'S ALL RIGHT, MISS! MY NAME IS BORATE. MY BOY IS CHAMKA.
POOR THING... YOUR HANDS ARE SO COLD.
MOTHER ...
"TAKIKO, DEAR, YOUR LITTLE HANDS ARE GOING TO GET FROST-BITE."
"LET MOTHER WARM THEM UP FOR YOU."
MA!! LISTEN, SHE'S THE BOUNTY'S--
BOUNTY-HUNTING? I'VE BEEN WORRIED SICK EVER SINCE YOU UP AND LEFT HOME...
Ah...

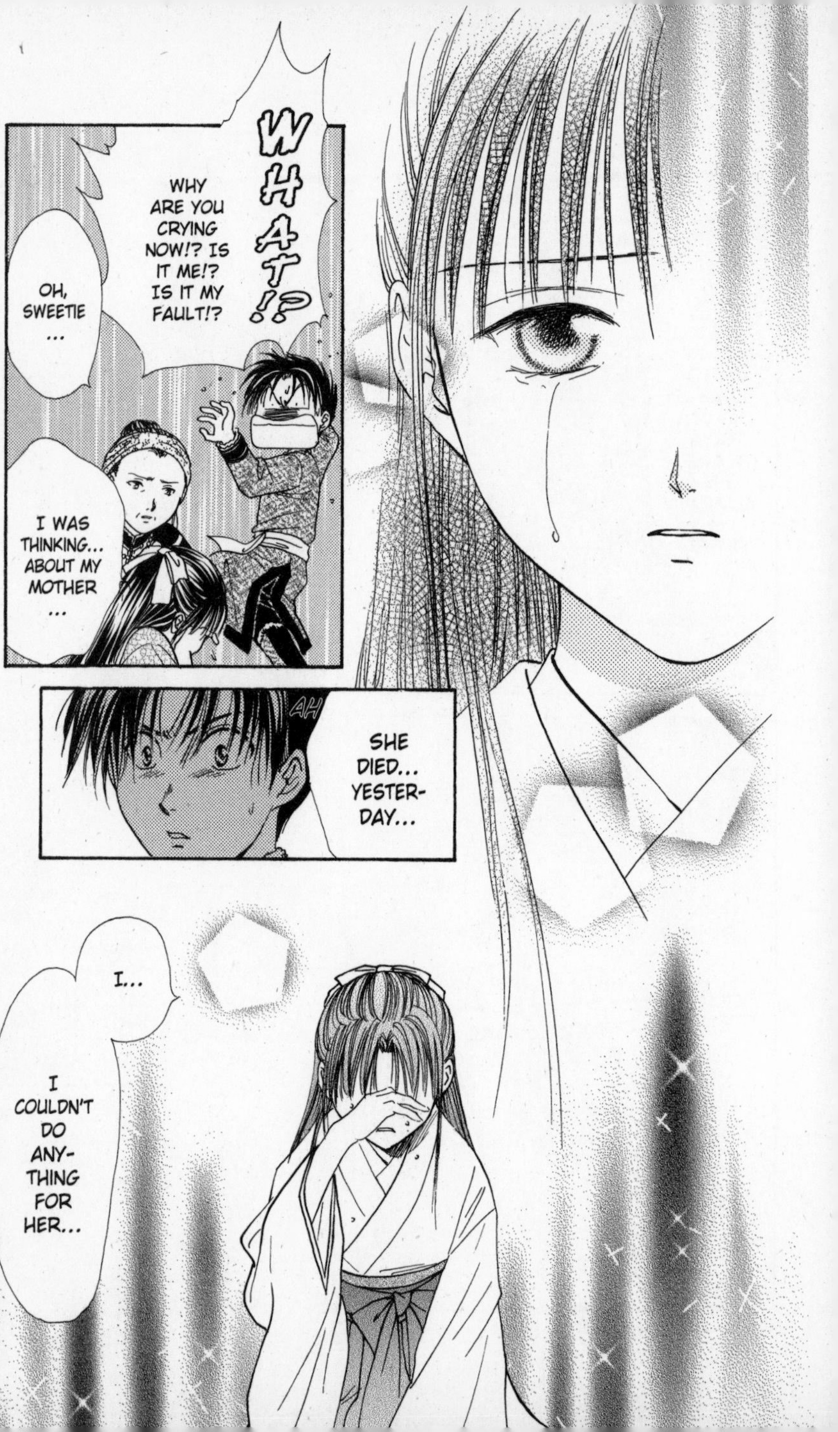
WHAT!?
WHY ARE YOU CRYING NOW!? IS IT ME!? IS IT MY FAULT!?
OH, SWEETIE...
I WAS THINKING... ABOUT MY MOTHER...
AH
SHE DIED... YESTERDAY...
I...
I COULDN'T DO ANYTHING FOR HER...

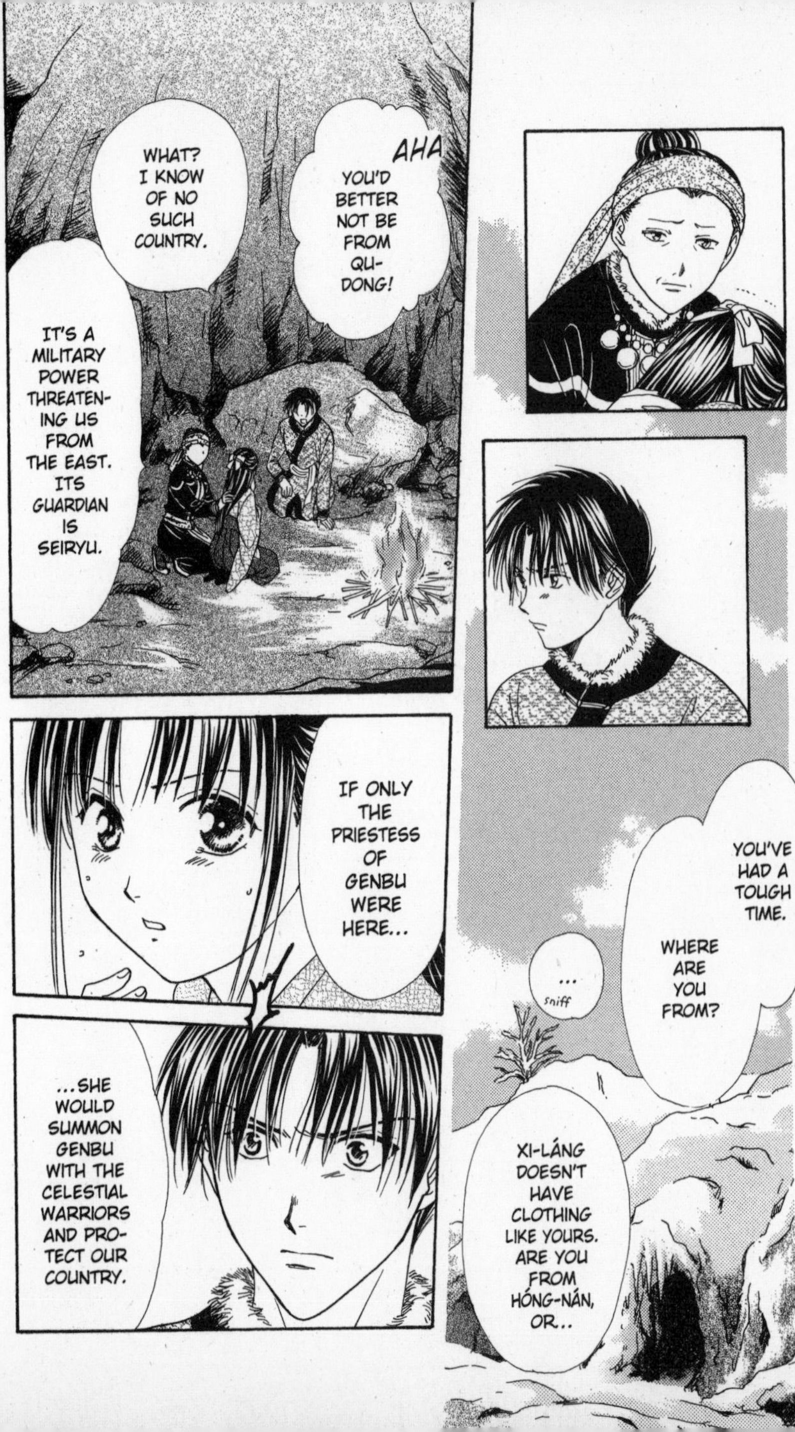

...
YOU'VE HAD A TOUGH TIME.
WHERE ARE YOU FROM?
... sniff
XI-LÁNG DOESN'T HAVE CLOTHING LIKE YOURS. ARE YOU FROM HÓNG-NÁN, OR..
AHA
YOU'D BETTER NOT BE FROM QU-DONG!
WHAT? I KNOW OF NO SUCH COUNTRY.
IT'S A MILITARY POWER THREATEN-ING US FROM THE EAST. ITS GUARDIAN IS SEIRYU.
IF ONLY THE PRIESTESS OF GENBU WERE HERE...
...SHE WOULD SUMMON GENBU WITH THE CELESTIAL WARRIORS AND PRO-TECT OUR COUNTRY.

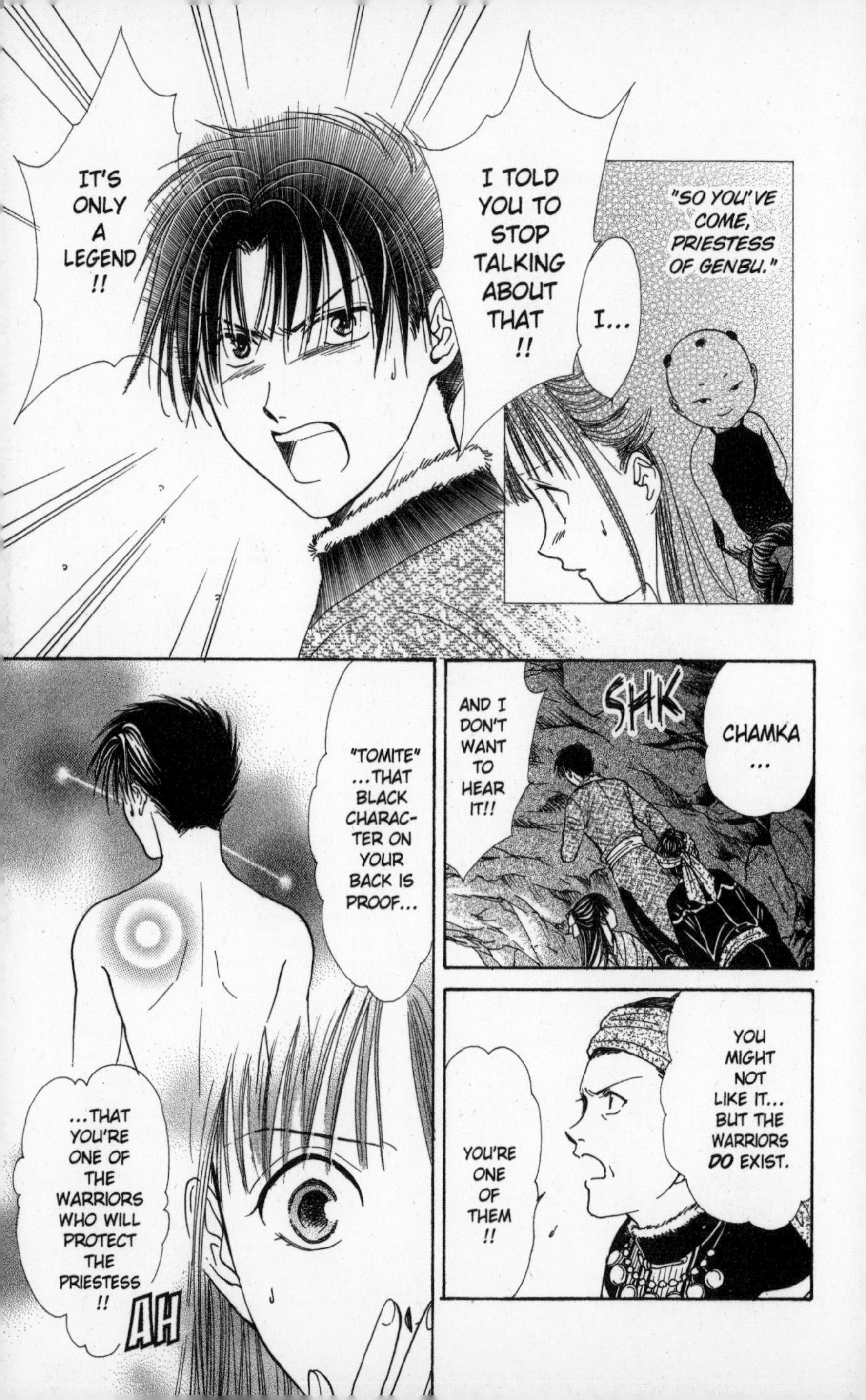
"SO YOU'VE COME, PRIESTESS OF GENBU."
I...
I TOLD YOU TO STOP TALKING ABOUT THAT!!
IT'S ONLY A LEGEND!!
CHAMKA...
SHK
AND I DON'T WANT TO HEAR IT!!
YOU MIGHT NOT LIKE IT... BUT THE WARRIORS *DO* EXIST.
YOU'RE ONE OF THEM!!
"TOMITE"...THAT BLACK CHARACTER ON YOUR BACK IS PROOF...
...THAT YOU'RE ONE OF THE WARRIORS WHO WILL PROTECT THE PRIESTESS!!
AH

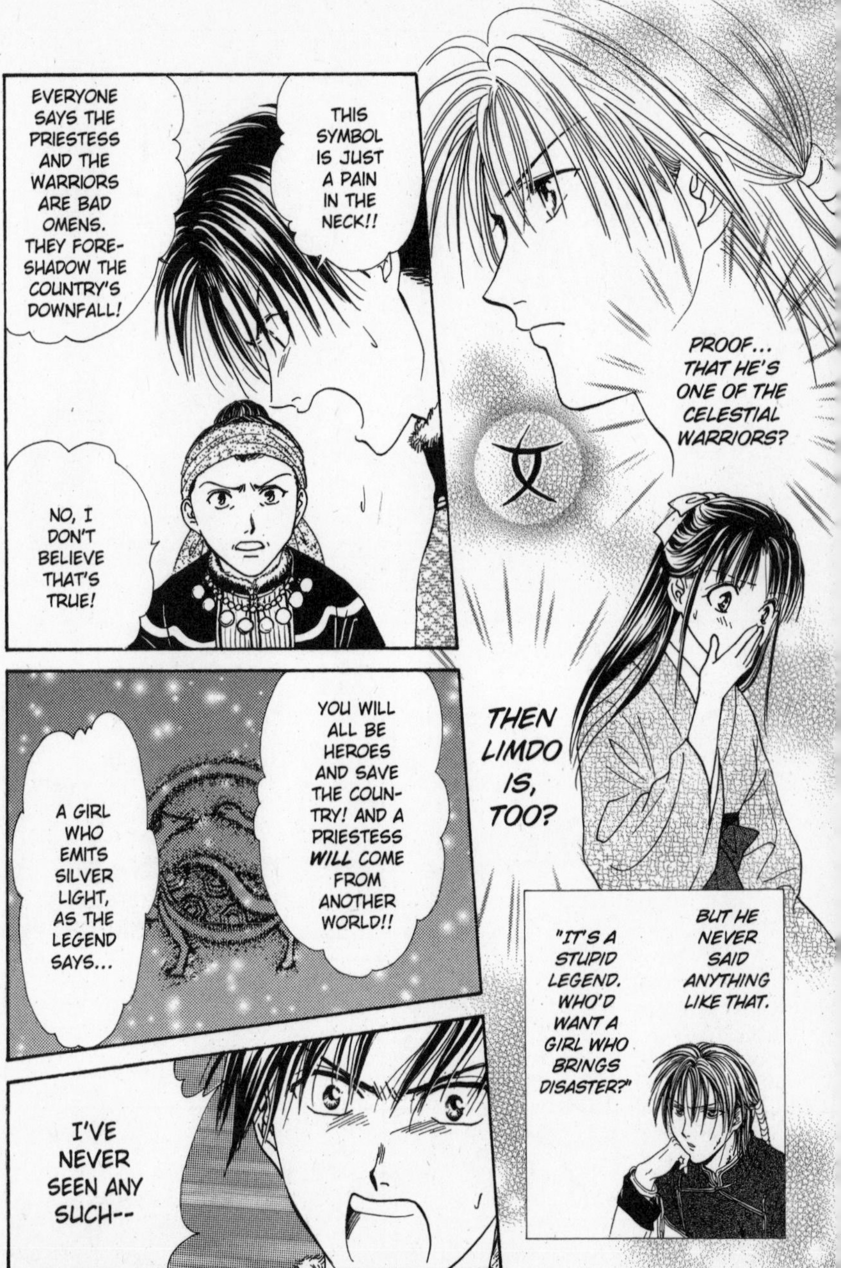
PROOF... THAT HE'S ONE OF THE CELESTIAL WARRIORS?
THEN LIMDO IS, TOO?
BUT HE NEVER SAID ANYTHING LIKE THAT.
"IT'S A STUPID LEGEND. WHO'D WANT A GIRL WHO BRINGS DISASTER?"
THIS SYMBOL IS JUST A PAIN IN THE NECK!!
EVERYONE SAYS THE PRIESTESS AND THE WARRIORS ARE BAD OMENS. THEY FORE-SHADOW THE COUNTRY'S DOWNFALL!
NO, I DON'T BELIEVE THAT'S TRUE!
YOU WILL ALL BE HEROES AND SAVE THE COUN-TRY! AND A PRIESTESS WILL COME FROM ANOTHER WORLD!!
A GIRL WHO EMITS SILVER LIGHT, AS THE LEGEND SAYS...
I'VE NEVER SEEN ANY SUCH--

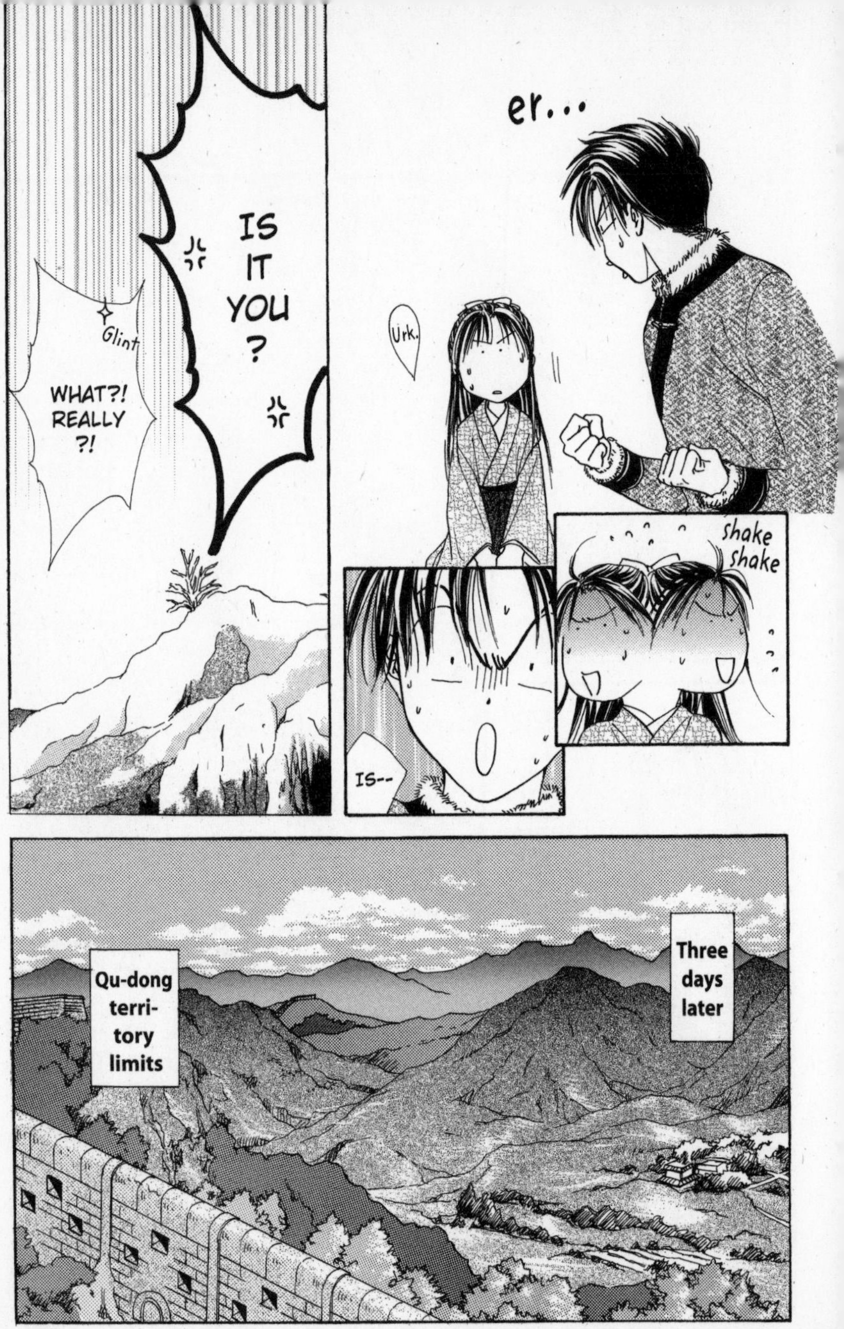

er...
Urk.
shake shake
IS--
IS IT YOU?
Glint
WHAT?! REALLY ?!
Three days later
Qu-dong territory limits

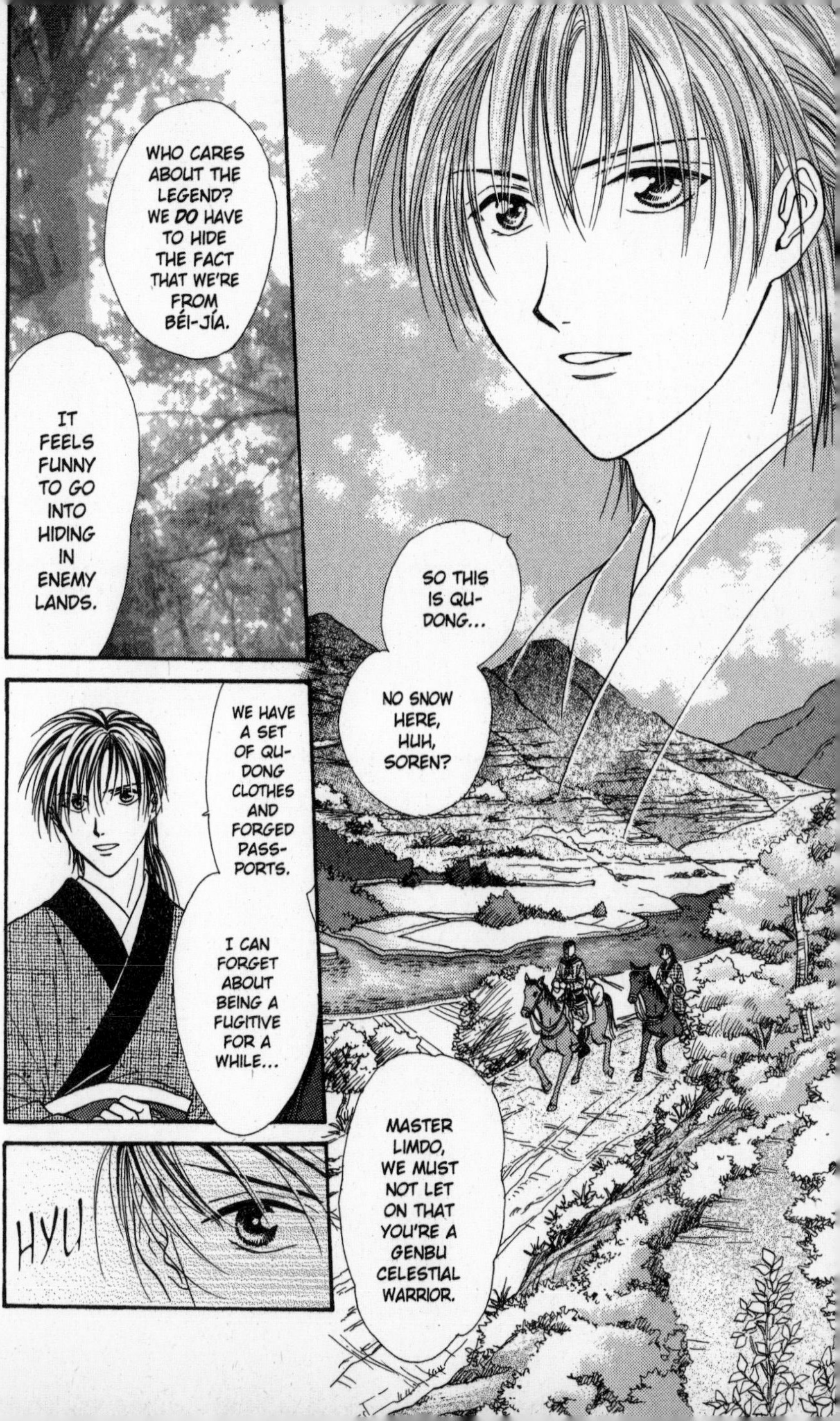
SO THIS IS QU-DONG...
NO SNOW HERE, HUH, SOREN?
MASTER LIMDO, WE MUST NOT LET ON THAT YOU'RE A GENBU CELESTIAL WARRIOR.
WHO CARES ABOUT THE LEGEND? WE *DO* HAVE TO HIDE THE FACT THAT WE'RE FROM BÉI-JÍA.
IT FEELS FUNNY TO GO INTO HIDING IN ENEMY LANDS.
WE HAVE A SET OF QU-DONG CLOTHES AND FORGED PASS-PORTS.
I CAN FORGET ABOUT BEING A FUGITIVE FOR A WHILE...
HYU

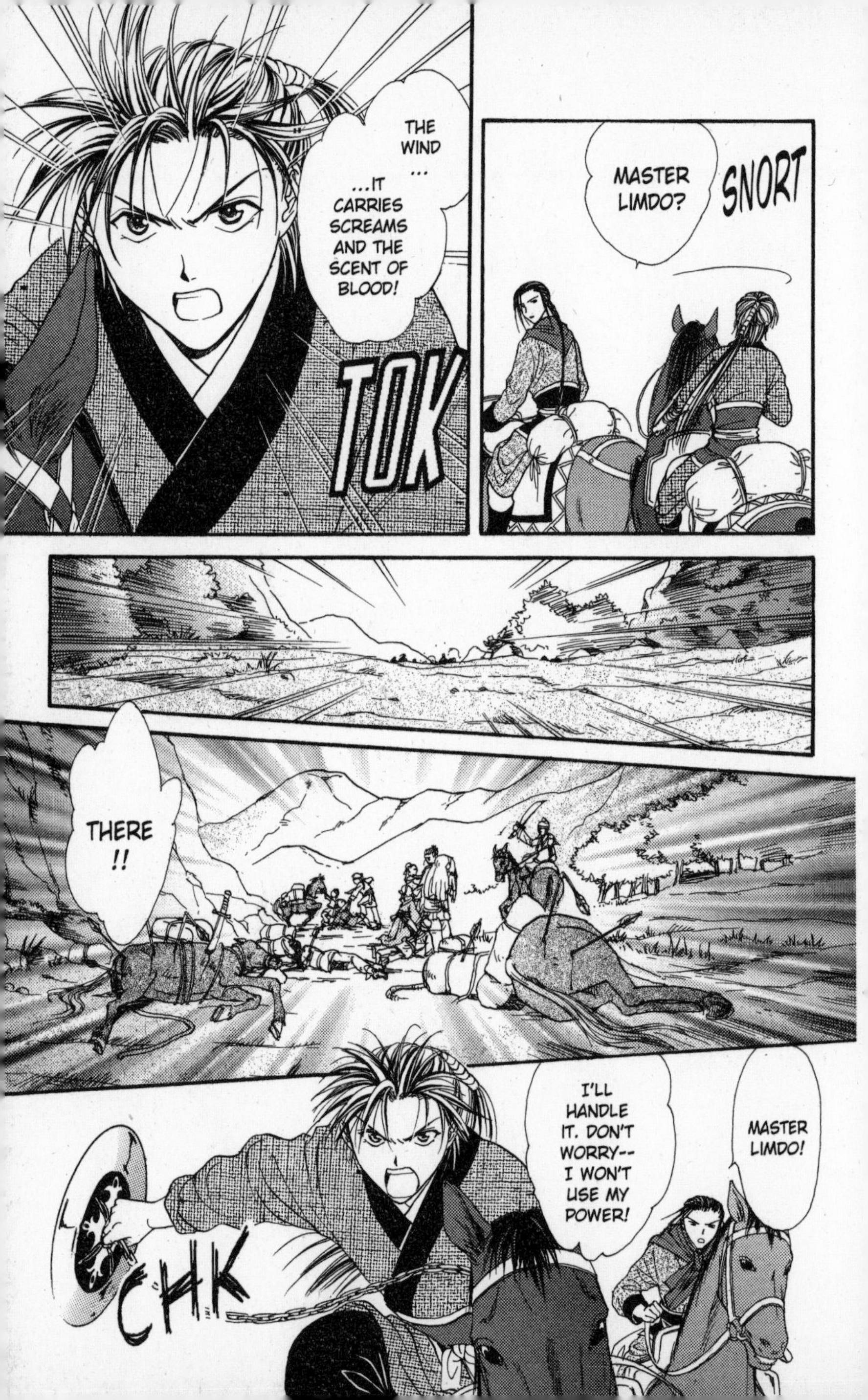
MASTER LIMDO?
SNORT
THE WIND ... ...IT CARRIES SCREAMS AND THE SCENT OF BLOOD!
TOK
THERE !!
MASTER LIMDO!
I'LL HANDLE IT. DON'T WORRY-- I WON'T USE MY POWER!
CHK

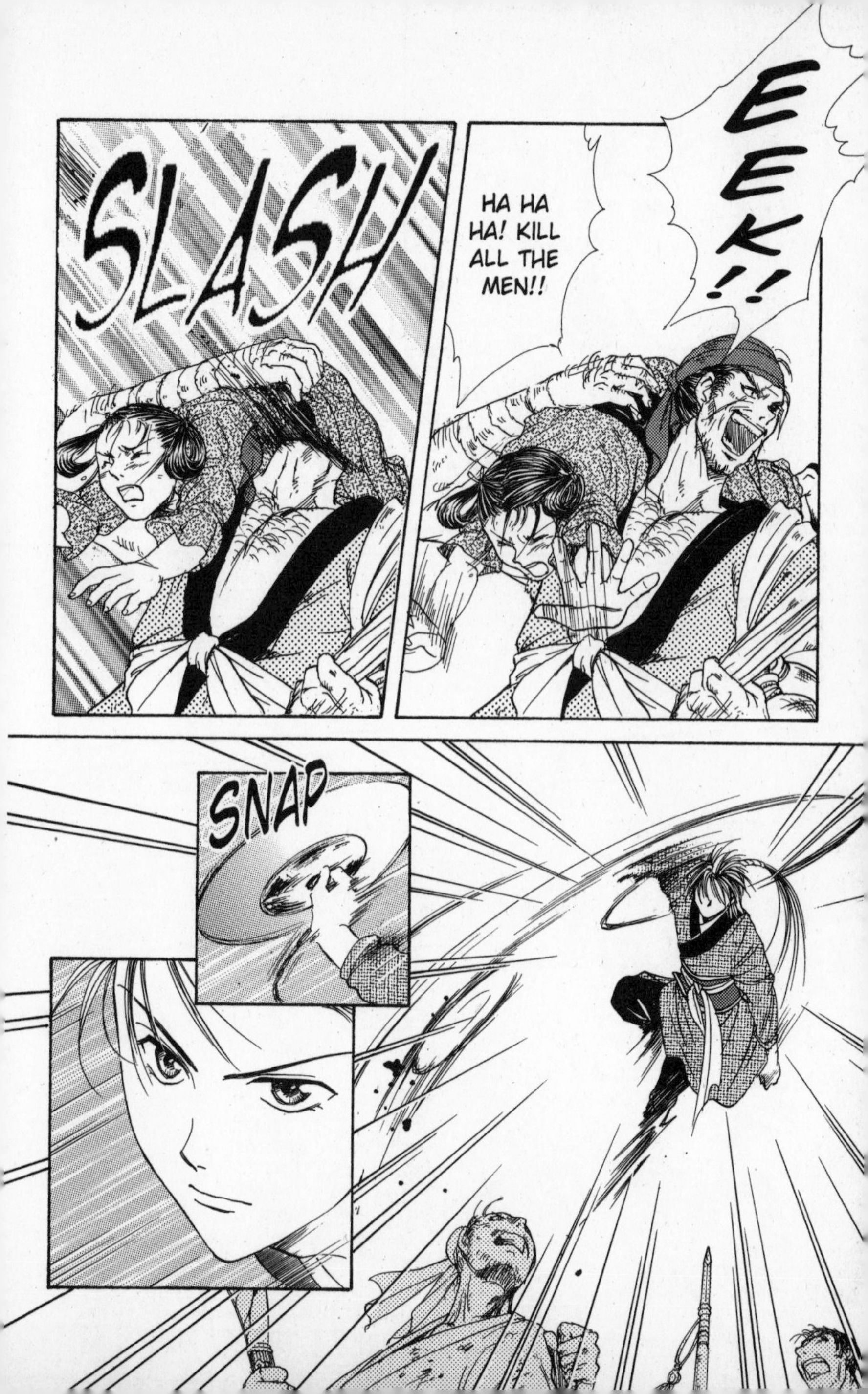
EEK!!
HA HA HA! KILL ALL THE MEN!!
SLASH
SNAP

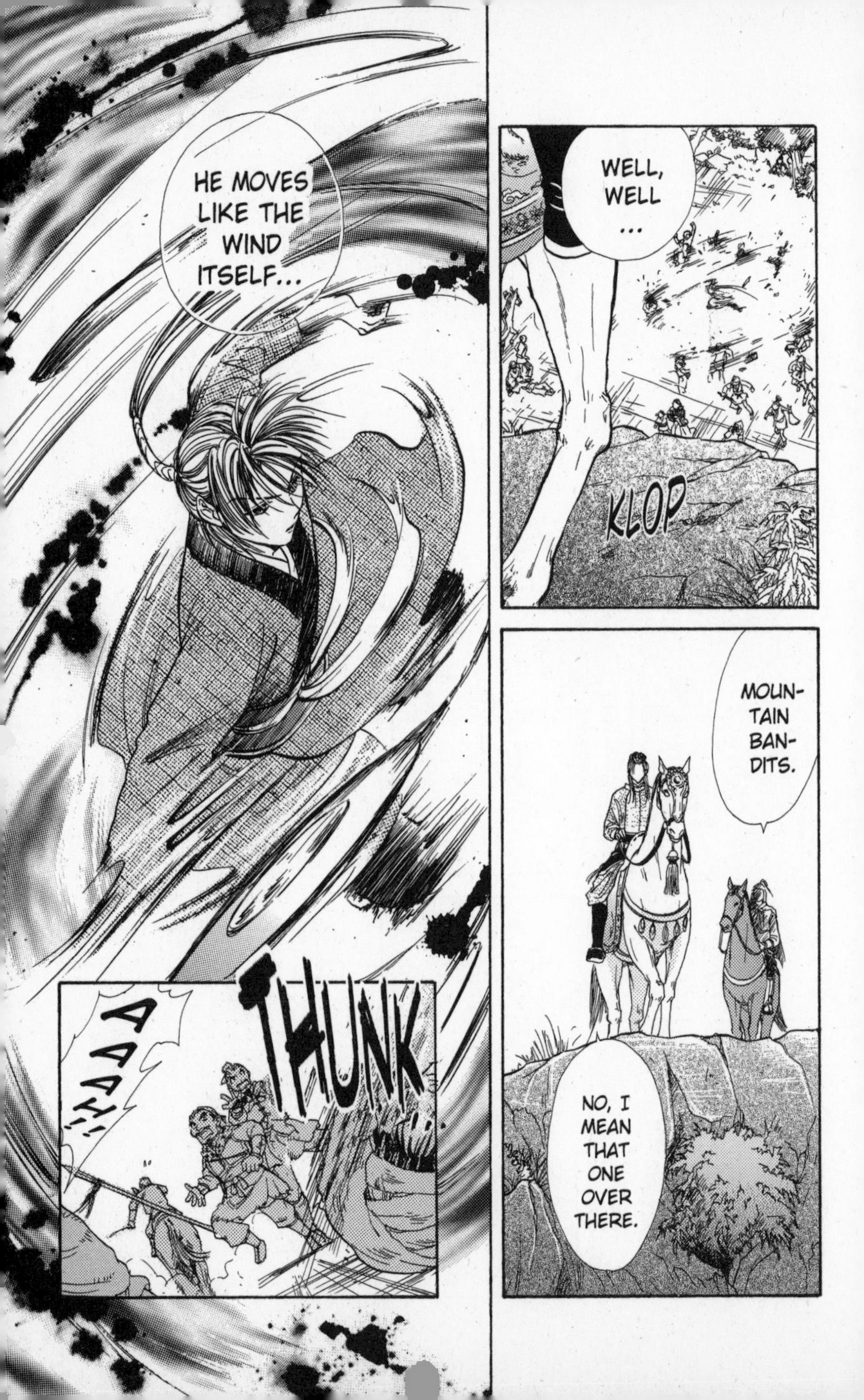
WELL, WELL ...
KLOP
MOUN-TAIN BAN-DITS.
NO, I MEAN THAT ONE OVER THERE.
HE MOVES LIKE THE WIND ITSELF...
THUNK
AAAAH!!

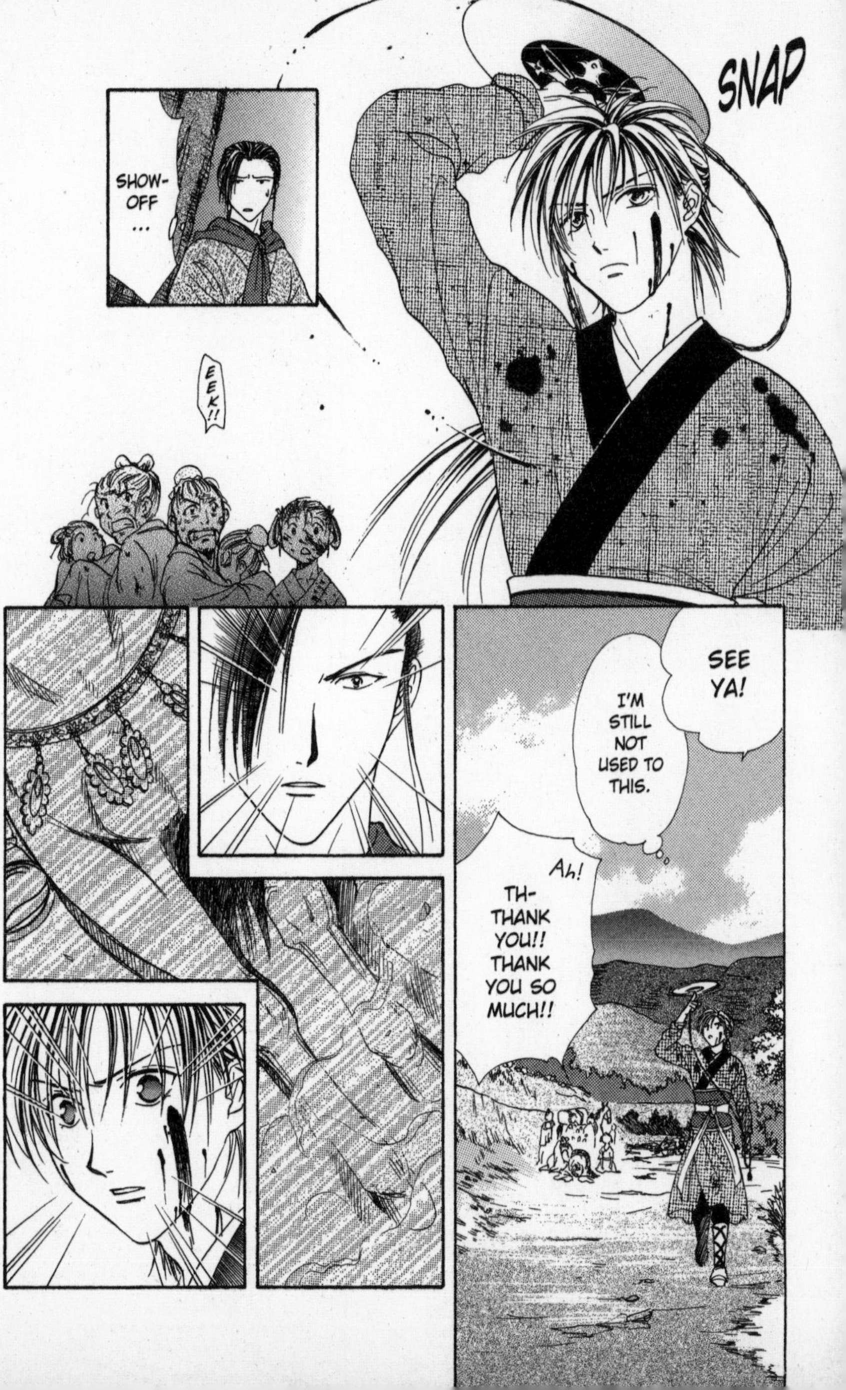
SNAP
SHOW-OFF ...
EEK!!
SEE YA!
I'M STILL NOT USED TO THIS.
Ah!
TH-THANK YOU!! THANK YOU SO MUCH!!

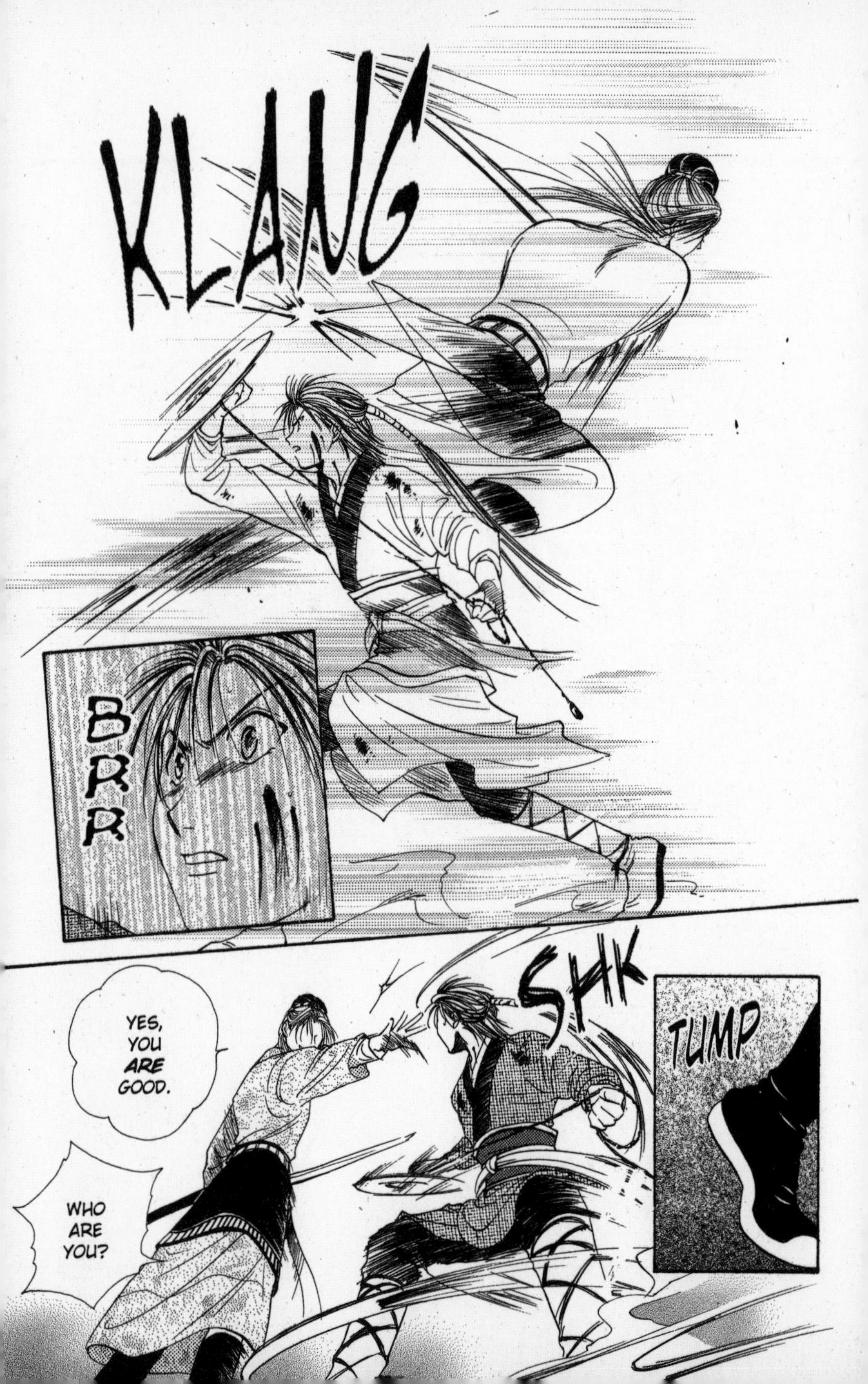
KLANG
BRRR
TUMP
SHK
YES, YOU ARE GOOD.
WHO ARE YOU?

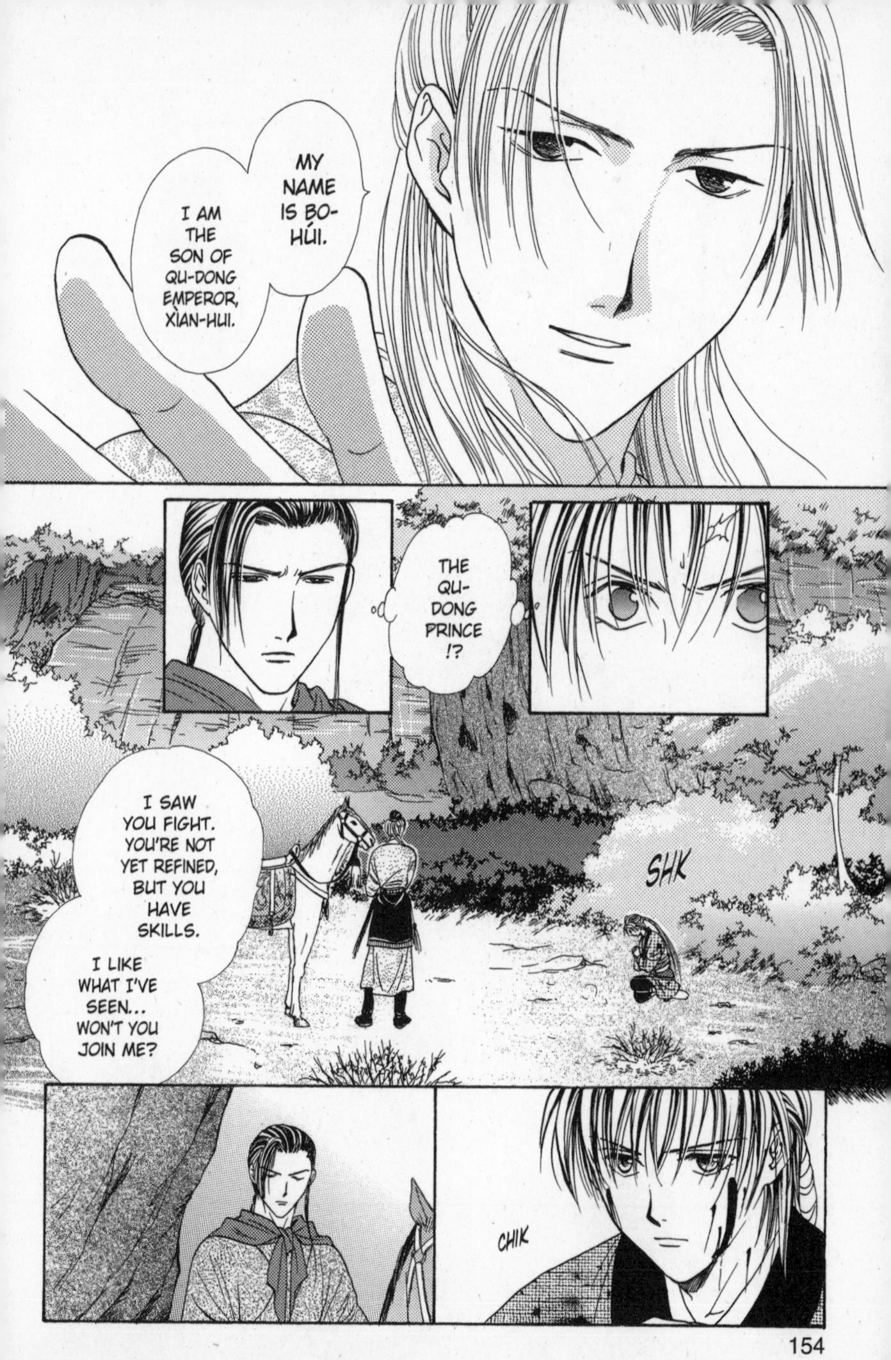
MY NAME IS BO-HÚI.
I AM THE SON OF QU-DONG EMPEROR, XÌAN-HUI.
THE QU-DONG PRINCE !?
SHK
I SAW YOU FIGHT. YOU'RE NOT YET REFINED, BUT YOU HAVE SKILLS.
I LIKE WHAT I'VE SEEN... WON'T YOU JOIN ME?
CHIK

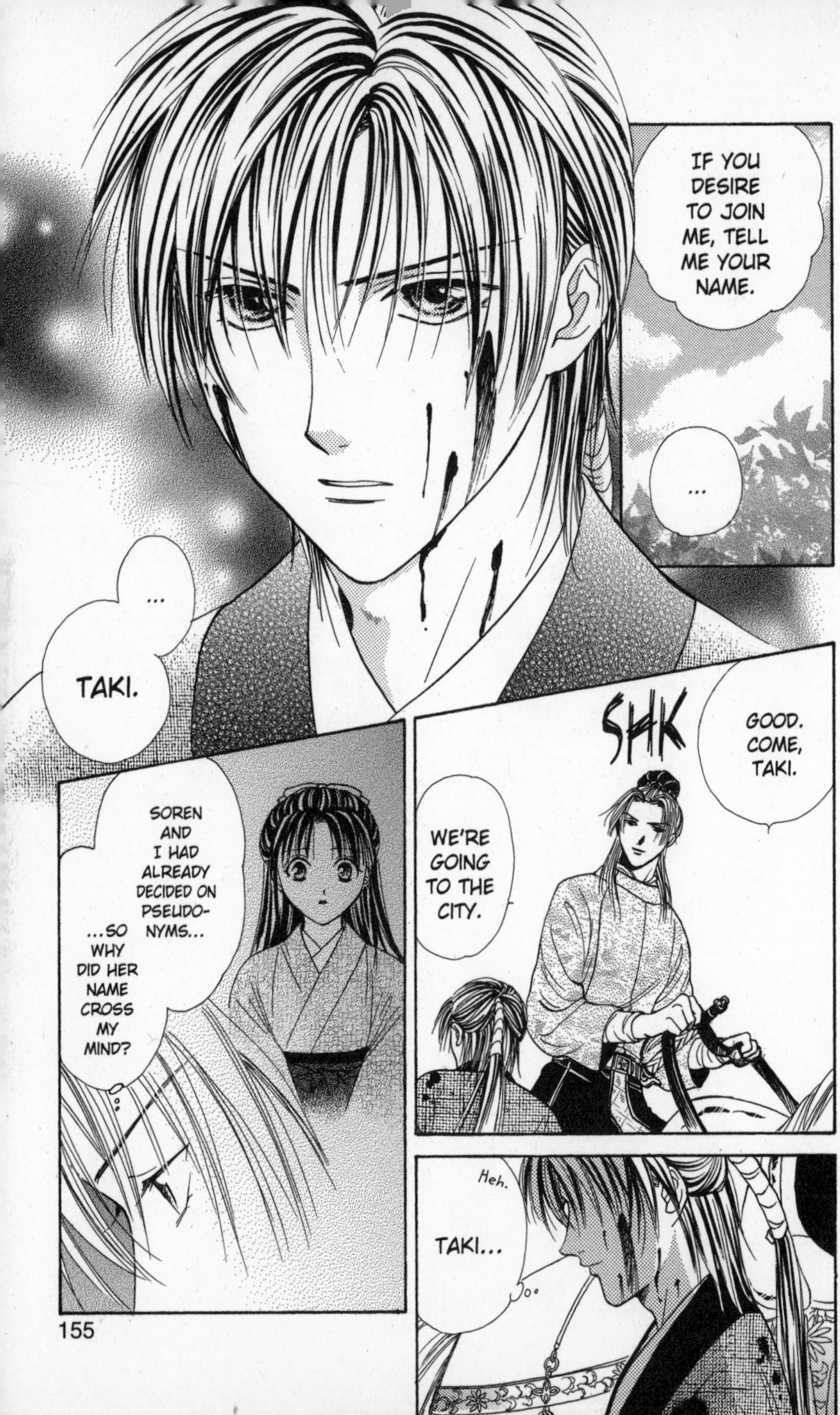
IF YOU DESIRE TO JOIN ME, TELL ME YOUR NAME.
...
...
TAKI.
SHK
GOOD. COME, TAKI.
WE'RE GOING TO THE CITY.
Heh.
TAKI...
SOREN AND I HAD ALREADY DECIDED ON PSEUDO-NYMS...
...SO WHY DID HER NAME CROSS MY MIND?

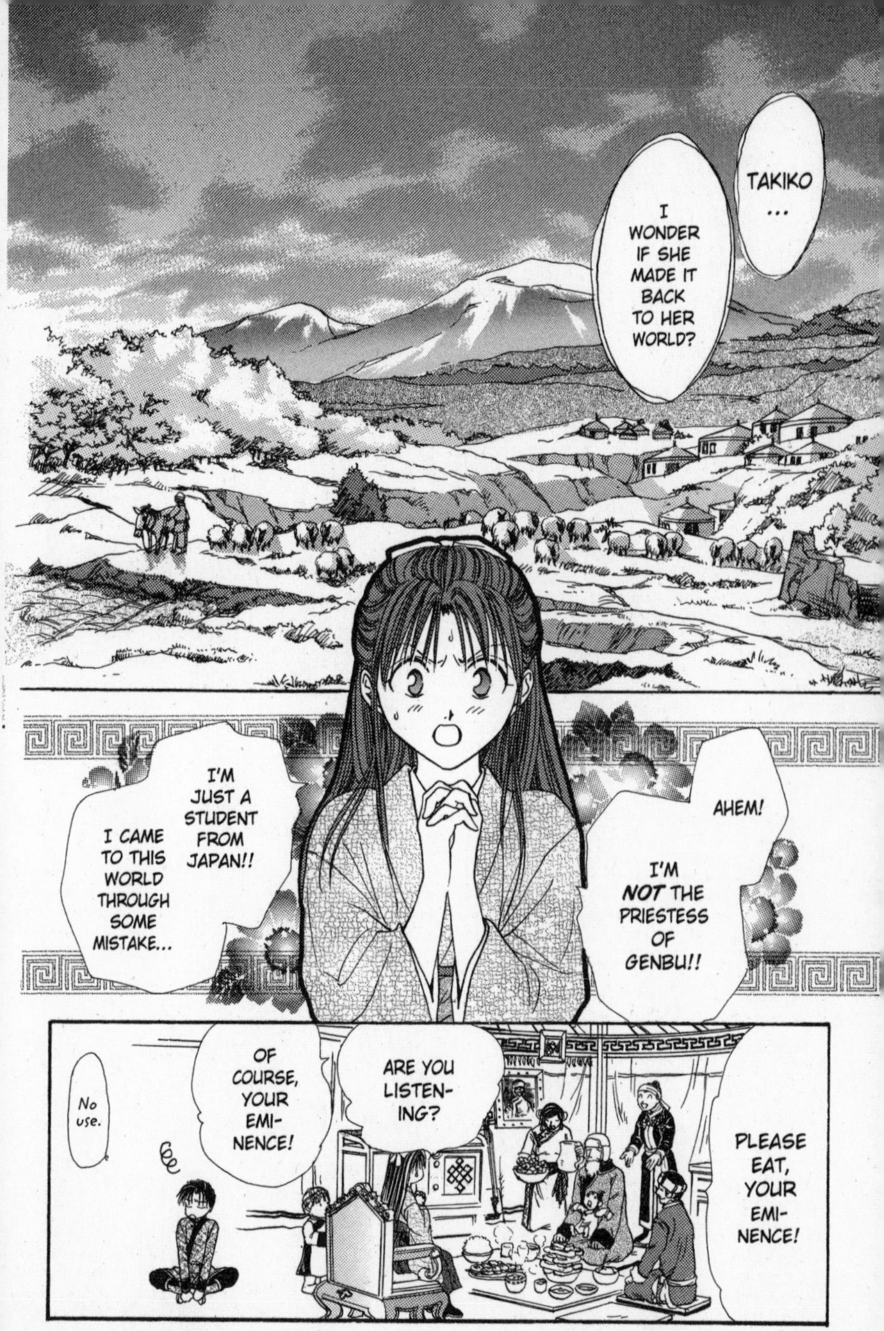
TAKIKO...
I WONDER IF SHE MADE IT BACK TO HER WORLD?
AHEM!
I'M **NOT** THE PRIESTESS OF GENBU!!
I'M JUST A STUDENT FROM JAPAN!!
I CAME TO THIS WORLD THROUGH SOME MISTAKE...
PLEASE EAT, YOUR EMINENCE!
ARE YOU LISTENING?
OF COURSE, YOUR EMINENCE!
No use.

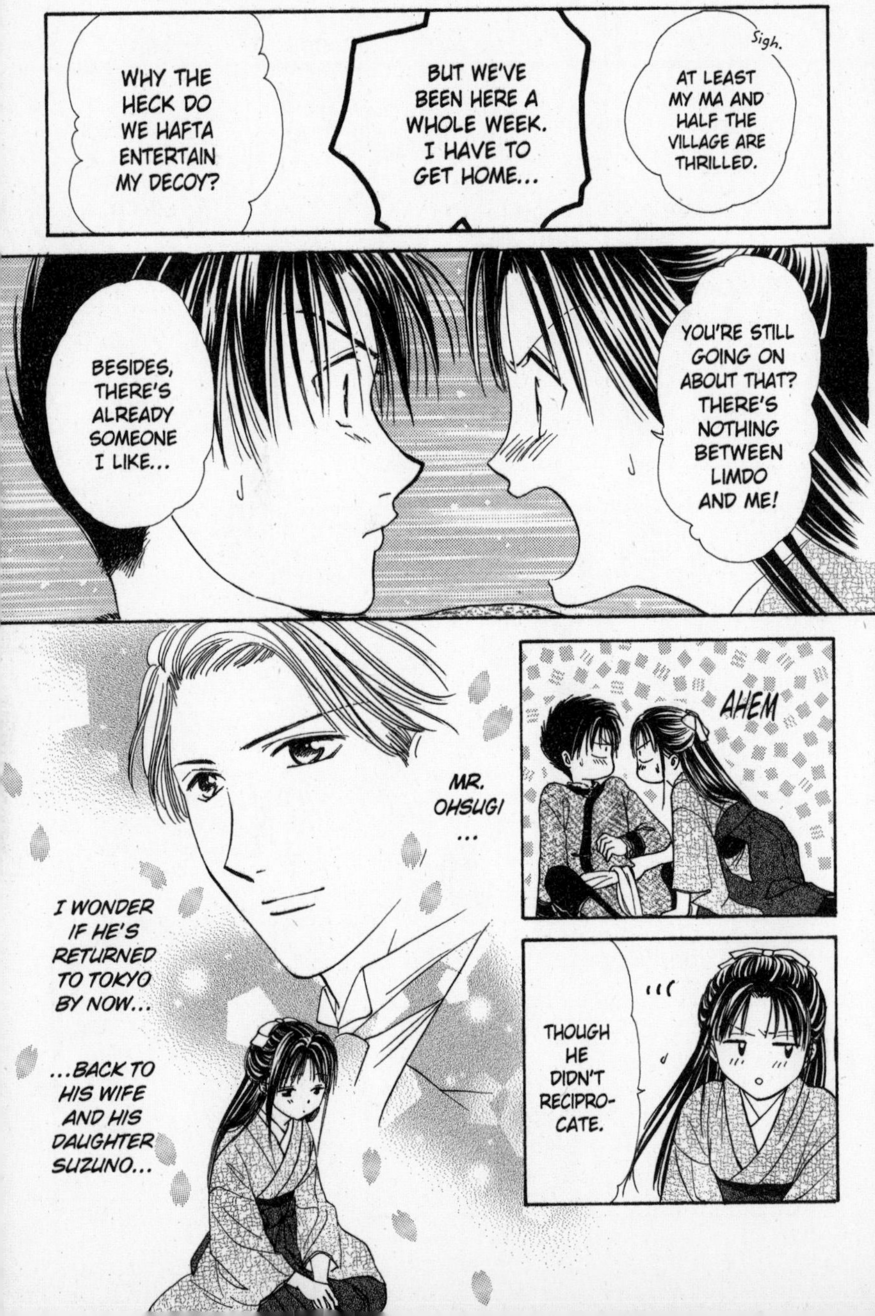
Sigh.
AT LEAST MY MA AND HALF THE VILLAGE ARE THRILLED.
BUT WE'VE BEEN HERE A WHOLE WEEK. I HAVE TO GET HOME...
WHY THE HECK DO WE HAFTA ENTERTAIN MY DECOY?
YOU'RE STILL GOING ON ABOUT THAT? THERE'S NOTHING BETWEEN LIMDO AND ME!
BESIDES, THERE'S ALREADY SOMEONE I LIKE...
AHEM
...
THOUGH HE DIDN'T RECIPRO-CATE.
MR. OHSUGI ...
I WONDER IF HE'S RETURNED TO TOKYO BY NOW...
...BACK TO HIS WIFE AND HIS DAUGHTER SUZUNO...

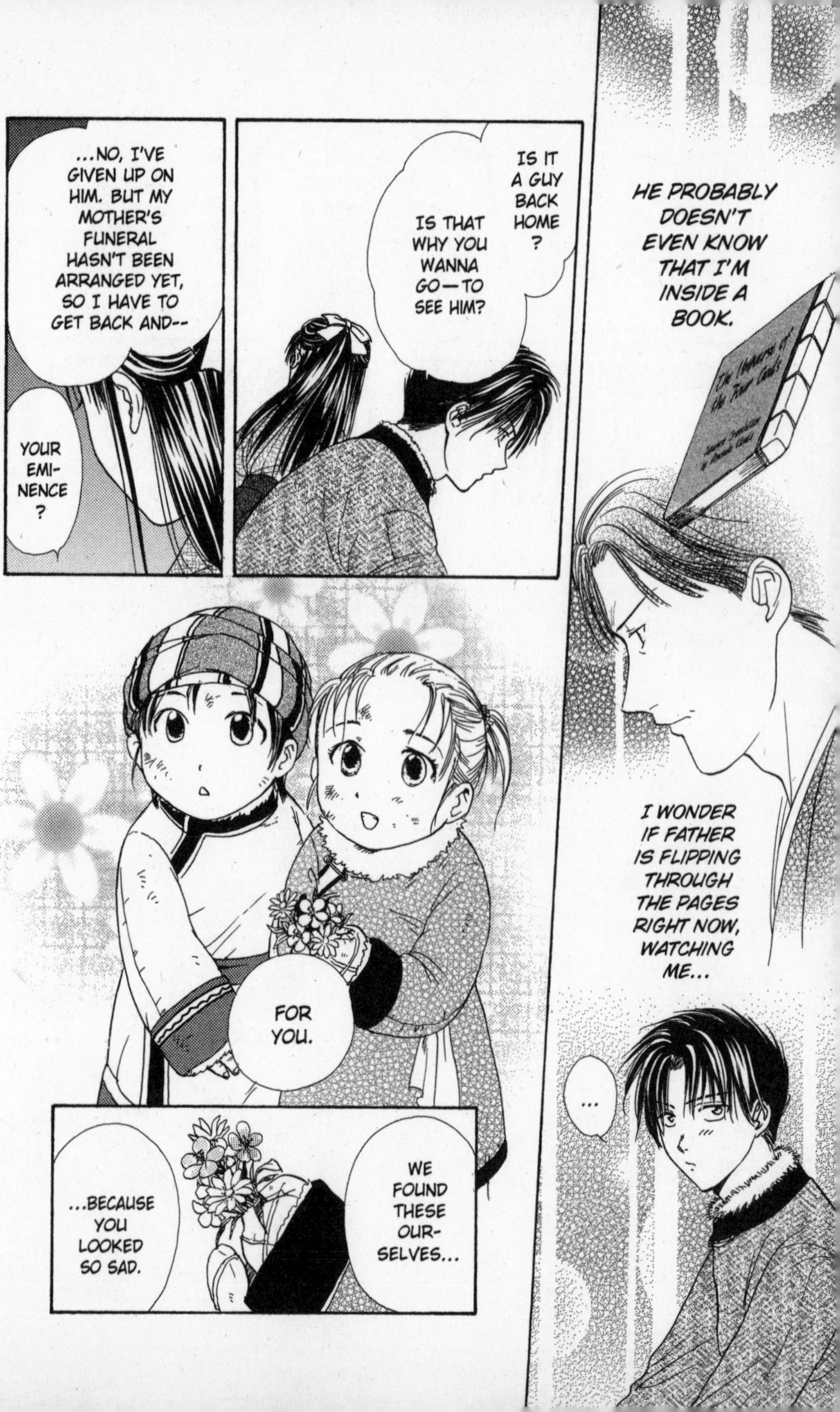
HE PROBABLY DOESN'T EVEN KNOW THAT I'M INSIDE A BOOK.
I WONDER IF FATHER IS FLIPPING THROUGH THE PAGES RIGHT NOW, WATCHING ME...
...
IS IT A GUY BACK HOME?
IS THAT WHY YOU WANNA GO—TO SEE HIM?
...NO, I'VE GIVEN UP ON HIM. BUT MY MOTHER'S FUNERAL HASN'T BEEN ARRANGED YET, SO I HAVE TO GET BACK AND--
YOUR EMINENCE?
FOR YOU.
WE FOUND THESE OURSELVES...
...BECAUSE YOU LOOKED SO SAD.

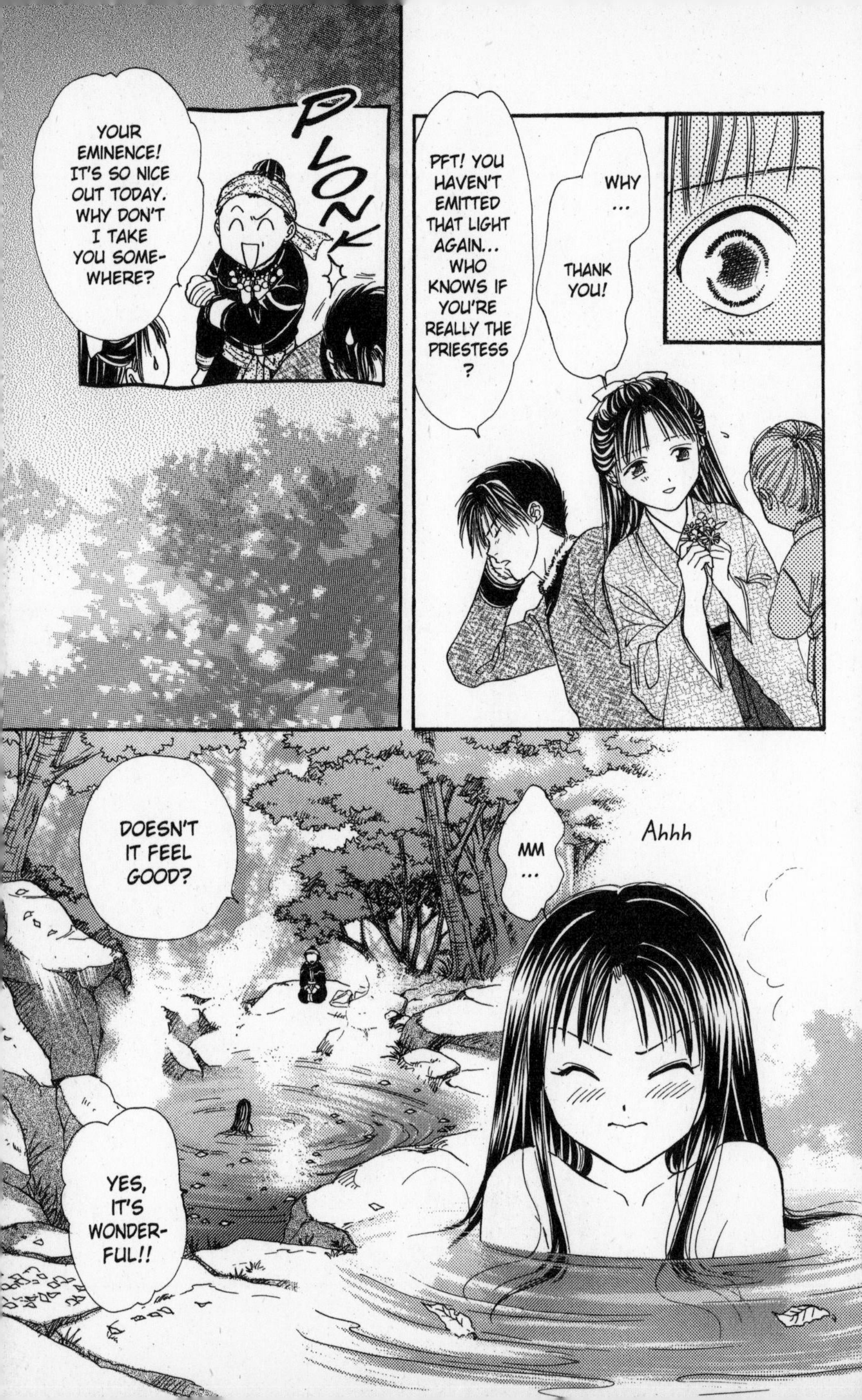
WHY ... THANK YOU!
PFT! YOU HAVEN'T EMITTED THAT LIGHT AGAIN... WHO KNOWS IF YOU'RE REALLY THE PRIESTESS?
PLONK
YOUR EMINENCE! IT'S SO NICE OUT TODAY. WHY DON'T I TAKE YOU SOME-WHERE?
Ahhh
MM ...
DOESN'T IT FEEL GOOD?
YES, IT'S WONDER-FUL!!

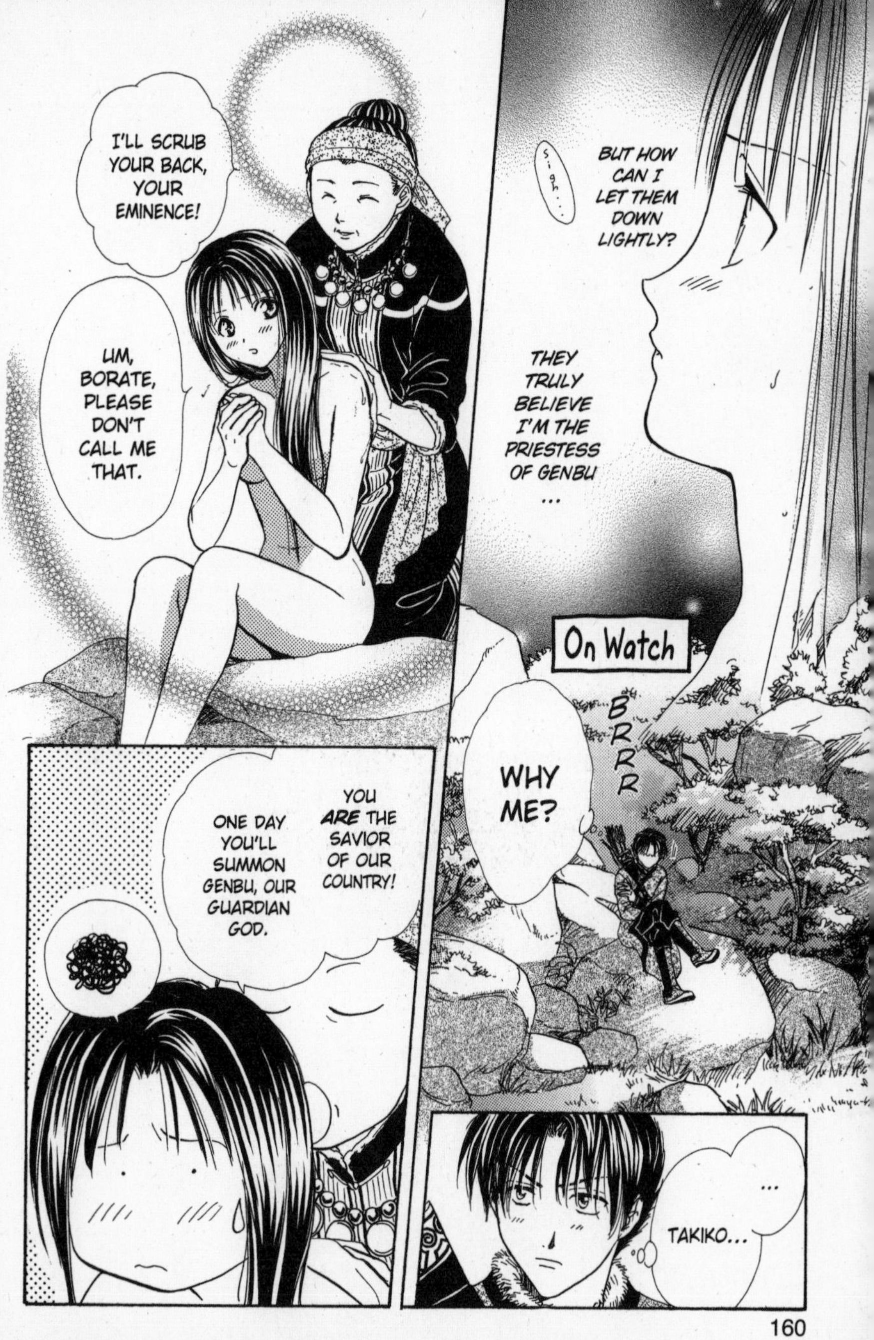

I'LL SCRUB YOUR BACK, YOUR EMINENCE!
UM, BORATE, PLEASE DON'T CALL ME THAT.
YOU ARE THE SAVIOR OF OUR COUNTRY!
ONE DAY YOU'LL SUMMON GENBU, OUR GUARDIAN GOD.
sigh...
BUT HOW CAN I LET THEM DOWN LIGHTLY?
THEY TRULY BELIEVE I'M THE PRIESTESS OF GENBU...
On Watch
WHY ME?
BRRR
...
TAKIKO...

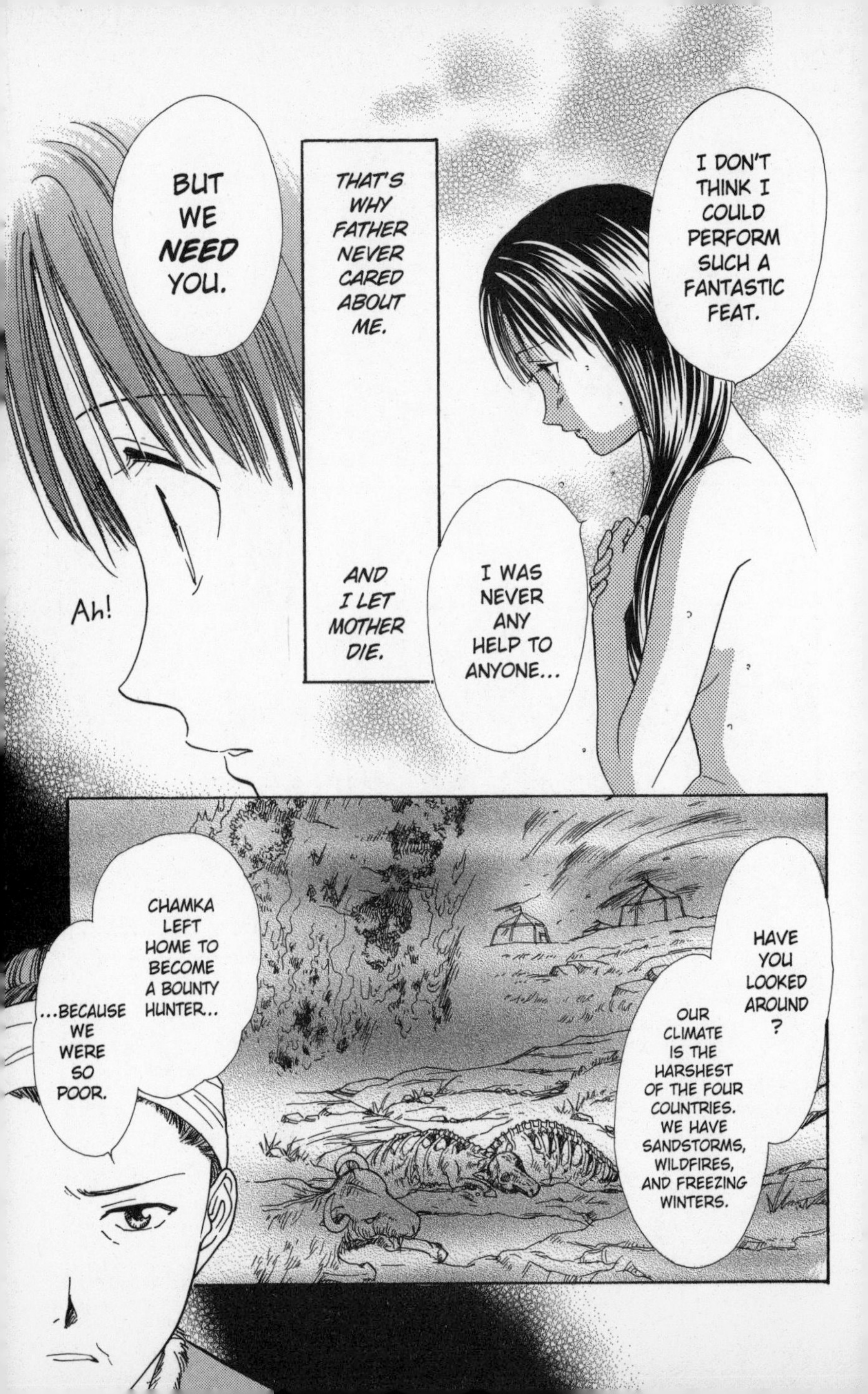
I DON'T THINK I COULD PERFORM SUCH A FANTASTIC FEAT.
THAT'S WHY FATHER NEVER CARED ABOUT ME.
I WAS NEVER ANY HELP TO ANYONE...
AND I LET MOTHER DIE.
BUT WE NEED YOU.
Ah!
HAVE YOU LOOKED AROUND?
OUR CLIMATE IS THE HARSHEST OF THE FOUR COUNTRIES. WE HAVE SANDSTORMS, WILDFIRES, AND FREEZING WINTERS.
CHAMKA LEFT HOME TO BECOME A BOUNTY HUNTER...
...BECAUSE WE WERE SO POOR.

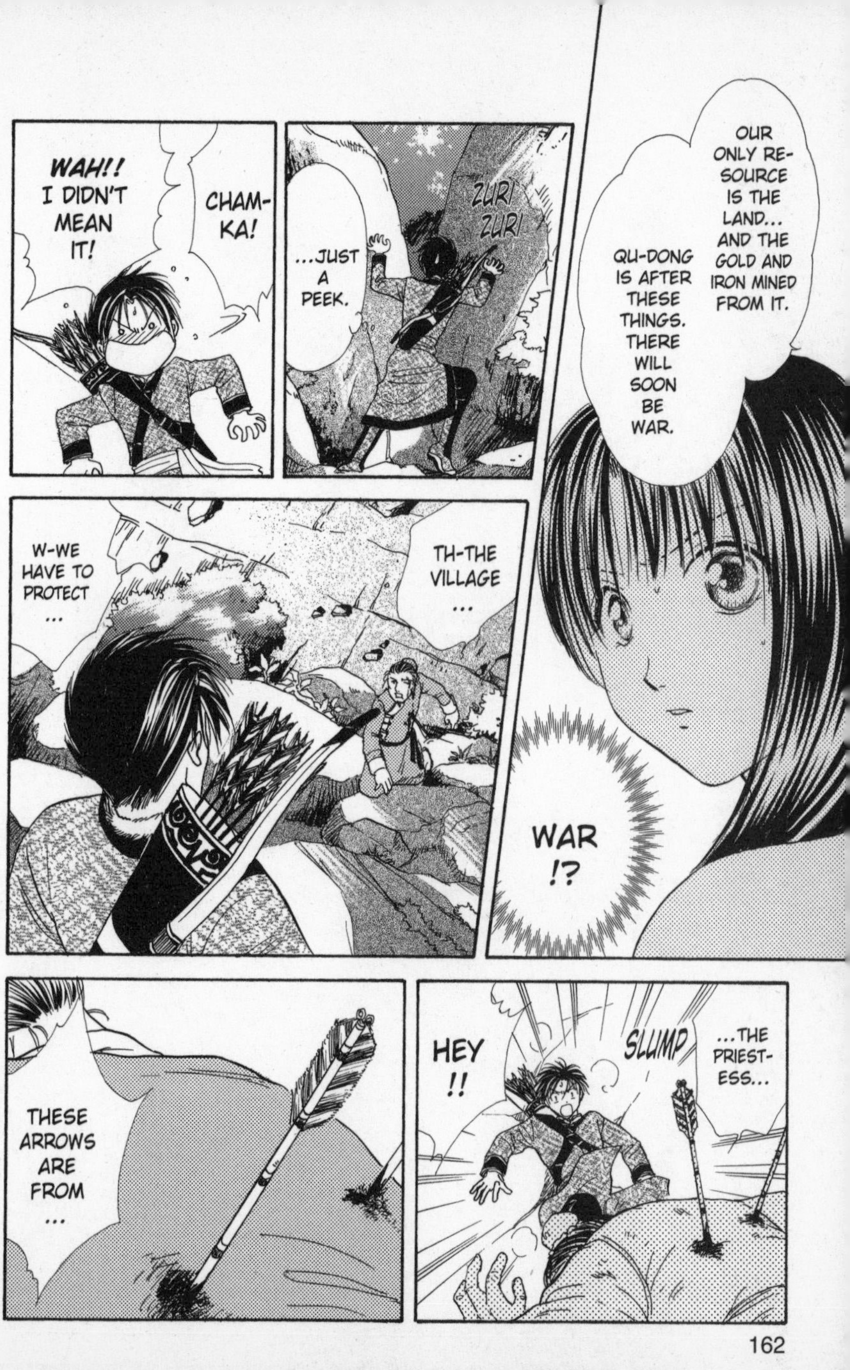
OUR ONLY RESOURCE IS THE LAND... AND THE GOLD AND IRON MINED FROM IT.
QU-DONG IS AFTER THESE THINGS. THERE WILL SOON BE WAR.
WAR !?
ZURI ZURI
...JUST A PEEK.
CHAMKA!
WAH!! I DIDN'T MEAN IT!
TH-THE VILLAGE ...
W-WE HAVE TO PROTECT ...
...THE PRIESTESS...
SLUMP
HEY !!
THESE ARROWS ARE FROM ...

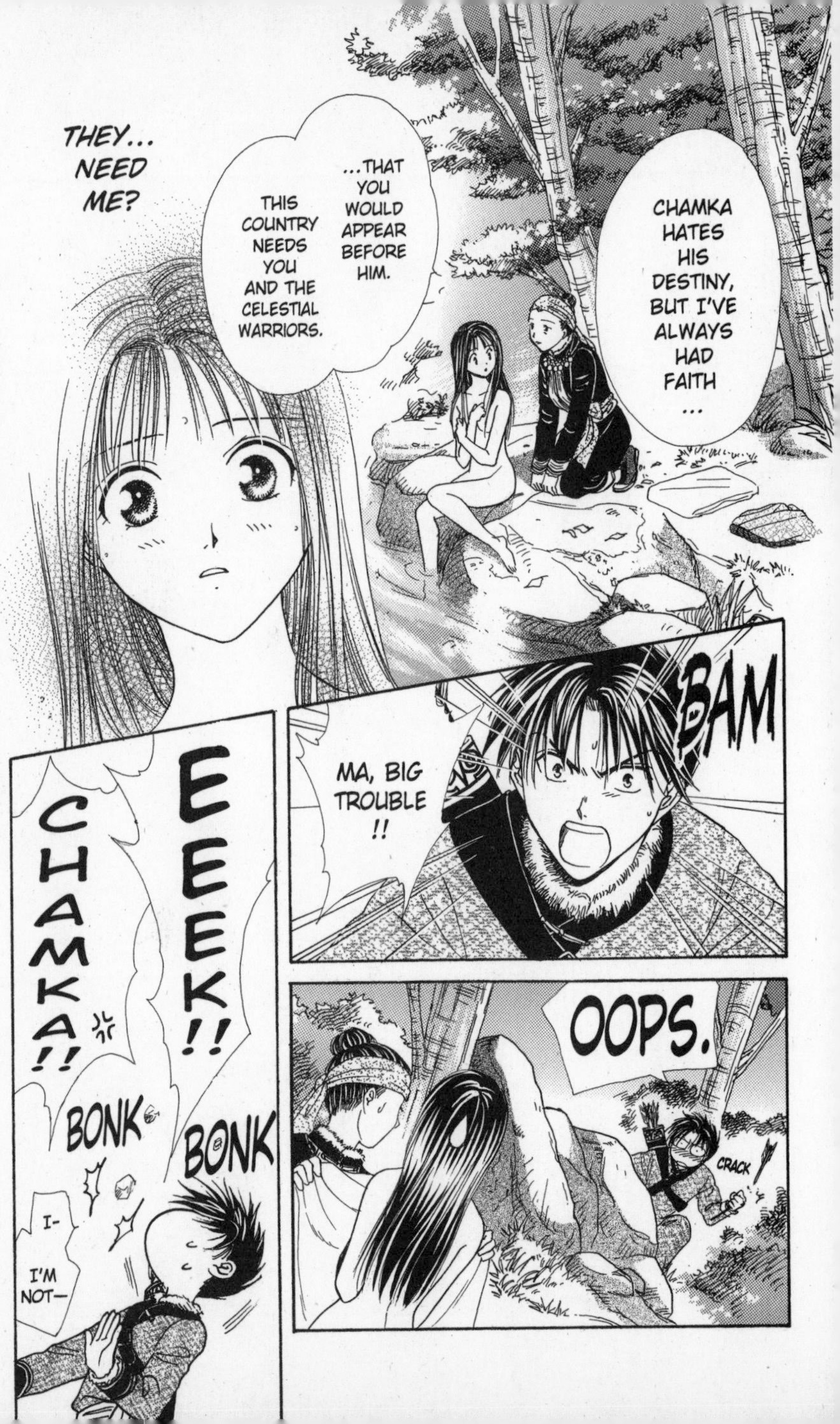
CHAMKA HATES HIS DESTINY, BUT I'VE ALWAYS HAD FAITH ...
...THAT YOU WOULD APPEAR BEFORE HIM.
THIS COUNTRY NEEDS YOU AND THE CELESTIAL WARRIORS.
THEY... NEED ME?
BAM
MA, BIG TROUBLE !!
OOPS.
CRACK
EEEEK!!
CHAMKA!!
BONK
BONK
I-
I'M NOT—

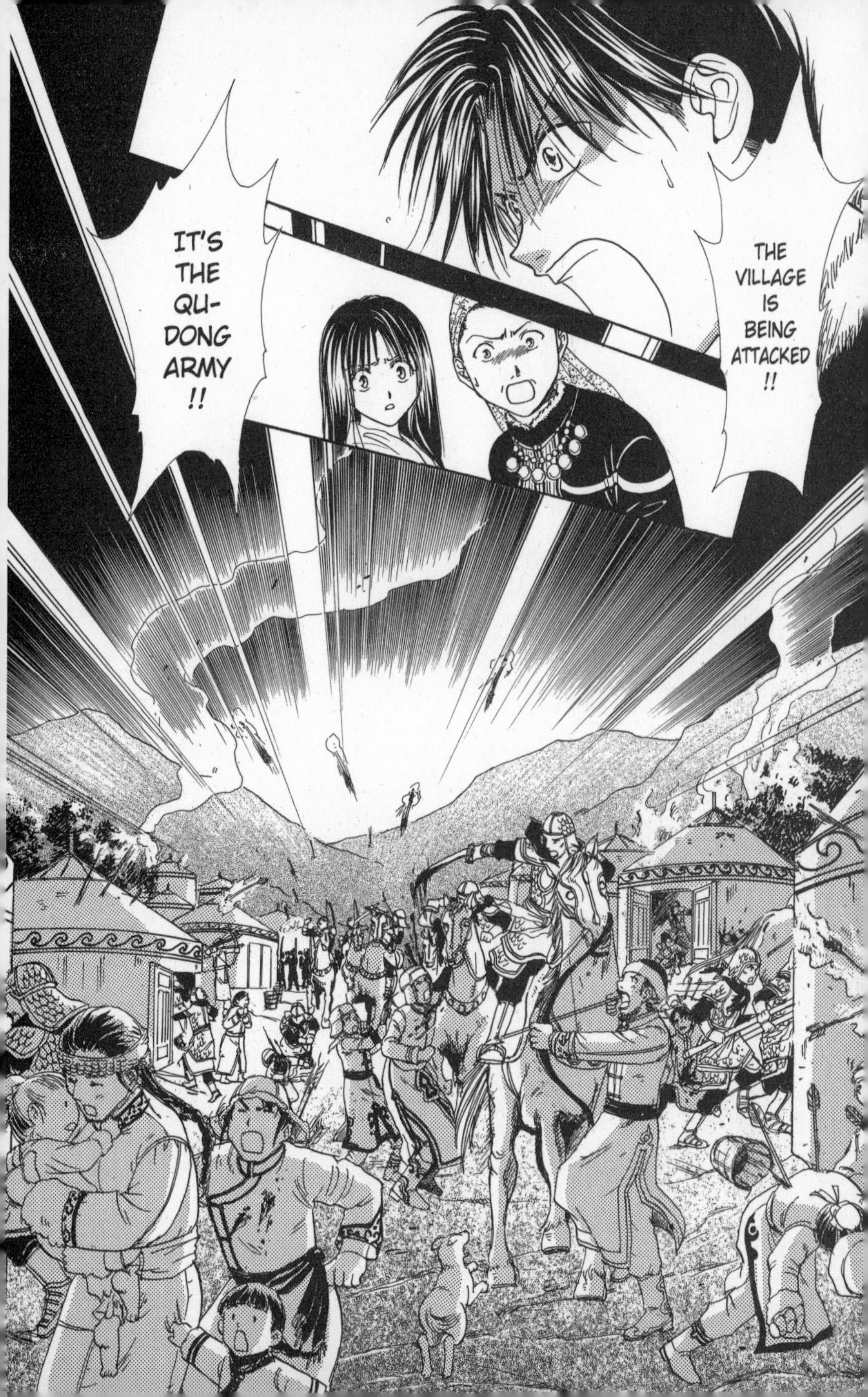
THE VILLAGE IS BEING ATTACKED!!
IT'S THE QU-DONG ARMY!!

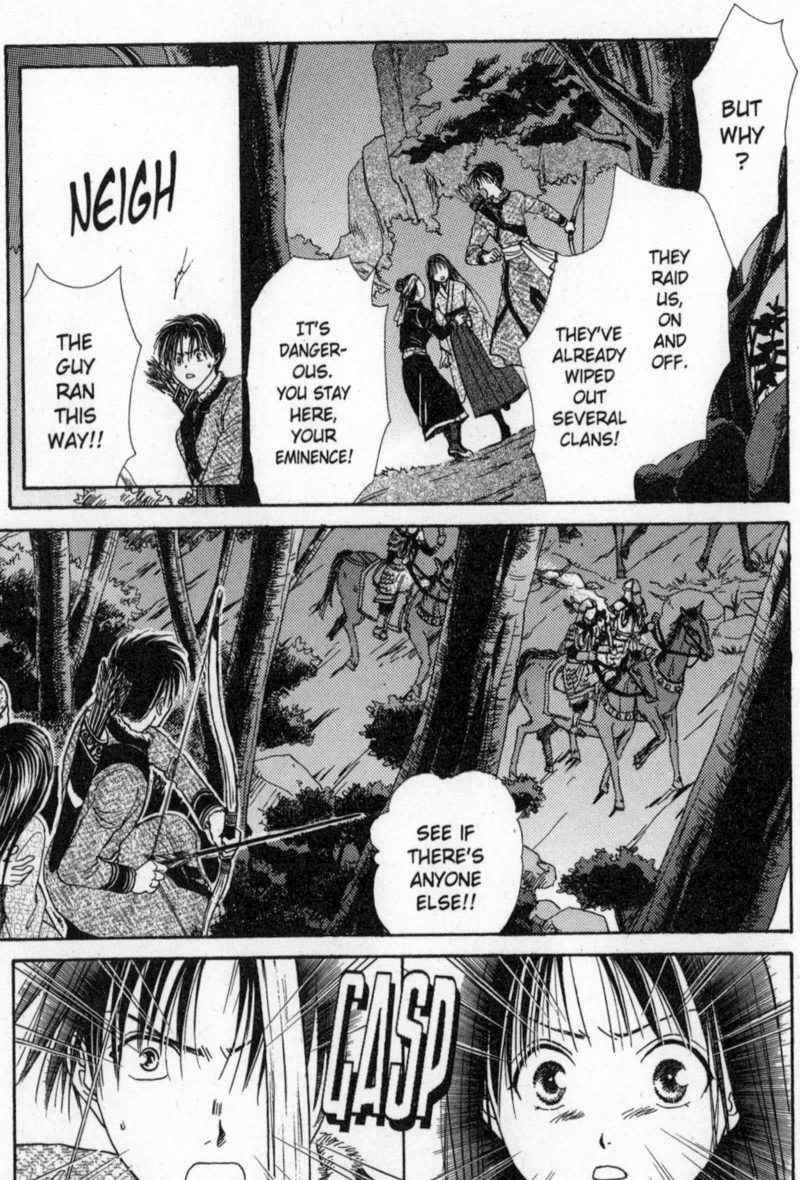
BUT WHY?
THEY RAID US, ON AND OFF.
THEY'VE ALREADY WIPED OUT SEVERAL CLANS!
IT'S DANGER-OUS. YOU STAY HERE, YOUR EMINENCE!
NEIGH
THE GUY RAN THIS WAY!!
SEE IF THERE'S ANYONE ELSE!!
GASP

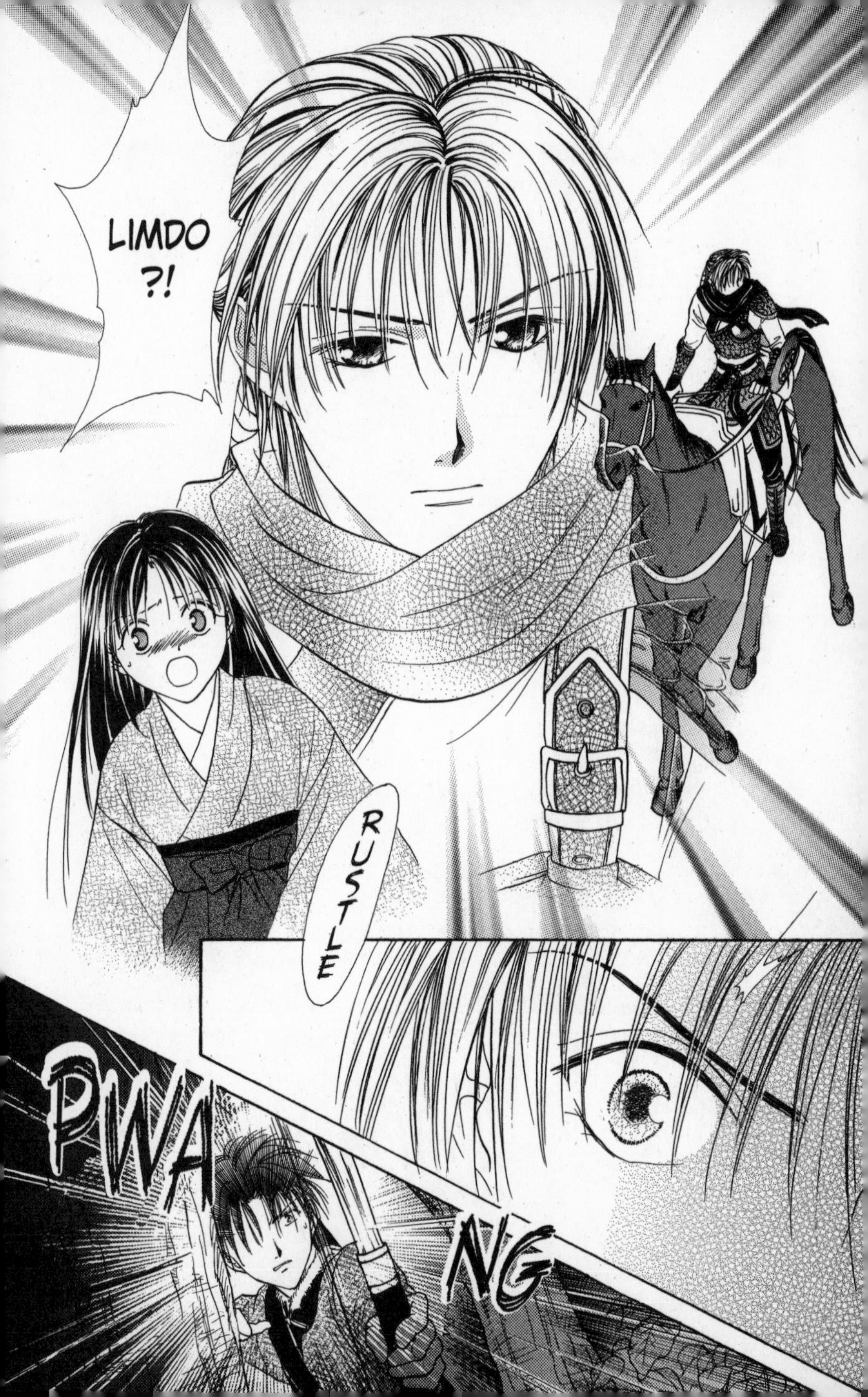
LIMDO ?!
RUSTLE
PWANG

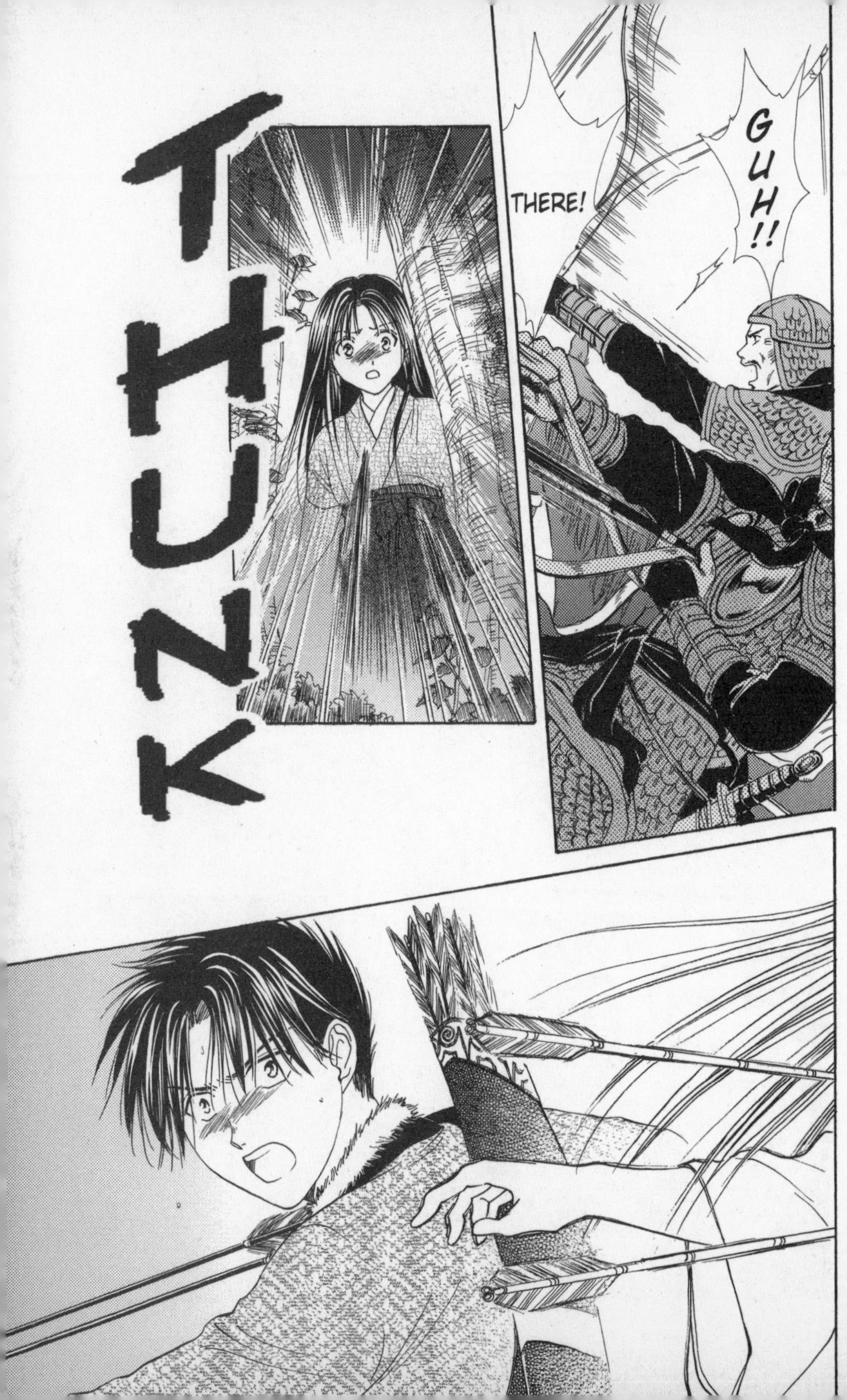
GUH!!
THERE!
THUNK

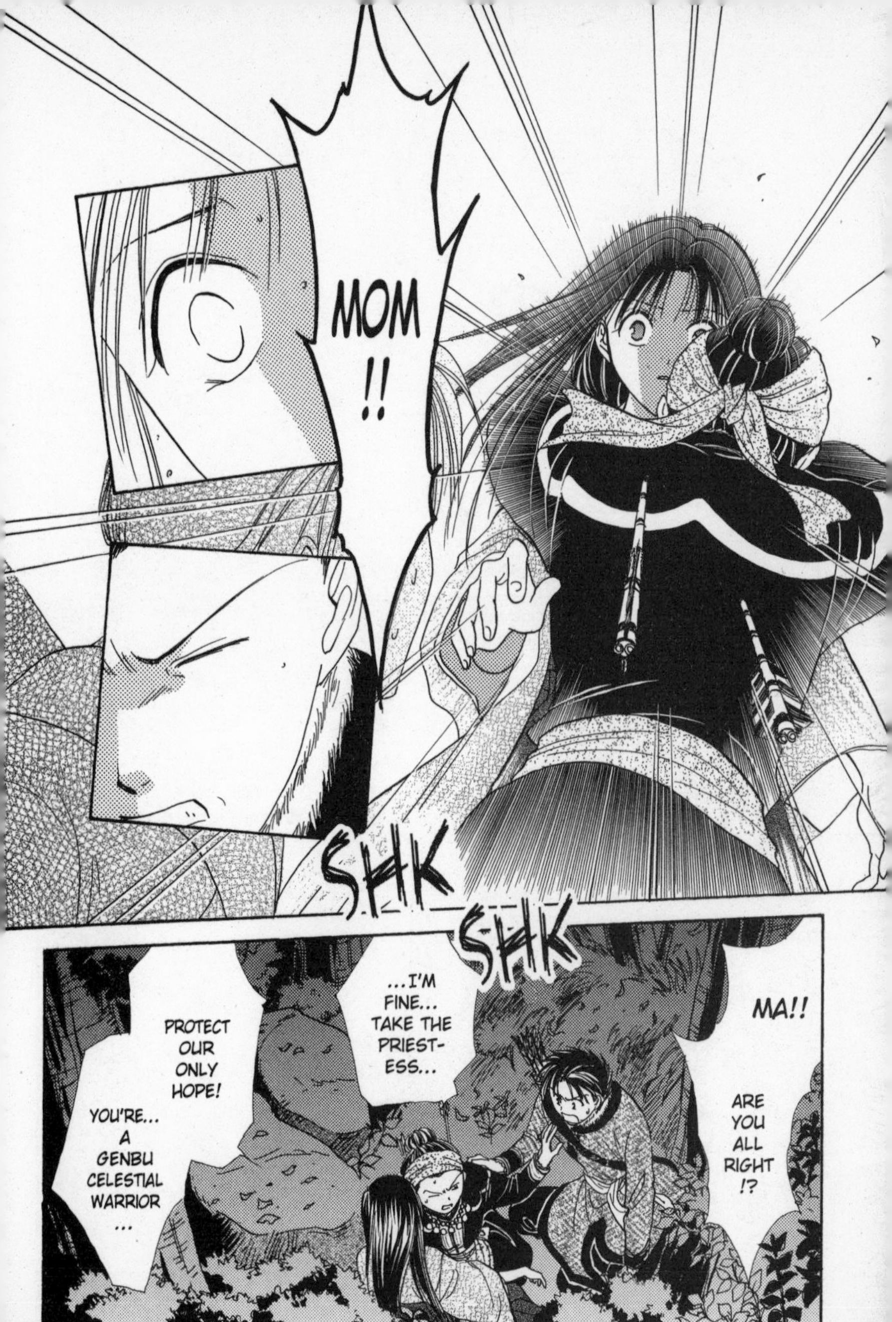
MOM!!
SHK
SHK
MA!!
ARE YOU ALL RIGHT!?
...I'M FINE... TAKE THE PRIEST-ESS...
PROTECT OUR ONLY HOPE!
YOU'RE... A GENBU CELESTIAL WARRIOR...

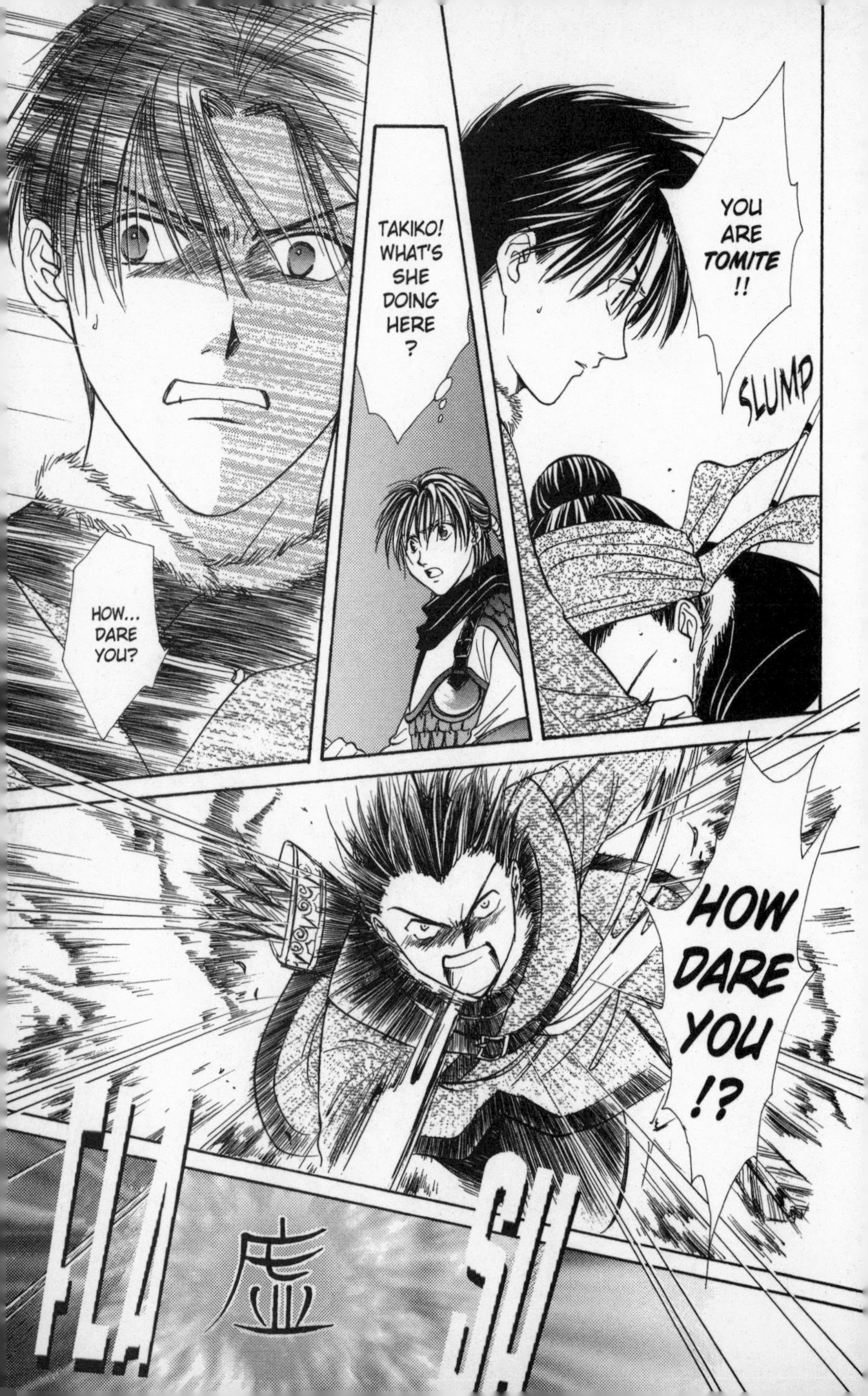
YOU ARE TOMITE !!
SLUMP
TAKIKO! WHAT'S SHE DOING HERE ?
HOW... DARE YOU?
HOW DARE YOU !?
FLA
虚
SH

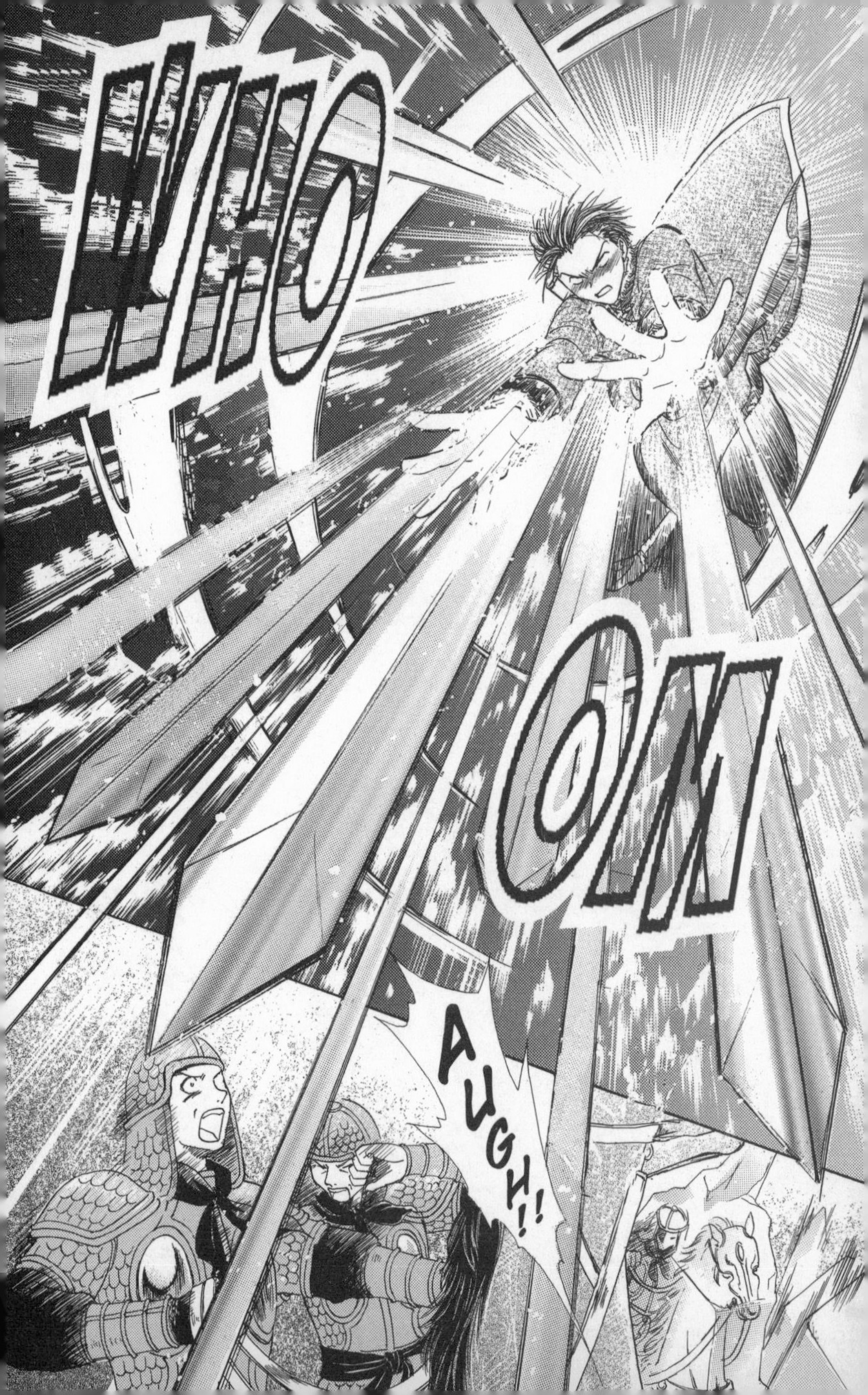
WHO
OM
AUGH!!

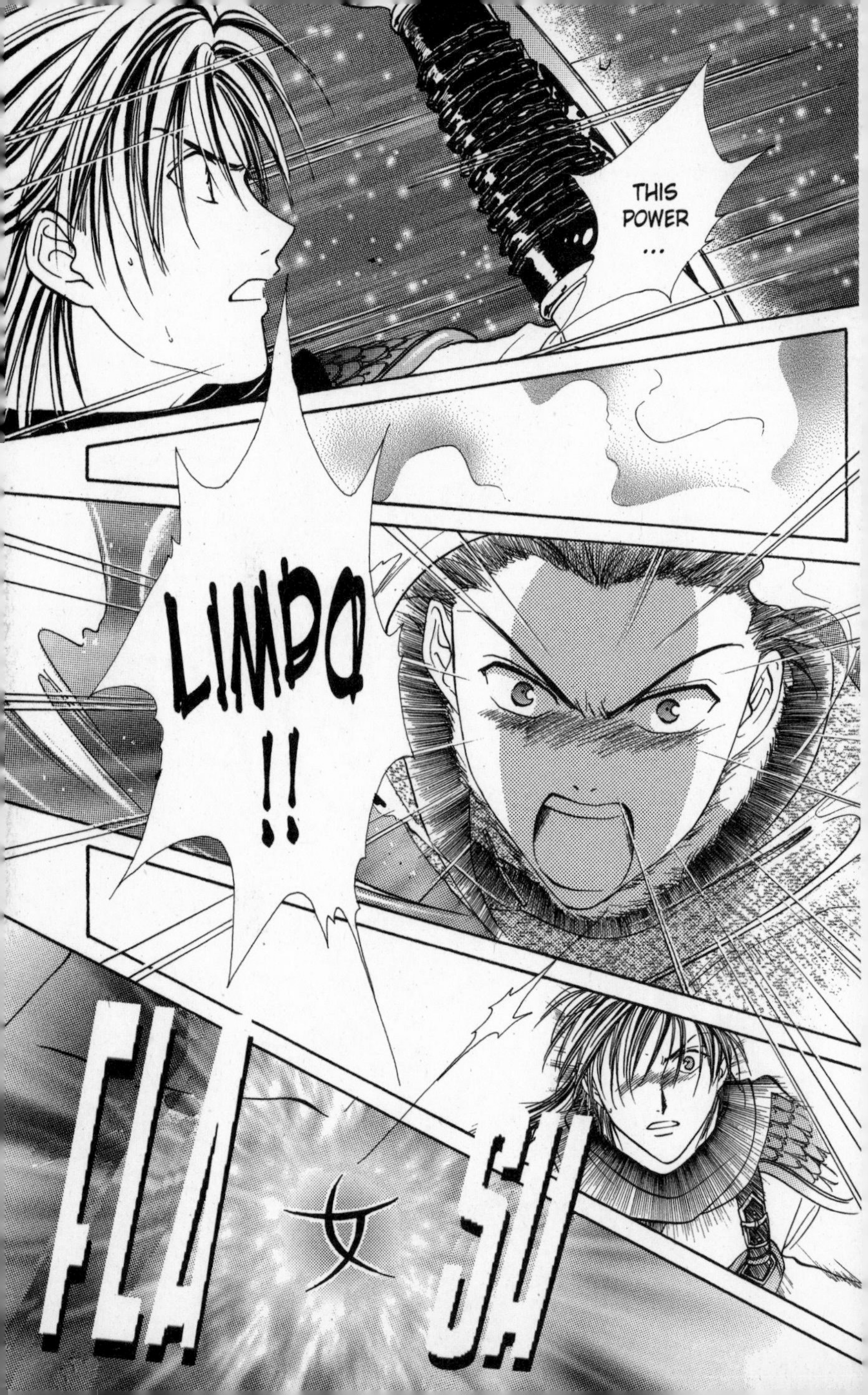
THIS POWER ...
LIMBO !!
FLA SH

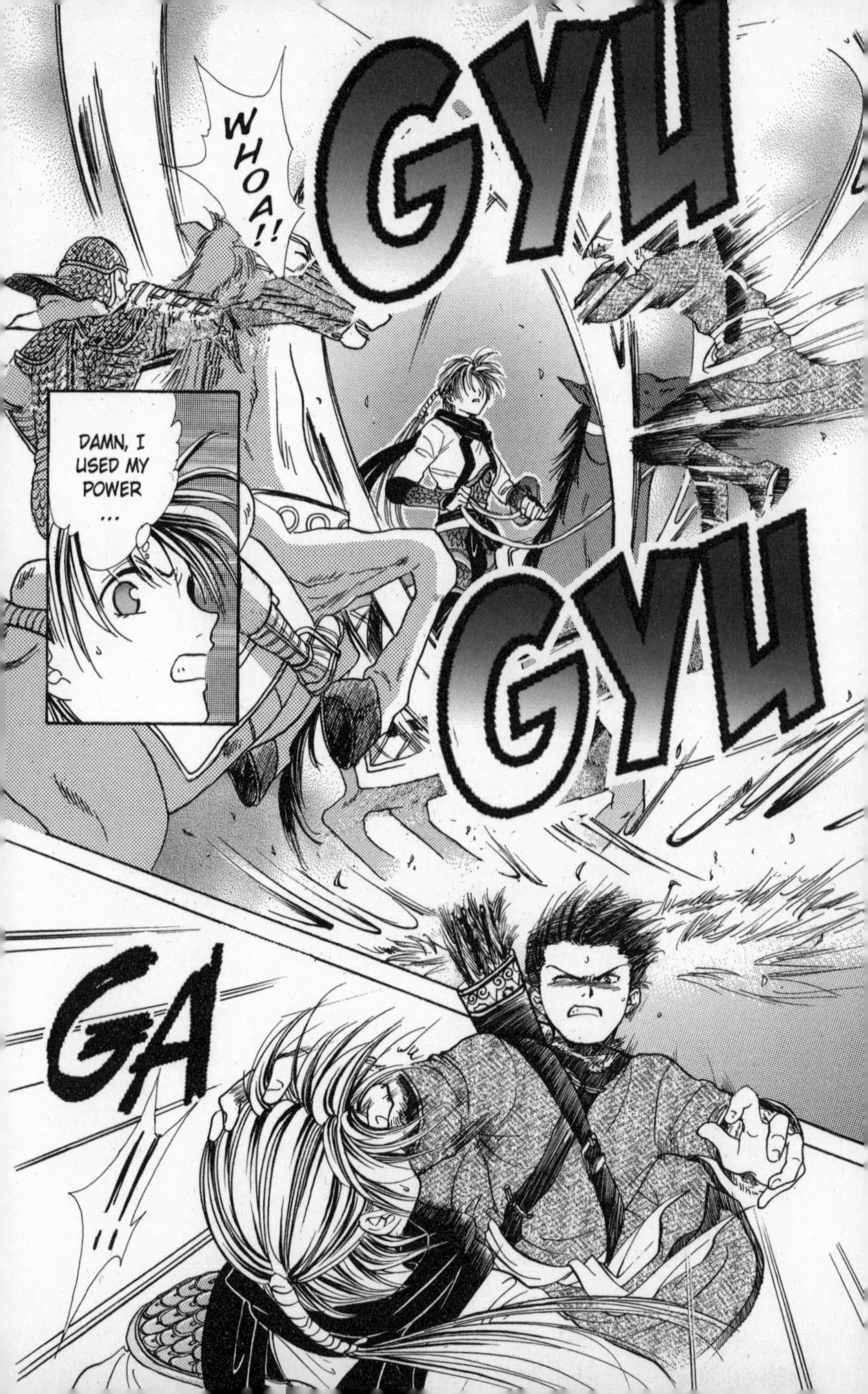
GYH
WHOA!!
GYH
DAMN, I USED MY POWER ...
GA

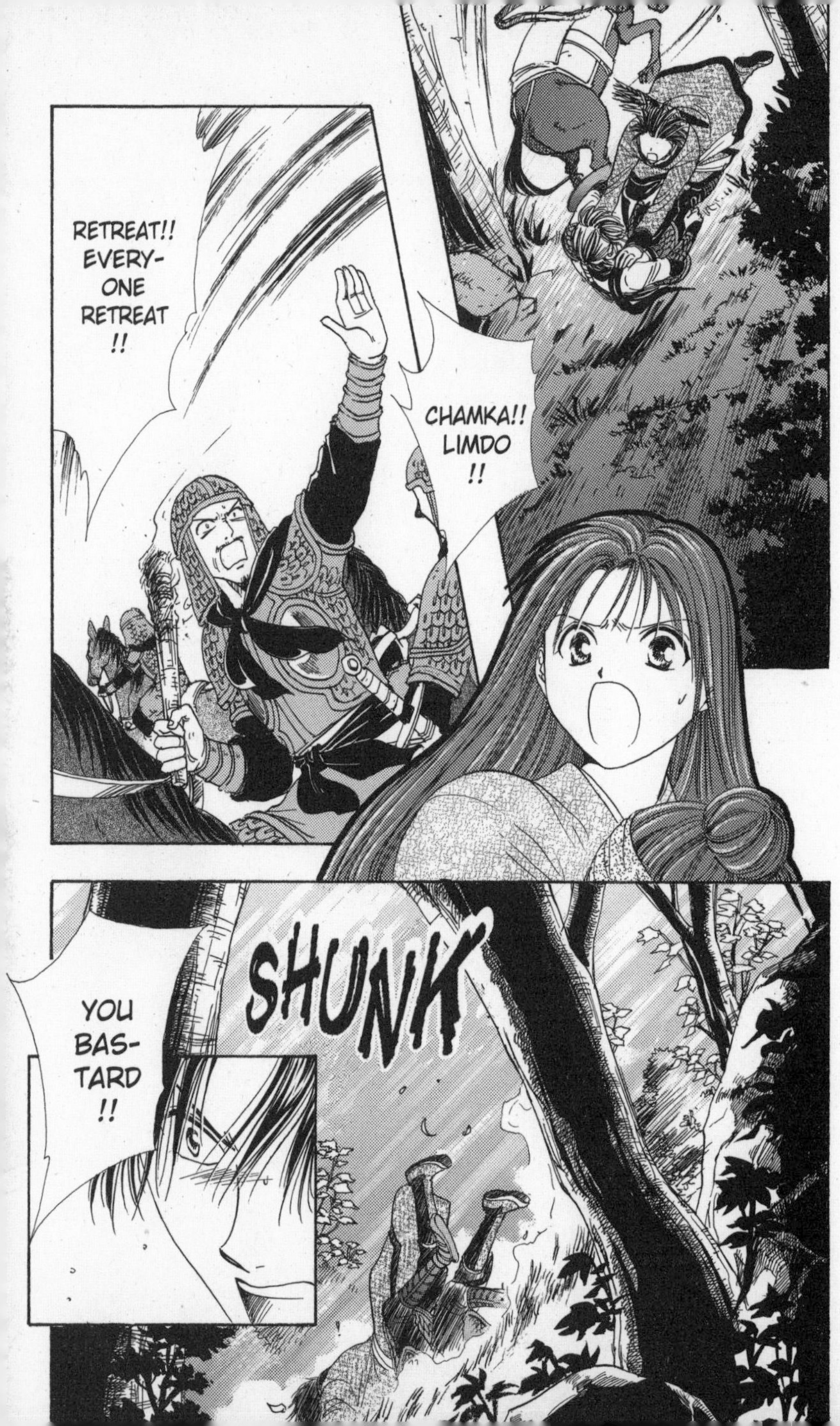
CHAMKA!! LIMDO!!
RETREAT!! EVERY-ONE RETREAT!!
SHUNK
YOU BAS-TARD!!

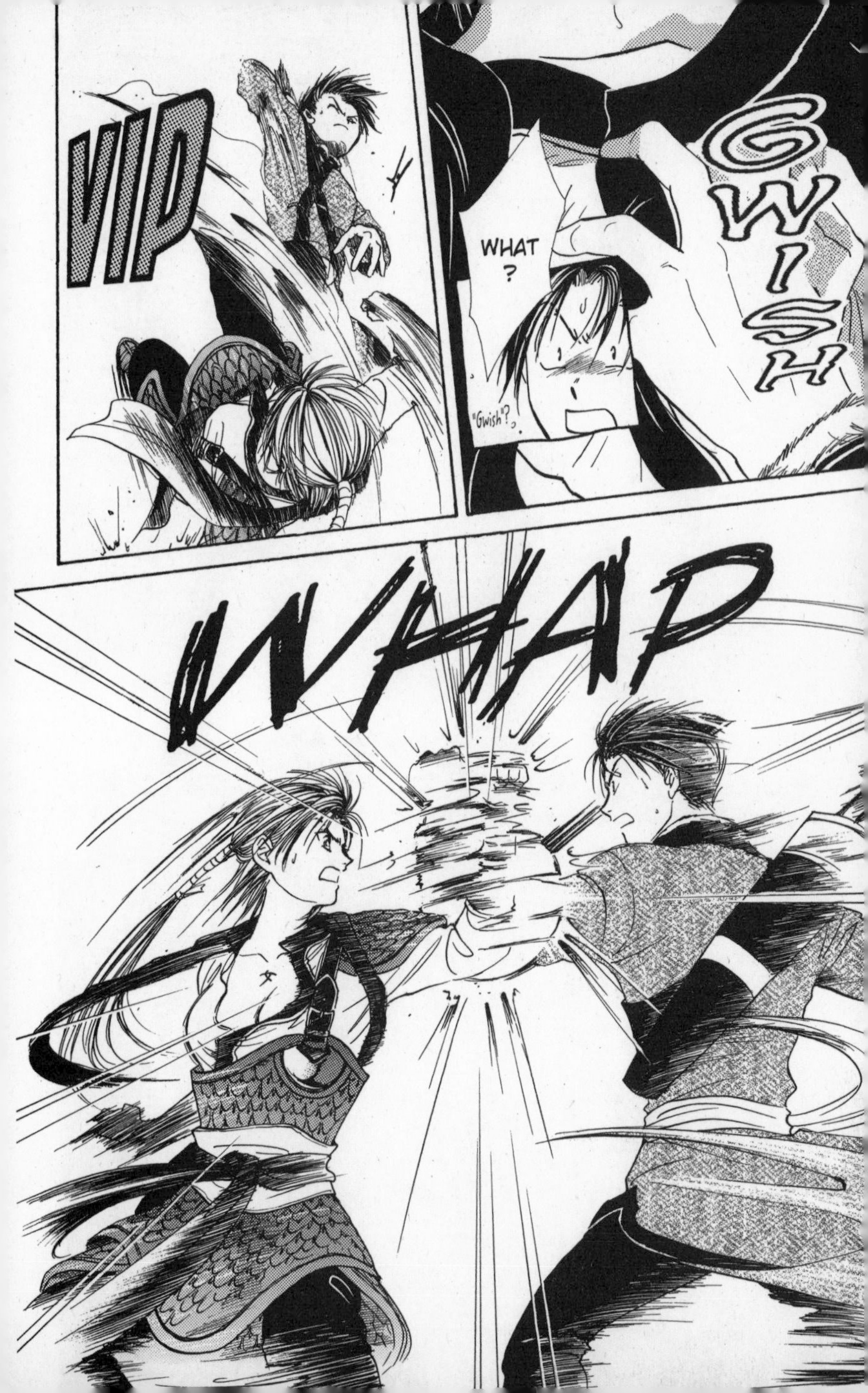
GWISH
WHAT?
"Gwish"?
VIP
WHAP

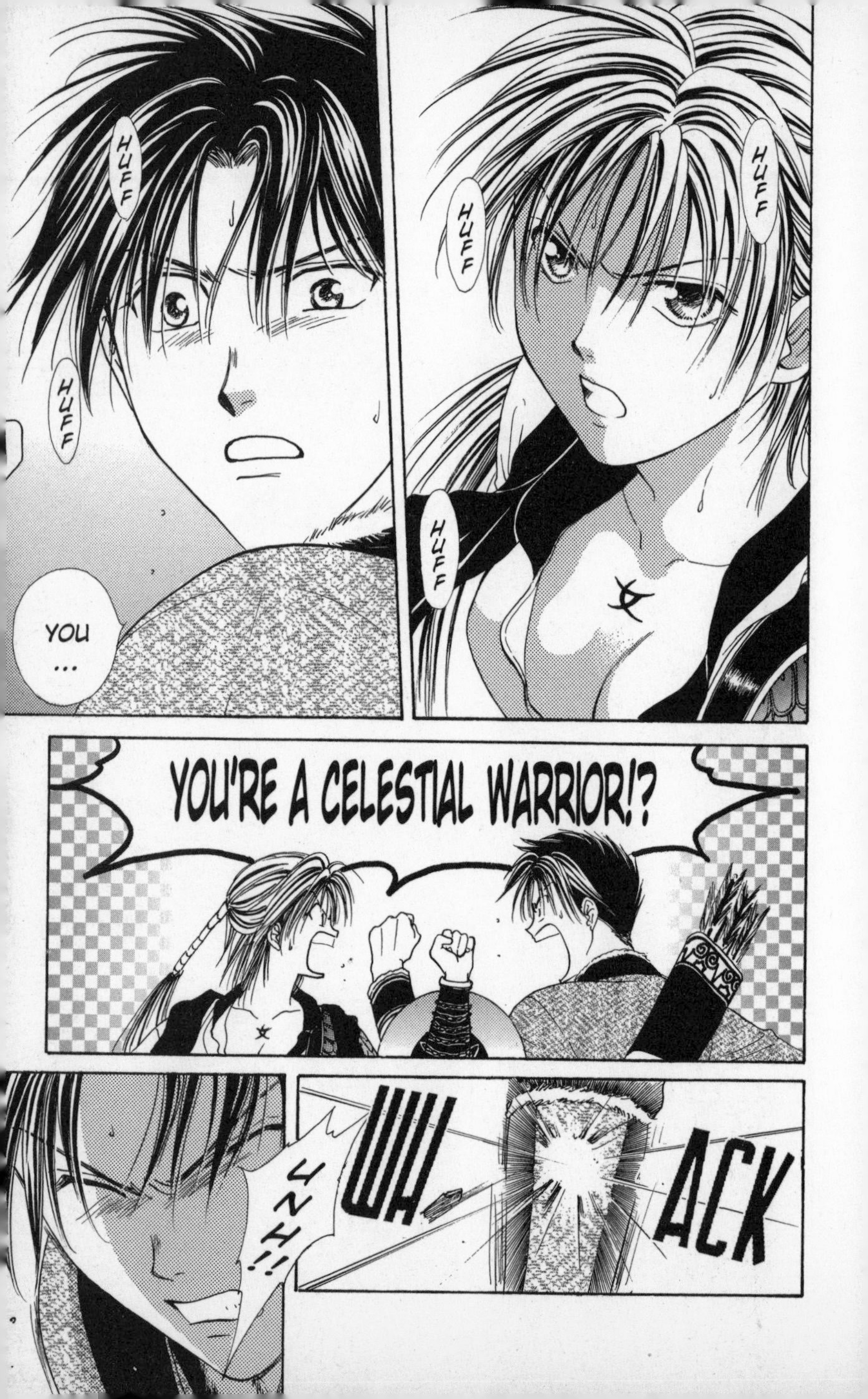

HUFF
HUFF
HUFF
HUFF
HUFF
YOU ...
YOU'RE A CELESTIAL WARRIOR!?
WHACK
UNH!!

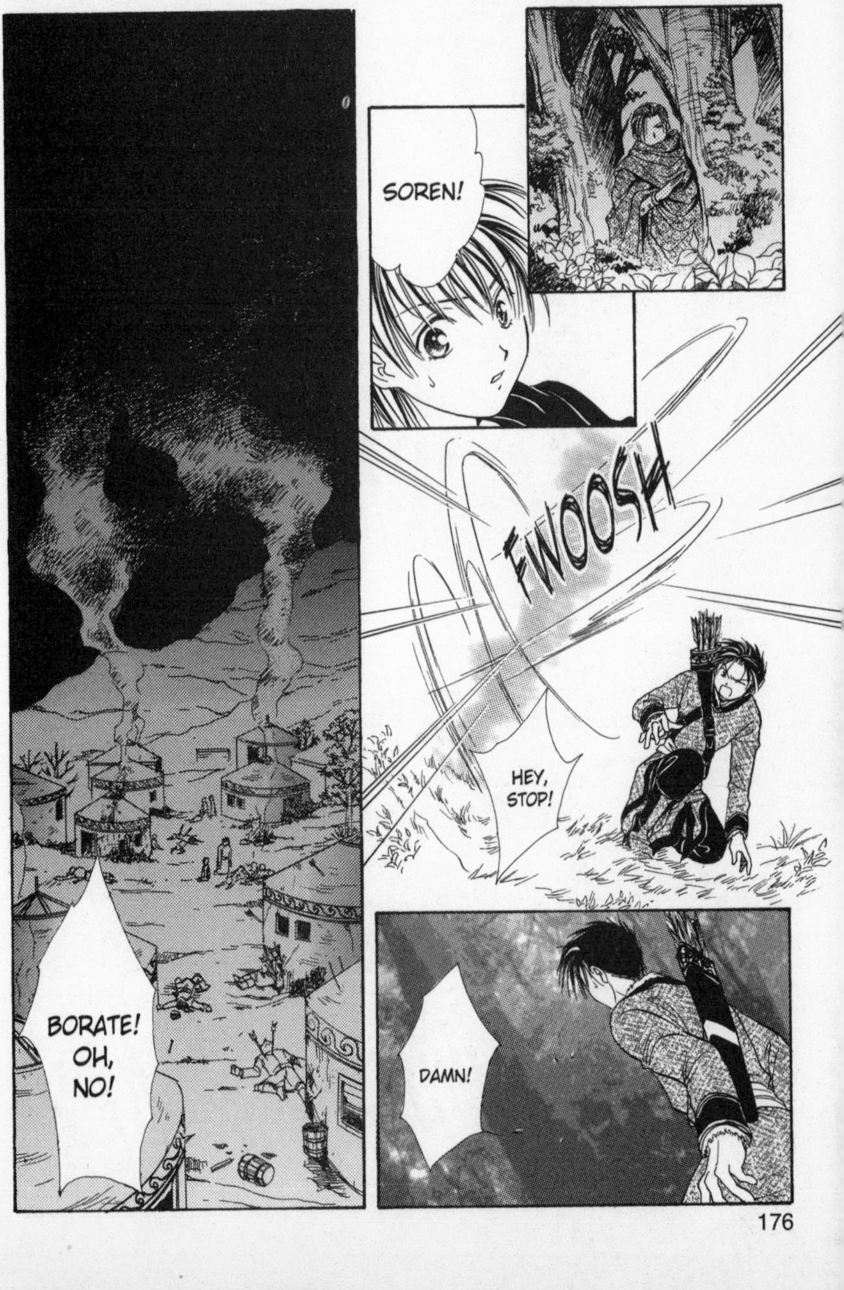
SOREN!
FWOOSH
HEY, STOP!
DAMN!
BORATE! OH, NO!

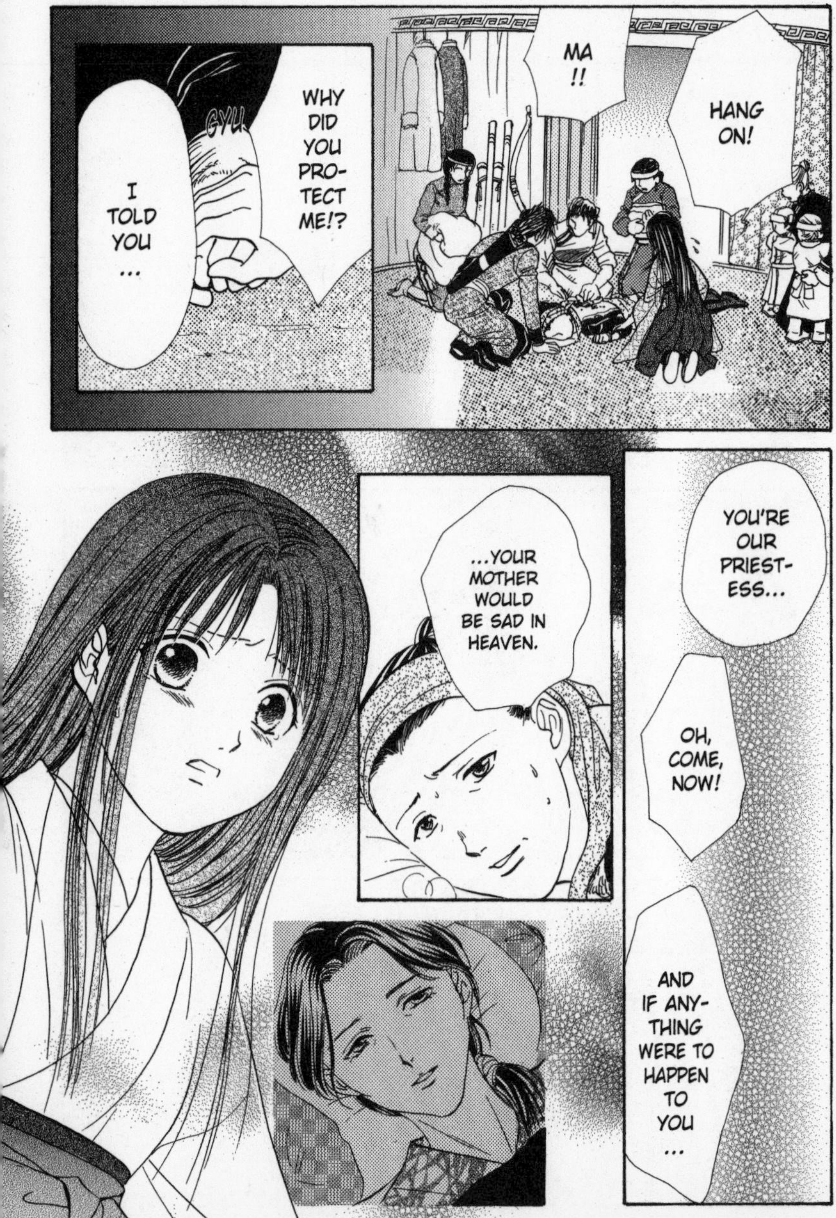
HANG ON!
MA !!
WHY DID YOU PRO-TECT ME!?
GYU
I TOLD YOU ...
YOU'RE OUR PRIEST-ESS...
OH, COME, NOW!
AND IF ANY-THING WERE TO HAPPEN TO YOU ...
...YOUR MOTHER WOULD BE SAD IN HEAVEN.

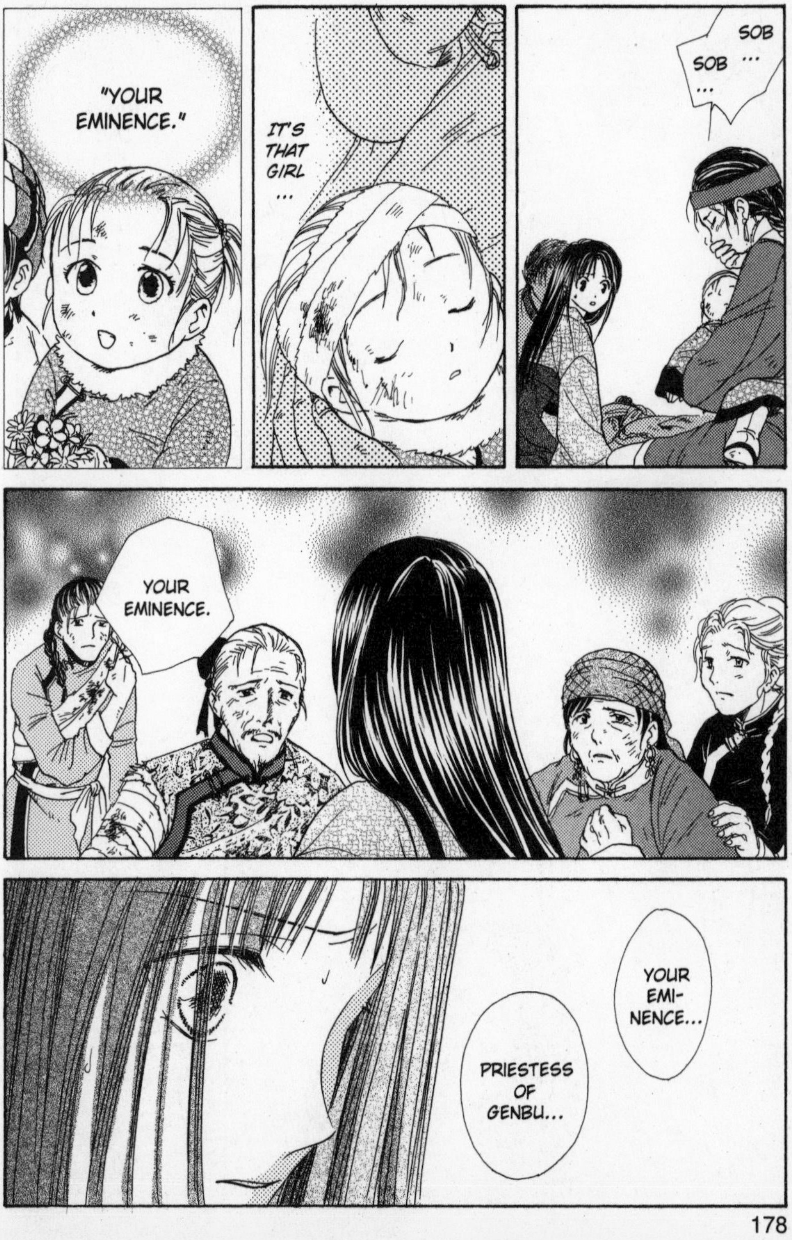
SOB ...
SOB ...
IT'S THAT GIRL ...
"YOUR EMINENCE."
YOUR EMINENCE.
YOUR EMI-NENCE...
PRIESTESS OF GENBU...

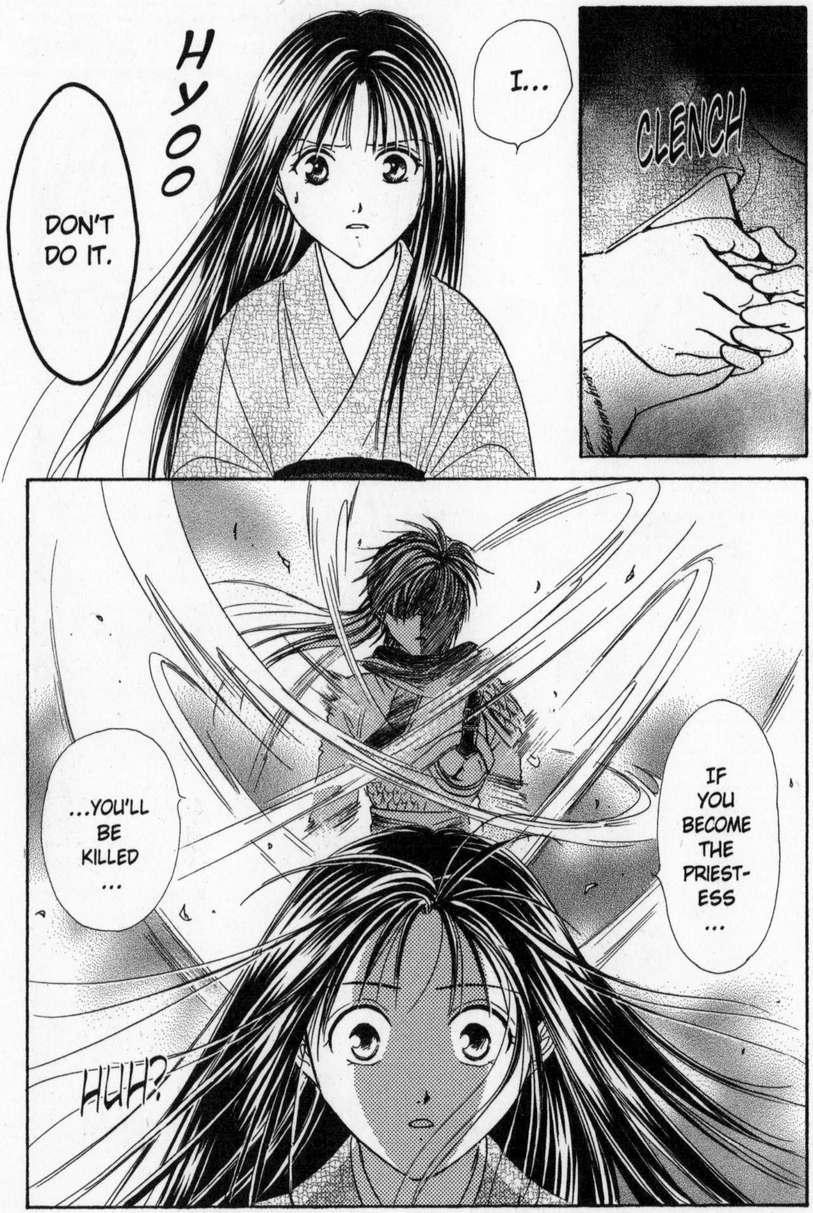
CLENCH
I...
HYOO
DON'T DO IT.
IF YOU BECOME THE PRIEST-ESS...
...YOU'LL BE KILLED...
HUH?

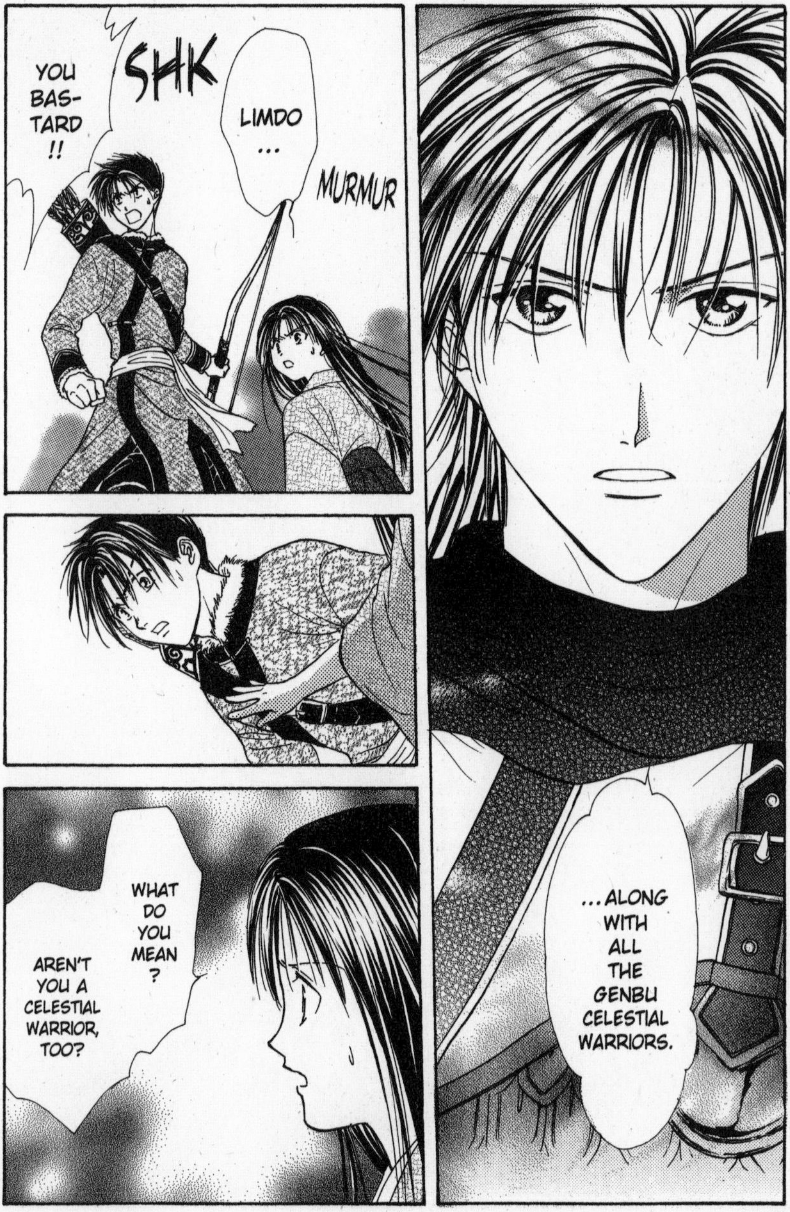
...ALONG WITH ALL THE GENBU CELESTIAL WARRIORS.
LIMDO...
MURMUR
SHK
YOU BASTARD!!
WHAT DO YOU MEAN?
AREN'T YOU A CELESTIAL WARRIOR, TOO?

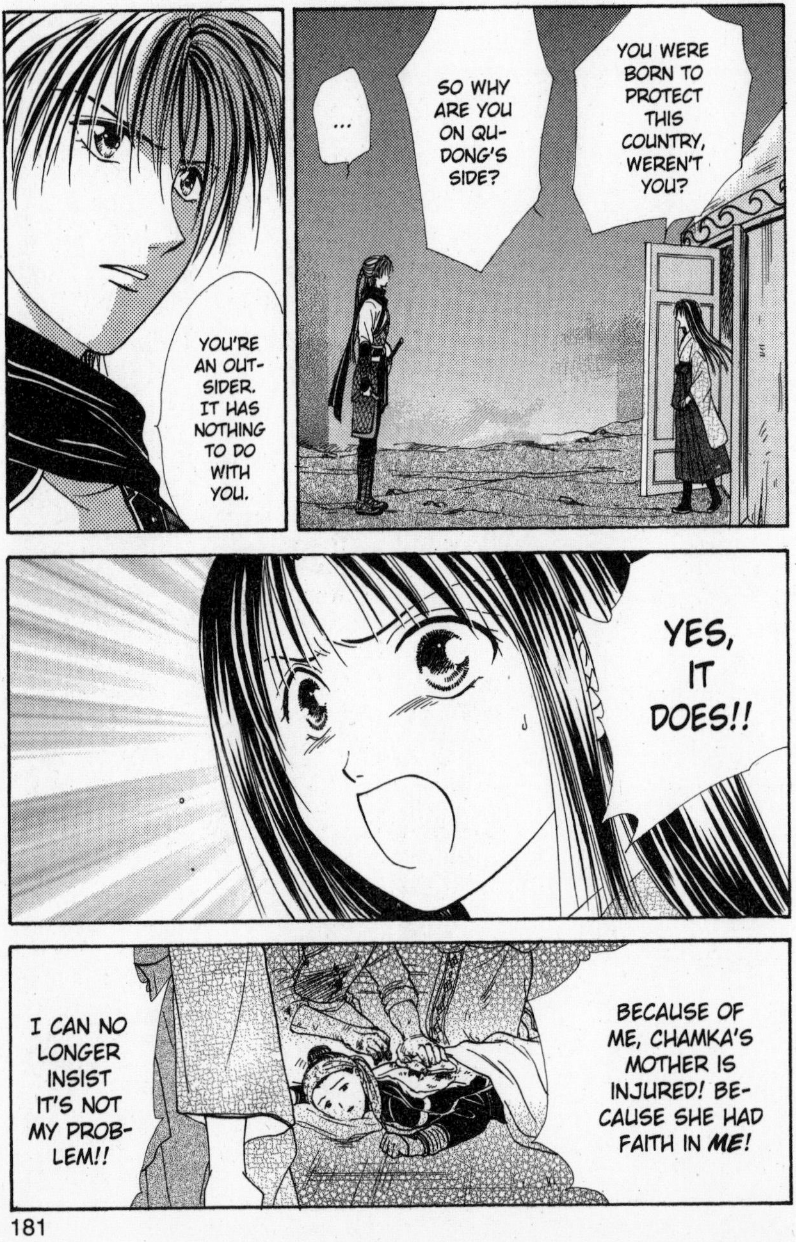

YOU WERE BORN TO PROTECT THIS COUNTRY, WEREN'T YOU?
SO WHY ARE YOU ON QU-DONG'S SIDE?
...
YOU'RE AN OUT-SIDER. IT HAS NOTHING TO DO WITH YOU.
YES, IT DOES!!
BECAUSE OF ME, CHAMKA'S MOTHER IS INJURED! BE-CAUSE SHE HAD FAITH IN *ME*!
I CAN NO LONGER INSIST IT'S NOT MY PROB-LEM!!

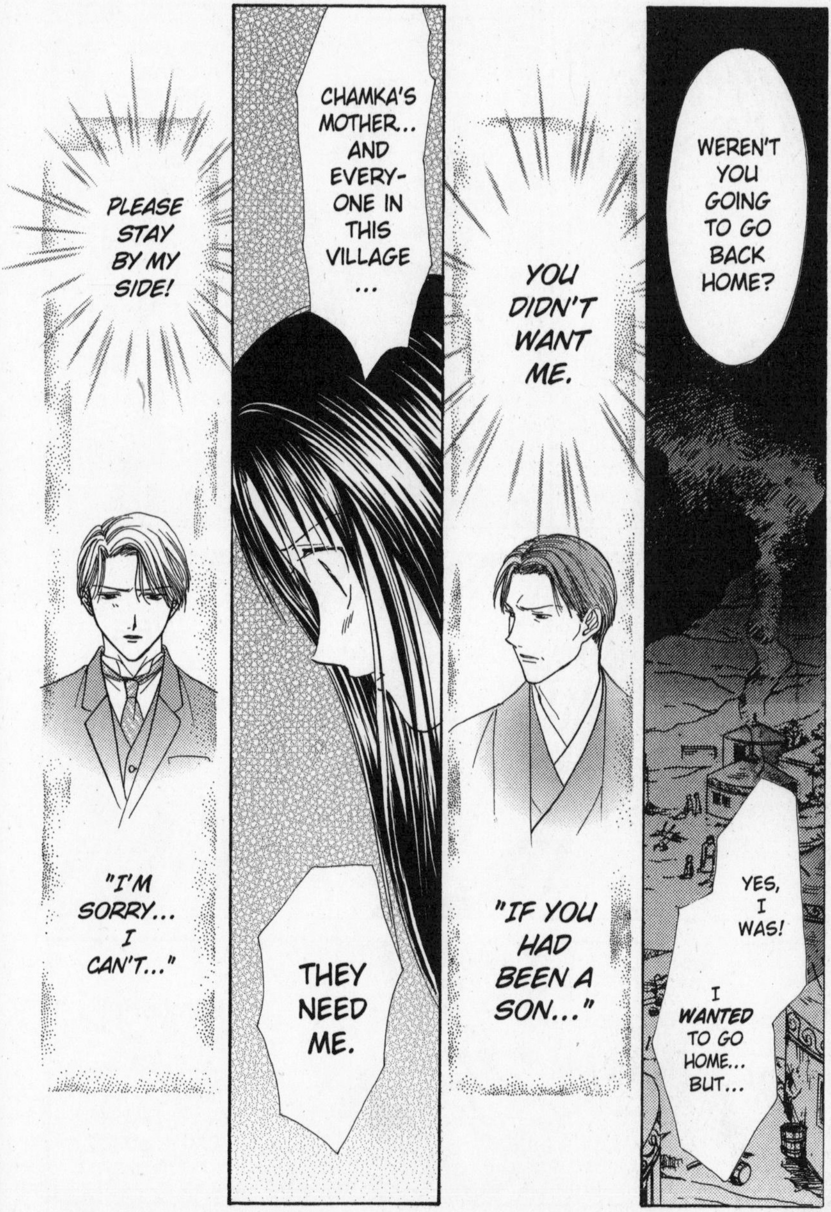
WEREN'T YOU GOING TO GO BACK HOME?
YES, I WAS!
I WANTED TO GO HOME... BUT...
YOU DIDN'T WANT ME.
"IF YOU HAD BEEN A SON..."
CHAMKA'S MOTHER... AND EVERYONE IN THIS VILLAGE ...
THEY NEED ME.
PLEASE STAY BY MY SIDE!
"I'M SORRY... I CAN'T..."

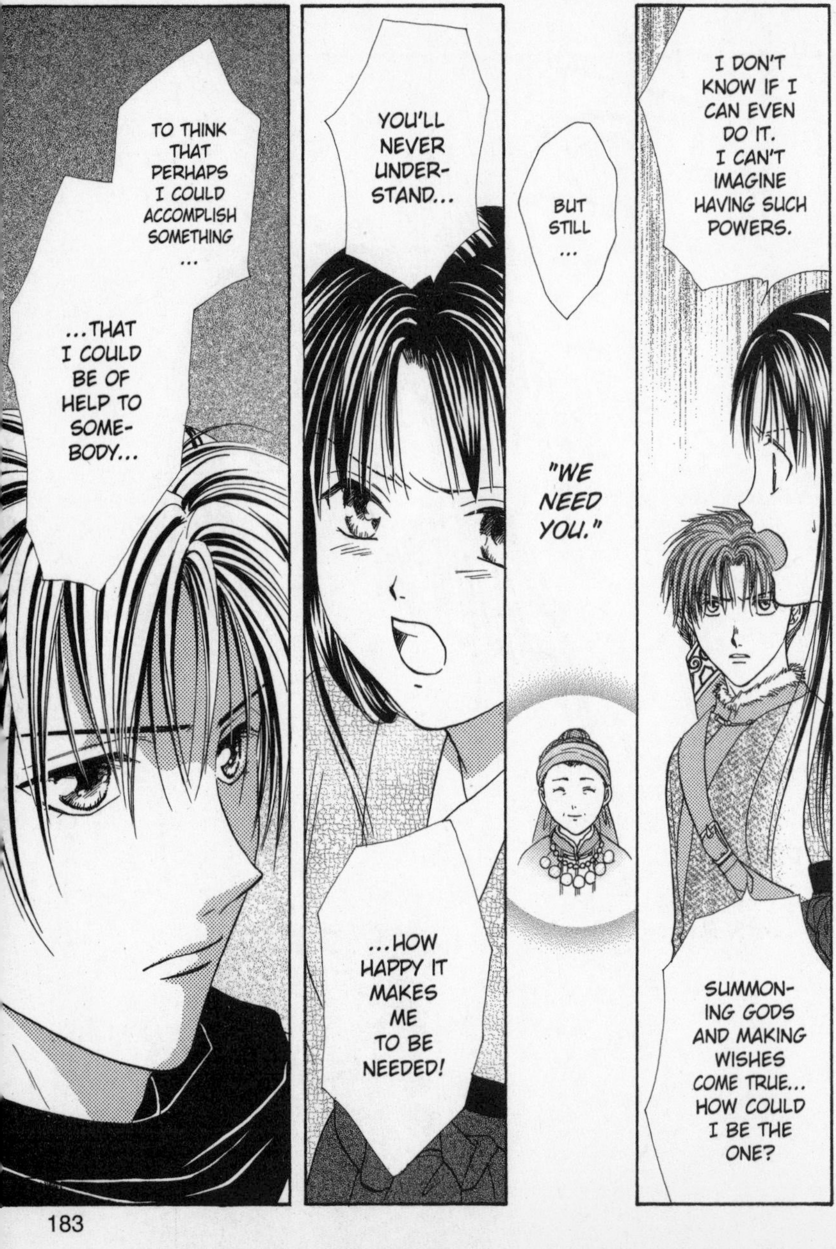
I DON'T KNOW IF I CAN EVEN DO IT. I CAN'T IMAGINE HAVING SUCH POWERS.
SUMMONING GODS AND MAKING WISHES COME TRUE... HOW COULD I BE THE ONE?
BUT STILL ...
"WE NEED YOU."
YOU'LL NEVER UNDERSTAND...
...HOW HAPPY IT MAKES ME TO BE NEEDED!
TO THINK THAT PERHAPS I COULD ACCOMPLISH SOMETHING ...
...THAT I COULD BE OF HELP TO SOMEBODY...

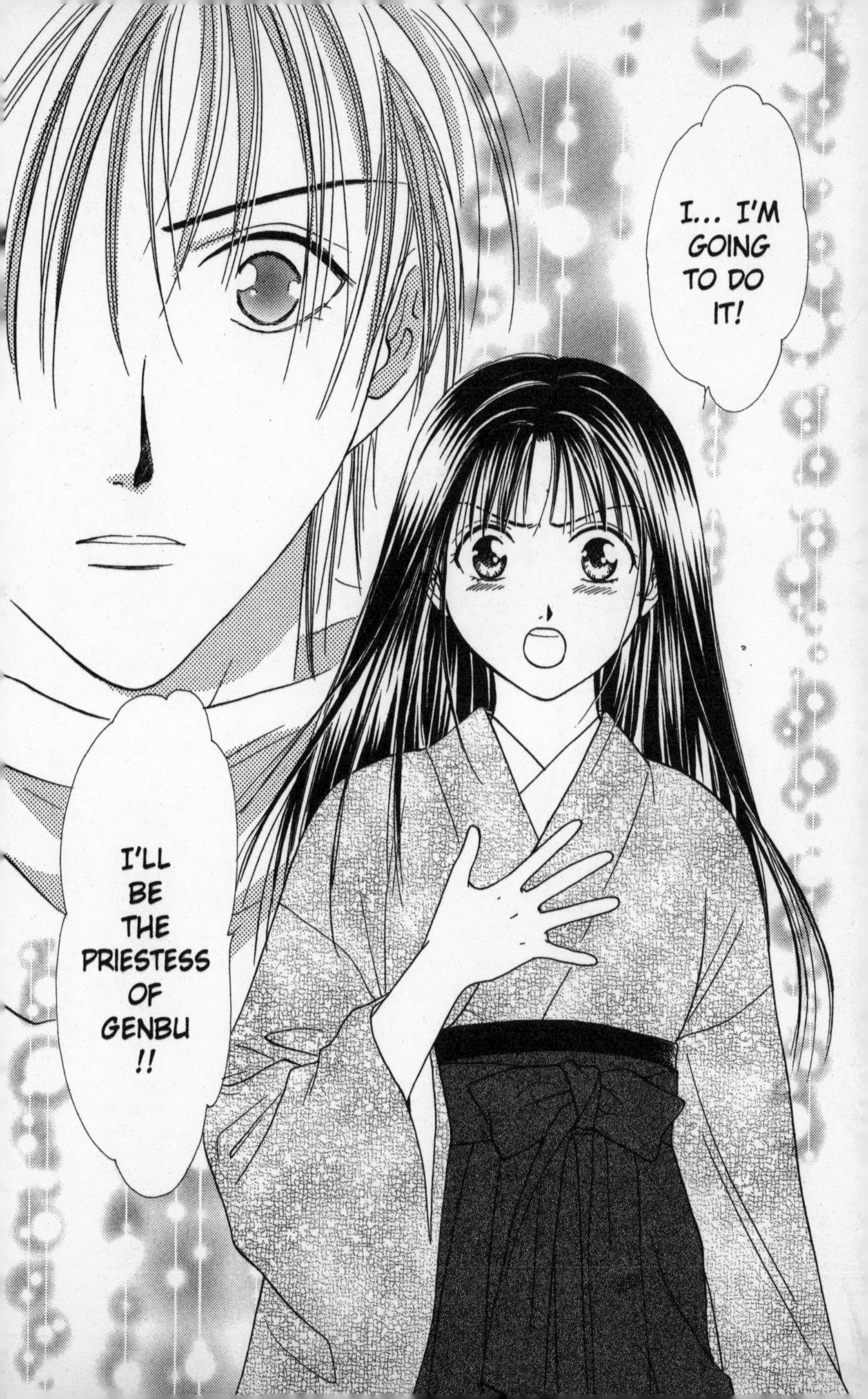
I... I'M GOING TO DO IT!
I'LL BE THE PRIESTESS OF GENBU !!

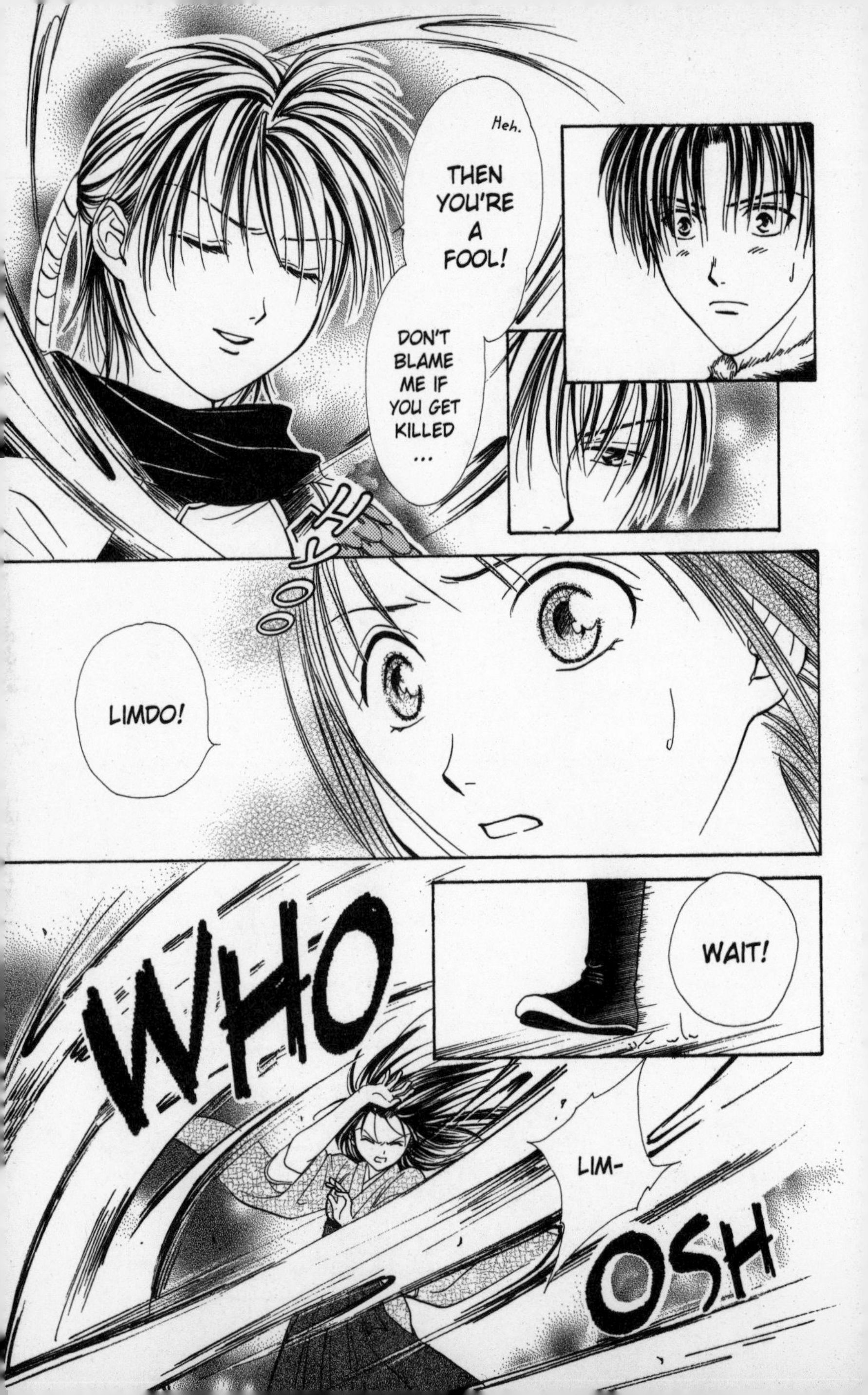
Heh.
THEN YOU'RE A FOOL!
DON'T BLAME ME IF YOU GET KILLED ...
HYOO
LIMDO!
WAIT!
WHOOSH
LIM-

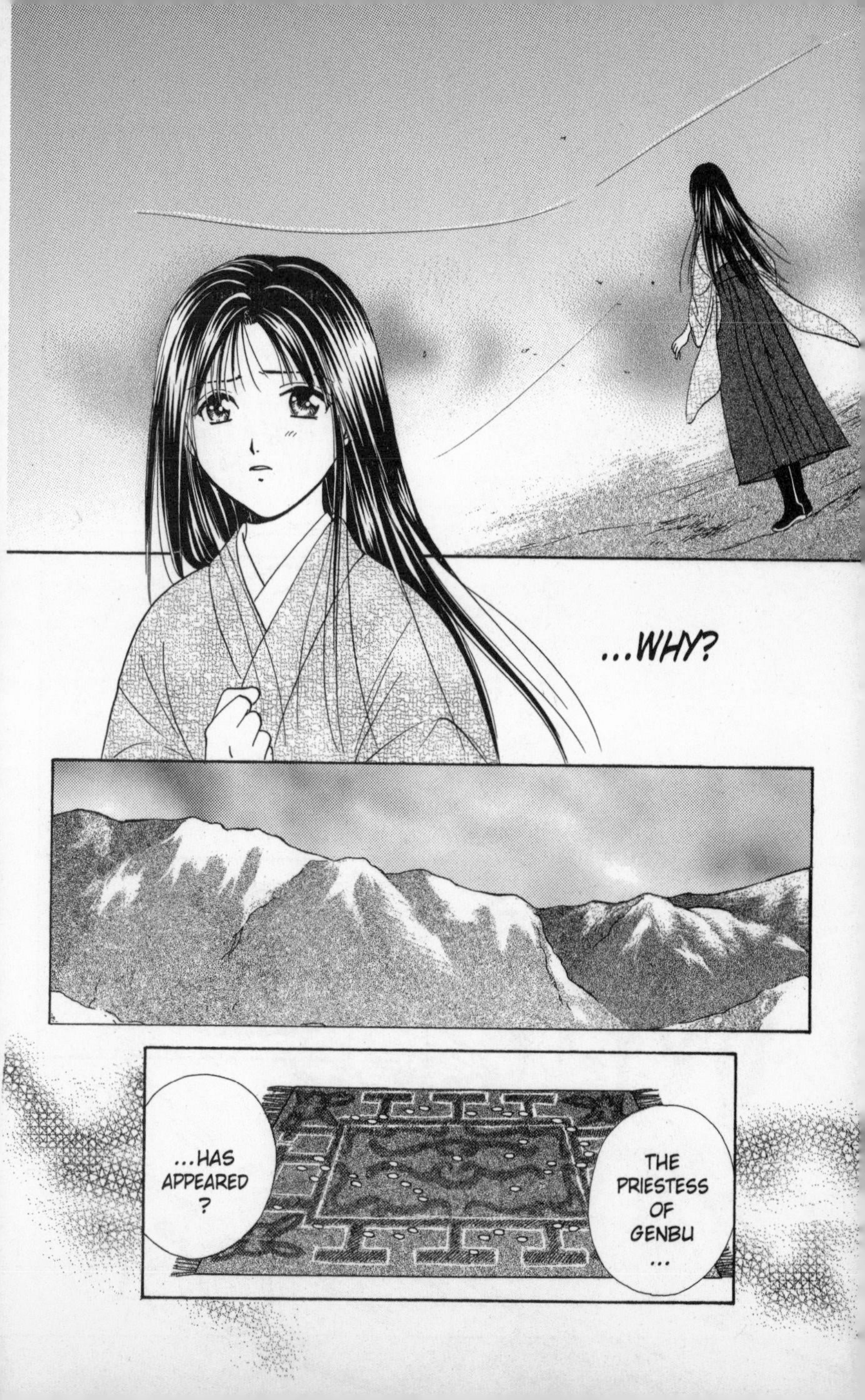
...WHY?
THE PRIESTESS OF GENBU ...
...HAS APPEARED ?

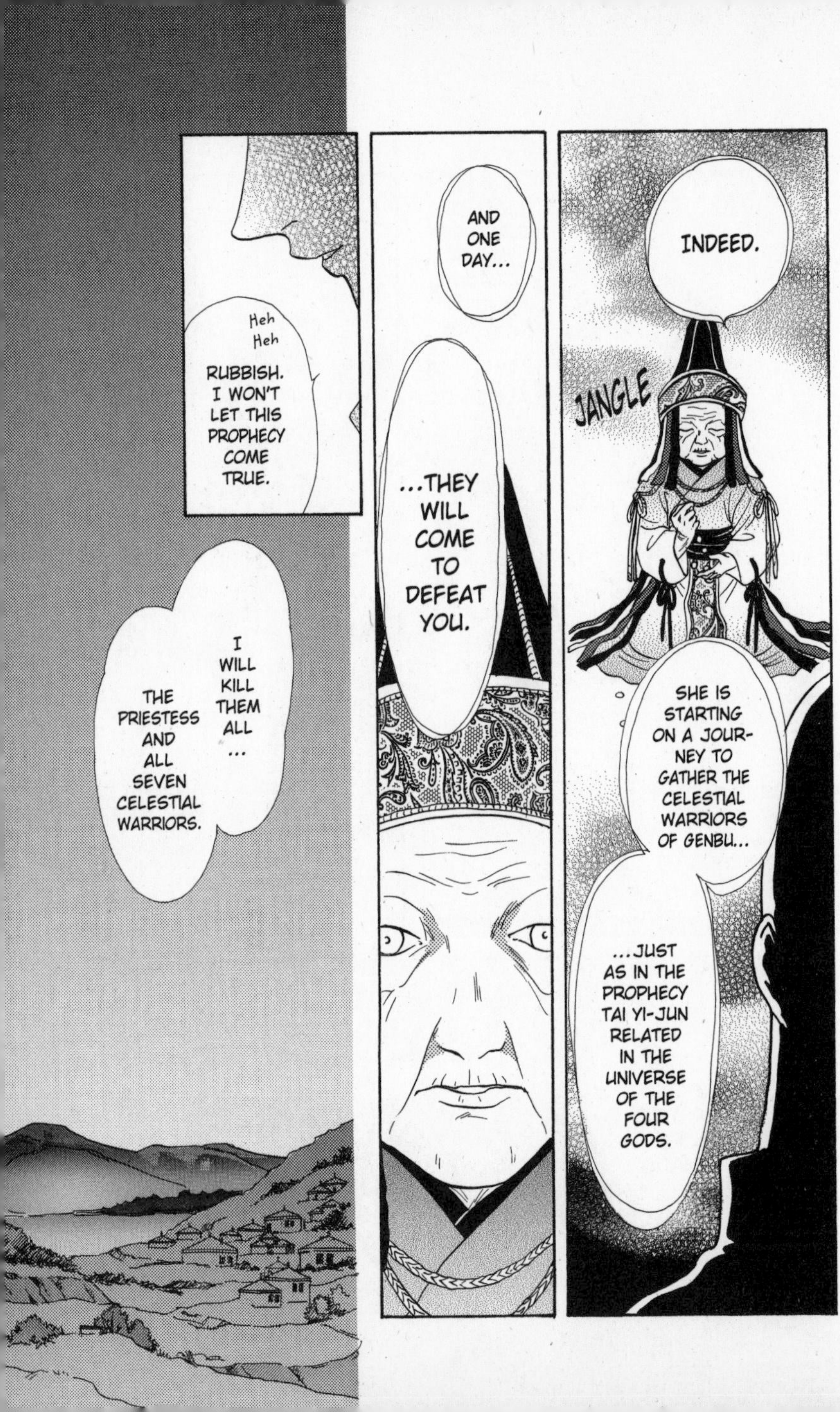
INDEED.
JANGLE
SHE IS STARTING ON A JOURNEY TO GATHER THE CELESTIAL WARRIORS OF GENBU...
...JUST AS IN THE PROPHECY TAI YI-JUN RELATED IN THE UNIVERSE OF THE FOUR GODS.
AND ONE DAY...
...THEY WILL COME TO DEFEAT YOU.
Heh Heh
RUBBISH. I WON'T LET THIS PROPHECY COME TRUE.
I WILL KILL THEM ALL...
THE PRIESTESS AND ALL SEVEN CELESTIAL WARRIORS.

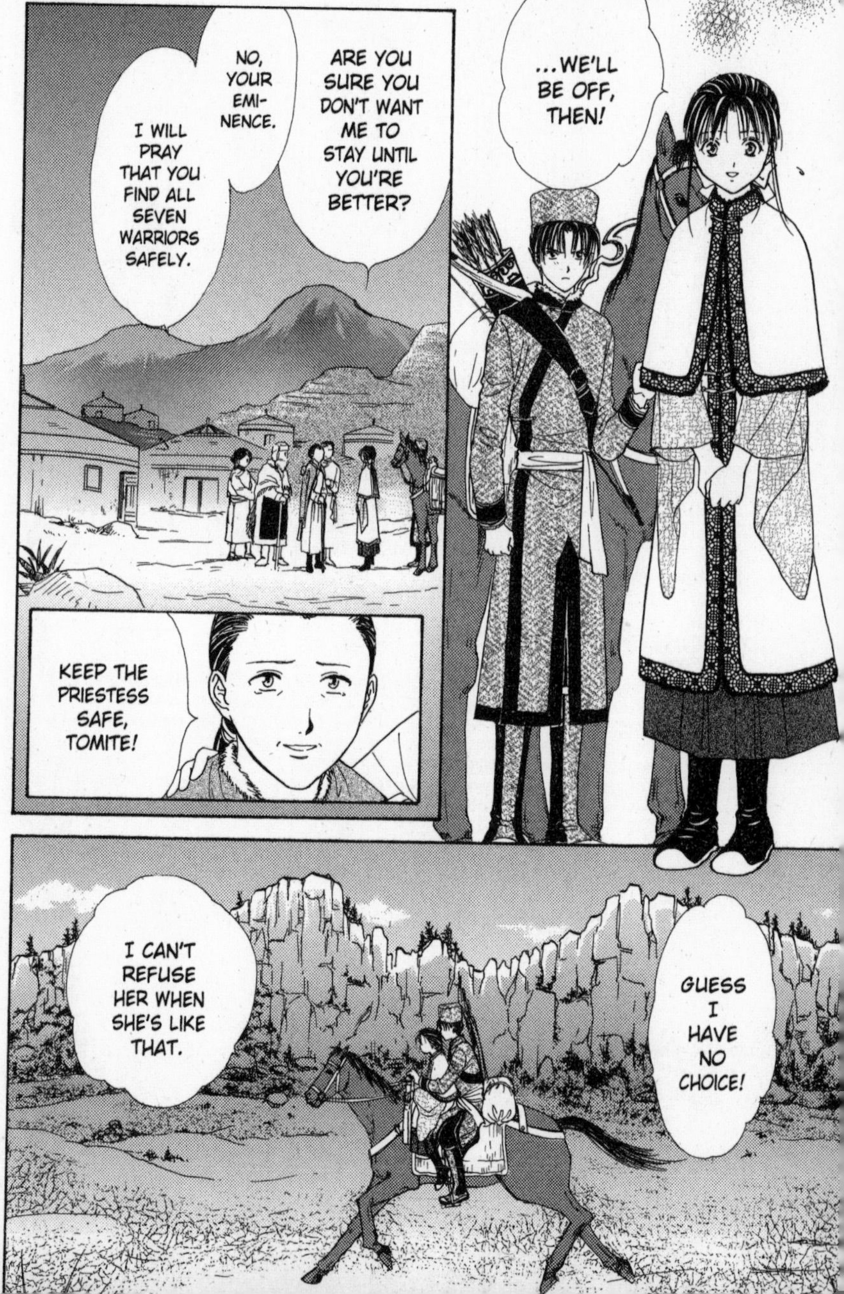
...WE'LL BE OFF, THEN!
ARE YOU SURE YOU DON'T WANT ME TO STAY UNTIL YOU'RE BETTER?
NO, YOUR EMI-NENCE.
I WILL PRAY THAT YOU FIND ALL SEVEN WARRIORS SAFELY.
KEEP THE PRIESTESS SAFE, TOMITE!
GUESS I HAVE NO CHOICE!
I CAN'T REFUSE HER WHEN SHE'S LIKE THAT.

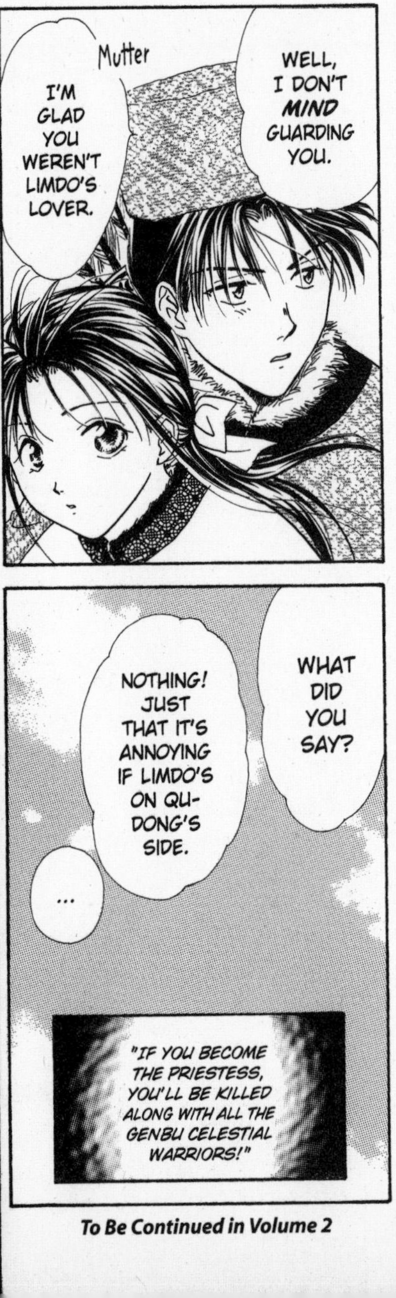
WELL, I DON'T **MIND** GUARDING YOU.
Mutter
I'M GLAD YOU WEREN'T LIMDO'S LOVER.
WHAT DID YOU SAY?
NOTHING! JUST THAT IT'S ANNOYING IF LIMDO'S ON QU-DONG'S SIDE.
...
"IF YOU BECOME THE PRIESTESS, YOU'LL BE KILLED ALONG WITH ALL THE GENBU CELESTIAL WARRIORS!"

To Be Continued in Volume 2

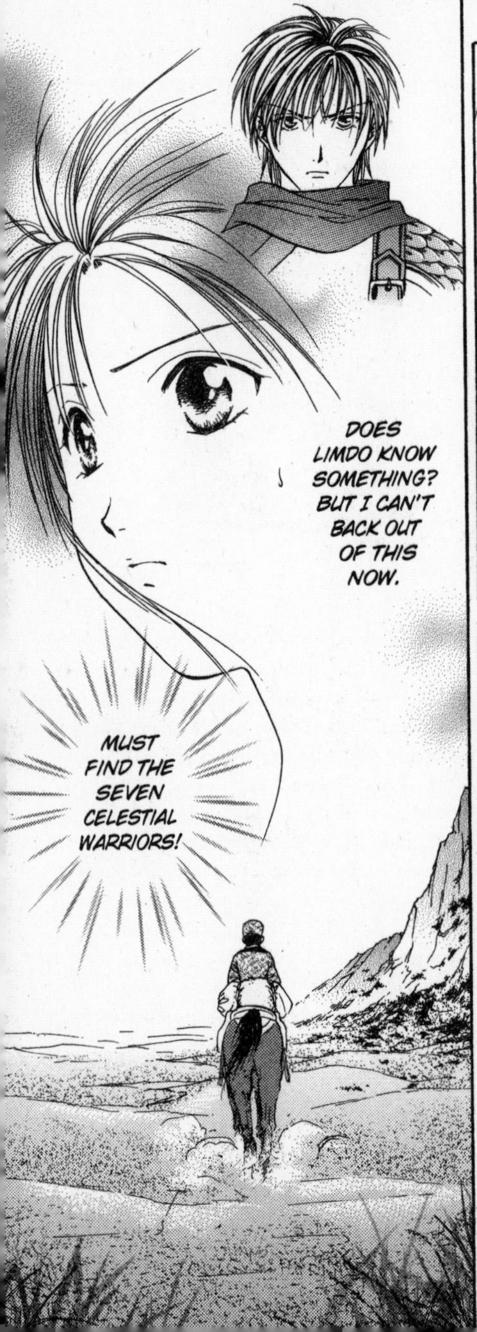
DOES LIMDO KNOW SOMETHING? BUT I CAN'T BACK OUT OF THIS NOW.
MUST FIND THE SEVEN CELESTIAL WARRIORS!

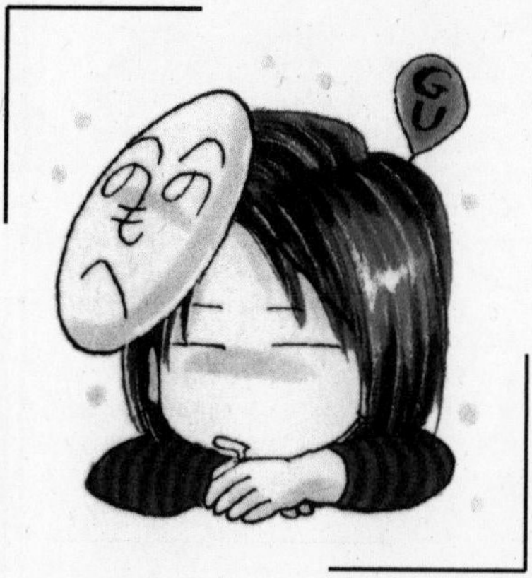
GU

Yuu Watase was born on March 5 in a town near Osaka, Japan, and she was raised there before moving to Tokyo to follow her dream of creating manga. In the decade since her debut short story, Pajama De Ojama (An Intrusion in Pajamas), she has produced more than 50 compiled volumes of short stories and continuing series. Her latest work, *Absolute Boyfriend*, was serialized in Japan in the anthology magazine *Shôjo Comic* and is currently being serialized in English in *Shojo Beat* magazine. Watase's other beloved series *Alice 19th*, *Imadoki!*, and *Ceres: Celestial Legend* are now available in North America in English editions published by VIZ Media.

Fushigi Yûgi:
Genbu Kaiden Vol. 1

The Shojo Beat Manga Edition
STORY AND ART BY
YUU WATASE

English Adaptation/Shaenon Garrity
Translation/Lillian Olsen
Touch-up Art & Lettering/Walden Wong
Design/Amy Martin
Editor/Ian Robertson

Editor in Chief, Books/Alvin Lu
Editor in Chief, Magazines/Marc Weidenbaum
VP of Publishing Licensing/Rika Inouye
VP of Sales/Gonzalo Ferreyra
Sr. VP of Marketing/Liza Coppola
Publisher/Hyoe Narita

Printed in the U.S.A.

Published by VIZ Media, LLC
P.O. Box 77010
San Francisco, CA 94107

Shojo Beat Manga Edition
10 9 8 7 6 5
First printing, June 2005
Fifth printing, December 2007

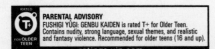

PARENTAL ADVISORY
FUSHIGI YÛGI: GENBU KAIDEN is rated T+ for Older Teen.
Contains nudity, strong language, sexual themes, and realistic
and fantasy violence. Recommended for older teens (16 and up).
ratings.viz.com

store.viz.com

Tell us what you think about Shojo Beat Manga!

Our survey is now available online. Go to:

shojobeat.com/mangasurvey

Help us make our product offerings better!